CLARENDON LIBRARY OF LOGIC AND PHILOSOPHY

General Editor: L. Jonathan Cohen

WORKS AND WORLDS
OF ART

WORKS AND WORLDS OF ART

BY

NICHOLAS WOLTERSTORFF

CLARENDON PRESS . OXFORD
1980

Oxford University Press, Walton Street, Oxford OX2 6DP

OXFORD   LONDON   GLASGOW
NEW YORK   TORONTO   MELBOURNE   WELLINGTON
KUALA LUMPUR   SINGAPORE   HONG KONG   TOKYO
DELHI   BOMBAY   CALCUTTA   MADRAS   KARACHI
NAIROBI   DAR ES SALAAM   CAPE TOWN

© *Nicholas Wolterstorff 1980*

Published in the United States by
Oxford University Press, New York

British Library Cataloguing in Publication Data

Wolterstorff, Nicholas
    Works and worlds of art. – (Clarendon library of logic and philosophy).
    1. Aesthetics
    I. Title
    701   BH201   79–41806

    ISBN 0–19–824419–3 hardback
            0–19–824426–6 paperback

Printed in the United States of America

Preface

Mimesis, perhaps best translated as representation, was thought by Aristotle to constitute the essence of art. On that it seems to me he was mistaken. Some art is abstract, or pure; nothing is represented thereby. But though representation is not essential to art, certainly it is pervasive and fundamental in art. It is to be found in all the arts, though not, indeed, in every *work* of art.

My project here is to construct a theory concerning the nature of *mimesis* in art. Two ideas lie at the heart of my suggestion. Representation is commonly understood to be a relation between symbols of a certain sort and that which they symbolize. I suggest, instead, that at its root representation is an *action* performed by human beings. Thus my theory stands more in the line of contemporary theories of action than in the line of contemporary theories of symbols. Secondly, the heart of representation, no matter in which of the arts it occurs, lies not in composing a copy of the actual world but rather in using some artefact to project a world distinct from our actual world. Representation, or mimesis, is world projection. An implication of this approach is that art is here seen more from the side of the artist than from the side of the spectator.

Throughout this century, aesthetics has been a somewhat turgid backwater alongside the main currents of philosophy. I hope that this discussion will make some contribution toward bringing it back into the mainstream.

Grand Rapids, Michigan
June 1979

Acknowledgements

My thanks are due above all to my philosophical colleagues at Calvin College, and especially to Alvin Plantinga, for their incisive criticisms of earlier drafts of this book and helpful suggestions for improvement. Without their contributions, this book would be considerably different, and much inferior. Sometimes they despaired of ever seeing an end to the project. I shall not say that that despair was always unwarranted! My thanks are due also to my graduate students at the University of Notre Dame and Temple University, who shared in the formation of these ideas. And to Kendall Walton and Robert Howell, with whom I have discussed many of these ideas over a good number of years.

A senior fellowship and a summer stipend from the National Endowment for the Humanities proved essential in giving me the time free from teaching to work on the book, as did a sabbatical leave from Calvin College. To both of them, my thanks.

Some of the material in this book has previously appeared in published form. Material from *Poetics* is reprinted by permission of the Editor. Material from the *Journal of Aesthetics and Art Criticism* is reprinted by permission of the Editor. Material from *Noûs* is copyright © 1975 by Indiana University, and is reprinted by permission of the Editor.

In addition I reproduce some passages from Nelson Goodman, *Languages of Art* (Hackett Publishing Company Inc., 2nd edn., 1976), which are reprinted by permission of Nelson Goodman.

Contents

Introduction

In the following essay I discuss one of the fundamental actions that works of art serve to perform—the action of *world projection* as I shall call it. Hugo Van Der Goes, by way of his *Adoration of the Shepherds* now hanging in the Uffizi in Florence, projected a world containing shepherds, oxen, a barn, angels, Mary, Joseph, etc. That is one illustration of the action I have in mind. I shall look at the nature of the entities used to perform the action—namely, artefacts of art. I shall look at the nature of that which is projected—worlds. And I shall look at the nature of the action itself—projection.

Works of art serve to perform an enormous variety of actions, both in fact and by the intent of their makers. That is true for our society. It is true for all others as well. Artistically man acts. So my topic of discussion is one, but only one, from among all the different actions that works of art serve to perform. To introduce the discussion I shall sketch out, in Part One, a general schematism for thinking of the role of art in action.

Aesthetic inquiry since its origins in the eighteenth century has rarely set art in the context of action. In one major tradition it has focused on the work of art itself and the aesthetic experience of the beholder. In another, it has focused on the artist's experience of creation. In none has it explicitly focused on the role of art in action.

Admittedly it is possible to regard my project in a conservative light with respect to these modern traditions. For whatever else the aesthetic experience may be, it is an experience attained in and by submitting some entity to the *action* of aesthetic contemplation. And whatever else the creative experience may be, it is an experience attained in and by performing the *action* of artistic creation. So certain facets of the role of art in action have in fact been the concern of modern aesthetics. In exploring the action of world projection I am acting in continuity with the tradition.

But to regard my project in this conservative light is to miss some fundamental differences. In the first place, it is no accident that modern aesthetics, in both of its major traditions, has thought in terms of *experience* rather than in terms of *action*. Thereby it has reflected its Cartesian inheritance, shared with the rest of modern philosophy. Ever since the Cartesian turn, man as centre of consciousness rather than man as agent in the world has constituted a basic orientation of Western philosophy. Today this phase of our Cartesian inheritance is wearing thin. Recent years have seen a rise of interest in the formation of theories of action. This essay, by placing art in the context of man as agent in the world rather than in the context of man as experiencer, participates in this incipient anti-Cartesianism.

Then too, one must differentiate the structurally diverse ways in which art enters into action. The action of world projection, on which I shall concentrate, is an action performed *by way of* creating, or performing some action on, some art artefact. The artefact serves as *instrument* of that action. It is *used to perform* that action. The action of artistic creation is structurally different. It does not consist in *using* a work of art to *do* something but, rather, in bringing a work of art into existence or bringing it about that some entity becomes a work of art. And the action of aesthetic contemplation is structurally different yet. It too is not an action performed *by way of* creating, or acting on, some work of art. But in distinction from artistic creation it is itself an example of *doing something to* some work of art. Works of art are *objects of* the action of aesthetic contemplation. (These structural differences will be explored in some detail in Section I I I of Part One.)

Just as it is no coincidence that modern aesthetics, in both of its major traditions, has thought in terms of experience, so too it is no coincidence that one of its traditions has focused on the creation rather than on the uses of art. That focus reflects the widespread conviction that in artistic creation man transcends the routines of ordinary social existence, transcends also the use of works of art for the performance of various actions, and experiences something of higher value. The tradition has been protean in the forms it has assumed. But the Romantic form has for some time been dominant. Artistic creation, so it is said, consists in expressing one's emotions. By providing us a means for expressing the inner life of Emotion it offers an alternative to the routines of Reason.

Of course it is true that emotions can be expressed by creating and performing works of art. But the underlying perspective of the following essay is emphatically not that of the Romantic inheritance. The perspective is not that of the human being expressing his inner emotional self by the creation of art. It is rather that of the human being composing artefacts whereby he acts in various ways with respect to his surrounding reality and enables members of society to do so as well. This expansion of perspective reflects the conviction that the expression of emotion is but one among other reasons for the creation of works of art, and in the total body of the world's art, a thoroughly subordinate reason. The fundamental (though not exclusive) value of artistic creation lies not in what is inherent in the action of creation itself but in its providing us with instruments and objects of action generally. Some of what we find worth doing would have to remain undone if we had no works of art. Much could be done only haltingly and limpingly.

The fact that in the other major tradition of modern aesthetics the focus has been on the action of aesthetic contemplation is also to be accounted for by deep-lying cultural attitudes. For that focus reflects the conviction, first articulated in the eighteenth century, that what is of paramount importance in the realm of the arts is just the delight to be found in aesthetic contemplation of works of art. Indeed, this tradition is so strong that no doubt some of my readers will have found it vaguely offensive, or strangely beside the point, to talk about the *uses* of art.

The tradition comes in two versions. Sometimes it is held that art in general is *intended* for aesthetic contemplation—that music is for listening to, painting for looking at, poetry for reading. 'The most evident characteristic of a work of art', says Paul Valéry, 'is its uselessness.' Alternatively, sometimes it is admitted that the range of intended uses for works of art is broader than this; but then it is insisted that of all the uses works of art serve and are intended to serve, aesthetic contemplation is the one of greatest value.

The following essay reflects a repudiation of this tradition as well. Of course it is true that aesthetic contemplation is an action of great value in human life. Furthermore, part of the importance of world projection lies in the fact that it significantly enlarges the scope for aesthetic contemplation. Apart from this there would be, for example, no stories from which to take aesthetic delight. Yet man as *agent* who makes use of works of art in a wide variety of actions, rather than man as *contemplator* of works of art, is our basic perspective. In that is reflected the conviction that aesthetic contemplation is neither the invariant purpose behind the creation of works of art, nor always what is most worth doing with them. Serving as objects of aesthetic contemplation is one among other roles that works of art play in human life—not always the intended one, not always the most important one, and as it happens, not the one on which I will focus in this essay.

In order to see that it is not always the intended role, notice, first, that there are a number of quite different concepts commonly associated with the phrase 'work of art'. One is that of *an instance of one of the fine arts*. Another is that of *an instance of one of the fine arts which is a satisfying object for aesthetic contemplation*. Whichever concept we use, however, it proves not to be the case that works of art are in general intended for aesthetic contemplation.

In his instructive essay, 'The Modern System of the Arts',[1] Paul Oskar Kristeller traces the emergence of our modern catalogue of the arts, showing that it was in the eighteenth century that writers first began to group together painting, sculpture, architecture, music, and poetry as fine arts. Until that time people would have felt, for example, that music has closer affinities with mathematics that it has with painting. Today we would differentiate—as eighteenth-century writers customarily did not—poetry from fiction and drama, and would regard all three as arts. And we would probably add the new phenomena of film and ballet dance. But otherwise what we today regard as paradigmatic examples of a major fine art do not differ much from what our eighteenth-century forebears so regarded. At most, we might wonder whether perhaps architecture is a borderline rather than a paradigmatic example.

---

[1] In P. O. Kristeller, *Renaissance Thought: II* (Harper Torchbooks: New York, 1965).

Now the arts all manifest themselves in *instances*, in *works*—works of music, works of visual art, etc. Thus it is that we can conceive of a work of art as an instance of one of the major fine arts. When we do thus conceive of a work of art, is it true that works of art are in general intended for aesthetic contemplation? Quite to the contrary. The action of aesthetic contemplation appears as merely one among a multiplicity of actions in which works of art, thus conceived, serve and are intended to serve. In many, if not most, cases it was never intended by the artist that his work should serve as an object of aesthetic contemplation. And when it was so intended, seldom was this the sole use intended. The situation is not substantially changed if, alternatively, we conceive of a work of art as an instance of one of the fine arts which is a satisfying object for aesthetic contemplation. For not even all of such objects were *intended* to serve as objects of aesthetic contemplation—witness the world's tomb art.

Of course, it's possible to conceive of a work of art not as an instance of one of the fine arts which is a satisfying object for aesthetic contemplation, but rather, as *an instance of one of the fine arts such that the primary intent behind its creation was that it should serve as an object of aesthetic contemplation.* When that is how we conceive of a work of art, then obviously we get the result that works of art are invariably intended for aesthetic contemplation. But it should be noted that on this concept, vast stretches of what we normally take to be works of art are excluded from the realm of art. There are hymns, for example, which are works of art. But the intended use of a hymn is not to serve as object of aesthetic contemplation but to be sung by an entire cultic gathering in order to give praise to its god. The small clay figurines made by ancient Mexicans and now being unearthed from burial sites had as their intended use to accompany the dead in their afterlife. And if the standard view concerning the paintings in the Lascaux caves is correct, these too did not serve as objects of aesthetic contemplation but were intended, in magical fashion, to help achieve success in the hunt.

There are those who would grant this point that works of art are not in general *intended* for aesthetic contemplation but who would insist that, none the less, of all the actions which they serve, this is the most *valuable*. Then again justification is given to that tradition of aesthetic inquiry in which the focus is on the action of aesthetic contemplation and its objects.

I myself see no reason for thinking this true. The worth of aesthetic contemplation is something I would be among the last to deny. I would feel profoundly impoverished if I no longer had available to me things in contemplation of which I could find aesthetic delight. But to elevate the action of aesthetic contemplation above all other functions of art—for that I see no justification.

We are touching here on religious issues. A religious or quasi-religious aesthetic mysticism has often provided the rationale in the modern world for the ennoblement of aesthetic contemplation. Such mysticism I do not share. The vision was never better expressed than by Clive Bell in these well-known words:

Art transports us from the world of man's activity to a world of aesthetic exaltation. For a moment we are shut off from human interests; our anticipation and memories are arrested; we are lifted above the stream of life...

Provided that there be some fraction of pure aesthetic emotion, even a mixed and minor appreciation of art is, I am sure, one of the most valuable things in the world—so valuable, indeed, that in my giddier moments I have been tempted to believe that art might prove the world's salvation.

But if an object considered as an end in itself moves us more profoundly (i.e., has greater significance) than the same object considered as a means to practical ends or as a thing related to human interests—and this undoubtedly is the case—we can only suppose that when we consider anything as an end in itself we become aware of that in it which is of greater moment than any qualities it may have acquired from keeping company with human beings. Instead of recognizing its accidental and conditioned importance, we become aware of its essential reality, of the God in everything, of the universal in the particular, of the all-pervading rhythm. Call it by what name you will, the thing that I am talking about is that which lies behind the appearance of all things—that which gives to all things their individual significance...[2]

In all societies, instances of the arts have been used to perform the action on which I shall concentrate, that of world projection. The reasons for this action's being so pervasively

[2] From chap. I of Clive Bell, *Art* (Capricorn Books: New York, 1958).

practised and so obviously prized are multiple and various. There can be no doubt, though, that in the whole body of the world's art it was and is an action vastly more pervasive than the action of aesthetic contemplation, and that it is an action for the sake of which much of man's artistic creation has been undertaken. Thus in discussing this action we are focusing on something pervasive and fundamental in the arts.

I begin the discussion by setting forth in Part One a general schematism for the role of works of art, and of cultural artefacts generally, in human action. From all the actions in which works of art play a role I then single out for detailed attention in the remainder of our discussion, the action which I am calling *world projection*. This action I understand as constituting the heart of representation, or *mimesis*—when that is understood as something that takes place in all the arts (though not with each work in all the arts). In Part Two I look at the ontological nature of the artefacts of art; for it is by the appropriate use of these that world projection is accomplished. In Part Three I look at the nature of the worlds projected. In Part Four I develop a fully general theory concerning the nature of the action of world projection. In Part Five I look at how world projection is accomplished in the medium of dramatic production. In Part Six, how it is accomplished in the medium of picturing. And lastly, in Part Seven I offer some brief reflections on why we human beings find it worthwhile engaging in this action of world projection.

Though each part of the theory is meant to have application to all the arts, I found that the discussion became too diffuse when at each major point I tried to use examples from all the arts. Accordingly, I have adopted the strategy of taking most of my examples in each Part from a single art, but then varying the art from Part to Part. In Part Two the examples are taken dominantly from music; in Part Three, from literature; in Part Five, of course, from drama; and in Part Six, from visual representation. The other Parts remain relatively general with respect to examples. I regret that architecture—my favourite art—has mainly been left out.

Perhaps I should say, lastly, that the concept of work of art that I shall consistently use is that of an instance of one of the major fine arts.

PART ONE

Art in Action

I. *Doing One Thing by Doing Another*

My purpose in this essay is to analyse the nature of world projection, not to develop a fully articulated theory concerning the role of works of art in action. For the purposes of my analysis, though, it will be helpful to construct at least a schematism for understanding the role of art in action, and then to suggest where in the schematism we should place various important actions in which works of art play a role. That, accordingly, will be my goal in this Part.

Let me make the ontological assumption that there are such entities as actions. That is to say, let me assume that in addition to there being animals which walk there is the action of walking, that in addition to there being persons who think there is the action of thinking, etc. I readily concede that this is a controversial assumption. But here it will not be possible to offer a defence.[1]

A thoroughly plausible view as to a necessary condition for the identity of actions is that any action A is identical with any action B only if it is impossible that there be something which exemplifies A and not B or B and not A.[2] Accordingly, with that criterion in mind imagine a situation in which

---

[1] For a defence see my *On Universals* (Univ. of Chicago Press: Chicago, 1970).

[2] For suppose it is possible, for specific A and specific B, that there be something which exemplifies A and not B or B and not A. That is just to say that in some possible world W there is some entity α such that in W, A has the property of being exemplified by α and B lacks the property of being exemplified by α, or vice versa. But then in world W, A and B are distinct—by the Principle of the Indiscernibility of Identicals (the Principle of the Distinctness of Discernibles). Secondly, I take it to be true, for any x and any y, that if that entity which is x and that entity which is y are distinct in any possible world, then they fail to be identical in every possible world. And so we get our conclusion: any action A is diverse from any action B if it is possible that there be something which exemplifies A and not B or B and not A.

I issue the request to open the door, and that I do so by uttering the English sentence, 'Would you open the door?' By the criterion of action-diversity offered, I will in that situation have performed two distinct actions: that of issuing the request to open the door, and that of uttering the English sentence, 'Would you open the door?' For one can utter that sentence without issuing that request—for example, one can utter it just to offer an example of an English sentence. And conversely, one can issue that request without uttering that sentence—for example, one can issue it by uttering some French sentence.

Equally, though, it is clear that in the situation imagined these two actions stand in an important relation to each other—one in which they do not necessarily but only contingently stand. Or to articulate the structure of the situation more fully: it is clear that in this situation the *three* of us—I and these two actions—contingently stand in an important relation to each other: the relation, namely, of me performing the one action *by* performing the other.

I said that in the situation described I and these two actions *contingently* stand in the relation of my performing the one by performing the other. What I had in mind when I said that is that I might not have performed either of these actions. Contingency enters at a second point as well, however. For I might have performed the action of uttering the sentence without performing the action of issuing the request. In that regard, the situation imagined differs from the following situation: by running a mile in six minutes this morning I ran a *half*-mile within six minutes. For though indeed I need not have run either a mile or a half-mile, it is impossible that I should have performed the action of running a mile in six minutes and not thereby have performed the action of running a *half*-mile within six minutes.

It does not seem to me to be a misuse of English to say, as I just did, that *by* running a mile in six minutes I ran a *half*-mile within six minutes. Probably it is more apt, however, to use the word 'in' to express the relation: in running a mile in six minutes I ran a half-mile within six minutes. But be that as it may, from now on when I say that someone performed one action *by* performing another, I wish to be understood as implying that it is possible for someone to perform the latter action without thereby performing the former.[3]

And now let me borrow from Alvin Goldman, in his book *A Theory of Human Action*,[4] to say that in the situation first imagined I *generated* the action of issuing the request to close the door by the action of uttering the sentence, 'Would you close the door?' And in general,

Def. 1: An agent P generated ψ-ing by ϕ-ing at t =df P performed the action of ψ-ing by performing at t the action of ϕ-ing.

If an action is performed without being generated by any action, let us say that it is performed *foundationally*. I shall be saying a good deal more about the phenomenon of action-generation. But let me drop that topic for just a moment, to call attention to an important ambiguity in the use of the word 'action'. By an action one might mean *an attribute* of a certain sort. For example, *running* and *knowing the multiplication tables up to 12* are both attributes. The former, however, is an action, whereas the latter is not. By an action though, one might also mean *an instance* of some attribute—specifically of some attribute which is an action. That is to say, by an action one might mean *an event* of a certain sort. Some particular event consisting of *John's running* would be an example. However, that entity which is John's knowing the multiplication tables up to 12 would not be an example. For no attribute of which this is an instance is an action-attribute.

Now in English we have the word 'act' in addition to the word 'action'. I shall make use of this fortunate fact by using the word 'action' exclusively for attributes of a certain sort—*action*-attributes; and by using the word 'act' exclusively for event of a certain sort—those which are instances of action-attributes.

I should perhaps, at this point, express my awareness that the assumption that there are such entities as acts, distinct from actions, is no less controversial than the assumption that there

---

[3] Later I shall relax this stipulation, to allow for such cases as: by checkmating his opponent's king in chess, John won at chess. It is impossible that John should perform the former of these and not the latter. See Part Four, Section III.

[4] Alvin Goldman, *A Theory of Human Action* (Prentice-Hall: Englewood Cliffs, N.J., 1970).

are such entities as actions. It would be interesting to see what
can be said for and against the assumption. But that is here
impossible.[5] Perhaps all that I want to say in what follows could
be recast so that the existence of acts is not assumed. Perhaps
also it could be recast so that acts but not actions are assumed to
exist. But I shall be ontologically profligate and assume the
existence of entities of both categories.

Let us now return to my initial thought-example. If I issue
the request to open the door by uttering the English sentence,
'Would you open the door?' then there is in existence at the time
in question an instance of each of the two actions of issuing the
request to open the door and of uttering the English sentence,
'Would you open the door?' Specifically, there are in existence
an act consisting of *my* issuing the request to open the door, and
an act consisting of *my* uttering the English sentence, 'Would
you open the door?' Let us, conserving terminology, use 'to
generate' when speaking of acts as well as when speaking of
actions, saying that the former act, the act of uttering the
sentence, generated the latter act, the act of my issuing the
request. In general: suppose that some person P generated
ψ-ing by ϕ-ing at some time t. Let us then say that the act of P's
ϕing which took place at t *generated* an act of P's ψ-ing.[6]

As I conceive the relation between acts and actions, a single
act may be an instance of two different actions. And I shall not
deny (though also I shall not affirm) that this may be the case
even if someone generated the one action by the other. Thus I
shall not assume that from 'Act A generated act B' it follows
that A is not identical with B. I do assume throughout, however, that act-generation is a transitive relation.

I shall not here attempt an explanation of the concept of
action-generation, for we do already have the concept. It is one

[5] For a defence, see my 'Can Ontology Do Without Events?' In *Essays on the Philosophy
of Roderick M. Chisholm*, ed. Ernest Sosa (Rodopi: Amsterdam, 1979), pp. 177–205.
[6] My definition of 'generates' as it applies to acts is more roundabout than is
Goldman's. It appeals to a prior definition of 'generates' as it applies to actions. The
reason for the difference is that Goldman speaks of acts as *done by* agents. It seems clear
to me, however, that it is actions and not acts that are done by agents. If I ask what it is
that John is doing (what action it is that he is performing), the answer is 'playing the
Brahms sonata', not 'John's playing the Brahms sonata.' Thus the ordinary concept of
doing one thing by doing another is a concept of *action* generation, not of act generation.
Another difference is that Goldman assumes that no act can be an instance of two
different actions.

of our ordinary concepts. Neither shall I attempt an analysis of the concept. Our need in this essay is only for the *use* of the concept; an analysis would be superflous. A few observations, though, are in order.

One thing's being done by the doing of another is not confined to cases in which the agent of the two doings is a single person. A team, for example, can do one thing by doing another. Neither is it confined to cases in which the agent of the two doings is identical. An organization can do something by way of some official of the organization doing something. And one person can do something by way of someone else doing something 'on his behalf'. Further, a person may do something by coming into a certain state rather than by performing a certain action. States of agents as well as acts of agents are capable of generating acts. For example, Michael might win the game by being the last to have a battleship remaining on the board. If one were going to construct an analysis of our ordinary concept of action generation, the full range of different types of cases would have to be taken into account. However, since it is only the cases of some single person doing one thing by doing another that will fall within our purview in the following essay, I have defined '——generates ...' in such a way that it covers only such cases.

Every case of action-generation presupposes the truth of some particular subjunctive conditional. It is because it was true at the time that I would issue the request if I would utter the sentence (in circumstances of a certain sort), that I performed the action of *issuing the request* by performing the action of *uttering the sentence*. It is because it was true at the time that John would cause delight in his old teacher if he would play the Brahms sonata, that by performing the action of *playing the Brahms sonata* he performed the action of *delighting his old teacher*. Later I shall have some words to say on what makes such subjunctive conditionals true.

Goldman contends that if act *A* generates act *B*, then *B* is wholly simultaneous with *A*. Such a contention must face the fact that though by pulling the trigger I kill the horse, yet the horse may actually die several days after I pull the trigger. Perhaps the act of my killing the horse can be analysed in such a way as to make it evident that it was indeed wholly simultaneous with my pulling the trigger. But since the truth on this matter will not make a difference to my subsequent claims, I shall not take a stand on the issue. However, to avoid undue complications in some of my subsequent formulations, I shall sometimes speak as if I did indeed believe that act-generation holds only between wholly simultaneous acts.

An example of action-generation to which I have thus far made repeated reference is this

(1) By uttering the English sentence, 'Would you close the door?' I issued the request to close the door.

And another example to which I have alluded is this one:

(2) By playing the Brahms sonata, John delighted his old teacher.

A bit of reflection on these two examples suffices to make it clear that action-generation comes in at least two importantly different species, each of these examples being an example of one such species.

Example (2) is an example of what may be called *causal* generation. The generated act of John's delighting his old teacher consists of (i.e., is identical with) the act of John's bringing about the event of his old teacher's being delighted. And the event of his old teacher's being delighted is *caused* by the generating act of John's playing the Brahms sonata. When acts are thus related we have an example of what may appropriately be called *causal* generation. Let us first have a definition of 'causal generation' as applying to a relation which holds among the members of a pair of actions and an agent:

Def. 2: An agent P *causally* generated ψ-ing by ϕ-ing at t =df
  (i) P generated ψ-ing by ϕ-ing at t; and
  (ii) P's act of performing the action of ϕ-ing causes some event E such that the act of P's ψ-ing is identical with an act of P's bringing about E.

We can now easily explain what constitutes causal generation as a relation holding between acts: if P causally generates ψ-ing by ϕ-ing, then the act of P's ϕ-ing causally generates an act of P's ψ-ing.

It is important to notice that when some act A of some agent

P causally generates some act B, A does not cause B. Rather, A causes some event E such that B consists of P's bringing about E. The act of John's playing the Brahms sonata does not cause the act of John's delighting his old teacher. It causes the event of John's old teacher being delighted.

The species of action-generation illustrated in the other example, our initial one, I shall call *count*-generation. I do so because my uttering the sentence, 'Would you close the door?' *counts as* my issuing the request to close the door. In general:

Def. 3: An agent P *count*-generates ψ-ing by ϕ-ing at t =df
  (i) P generates ψ-ing by ϕ-ing at t; and
  (ii) P's act of performing the action of ϕ-ing counts as an act of P's ψ-ing.

That explains count-generation as a relation holding between an agent and the members of a pair of actions. The explanation of count-generation as a relation holding between acts is, once again, easily come by: if P count-generates ψ-ing by ϕ-ing, then the act of P's ϕ-ing count-generates an act of P's ψ-ing.

But what is it for P's act of performing the action of ϕ-ing to *count as* an act of P's ψ-ing? Specifically, what is it for my act of uttering the English sentence, 'Would you open the door?' to *count as* my issuing the request to open the door? Since the concept of count-generation will occupy a central place in our account of world projection, it will be important to have an answer to this question. I shall postpone the answer, however, until the opening of Part Four.

It will prove illuminating to follow Goldman's lead in constructing diagrams of action-generation. We are to draw pairs of circles one above the other and connected by a solid line. Then to say that someone generated ψ-ing by ϕ-ing at some time we put a name of ϕ-ing opposite the lower circle and a name of ψ-ing opposite the higher circle. And to signify the species of generation we put, opposite the line connecting the two circles, '*ca*' for causal-generation and '*co*' for count-generation. The diagram for John delighting his old teacher by playing the Brahms sonata is illustrated below.

○ delighting his old teacher

ca

John ○ playing the Brahms sonata

One can of course also construct chains of such diagrams. But then, if the transitivity of act-generation is to be respected, it must be remembered that if the sign of ϕ-ing has immediately above it in the diagram a sign for ψ-ing, and if in turn the sign for ψ-ing has immediately above it in the same diagram a sign for χ-ing, this indicates not only that the person in question generated ψ-ing by ϕ-ing and χ-ing by ψ-ing, but also χ-ing by ϕ-ing. An example of such a diagram is shown below.

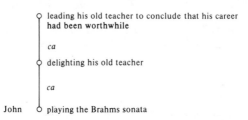

Let us call all such diagrams, no matter what their length, *action-trees*.

II. *Action-Plans*

On the evening of 29 May 1913, in the Théâtre des Champs-Élysées in Paris, one of the great music scandals of all time took place. It was the première performance of Stravinsky's *Rites of Spring*, with Pierre Monteux as conductor and Nijinsky as choreographer. Monteux had scarcely given his opening beat when confusion began to reign among the dancers on stage, and shortly thereafter enraged pandemonium broke loose in the hall. The orchestra played bravely on, and the uproar continued unabated. I think it can be said, in summary, that by composing *Rites of Spring* and getting it performed, Stravinsky incensed that evening's audience. What has also proved true, though, is that by creating and publishing *Rites of Spring* Stravinsky gave aesthetic delight to many people. Here then are two cases of causal generation on Stravinsky's part.

In spite of that similarity, there is obviously a substantial structural difference between these two cases. Giving aesthetic delight to people was probably something that Stravinsky wanted to do, given his participation in the Western institution of high art. Incensing that evening's audience was probably not something that he wanted to do—though it's clear that he later took delight in recalling the episode. In turn, giving aesthetic delight to people may well have been something that Stravinsky wanted to do because he believed that thereby he would generate something else that he wanted to do—earn himself an income, bring himself fame, or whatever. Or, alternatively, it may have been something that he wanted to do for its own sake.

Let us try to give a generalized articulation to these and closely related distinctions by introducing the concept of an *action-plan* and exploring the various types of action-plans. The discussion will prove somewhat complex, and the general reader who is not interested in the 'fine print' of the theory may wish to jump ahead to the next Section. The discussion there can be understood without grasping the analysis in this section.

I start with some action A that some person P wants at time t_1 to do at time t_2. One possibility is that P believed at t_1 that he cannot perform A at t_2. Then P at t_1 has no action-plan for performing A at t_2. Alternatively, P may believe at t_1 that there is a chance that he can perform A at t_2; but there may be no action A' distinct from A such that P believes at t_1 that he might be able to perform A' at t_2 and that if he did so he might thereby generate A. In such a case, let us call the unit set, $\langle A \rangle$, P's *action-plan* at t_1 for performing A at t_2. But thirdly, there may be at least one ordered set of actions, $\langle A_1, \ldots, A_n \rangle$, such that P believes at t_1 that he might be able to perform A_1 at t_2 and that if he did so he might thereby generate $A, \ldots$, and believes that he might be able to perform A_n at t_2 and that if he did so he might thereby generate A_{n-1}.[7] In such a case, let us call the n + 1-tuple of actions, $\langle A, \ldots, A_n \rangle$, P's *action-plan* at t_1 for performing A at t_2. Let us call A, the *goal* of that action-plan. And let us call A_n, the *terminus* of the plan.

An action-plan of P at t_1 for doing A at t_2 may be a proper subset of a larger action-plan of P at t_1 for doing A at t_2, and it may be that in several different ways. For one thing, given an action-plan of P at t_1 for doing A at t_2, there may be some distinct action A' which P at t_1 also wants to do at t_2, and concerning which he believes that he might be able to perform

[7] For purposes of convenience in formulation I assume that a generated action occurs at the same time as its generating action, and that we all believe this.

A at t_2 and that if he did so he would probably thereby generate A'. On the other hand, there may be no such action A'. If there is not, let us call $\langle A, \ldots, A_n \rangle$ a *completed* action-plan of P at t_1 for doing A at t_2. Then on the other end, given an action-plan $\langle A, \ldots, A_n \rangle$ of P at t_1 for doing A at t_2, there may be some action, A_{n+1}, such that P at t_2 believes that he might be able to perform A_{n+1} at t_2 and that if he did so he might thereby generate A_n. On the other hand, there may be no such action. If there is not, let us call the plan a *closed* action-plan of P at t_1 for performing A at t_2. And then lastly, two action-plans of P at t_1 may have the same goals and same termini, and yet the one may be a proper subset of the other. Schematically, for example, one action-plan of P at t_1, for performing A at t_2 might be $\langle A, A_1, A_2, A_3, A_4 \rangle$. And another might be $\langle A, A_1, A_4 \rangle$. An action-plan α of P at t_1 for doing A at t_2, which is such that there is no other action-plan of P at t_1 for doing A at t_2 that has the same terminus as α and of which α is a proper subset, may be called a *filled* action-plan of P at t_1 for doing A at t_2. Given the possibility of 'branchings' out from A_n (or from later actions) which meet again at A (or at earlier actions), P at t_1 may have more than one filled action-plan for doing A at t_2. One might be $\langle A, A_1, A_2, A_3, A_4 \rangle$, and another $\langle A, A_1, B_2, B_3, A_n \rangle$.

We can distinguish, among those things that some person P at t_1 wants to do, between those that he wants to do *merely instrumentally*, and those that he wants to do *for their own sake*. If P at t_1 wants to do A at t_2, but wants to do A at t_2 only for the reason that he believes that by doing A he will probably generate some other action A' which he wants to do at t_2, then P at t_1 wants to do A at t_2 *merely instrumentally*. On the other hand, if P at t_2 wants to do A at t_2, but if it's not the case that P at t_1 wants to do A at t_2 merely instrumentally, then P wants to do A *for its own sake*. A person may want to do something for its own sake, and also want to do it because he believes that thereby he will generate something else that he wants to do. Further, a person may want to do something for its own sake, without that action being the goal of any action-plan of his. For it may be that he believes that he cannot do it. It must be noticed that it is not necessary, if $\langle A, \ldots, A_n \rangle$ is to be an action-plan of P at t_1, that A be an action that P wants to do for its own sake.

Now suppose that P at t_1 has a filled action-plan, $\langle A, \ldots, A_n \rangle$, for doing A at t_2; and suppose he believes, concerning some action A' which is not a member of $\langle A, \ldots, A_n \rangle$, that if he performs $\langle A, \ldots, A_n \rangle$ at t_2 he might generate A'. We may say of A' that, relative to $\langle A, \ldots, A_n \rangle$ at t_2, it is a *consequence anticipated* by P at t_1. Suppose that in addition A' is not something that P at t_1 wants to do at t_2. Then we may say of A' that, relative to $\langle A, \ldots, A_n \rangle$ at t_2, it is an *unwanted* consequence anticipated by P at t_1.[8]

Suppose, for example, that John has an action-plan for delighting his old teacher at a certain time, one whose terminus is playing the Brahms sonata. John may well believe that by playing the Brahms sonata at that time he will bore his sister. But relative to his filled action-plan, boring his sister will be only a consequence anticipated by John. For certainly John will not believe that by boring his sister he will delight his old teacher. Indeed, boring his sister may well be a consequence *unwanted* by John—though on the other hand, it might be the goal of distinct action-plan whose terminus is also playing the Brahms sonata.

P at t_1 may have *alternative strategies* for doing A at t_2. That is to say, at t_1 P may have at least two different action-plans for doing A at t_2, such that there is no action concerning which he believes that by performing it at t_2 he might generate all members of both. So from among the alternative strategies of P for doing A, we want to pick out those which he *tries to implement*—if he does try to implement any. Suppose that P at t_2 wants to do A at t_2, that P at t_2 has an action-plan for doing A at t_2 which has A_n as terminus, and that P at t_2 performs A_n for the reason that he wants to do A. Let us then say that P has *tried to implement* that action-plan at t_2 by performing its terminus, A_n. And if all the members on some action-plan that P tries to implement at t_2 are such that by performing A_n he *does* generate them, then P at t_2 *has implemented* that action-plan for doing A at t_2.

There is, of course, many a difference between the action-plans that we try to implement and the action generations which ensue. Suppose, once again, that an action-plan for doing A that P tried to implement has A_n as its terminus. By doing A_n, P will almost certainly generate all sorts of actions which he did not at the time believe he would generate. And

---

[8] The principle of double effect.

conversely, P may well fail to generate what he believed he would generate. He may even fail to generate the *goal* of an action-plan he tried to implement by doing A_n. By moving his fingers in such-and-such ways across the piano keyboard, thereby playing the Brahms sonata, John may annoy his old teacher, when what he wanted to do and what he expected to do by playing the Brahms sonata was to delight his old teacher.

We can now return to the Stravinsky example with which we began. No doubt *getting his work 'Rites of Spring' performed* was the goal of an elaborate action-plan of Stravinsky, one that he tried to implement. I suspect that the members of this plan were in turn members of an action-plan whose goal was *giving aesthetic delight to people*. But *incensing the audience* was perhaps not the goal of any action-plan of Stravinsky. And with respect to a filled action-plan that he tried to implement whose goal was *getting 'Rites of Spring' performed*, it was perhaps not even a consequence anticipated by him.

Following the model of our action-trees, we could easily devise ways of diagramming action-plans. More relevant to our purposes, however, will be ways of adding to our action-trees information about the matters that we have been discussing in this section. So begin with the action-tree illustrated below.

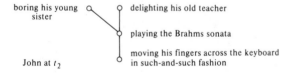

For any pair of actions on an action-tree, to indicate that at the time in question the agent believed that by performing the one he might generate the other and that he maybe *could* perform the one, draw an arrowed dotted line from the circle standing for the one to the circle standing for the other. If he did not believe that he might be able to perform the one and by performing it might generate the other, draw a double dotted arrowed line. The absence of a dotted and double dotted line between a pair of circles means that we are being told nothing one way or the other. (The reason for the arrow is that, though someone may generate A by performing A', he may have believed that he might generate A' by performing A.) An example is show below.

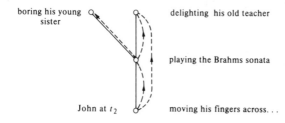

The example tells us that by *moving his fingers in such-and-such fashion* John generated the action of *playing the Brahms sonata*; and that by doing that he in turn generated the actions of *delighting his old teacher* and of *boring his young sister*. In addition it tells us that at t_2 John believed that he might delight his old teacher by playing the Brahms sonata and also by moving his fingers across the keyboard in such-and-such fashion, that he also believed that he might play the Brahms sonata by moving his fingers, and that he thought he might bore his sister by playing the Brahms sonata. As to whether he believed that he might bore his sister by moving his fingers in such-and-such fashion, we are told nothing one way or the other. (Though it's obvious that in fact he did believe this.)

Lastly, to inform us that one or more of the actions indicated on an action-tree was one that the agent wanted to do at the time in question, we put a W in the appropriate circle, and to indicate that it was not one that he wanted to do, we put in a W with a bar over it. To indicate that it was something he wanted to do for its own sake, we add to the W an S; and to indicate that he wanted it merely instrumentally, we add an I. An example, is shown below.

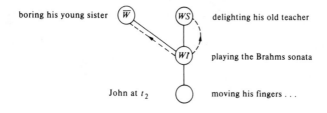

The example tells us that John delighted his old teacher and bored his young sister by playing the Brahms sonata, and that he did this in turn by moving his fingers across the keyboard in such-and-such fashion. It tells us in addition that John wanted to play the Brahms sonata only instrumentally, but that he wanted to perform the action of delighting his old teacher for its own sake. Concerning the action of boring his young sister it tells us in addition that John at t_2 did not want to do that. However, he believed that he would do it by playing the Brahms sonata, though he believed that he would also delight his old teacher. Thus boring his young sister was an unwanted though anticipated consequence of playing the Brahms sonata. Concerning other matters, the diagram is silent.

III. *A Schematism for the Role of Art in the Actions of the Artist*

By using the concepts explored and formulated in the preceding two sections we can arrive at a schematic understanding of the role of art in action. That is to say, we can arrive at an understanding of the structurally diverse ways in which art plays a role in action.

To show how the concepts discussed can be used for this purpose, I shall select various examples of actions in which works of art play a role, and show the structural similarities and differences among them. Some of the examples will be actions whose nature has been hotly debated among aestheticians. Accordingly, in order to state the structural affinities and non-affinities of these with other actions we shall have to commit ourselves on some controversial issues. Some of these commitments may appear dogmatically taken, since to enter fully into the debates concerning the proper analysis of each of these would take us far away from our main goal in this essay. However, by dealing with some of these controversial examples the relevance of the schematism to actions on which theorists have found it important to reflect will become evident.

Our discussion will also have this more specific benefit: by seeing how world-projection differs structurally from a variety of other actions, some of them liable to be confused with it, we will be better situated for discussing this action in the remainder of the essay. My choice of certain examples will have this benefit in view.

Central to the ways in which works of art play a role in action is their serving as *objects* of action. Let me explain. Certain of the actions that we perform are relational actions. For their instantiation they require that something be related to something in a certain way. The action of *kicking* is an example. So consider an instance of some such action, for example, my kicking my desk, then consider that correlative set of entities which exemplify the action. In our example, that set will be the one whose members are me and my desk. We may call that member (those members) of the set which performs (perform) the action, the *agent*(*s*) of the action, for that instance of it. And any member of the set which occurs in some capacity other than that of performing the action may be called the *object*(*s*) of the action, for that instance of it. In our example, I am the agent and my desk is the object. Throughout my discussion, when I speak of some entity as *used to perform* some action, what I shall mean is that that entity is an *object* of the action, for that instance of it. (When I kick myself, then the set has just one member, myself; and I am both agent and object of the action of kicking, for that instance of it.)

A convenient way of displaying, on an action-tree, that something is an object of some action is to put a box around the expression which denotes that object. Thus the bottom line on an action-tree might look like this:

John ○ playing [the Brahms sonata]

That shows that John is the agent, and the Brahms sonata the object, for some instance of the relational action of *playing*.

It will be convenient to speak of the agents and objects of *acts* as well as of the agents and objects of actions. The idea can readily be explained. If P is the agent of some relational action R, for some instance r of R, then let us say that P is the *agent* of the act r. And if O is an object of R for r, then let us say that O is an *object* of the act r. Suppose, for example, that on some occasion I contemplate the *Rokeby Venus*. I am then the agent and the *Rokeby Venus* is the object of the action of *contemplating*,

for that particular instance of the action. Also, I am the agent
and the *Rokeby Venus* is the object of that particular act which
consists of *my contemplating the 'Rokeby Venus'*.

If we bring to mind the concept of action-generation, then we
see at once that there are two additional ways in which works of
art play a role in action. For example, when John, as agent,
performs on the Brahms sonata, as object, the action of playing,
then he generates the action of delighting his teacher. In such a
case, let us say that the work of art serves as *instrument* of the
generated action. Thus, in the example offered, the Brahms
sonata serves as instrument of the action of delighting John's
teacher. When I say, in what follows that a work of art *functions*
in the performance of some action, I shall mean that it serves as
instrument for the performance of that action. An action-tree
depiction of a work of art serving as instrument of some action is
shown below.

$$
\begin{array}{ll}
\circ & \text{delighting his old teacher} \\
| & \\
\text{John} \quad \circ & \text{playing} \quad \boxed{\text{the Brahms sonata}}
\end{array}
$$

Thirdly, sometimes an action for which some work of art serves
as object is itself generated by performing some other action. By
applying paint to canvas Titian generated the action of creating
the *Rokeby Venus*. This can be depicted in the diagram below.

$$
\begin{array}{ll}
\circ & \text{creating} \quad \boxed{\text{the \textit{Rokeby Venus}}} \\
| & \\
\text{Titian} \quad \circ & \text{applying paint to canvas}
\end{array}
$$

For our purposes it will not be necessary to give any special
name to the relation which holds, in such cases as this, between
the generating action and the work of art which serves as object
for the generated action.

I begin by considering, in this section, some of the actions of
which the artist is agent. Let us have before us a concrete
example. Among the masterpieces in the Louvre is one by
Rembrandt in which he represented Bathsheba bathing. That
it is Bathsheba we know from the title, *Bathsheba*. And that she is
bathing is plain for all to see. Apparently Rembrandt's model
for this particular painting was his own beloved Hendrickje.

Adding to these facts what is generally known about Rembrandt, we can say the following: Rembrandt, by performing the action of

(1) applying paint to canvas,

generated the action of

(2) producing a rendering of Hendrickje,

and thereby generated the action of

(3) creating the painting *Bathsheba*.

In turn, by performing (3) Rembrandt generated the actions of

(4) representing Bathsheba as bathing,
(5) projecting a world which includes a woman bathing,
(6) giving aesthetic delight to people,
(7) embarrassing Hendrickje, and
(8) getting his smock dirty.

Let us also consider how Rembrandt's

 (9) revealing his fondness for strong chiaroscuro, and
(10) expressing his aversion to the Renaissance cult of the ideal body

are related to his performing the action (3).

The only action, from actions (1)–(8), of which the painting *Bathsheba* was object is (3). All the others are either actions by which Rembrandt generated (3) or actions which his performing of (3) generated.

Since it is such actions as (4) and (5) that will be the focus of our discussion in this essay, let us begin with them. Both are actions which Rembrandt count-generated by performing (3). *Rembrandt's creating the painting 'Bathsheba'* counts as *Rembrandt's representing Bathsheba as bathing*, and also as *Rembrandt's projecting a world which includes a woman bathing*.[9] Furthermore, both are probably occurrences of actions which Rembrandt tried to generate and believed he maybe could. Probably each of these actions was the goal of some action-plan that Rembrandt tried to implement.

[9] Actually, it's not just his creating the painting, but his creating it in such-and-such a context, that counts as those two other acts.

Commonly writers on the arts blur together the action of representing something (in the sense of 'represent' according to which Rembrandt represented Bathsheba) with the action of producing a rendering of some thing, as in our action (2). What helps to induce the blur is that often what is represented is identical with what is rendered. What helps even more to induce the blur is that the word 'represent' is used as appropriately in the one case as in the other. It is perfectly correct to say that Rembrandt represented Hendrickje by his production of the painting *Bathsheba*, as well as to say that he represented Bathsheba.

The case before us helps to make clear, however, that the action of representing, when by that we mean the action which Rembrandt performed on Bathsheba, is distinct from the action of rendering. For Hendrickje is rendered but Bathsheba is not. What also makes clear the diversity of these actions is that, in other cases, some particular person is represented without anyone at all being rendered, and in yet others, some particular person is rendered without there being any person at all who is represented. The sculptor of the door jambs at Moissac who so stunningly represented the prophet Jeremiah did not—if he worked as did most medieval sculptors—use anyone as model to be rendered. And though Leonardo apparently created his *Mona Lisa* by using some particular woman as model, he did not thereby represent any particular woman.

Furthermore, consider any case in which by rendering E_1 someone has created a painting whereby he represents E_2. It is always possible for him to have created that very same paint-on-canvas object, and to have represented E_2 thereby, without having rendered E_1 or anything else. And likewise, it is always possible for him to have created that very same paint-on-canvas object and to have done so by rendering E_1, without thereby having represented E_2 or anything else. Rembrandt could have produced his painting *Bathsheba*, and could thereby have represented Bathsheba, without rendering Hendrickje. He could hardly have used Bathsheba herself, since of her appearance he knew virtually nothing. But he could have used someone other than Hendrickje, or no one at all. On the other hand, by rendering Hendrickje he could have produced his *Bathsheba* painting and have represented someone other than Bathsheba thereby, or have represented no one. He could, for one thing, have represented Hendrickje.

To create a painting by producing a rendering of something is to engage in a form of guided making. It is to produce a painting by trying to render one and another feature of one's model in paint—to produce an 'equivalent' in paint-on-canvas of whatever features of one's model one is trying to render.[10] And that in turn is to allow one's laying down of paint onto canvas to be guided in a certain characteristic way. By performing the action of rendering Hendrickje, Rembrandt *causally generated* the action of creating the painting *Bathsheba*, while in turn he *causally generated* the former of these actions by applying paint to canvas. Furthermore, producing a rendering of Hendrickje was no doubt the goal of an implemented action-plan of Rembrandt.

The supplemented action-tree for what we have discussed thus far then is shown in the diagram below.

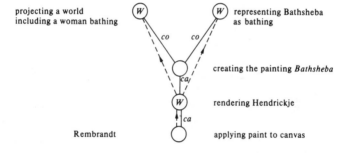

[10] Rendering occurs far less often in the representational arts than a modern Western observer might suppose. With the exception of the post-Renaissance West it has been a very subsidiary mode of artistic production. Why it gained dominance in our culture some four centuries ago, and why it is now receding in dominance, are important questions which to my knowledge have never been satisfactorily answered. Perhaps the coming of the photograph explains the latter. But the usual aside to be found in art history books, to the effect that the former was the result of Aristotelian thought entering Western culture, is too speculative to be satisfying.

A puzzling feature of intellectual history is Plato's assuming that the painter creates only by rendering. It was probably not even *characteristic* of the Greek artists that they created by rendering. Yet the charges that Plato brings against the painter in Book Ten of his *Republic* quite clearly presuppose that the painter is one who renders.

To produce a painting by making a rendering of something must be distinguished from producing a painting by making a copy of something, though the latter too is a form of guided making. Van Gogh produced one of his paintings by making a copy of Millet's *The Cornfield*. What he copied was itself a painting. It was not a cornfield.

It is worth noting, parenthetically, that the distinction between representing and rendering is as important for an understanding of photographs as it is for an understanding of paintings. The camera provides us with a mechanical device for producing renderings of things. The resultant artefacts—photographs or illuminated pictures—may also be used to represent things. But only sometimes will that which they are used to represent be identical with what they are renderings of. In some of the Walt Disney cartoons, for example, a talkative insouciant fowl called 'Donald Duck' is represented. (Donald Duck is of course represented without *there being* some entity, Donald Duck, which is thereby represented.) But in producing the photographs no fowl at all was photographically rendered. Rather, a sequence of drawings was photographically copied. Yet it is Donald Duck, not some drawing, which is represented. In somewhat similar fashion we must distinguish, in non-cartoon fictional cinema, between the actor who is photographically rendered and the character which is represented. The director creates the film by photographically rendering some actor. And in turn, by creating the film he produces a representation of some character.[11]

Let us move on to action (6) on my list, that of giving aesthetic delight to people. Rembrandt generated this action by creating the painting *Bathsheba*. It is in that respect structurally similar to the action of representing Bathsheba as bathing. In contrast, however, it is *causally* generated. For the act of Rembrandt's giving aesthetic delight to people consists in Rembrandt's bringing about the event of people being aesthetically delighted; and this event is caused by the act of Rembrandt's creating the painting *Bathsheba*. The act causally

---

[11] André Bazin, in his suggestive essay 'The Ontology of the Photographic Image', in *What is Cinema?* (Univ. of California Press: Berkeley, 1967), wholly misses the fact that in film as in painting representation is a phenomenon distinct from rendering. He says, for example, that 'Photography and cinema . . . are discoveries that satisfy once and for all, in its very essence, our obsession with realism.' (p. 12.) What he means is that photographs and films are (by and large) produced by rendering or copying something, mechanically so. But that has little to do with *realism* in the sense of that word which is relevant to art and aesthetics. This is clear from the fact that there are non-realistic as well as realistic films. The realism or non-realism of a film inheres in its representational dimension, not in its renditional dimension.

contributes to the existence of that event. Nothing similar holds for the act of Rembrandt's representing Bathsheba as bathing. This does not consist in Rembrandt's bringing about some event which is a causal effect of the act of Rembrandt's creating the painting *Bathsheba*.

Action (7), embarrassing Hendrickje, and action (8), getting his smock dirty, are like (6) in the respects mentioned. All are causally generated by (3). There are the following differences, however. In all likelihood (6) was the goal of an action-plan that Rembrandt tried to implement. But neither the action of *embarrassing Hendrickje*, nor that of *getting his smock dirty*, was the goal of any action-plan whatsoever. Of these, in turn, *getting his smock dirty* was no doubt an anticipated consequence of one of Rembrandt's action-plans—and more specifically, of one that he tried to implement. But we may suppose that *embarrassing Hendrickje* was not even an anticipated consequence of any action-plan that he tried to implement. The action-tree is shown below.

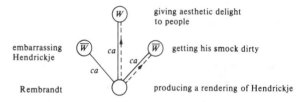

In general, by creating some work of art an artist generates an enormous multiplicity of actions. Some of these he may have wanted to generate, others not. To his generation of some he may be averse, to that of others, not. His generation of some he will have anticipated, others, not. Of his generation of some he will learn, of his generation of others he will never learn. The artist creates his work, the waves of history catch it up. To a great extent what he does is unintended, unwelcome, unanticipated, or unknown.

When we get to (9), the action of *revealing his fondness for strong chiaroscuro*, and to (10), the action of *expressing his aversion to the Renaissance cult of the ideal body*, we enter a hornets' nest of controversy—as anyone knows who has read the literature in aesthetics of the past 75 years. Part of the controversy is focused on claims concerning the significance of self-revelation and self-expression in the arts, with the Romantic tradition regarding at least the latter as indispensable to, if not definitive of, artistic creation. But another part of the controversy is focused on the *nature* of these actions. Controversies of the former sort can here be put to one side. Those of the latter sort we shall have to enter. For we want to know what position self-revelation and self-expression occupy in the structure of art in action. To answer that, we have to know what they are.

Let us begin with an example of expression drawn from outside art. Suppose that Mary has nursed Rebecca through a siege of pneumonia and that Rebecca now wishes to express her gratitude to Mary. She contemplates various ways of doing so, among them these:

(1) by saying that she is very grateful,
(2) by sending Mary a 'Thank you' card,
(3) by taking care of Mary's children for a week, and
(4) by sending over a favourite shrub from the local nursery.

I take it that all of these are in fact ways in which Rebecca can express her gratitude. She cannot discard one or more on the ground that her gratitude cannot be expressed in that way. Her choice among them has to be made by deciding which, in the situation, is the *best* way of expressing her gratitude.

What is it that makes all four of them ways for Rebecca to express her gratitude? For one who knows the etymology of 'express' (Latin, *exprimere*, to squeeze or press out), the thought at once comes to mind that to express one's gratitude is to reveal it, to manifest it, to show it, to evince it. For Rebecca to express her gratitude by taking care of Mary's children is for Rebecca to *reveal* her gratitude by taking care of Mary's children.

No doubt what is expressed by someone is in many cases also thereby revealed by that person, and vice versa. But self-revelation and self-expression cannot simply be identified. For it is possible that a person reveal some one of his states of consciousness without therein expressing it, and that he express some one, without therein revealing it. Suppose, for example, that someone is giving his first public speech and that he feels nervously apprehensive. He might then reveal his apprehension by gripping the podium so hard that his knuckles turn white. But he would not thereby have *expressed* his apprehension. He would instead have *betrayed* it.[12] Then too, one can reveal, though one cannot express, things about oneself other than one's states of consciousness. By speaking as he does, Jimmy Carter reveals that he comes from the American South.

Let us begin with a scrutiny of self-revelation, and then move on to self-expression. First, suppose that nobody actually concludes on the basis of the white knuckles that the speaker is nervously apprehensive. Might the speaker none the less have revealed his nervous apprehension by gripping the podium so hard that his knuckles turn white? Can one reveal one's so-and-so by doing such-and-such without revealing it *to* anybody? Can revelation take place without someone discerning of what the revelatory action is revelatory?

I think the situation here is that two different concepts are associated with the English word 'reveal'. On one of them—call it the *non-transmittal* concept–one can reveal one's state of consciousness without revealing it *to* anyone. On the other—call it the *transmittal* concept—that cannot be. On the transmittal concept, nothing is revealed until someone apprehends what is revealed.

It is easy to see how to begin the analysis of the non-transmittal concept of self-revelation. In the first place, one can reveal one's apprehension only if one *is* apprehensive. One can't reveal what one isn't. Secondly, one can reveal some state of self by gripping the podium so hard that one's knuckles turn white only if one *does in fact* grip the podium so hard that one's knuckles turn white. One can't reveal something by doing something that one doesn't do.

But obviously something more is needed. The core of self-revelation consists in some sort of relation, some sort of connection, between the revealed state of self and the revealing act. What might that connection be? I suggest that it is two-fold: the revealer must perform the revealing act *because* he is in that state or *for the reason* that he wants someone to know that he is. And the revealing act must be *good evidence* for the existence of the revealed state.

[12] Cf. R. G. Collingwood, *The Principles of Art* (Oxford Univ. Press: Oxford, 1970), pp. 121–4; and Wm. P. Alston, 'Expressing', in Max Black (ed.), *Philosophy in America* (Cornell Univ. Press: Ithaca, N.Y., 1965).

So I suggest the following as an analysis of non-transmittal self-revelation:

S reveals his f-ness at t if and only if:
  (i) S is-f at t; and
  (ii) there is some action ϕ-ing such that
    (a) S performs the action of ϕ-ing at t (not necessarily intentionally),
    (b) S's ϕ-ing is a perceptible act,
    (c) S performs the action of ϕ-ing because S is-f, or for the reason that S wants someone to know he is-f, and
    (d) the act of S's ϕ-ing is good evidence (to a suitable qualified observer) of S's f-ness.

An analysis of the transmittal concept of self-revelation is now easily arrived at. S reveals his f-ness to P if and only if (i) and (ii) hold as above, and (ii) (e): P infers that S is-f on the basis of P's belief that S is ϕ-ing (plus suitable background beliefs). Transmittal revelation occurs when someone actually takes up the good evidence by making the appropriate inference.

A natural question to raise about this analysis is whether either (ii) (c) or (ii) (d) is superfluous. I think neither is. Consider first the need for proviso (ii) (d), the good evidence proviso. It's probably true that Rembrandt painted Bathsheba as he did because of his fondness for chiaroscuro. But Rembrandt's painting *Bathsheba* does not reveal this fondness. And the reason it does not do so is that Rembrandt's painting of this one picture is only *slim* evidence of his fondness for chiaroscuro. A whole series of strongly chiaroscuro-ed paintings would provide good evidence, but not one painting by itself.

How about the other way round? Does the good evidence proviso render the 'because' proviso superfluous? No. For there are cases in which S's ϕ-ing constitutes good evidence for S's f-ness even though S did not perform the action of ϕ-ing *because* he is-f, nor for the reason that he wants someone to know that he is-f; and such situations do not constitute cases of revealing. For example, S's sitting in church at a certain time may be good evidence (to a qualified observer) that S is feeling resentful at that time. But S is not revealing his resentment by sitting in church. And the factor missing is just that S is sitting in church neither *because* he is feeling resentful nor *for the reason* that he wants someone to know that he is.[13]

My reason for proposing this analysis of self-revelation was that I wanted to discover how this oft-discussed action fits into our schematism for the role of cultural artefacts in human action. If my analysis is anywhere near correct, the conclusion must be that self-revelation is neither a causally generated nor a count-generated action. Always self-revelation is generated; never is it performed foundationally. But the analysis shows that the connection between self-revelation and some action whereby someone generates it fits neither the pattern of causal generation nor that of count-generation. It is more complex than either.

What remains is a consideration of how self-expression fits into our schematism. For this, too, we need an analysis of the action before we can draw our conclusions.

The beginning of an analysis of self-expression goes exactly like the beginning of an analysis of self-revelation. To express her gratitude by saying that she is grateful, Rebecca must *in fact be* grateful, and must *in fact perform* the action of saying that she is grateful. So the difference between self-revelation and self-expression lies, in part at least, in the different 'hook-up' between the state of self and the generating act. What is the connection in the case of self-expression?

Consider these two claims:

(a) He expressed his disgust by asserting that he was disgusted, and

(b) He expressed his disgust by uttering the words 'I'm disgusted'.

One can of course assert that one is disgusted when one is not. But one cannot do so knowingly and sincerely. This is an action such that one cannot perform it knowingly and sincerely unless one is disgusted. In turn, one can utter the words 'I'm disgusted' without asserting that one is disgusted. But if one's uttering 'I'm disgusted' *counts as* one's asserting that one is

---

[13] Incidentally, the 'because' in proviso (ii) (c) must cover both reasons and causes. For proviso (ii) (c) must apply to the case in which the *cause* of S's gripping the podium so hard that his knuckles turn white is S's nervous apprehension, and the case in which the *reason* for Rembrandt's painting a whole series of pictures as he did is his fondness for chiaroscuro.

disgusted, then by uttering these words one has count-generated an action which one cannot perform knowingly and sincerely without being disgusted.

These facts about doing things knowingly and sincerely seem to me crucial in the analysis of (a) and (b). I suggest that the person expressed his disgust by asserting that he was disgusted if he was disgusted, if he did assert that he was disgusted, and if he could not knowingly and sincerely perform that action unless he were disgusted. Similarly, the person expressed his disgust by uttering the words 'I'm disgusted' if he was disgusted, if he did utter these words, and if his uttering those words counts as his performing some action which he could not knowingly and sincerely perform unless he were disgusted. In general, this can be said:

S expresses his f-ness at t if:
    (i) S is-f at t,
   (ii) S's f-ness is a state of consciousness, and
  (iii) there is some action ϕ-ing such that
       (a) S performs the action of ϕ-ing at t, and
      (b) either S cannot knowingly and sincerely perform the action of ϕ-ing at t unless S is-f at t, or there is some action ψ-ing such that S's ϕ-ing counts as S's ψ-ing and S cannot knowingly and sincerely perform the action of ψ-ing at t unless he is-f at t.

But one is not limited, in expressing some state of consciousness, to those actions which have the presence of such a state of consciousness as a sincerity condition. For consider such cases as these:

  (c) Rebecca expressed her gratitude to Mary by sending over a shrub from the local nursery, and
  (d) John Cage expressed his Buddhist convictions by adopting aleatory techniques in his music.

Here the issue of doing something knowingly and sincerely does not even arise. Instead, what we have in these cases is the phenomenon of someone wanting to do and actually doing something which he believes to be, and which is in fact, inherently *fitting* (congruent) to his state of consciousness. Rebecca fetched about for some action which would be inherently fitting to her feeling of gratitude, and hit on sending over a favourite shrub. And John Cage fetched about for some strategies in music which would inherently fit his Buddhist convictions, and hit on chance techniques. So I suggest this analysis: Cage expressed his Buddhist convictions by adopting aleatory techniques in his music if Cage did have Buddhist convictions, if he did adopt aleatory techniques in his music, if those techniques are inherently fitting to his Buddhist convictions, and if he adopted those techniques because he wanted to do or produce something inherently fitting to his Buddhist convictions and believed that the use of aleatory techniques would satisfy this goal.

I think that we have covered the full range of strategies for self-expression. To express some one of one's states of consciousness one must either do or produce something which is inherently fitting (congruent) to that state of consciousness, or one must do something which one cannot knowingly and sincerely do unless one is in that state of consciousness. Thus:

S expresses his f-ness at t if and only if:
   (i) S is-f at t,
   (ii) S's f-ness is a state of consciousness, and
   (iii) there is some action ϕ-ing such that S performs the action of ϕ-ing at t, and one or other of the following is true:
      (a) S cannot knowingly and sincerely perform the action of ϕ-ing at t unless s is-f at t, or there is some action ψ-ing such that S's ϕ-ing counts as S's ψ-ing and S cannot knowingly and sincerely perform the action of ψ-ing at t unless he is-f at t; or
      (b) at t S wants to do or produce something significantly fitting (congruent) to his f-ness, he believes that ϕ-ing will satisfy this goal, and ϕ-ing does in fact satisfy this goal.

If these analyses are correct, then self-expression differs from self-revelation in at least four important respects.

(1) The action by which one expresses one's self must be done intentionally, or at least must be an action on which there are conditions of knowledgeability and sincerity. No such requirement holds for revelation. The revealing action may

have been one done intentionally, or one on which there are knowledgeability and sincerity conditions. But it need not have been of that sort. The speaker who revealed his nervous apprehension did not intend to grip the podium so tightly that his knuckles turned white, neither are there any conditions for performing that action knowingly and sincerely. Such non-intentionally performed actions as writhing in pain and grimacing may be revelatory; they cannot be expressional. In that difference lies the principal divergence between revelation and expression.

(2) Self-revelation requires that the revealing act be *good evidence* for the revealed state of consciousness. There is no requirement that the expressing act be good evidence for the expressed state. Cage may well have expressed his Buddhist beliefs by using aleatory strategies even though the mere presence of those strategies in his music is not good evidence for his holding those beliefs.

(3) It is not required for self-expression that the expressing act be perceptible, whereas it is required for self-revelation that the revealing act be perceptible. What comes to mind here are the Croce–Collingwood discussions concerning expression, in which it is claimed that expressing may be done wholly in one's mind. That seems correct, though I think it happens far less often than Croce and Collingwood suggest. One can express one's gratitude to God by reciting mentally a prayer of thanksgiving. Revelation involves making perceptible, expression does not.[14]

(4) Lastly, the only candidates for self-expression are states of consciousness—one's feelings, one's thoughts, one's attitudes, one's beliefs, etc. The scope of self-revelation is

---

[14] Incidentally, we can also make sense of the Collingwood claim that the expression of emotions involves clarification of those emotions. That seems to me not to be a necessary condition for expressing one's emotions. But in trying to express some one of one's emotional states—whether by trying to do something which is fitting to that emotional state, or by trying to do something whose knowing and sincere performance requires that one be in that emotional state—one may be forced to clarify that emotional state to oneself. 'When a man is said to express emotion, what is being said about him comes to this. At first he is conscious of having an emotion, but not conscious of what this emotion is. All he is conscious of is a perturbation or excitement, which he feels going on within him, but of whose nature he is ignorant. While in this state, all he can say about his emotion is: "I feel ... I don't know what I feel." From this helpless and oppressed condition he extricates himself by doing something which we call expressing himself.' R. G. Collingwood, *The Principles of Art*, p. 109.

broader. Any non-perceptible state of oneself is a candidate for self-revelation—one's origins, one's having a sore knee, etc.

Now for the point that we wished to lead up to. How is Rembrandt's performance of action (3), *creating the painting 'Bathsheba'*, related to his performance of action (10), *expressing his aversion to the Renaissance cult of the ideal body*? Well, if our analysis of self-expression is approximately correct, then in cases of self-expression as well as in cases of self-revelation we are confronted with two acts joined by act-generation; but the mode of generation is different from, and more complex than, either count-generation or causal generation. When Rebecca expressed her gratitude by sending over a 'Thank you' note, her act of sending over the note neither count-generated nor causally generated her act of expressing her gratitude. Still, never is self-expression performed foundationally. Always it is generated.

IV. *The Role of Art in the Actions of the Public*

In developing my schematism for the role of art in action I have thus far looked at matters exclusively from the standpoint of the artist, discussing the structurally diverse roles which his composition can play in his actions. Quite obviously the same basic structure holds for the role of a work of art in the actions of the public. There is no point labouring the obvious. But two matters pertaining to the relation *between* the actions of the artist and the actions of his public are worth discussing.

Sometimes an artist's use of his work to perform some action *presupposes* that the work also functions or is used in a certain way in the actions of his public. For example, look once again at the action Rembrandt performed of giving people aesthetic delight, an action he generated by creating his painting *Bathsheba*. His generation of this action by creating *Bathsheba* presupposes that people will aesthetically contemplate the painting *Bathsheba*. And if Rembrandt believes that by creating a painting of Bathsheba he will generate the action of giving people aesthetic delight, he must also believe that people will submit his painting to the action of aesthetic contemplation.

The structure here can easily be clarified. The act of Rembrandt's giving people aesthetic delight consists of

Rembrandt's bringing about the event of people being aesthetically delighted. This event is caused by the act of *Rembrandt's creating 'Bathsheba'*. But this is not and cannot be the sufficient cause. What is also required, as a causal factor, is acts of people aesthetically contemplating *Bathsheba*. The event, like all events, has multiple causes.

Secondly, we have spoken of the artist as creating a work *for certain uses or functions*; likewise we might have spoken of the distributor as distributing a work *for certain uses or functions*. (We might also have spoken of the performer thus.) These phenomena, creating a work for certain uses or functions, and distributing a work for certain uses or functions, are obviously fundamental to a sociology of art. But what do they consist of?

To simplify the discussion, let us concentrate on the artist. Once we know what it is for him to create his work for such-and-such use or function we can easily make the appropriate applications to the distributor.

A factor that must at once be brought into consideration is that an artist may produce a work for use or function in the actions of a limited group of people. He need not make the work for the populace at large. Striking examples of this are those in which the creators of tomb art made their artefacts to be used by the dead in their afterlife.

We must also bring into consideration the fact that a work of art may function in, or be used to perform, actions for which it was never made. Rembrandt's works have functioned in securing financial gain to their owners. Rembrandt probably knew, or if not knew, at least expected, that his works would thus function. He may even have believed that they would serve that function well. But he did not produce them *for* that function. So what is it for him to have made his works for a certain use or function?

In being made for certain uses or functions works of art are like cultural artefacts generally, and it will help to look away from art for just a moment to consider some non-art artefacts—say, barbiturate sleeping pills. The manufacturer of barbiturate sleeping pills knows that his product can function effectively for committing suicide. Not only does he know this; he probably expects that some of his production will in fact function thus. But he does not make his pills *for* committing suicide. He makes them for inducing sleep in people. And he makes them to function thus for people who can tell whether the prospective taker lacks the 'negative indications'. To do all this consists, I suggest, in something like the following: to want persons, who can tell whether some prospective taker has the negative indications, to have something for inducing sleep in people; to believe that those persons who are thus discerning can satisfactorily use barbiturate pills for that purpose; and to produce barbiturate pills for the reason that one wants that and believes that.[15]

So also, for Rembrandt to produce his painting *Bathsheba* for the Dutch bourgeoisie for use as an object of aesthetic contemplation is, I suggest, for Rembrandt: to want the Dutch bourgeoisie to have something (additional) to serve as object of aesthetic contemplation, to believe that *Bathsheba* can be used satisfactorily for that purpose by them, and to produce *Bathsheba* for the reason that he wants that and believes that. So in general: to produce x for use or functioning in action A by members of set α, is to want the members of α to have something (additional) for use or functioning in A, to believe that x can satisfactorily be used by or function for the members of α in performing A, and to produce x for the reason that one wants that and believes that.

We wanted our analysis to be such that, on the analysis, a person could know or expect that his work would be used or function in a certain way without having made his work for that use or function. This result is in fact secured. A composer may know that his work will function to create a soothing auditory background in dining establishments. He may even want people to have works which satisfactorily serve that function, and may believe that his own work will do so. But it may still be that he did not produce *his* work for the reason that he wanted people to have something (additional) which could satisfactorily function thus. Unless that too holds, he does not, on the analysis, produce his work *for* creating a soothing background in dining establishments.

Someone might hesitate to accept the analysis because of the phenomenon of the charlatan. The charlatan maker of some patent medicine does not believe that his product can

---

[15] I except the case in which S *compels* P to make x for such-and-such use.

satisfactorily function for curing piles. But may it not still be the case that he makes it *for* curing piles? The answer, I think, is 'No'. He does not make his product for curing piles. He makes it for lining his own pockets with money. What he believes is that his product will satisfactorily serve *that* function.

An understanding of what it is to make a work of art for some use or function is indispensable to an adequate sociology of art. It is also indispensable to an adequate history of art—if not, indeed, to art criticism. For how an artist makes his work is, in part, determined by what he makes it for. If we do not know what uses or functions he made it for, there will characteristically be features of his work such that we do not know why he made them as he did. There may in fact be features of the work that we wholly overlook. The result may well be that our aesthetic delight is diminished from what it might otherwise have been.

PART TWO

Works

I. *Preliminaries*

Olivier Messiaen's composition for orchestra, *Et Exspecto Resur-rectionem*, has five sections, each of which is a setting of a passage from St John's *Apocalypse*. To say that each is a setting of a passage is to say, I think, that Messiaen used his music to project the very same state of affairs that St John projected with his words. How music can be used to perform such an action is a topic to be taken up later. Here let us ask: what is the work of art that Messiaen composed and which he entitled *Et Exspecto Resurrectionem?* Does it consist just of the sounds he composed? Or does it consist of the sounds along with the world projected?

In the Introduction I said that the concept of work of art that I would use throughout is that of *an instance of one of the major fine arts*. The word 'instance' is a rather ambiguous word, however. In all the arts there are perceptible artefacts; these can always with reason be regarded as instances of the art. Shortly we shall see that, in turn, these perceptible artefacts can in some cases be differentiated into occurrence-works and occurrences thereof. Secondly, when a world is projected with a perceptible artefact, there is the pair whose members are the artefact and the world; and this too can with reason be regarded as an instance of the art. Thirdly, in such arts as poetry, fiction, and drama, the world projected can by itself be regarded, with reason, as an instance of the art. (That is perhaps how we are thinking when we regard ourselves as presented with the same piece of litera-ture that we were presented with on an earlier occasion, even though the perceptible artefact—the text—that we are presented with is only a translation of that with which we were presented earlier and thus not identical with it.)

Which of all these possibilities do I have in mind when I speak of *instances* of the arts? All of them. Different as they are, I

shall regard entities of all these different sorts as *instances* of the
arts. Accordingly, all will be spoken of as *works of art*.

Our project is to explore the projection of worlds by way of
artefacts of art. We begin our exploration with an inquiry, in
this Part, into the nature of the perceptible artefacts used to
perform such projection. Accordingly, in this Part we shall not
be inquiring into the nature of works of art generally. We shall
not be inquiring into the nature of those projected worlds which
are works of art; that inquiry will be conducted in the next Part,
Part Three. Neither shall we here be inquiring into the nature of
those works of art which are artefact-cum-world. The nature of
such works will become clear by the end of Part Three. Here, to
say it once again, our concern will only be with the nature
of those *perceptible artefacts* which are works of art – these
perceptible artefacts being what are used in the arts to
project worlds. The *text* of the literary work is here our concern;
not the world of the literary work, and also not the text-cum-
world.

II. *Some Distinctions among Artefacts of Art*

What sort of entity is the musical artefact? The dramatic? The
sculptural? The poetic? The cinematic? Are artefacts of art all
fundamentally alike in their ontological status? Are any or all of
them physical objects? Events? Mental states? Sets? Let us set
out toward the answers to these questions by making a rapid
survey of the terrain of the arts.

Performing some work of art consists of bringing about *a
performance* of it—that is to say, it consists of bringing about (in a
certain way) an occurrence of that which is performed.[1] Now
in several of the arts there is application for the distinction

---

[1] To be wholly precise I should add, 'or of bringing about (in a certain way) an
occurrence of the artefactual-component of an artefact-cum-world work'. I assume that
those works of art which are *worlds* cannot, strictly, be performed. There is nothing to
produce an occurrence of. What, then, the telling of a story (which is one species of a
world) consists of is something we shall see in Part Four. It probably should be
remarked that the phrase 'performance of...' can also be used as true of instances of
the *action* of performing something. Using the word in that sense, *the Beaux Arts Trio's
performing of Brahms' Trio in C Major, Opus 67 on 17 January 1976*, is a performance. I shall
try to avoid using the word in that sense, and confine myself to using it as true of
occurrences of *entities performed*.

between that which is a performance of something and that which is performed. In music, for example, one can distinguish between some performance of *Verklaerte Nacht* and the work performed by bringing about that performance—namely, Arnold Schoenberg's work *Verklaerte Nacht*. Similarly, in dance one can distinguish between some performance of *Swan Lake* and the work performed by bringing about that performance—namely, the ballet *Swan Lake*. So also in drama one can distinguish between some performance of *The American Dream* and the work performed, namely, Edward Albee's work *The American Dream*.

Some persons will be sceptical as to whether, in the cases cited and others of the same sort, we really do have two distinct entities—a performance and that which is performed. But assuming it to be true that the concept of a performance of something and the concept of something performed both have application to the arts, there are two sorts of considerations which force one to the conclusion that that which is performed on a given occasion is distinct from the performance of it.

In the first place, a thing performed and a performance thereof will always diverge in certain of their properties. For example, *having been composed by Schoenberg* is a property of *Verklaerte Nacht* but not of any performance of *Verklaerte Nacht*. On the other hand, *taking place at a certain time and place* is a property of every performance of *Verklaerte Nacht* but not of *Verklaerte Nacht itself*.

A second sort of consideration, one which is actually a specific application of the first, also leads to the conclusion that in certain of the arts one must distinguish between those entities which are performances and those entities which are works performed. This second sort of consideration hinges on applications of the concepts of identity and diversity. That which is performed on one occasion may be identical with that which is performed on another; George Szell, for example, may twice over have conducted a performance of *Verklaerte Nacht*. Thus there may be two distinct performances of one single musical work. But two distinct things cannot each be identical with some one thing. Thus the two distinct performances cannot both be identical with the work performed. But if one of them, call it *A*, was identified with the work performed, then the other, call it B, would, by virtue of being a performance of the work performed, be a performance of performance A. Not only that, but performance A would be capable of being performed on many other occasions as well. Both of these consequences seem impossible.

A performance of a work of art is an occurrence of it (or of the artefactual component of it). So let us henceforth call a work of art which can be performed, an *occurrence-work*. Let us likewise call a work whose artefactual component can be performed, in case it is an artefact-cum-world work, an *occurrence-work*. Most if not all occurrence-works are universals, in that they can have multiple occurrences. Lastly, let us keep in mind that occurrences of the perceptible artefacts of art are themselves perceptible artefacts of art.

The ontological status of occurrences seems relatively clear. That of occurrence-works, however, is immensely perplexing. Occurrences are events. They take place at a certain time, begin at a certain time, and end at a certain time, last for a certain stretch of time, and have temporal parts in the sense that each occurrence is half over at a certain time, three-quarters over at a certain time, one-eighth over at a certain time, etc. But what sort of entity is an occurrence-work, and in particular, an occurrence-work which is a perceptible artefact? That is something which we shall have to discuss in considerable detail. What should already be clear, though, is that occurrence-works are not events. Thus already we can answer one of our opening questions. The perceptible artefacts of art are not all alike in their ontological status.

In certain of the non-performing arts distinctions similar to the occurrence/ occurrence-work distinction have application. Consider for example graphic art prints. Here a commonly applied distinction is that between a particular impression and the work of which it is an impression; between, for example, the tenth impression of *Obedient unto Death* and the print of which it is an impression, namely, Georges Rouault's *Obedient unto Death*. And consider those cases in which sculpture is produced from a mould. Here a commonly applied distinction is that between a particular casting of, say *The Thinker* and the sculptural work of which it is a casting, namely, Rodin's *The Thinker*. Consider thirdly those cases in the field of architecture in which many different buildings are produced according to one set of specifications. Here a commonly applied distinction is that between a given example of, say, the Tech-Bilt House No. 1 and that of which it is an example, namely, the Tech-Bilt House No. 1.

It may be noticed that an impression of a work of graphic art, a casting of a work of sculptural art, and an example of a work of architectural art, are all enduring physical objects. That is why I have grouped these particular arts together. In order to have a convenient terminology, let us call the works of which there can be impressions, castings, or examples (as well as those works of whose artefactual components there can be such entities), *object-works*. And let us say that impressions, castings, and examples are *objects* of object-works. Thus as a counterpart to the occurrence/occurrence-work distinction we have the object/object-work distinction. As with occurrences, let us remember that those entities which are objects of the perceptible artefacts of art are themselves perceptible artefacts of art.

The considerations which impel us to distinguish between an object-work and those entities which are objects thereof are parallel to those which impel us to distinguish between an occurrence-work and those entities which are occurrences thereof. One consideration is again that of divergence in properties. *Having been pulled through the press last* may be a property of a given impression of Rouault's print *Obedient unto Death*; it is not a property of the print itself. A second consideration is again to be derived from applications of the concept of identity and diversity. There can be two different castings of the same one sculptural work; and neither both of these castings together nor either one singly can be identified with the work. In the case of object-works there is yet a third sort of consideration which may be adduced, hinging on applications of the concepts of existence and non-existence. Any one of the several objects of an object-work can be destroyed without the object-work itself thereby being destroyed. I could, for example, perform the horrifying operation of burning my impression of Rouault's *Obedient unto Death*, but I would not thereby put the print itself out of existence.

The ontological status of the objects of object-works is

relatively unproblematic: they are physical objects. Of course plenty of things about the nature of physical objects remain unclear. Yet we know what they are, and it is clear that impressions, castings, and examples are to be numbered among them. But what is an object-work? What is *its* ontological status? That is something which we shall have to discuss in detail.

There remain literary works, films, and paintings to consider. A literary text can be both written down and 'sounded out'. There can be both copies of it and utterances of it. Now a copy is a physical object, whereas an utterance of something is an event. Further, the *copy of* relation seems closely similar to the *example of*, the *impression of*, and the *casting of* relations. Accordingly I shall say that a copy of a literary text is an object of it; and I shall add literary texts (along with the text-cum-world works of which they are the artefactual components) to the group of entities to be called object-works. But since an *utterance* of a literary work is an event, very much like a performance, I shall also include literary texts in the class of things to be called occurrence-works (along with the text-cum-world works of which they are the artefactual components). Thus literary works and literary texts are both occurrence-works and object-works.

Saying this, however, makes one want to look back to see whether we do not have good ground for saying that works of music and drama are also both occurrence-works and object-works. In the case of dramatic works I think it is clear that we must say 'No'. The artefactual component of a dramatic work is a pattern of actions. The actions will in all but the most unusual cases include speech actions. But in all but the most unusual cases they will include other sorts of actions as well. More importantly, that pattern of actions which is the artefactual component of a dramatic work will always include actions of *role-playing*. For these reasons, a reading aloud or a recitation of the script of a drama is not yet a performance of the drama. And a copy of the script for a drama is not a copy of the drama but a copy of the instructions for proper performance thereof. The script may of course be a literary work in its own right. And that work can have both readings aloud and copies. But the artefactual component of the dramatic work is not the script. And a copy of the script is not a copy of the artefactual component. The drama has no copies. All it can have is performances. Dramas are only occurrence-works.

Music presents a somewhat less clear situation. The crucial question is this: does a copy of the score stand to a work of music in a relationship similar enough to that in which a copy stands to a work of literature to justify us in calling a score-copy an object of the work? It seems to me not decisively clear one way or the other. What does seem clear is that a word can be both inscribed and uttered, whereas a sound cannot be inscribed but only sounded. The marks in a copy of a score are not instances of sounds but rather (instances of) instructions for producing sounds. Of course an inscription of some sequence of words can also be treated as instructions for the utterance of that sequence; yet at the same time it is genuinely an instance of those words. Some words, especially those in primitive cultures, are never written down; some, especially those in technical languages, are never sounded out. Yet most words have a dual manifestation. But suppose someone suggests that music should be thought of as being composed of *notes* rather than sounds; and then goes on to argue that notes, like words, can be both sounded out and written down. Obviously this is a suggestion worthy of further investigation. Whether it is true or false is not at once evident. But nothing that is said hereafter will depend essentially on whether it is true or false. So I shall continue to suppose that a work of music (or its artefactual component) consists of sounds.

The film seems to have a dual status similar to that of words. One and the same film may have many prints, a print being a physical object; and it may also have many showings, a showing being an occurrence. Thus a film, like a literary work, has claim to being regarded as both an object-work and an occurrence-work. There is this difference worth noting, though: a showing of a film will always occur by way of the showing of a certain print of the film, whereas the utterance of a literary work need not occur by way of the reading of some copy of the work. One can recite it from memory.

As for paintings, it seems that neither the object/object-work distinction nor the occurrence/occurrence-work distinction has application, nor does it seem that any close counterpart to these

distinctions has application. There is of course the distinction
between the work and reproductions of the work. But this is a
different distinction, as can be seen from the fact that one can
also have reproductions of each of the various impressions of a
print. What is lacking in painting is any counterpart to the
print/impression distinction. All one has is a counterpart to the
impression/reproduction distinction. The point may be put by
saying that all the impressions of a print are originals, none is a
reproduction. The conclusion must be that a painting is a
physical object. But more will be said on this matter later in our
discussion.

To say that a painting is merely a physical object is not to
deny that reproductions of paintings along with reproductions
of sculpture are entitled to being called 'works of art' in their
own right. So too are films, though for the most part they are
'reproductive' of incidents of role-playing and of visible events
and objects. And so too are recordings, though most recordings
are 'reproductive' of occurrences of sound. It is interesting to
note, however, that in the case of visual art reproductions and
sculpture reproductions one again often has application for the
print/impression or the work/casting distinction; and that in
the case of recordings (records), one can distinguish between
the recording on the one hand and the various discs of
the recording on the other, and in turn between a given disc
on the one hand and various playings of the disc on the
other.

We have spoken of the artefacts of art as perceptible; so a
word should be said about the relation between our perception
of an occurrence-work and our perception of the occurrences
thereof, and about the relation between our perception of an
object-work and our perception of the objects thereof. It has on
occasion been claimed that only occurrences and objects can be
perceived, not occurrence-works and object-works.[2] Surely this
is a highly paradoxical and implausible claim—that nobody,
for example, can hear Bach's *Musical Offering* and that nobody
can see the Tech-Bilt House No. 1. The situation seems rather
to be that one perceives (i.e., sees, hears, touches, or reads) an

---

[2] C. S. Peirce, *Collected Works of C. S. Peirce* (Harvard Univ. Press: Cambridge, 1933),
iv. 537; and C. S. Stevenson, 'On "What Is a Poem?"' in *Philosophical Review* (July
1957), p. 330.

occurrence-work or object-work by perceiving an occurrence or object of the work, and that only thus does one perceive the work.[3] In looking at a print one sees two things at once, the print and an impression thereof. In listening to a symphony one hears two things at once, the symphony and a performance thereof. Further, it is of immense importance for the critic to distinguish these two sorts of entities. For the very same predicate may be true of a musical performance and false of the work of which it is a performance.

To simplify our terminology, I shall henceforth call only those artefacts of art which are occurrence-works or object-works, *art works*. And both occurrences of art works and objects of art works will be called *examples* of art works. I shall continue to use 'work of art' to cover both works and their examples, along with such things as paintings which are neither. Perhaps here is also a good place to remark that the fact that the occurrence/occurrence-work distinction or the object/object-work distinction applies to a certain art does not imply that it applies *throughout* that art. There may be works of that art which are neither. Those works of music, for example, which are *total* improvisations (as distinguished from those which are improvisations on a theme) are neither occurrences of works nor occurrence-works themselves.[4]

---

[3] With this qualification: in the case of the temporal arts one can also perceive the work by perceiving a reproduction of an object or performance of it—though one hasn't then heard it live or seen it live. What I do not admit is that the musician who 'hears' a work by reading the score *really hears* it. He only *imagines* its sound.

[4] The general drift of the distinctions made above has been acquiring something of a consensus in recent years among those who have concerned themselves with the nature of works of art. See Andrew Harrison, 'Works of Art and other Cultural Objects' in *Proc. of the Aristotelian Society*, lxviii (1967–8), pp. 105–28: Margararet MacDonald, 'Art and Imagination', in *Proc. of the Aristotelian Society*, liii (1952–3), pp. 205–26; Joseph Margolis, *The Language of Art and Art Criticism* (Wayne State Univ. Press: Detroit, 1965), Chap. 4; C. L. Stevenson, 'On "What is a Poem?"' in *Phil. Review* (July 1957); R. Wellek and A. Warren, *Theory of Literature* (Harcourt, Brace & Co.: New York, 1956), Chap. XII; and Richard Wollheim, *Art and its Objects* (Harper & Row: New York, 1968). Very often writers have borrowed and generalized Peirce's type/token distinction only with reference to words and their written instances. But often all the things which I have labelled occurrence-works and object-works are called types, and all those which I have labelled occurrences or objects of such works are called tokens. Using this terminology our question can be put thus: what is the ontological status of those types which are the artefacts of art?

III. *Some Untenable Views on the Ontology of Art Works*

Let us begin by putting behind us certain common and tempting but none the less untenable views on the nature of art works. In the first place, art works cannot be identified with any physical objects. With what physical object, for example, might a work of music be identified? With the score? But in the case of scores we must also distinguish between the score and a copy thereof—which is just another example of the object/object-work distinction. So with the composer's autograph copy of the score? That the work of music is not to be identified with this physical object is clear from two facts: there may never have been such an object, since many musical works have never been scored; and even if there is or were such an object, it may be destroyed and the work remain in existence. In the case of graphic art the temptation is strong to identify the print with the plate that the artist prepares. But this identification should also be resisted; for the plate may be destroyed without thereby destroying the print. Thus it is in general the case that art works are not to be identified with physical objects.[5]

Are they then to be identified with entities of consciousness—that is, with entities whose existence at a certain time depends on their being an object of some act of consciousness at that time? Here it might be useful to look at the view propounded by R. G. Collingwood, namely, that an art work has the status of a thing imagined. Collingwood says this: 'The work of art proper is something not seen or heard, but something imagined.'[6] And further, 'The business "of an artist proper".' is 'for example, to make a tune. This tune is already complete and perfect when it exists merely as a tune in his head, that is, an imaginary tune. Next, he may arrange for the tune to be played before an audience. Now there comes into existence a real tune, a collection of noises. But which of these two things is the work of art? Which of them is the music? The answer is implied in what we have already said: the music, the work of art, is not the collection of noises, it is the tune in the composer's head. The noises made by the performers, and heard by the audience, are

---

[5] For a more detailed consideration of the view here rejected, see Wellek and Warren, op. cit.; and R. Wollheim, op.cit.

[6] R. G. Collingwood, op. cit., p. 142.

not the music at all; they are only means by which the audience, if they listen intelligently (not otherwise) can reconstruct for themselves the imaginary tune that existed in the composer's head.'[7]

What does not come through with any clarity in these passages from Collingwood is whether or not he holds that a condition of a tune's existing at a certain time is that it be the object of some act of consciousness occurring at that time—for example, the act of someone's imagining it. Suppose, though, that he does not hold that a tune is an entity of consciousness. Then we are told nothing positive as to the ontological status of art works. Though they cannot be perceived, they can be the object of acts of consciousness other than that of perception while yet existing independently of being the object of any such act. But entities of fundamentally different sorts fit this description: numbers, God, the equator.

Suppose then that Collingwood holds that art works are just entities of consciousness—though of a somewhat special sort, since they are not private to a single consciousness but can be shared among consciousnesses. A number of questions then come at once to mind. When one is 'imagining' the second movement of some quartet and no one else is 'imagining' any part of it, has the first movement then gone out of existence? And when one is 'imagining' the first occurrence of the second theme of the second movement and no one else is 'imagining' any part of it, has the first theme then gone out of existence? In short, does an entire work exist so long as someone is 'imagining' some part of it in the course of 'imagining' the whole? Or does only that fragment which someone is actively 'imagining' exist at the time it is actively imagined? Though the latter interpretation seems most in the spirit of the proposal, the former would seem to be the most charitable interpretation. Even so, it is clear that this view has the consequence that Beethoven's quartets, Rembrandt's prints, and Yeats's poems flit in and out of existence. For at some times these are and at other times these are not actually the object of some act of consciousnesses. But this consequence is surely false. Have not Beethoven's quartets, Rembrandt's prints, and Yeats's poems existed at least ever since their composition?

[7] Ibid., p. 139.

Let it be noted, though, that it does not follow from the fact that art works are not entities of consciousness that they cannot be composed in one's head. Perhaps musical and literary works can be. We shall have more to say on that later. And perhaps it is the conviction that they can be composed in one's head that has led some people to think of them as entities of consciousness. But from the proposition that an art work can be composed simply by 'imagining' it, without benefit of voice or limb, it does not follow that it depends for its existence (thereafter) on being consciously imagined by someone or other.

Another common but unsatisfactory view which deserves at least brief consideration is that occurrence-works and object-works are *sets* of their examples. The untenability of this suggestion can be seen by noticing that whatever members a set has, it has essentially,[8] whereas an occurrence-work or object-work might always have had different and more or fewer occurrences or objects than it does have; and by noticing that if set α has no members and set β has no members, then α is identical with β; whereas it is not the case that if art work γ has no examples and art work δ has no examples, then γ is identical with δ.

That there is but one null set is of course clear enough. But that a set cannot have had a different membership from what it does have is a fact apt to be confused with related but different facts. The property, *being a member of Carter's cabinet*, is a property shared in common by all and only the members of a certain set; the set, namely, whose members are all and only the members of Carter's cabinet. Let us for convenience's sake name this set, C. Now whoever has the property of being a member of Carter's cabinet has it only contingently. Accordingly that set which is C might have been such that some of its members lacked this property; indeed, all might have lacked it. Alternatively, persons who are not members of C might have had this property. Thus some other set than C might have been such that all and only its members have the property of being members of Carter's cabinet. But all of these facts pertaining to what might have been in place of what is are thoroughly compatible with the fact that C has its membership essentially. (See the next Section for a fuller discussion of these points.)

---

[8] For a defence of the view that sets have their memberships essentially, see my *On Universals*, pp. 178–80.

One other oddity of the view that art works are sets of their examples is worth noting. A generally unnoticed, but what I take to be genuine, fact about sets is that in order for some entity at a time t to bear to a certain set α the relation of being a member of α, the entity in question must exist at t. Sets cannot have as members entities that there aren't. Now if this is true, then there will be many different pairs of times such that the set of all and only those things which are copies of *Ulysses* at one of the times is distinct from the set of all and only those things which are copies of *Ulysses* at the other time. For, of course, copies of *Ulysses* come into and go out of being. Further, there will never be any such set as the set of all and only those things which are, were, or will be copies of *Ulysses*. For the destroyed copies are no longer available to be members of any set whatsoever. As copies of *Ulysses* come into and go out of existence, there is a whole flux of sets each of the sort that it has as members all and only those copies of *Ulysses* which exist at some particular time. With which of these, then, are we to identify *Ulysses*? The first? The last? The largest? The smallest? All of the available answers are equally implausible.

Our question remains unanswered: what is the ontological status of art works?

IV. *Of Works and Kinds*

One striking feature of the relationship between an art work and its examples is the pervasive sharing of predicates between them. Let me explain. Take some logical predicate[9] which in normal usage can be predicated of two distinct things in such a way as to assert something true in both cases. Let us say that in such a case those two things *share that predicate*. 'Is in the key of C minor' can be predicated truly of Beethoven's Opus 111 and also of most if not all performances of Beethoven's Opus 111; hence the work and those performances share the predicate. 'Has the figure slightly off-centre to the right' can be predicated truly of Rouault's *Obedient unto Death* and likewise of most if not all impressions of *Obedient unto Death*; hence the predicate is shared between work and impressions. 'Has "no" as its third word' can be predicated truly of Yeat's 'Sailing to Byzantium'

[9] For the concept of a *logical predicate* see my *On Universals*, Chap. I.

and also of most if not all copies of 'Sailing to Byzantium'; and so the predicate is shared. In this linguistic fact of the massive sharing of predicates between art works and their examples lies a clue as to the nature of art works.

Not every predicate which can be predicated truly of an art work, or which can be predicated truly of some or even all examples of some art work, is shared between the work and its examples. 'Is a performance' and 'is an occurrence' are never thus shared; nor are 'can be repeatedly performed' and 'can repeatedly occur'. Nor is 'composed by Hindemith' ever thus shared. 'Is thought about by me' is in some cases shared between a certain work and all its examples, in other cases it is shared between a certain work and only some of its examples, while in yet other cases a certain art work shares it with none of its examples. And 'has "no" as its third word' is unshared between the poem 'Sailing to Byzantium' and my particular copy of it, whereas it is shared between the poem and *most* copies of it.

Since the days of Aristotle philosophers have observed that between *natural kinds* and their *examples* there is also a massive sharing of predicates. 'Is an animal' is true of the horse. Likewise it is (or was) true of Bucephalus, and of all other horses. 'Has four feet' is true of the grizzly (*ursus horribilis*). Likewise it is true of the grizzlies in Brookfield Zoo. And so forth, on and on. Thus there is a striking linguistic similarity between art works and natural kinds.

Could it be that the similarity goes deeper than language? Could it be that art works and natural kinds are *ontological* allies? That is the thought that comes to mind. And that is in fact the thesis I shall articulate. To put it more stringently: art works and natural kinds are just two species of kinds. Of course the linguistic facts do not *confirm* this thesis. They only provide a clue. The confirmation must lie in the thesis fitting the ontological facts.

Unfortunately I cannot here presuppose any articulate grasp of the concept of a kind. So I shall myself have to make some general comments on the topic. In making these comments my aim, of course, is not to compose a full treatise on the topic of kinds. Remaining far short of that, I shall limit myself to matters directly relevant to our subsequent discussion. Thus at several points I shall state the assumptions I am making without developing any justification for those assumptions.

I assume in the first place that there is a function f—call it the *associate*-function—mapping properties onto kinds, and such that the value of f for any property *being a k* is the corresponding kind: K. Call K, the *kind-associate* of the property of *being a k*. Thus the property of being a horse has for its kind-associate the kind: Horse. The property of being a chair in this room has for its kind-associate the kind: Chair In This Room. And the property of being red (being a red thing) has for its kind-associate the kind: Red Thing. No doubt what comes first to mind when we think of kinds is natural kinds—the species, the genera, the phylla, of the botanical and zoological taxonomist. But I see no reason for denying that there is also the kind (type, sort): Chair In This Room. Once we have allowed this, then the assumption above seems plausible.

Is f also a one-to-one mapping of properties into kinds? Well, I dare say we all hold, for any K and any K', that if it is possible that there is something which is an example of K but not of K', or vice versa, then $K \neq K'$.[10] If there can be something which is an example of The Cat but not of The Domestic Cat, or vice versa, then The Cat is not identical with The Domestic Cat. But suppose this were regarded as both a necessary and sufficient condition of kind-identity, thus:

$K = K' \equiv$ it is impossible that there be something which is an example of K and not of K', and vice versa.

Then there would be situations in which two properties would have the same kind as their associate. For consider the property of being a rectangle with sides of equal length, and the property of being a rectangle whose diagonals are at right angles to each other. These, I take it, are distinct properties. The kind-associate of the first is: Rectangle With Sides Of Equal Length. That of the second is: Rectangle Whose Diagonals Are At Right Angles To Each Other. Now it is impossible that there be something which is an example of one of these kinds and not of the other. Accordingly, on the criterion being considered these

[10] This follows from the fact that Leibniz's Law holds in all possible worlds, coupled with the fact that if $x \neq y$ in one possible world, then $x \neq y$ in any possible world.

are identical. And then this one kind is the kind-associate of two distinct properties.

However, I think that the proposed criterion for kind-identity should be rejected. On this criterion, there is just one impossible kind (kind such that it is impossible that there be an example of it); and also just one necessary kind (kind such that it is impossible that there be something which is not an example of it). Now later in our discussion (in Part Three) I shall argue that the best way to construe the nature of fictional characters, and fictional entities generally, is to construe them as being kinds. And among fictional entities there are impossible ones, for example, the six characters in Pirandello's *Six Characters in Search of an Author*. A character couldn't possibly walk onto a stage, as Pirandello's six do; though of course an *actor* can. But if there were only one impossible kind, the six characters of Pirandello's play would be one. And that one would in turn be identical with the impossible buildings in the worlds of M. C. Escher's prints. These are consequences to be avoided. Accordingly I shall reject the proposed criterion for identity of kinds; and in its place I shall assume that our associate-function is a one-to-one mapping of properties into kinds.

To get the concept of a kind sharply before us it will be helpful to begin by contrasting kinds with sets. (Some of the points here made about sets will be brief recapitulations of points made in the preceding section.) So consider the property of being a chair in this room. By reference to this property I can specify certain sets; for example, the set of all and only those things which (presently) possess the property. But I can also specify this very same set without reference to this property. If the chairs in this room had names, I could specify the set by listing the chairs by name. Or if the chairs in this room were the only items of furniture in this room, I could specify the set as the set of all and only those things which are (presently) items of furniture in this room. For in specifying the members of a set one uniquely specifies the set. And that in turn is true because of the identity criterion for sets: set A = set B if and only if there is nothing which is a member of the one which is not also a member of the other.

Further, the set of all and only those things which are (presently) chairs in this room retains its membership across time as long as it exists, and necessarily so. No matter whether these chairs do or do not stay forever in this room, as long as that set exists it will have exactly these chairs as members—no others, no more, no fewer. So it is in general. It is impossible for the sets there are to change in their membership across time. More strongly yet: it is impossible for *there to be* a set which changes in its membership across time. The members which a set has at any time in some possible world are those which it has at every time (at which it exists) in that possible world.

Likewise sets retain their membership across possible worlds. The set of chairs (presently) in this room *could not* now have had other or more or fewer members than it does have. It is the set of just exactly those things, and necessarily so. Thus it is in general. All sets have their membership essentially. Indeed, it is impossible for *there to be* a set which does not have its membership essentially. Sets retain their memberships across all possible worlds in which they exist. When we put the point of this paragraph together with the point of the preceding one we get this: it is impossible that there should be a set whose membership at some time in some possible world is different from what it is at that or some other time (at which it exists) in that or some other possible world (in which it exists).

It does not follow, though, that sets exist necessarily. In fact, not all do. There are presently three chairs in this room. Now chairs do not exist necessarily. So suppose that only two of these chairs had ever existed. Then the set whose membership consists of exactly these three chairs would not have existed; for a set cannot have some entity as member unless that entity exists. Thus this set exists contingently.

Does it also come into and go out of existence? Certainly. For these three chairs have not always jointly existed, and will not always jointly exist. But there is a set which has these three specific things as members when and only when those three things exist. A set cannot have among its members at a certain time things that don't exist at that time.[11] Or to put it from the

---

[11] In general, I hold that something cannot have a property at a certain time unless it exists at that time. Since this principle will several times over be appealed to in our discussion, let us give it a name. Call it the Principle of Exemplification. For further discussion on the matter, see my 'Can Ontology Do Without Events?'

other side: an entity x bears to the set A the property of being a member of A only when x exists. And of course if x does not at a certain time have the property of being a member of A, then A at that time does not have the (converse) property of having x as a member. But as we have already seen, sets have their memberships invariantly across time, and essentially. So the conclusion must be that some sets become and perish.

What follows is that, though all sets have their memberships essentially, it is not in general the case that each of the members of a set is essentially a member thereof. One of these chairs might have existed and not have been a member of the set of all and only the chairs (presently) in this room. For there might have been no such set. But of course it couldn't be that *all three* members of this set should exist at a certain time and this one not be a member of the set at that time.

Though the set of all and only those things which are presently chairs in this room has its membership essentially, it is possible that something should be a member of this set and not be a chair in this room. One of the chairs in question might well not have been (presently) in this room. Yet that circumstance, had it obtained, would not have deleted that chair from membership in the set. For once again, the set in question just *is* the set whose members are those very chairs, no matter what property those chairs have or lack (except, of course, the property of belonging to the set and whatever others are entailed by that).

In most of these ways kinds are different from sets. Many of the differences flow from the necessary truth, concerning kinds, that some entity x is an example at t of the kind: K, if and only if x at t has the property of being a k. Or in other words: it's impossible that there be a kind whose examples at a certain time lack at that time the property-associate of the kind. So, for example, it's a necessary truth that something is an example at a certain time of the kind: Chair In This Room, if and only if at that time it has the property of being a chair in this room.

Of course there is variation across time as to what does in fact have the property of being a chair in this room. At some times nothing has it, right now three things have it, at other times other things have it. Thus it varies across time as to what is an example of the kind: Chair In This Room. Furthermore, different things might (presently) have had the property of being a chair in this room than do in fact have it. Thus many kinds do not have their examples essentially. Their exampleships vary across possible worlds as well as across times in our actual world.

Next, suppose once again that the only items of furniture in this room are those three chairs of which I have been speaking. In spite of that, the kind: Item Of Furniture In This Room, would not then be identical with the kind: Chair In This Room. That can easily be seen in this case by noticing that there *could* be something which is an example of the one and not of the other. Rather, the situation would be that these two distinct kinds would coincide in their exampleships at this moment in history. Thus, whereas a listing by name of the three chairs in this room would uniquely specify the set whose members are these three chairs, it would not uniquely specify a kind. In general, specification of the examples of a kind does not uniquely specify the kind.

The kind: Chair In This Room, might exist even if for a time there were no chair in this room. There would then exist that kind, but it would lack for examples. But if that is so, what then is the criterion for the existence of kinds? Well, the kind: K, exists just in case the property of which it is the associate exists. But that just shifts the problem. Under what conditions does a property exist? Without here offering the rationale, the propositions I shall assert with sentences of the form 'The property of *being-f* exists' (alternatively, 'there is the property of *being-f*') are those which are true if and only if either something is-*f* or something is not-*f*.[12] Thus, for example, the property of being a round square exists. For something is not a round square.

[12] A detailed rationale for this policy can be found in chapters 5 and 7 of my book *On Universals*. However, on two significant points my discussion in the book is deficient.

In the first place, it does not succeed in coping with the Russell Paradox for properties. It is worth seeing why it does not, and how the Paradox can be coped with. In the course of my discussion there I picked out a set of propositions which I called *predicate entailment principles*. These are principles of the form: 'If something is-*f*, then there is such a predicable as *being-f*.' I held that all such principles are true, necessarily true. And the proposition that they are true I called the General Predicate Entailment Principle (General PEP).

To understand what propositions I had in mind we must especially be aware of how 'is-*f*' functions in the formula. It functions as representing predicate expressions, i.e., expressions capable of functioning as logical predicates. I shall not here rehearse the definition offered of 'logical predicate'. What is important to observe, though, is a condition that I attached to something's being a predicate expression. It comes to this: a predicate expression cannot be both true and false at the same time of some one thing. (Here and throughout it must be understood that if some sign 'is-*f*' us used on one occasion with sense *S* and on another occasion with a distinct sense *S'*, and if on both occasions it is used as a logical predicate, then the sign used on one occasion is a different *predicate* from that used on the other. Diversity of senses is sufficient for diversity of predicates.)

To see the need for attaching the above cited condition to something's being a predicate expression, let us adapt one of Russell's old examples. Let us say that the expression 'was generally considered to be identical with the author of *Waverley*' is true of what some expression 'α' denotes just in case the proposition, *that α is identical with the author of 'Waverley'*, was generally thought to be true. And suppose we regarded that expression as a predicate expression. Then by the General Predicate Entailment Principle there is the property of being generally considered to be identical with the author of *Waverley*. Now surely the proposition 'The author of *Waverley* is identical with the author of *Waverley*' was generally considered to be true. Accordingly the expression 'was generally considered to be identical with the author of *Waverley*' was true of the author of *Waverley*. And if it stood for a property, namely, the property of being generally considered to be identical with the author of *Waverley*, the author of *Waverley* would have that property. But now consider the proposition 'Scott is identical with the author of *Waverley*'. Apparently at a certain point in history that was not generally considered to be true. Accordingly, then, the expression 'was generally considered to be identical with the author of *Waverley*' was not true of Scott. And if that expression is regarded as standing for a property, that of being generally considered to be identical with the author of *Waverley*, Scott would lack that property. However, Scott was in fact identical with the author of *Waverley*. Hence he would both have and lack that property, at the same time. But that is an impossibility. So that expression cannot be regarded as standing for that property. And we can easily forestall the difficulties if, in our general PEP formula, we lay down the condition that only predicate expressions can replace 'is-*f*', and if we lay down the stipulation that something is a predicate expression only if it cannot be both true and false at the same time of the same thing. Thus 'was generally considered to be identical with the author of *Waverley*', in the sense we have given it above, is not a predicate expression.

And now consider the Russell Paradox for properties. Take, for example, the fact that the property of being a horse does not exemplify itself. It looks as if, on the General PEP, there is then the property of not exemplifying itself. But in fact there is no such property. For let us ask concerning this very property—the property of *not exemplifying itself*—whether it exemplifies itself. If it does exemplify itself, then it does not exemplify itself. And if it does not exemplify itself, then it does. But that is impossible. So there is no such property.

At the time of writing *On Universals* I thought that the condition explained above on what counts as a predicate expression would prevent the General PEP from committing us to there being such a property as that of *not exemplifying itself*. For I thought that the condition attached to something's being a predicate expression would eliminate 'does not exemplify itself' as a candidate for predicatehood. But that was mistaken. For the defect of this expression is not that it can be both true and false of something at a single time. Its defect is rather that *if* it stood for the property of not exemplifying itself, it *would* be both true and false of that property. So we need a *Limited PEP*. Not all propositions of the form 'Something is-*f*' entail the corresponding propositions of the form 'There is such a thing as *being-f*.' We need to pick out that limited set of those that

With these general comments about kinds as background, we can now move on to formulate some definitions useful in our subsequent discussions. The basic undefined concept will be that of the relation, *being an example of*, it being understood that

---

do. Of course it is not difficult to pick out *a* set all of whose members do. But we want a set such that its members are all and only those in the larger set which entail their correspondents. Is it possible to pick this out?

Well, we have already seen that the decisive peculiarity of the predicate 'does not exemplify itself' is that if it stood for the property of not exemplifying itself, it would itself be both true and false of that property. So, generalizing, let us say that some predicate expression 'is-*f*' is not a *permissible* predicate expression if it is such that, if it stood for the property of *being-f*, it would be both true and false of that property. Then the Limited P E P is exactly like the General P E P, except that the expressions which can replace the sign 'is-*f*' are confined to *permissible* predicate expressions. Such predicate expressions as 'does not exemplify itself' and 'lacks the property of exemplifying itself' are not permissible predicate expressions. And in the criterion for the existence of properties offered in the text above we must keep in mind that what replaces the sign 'is-*f*' must always be a permissible predicate expression.

Let it be said, though, that the fact that there is no such property as not exemplifying itself does not imply that we do not say something true when assertively uttering such a sentence as 'The property of being a horse does not exemplify itself.' On the contrary, we can even give an ontological construal of what is claimed. What is claimed is that the property of being a horse *lacks* the property of exemplifying itself. The crux is that we cannot in general say that to lack the property of *being-f* is to have the property of *not-being-f*; and neither can we hold that for every property, *being-f*, there is the complement to that property, namely, *not-being-f*.

I was mistaken on one further matter in *On Universals*. I said that though many sentences of the form 'There is such an entity (predicable) as *f*-ness' can be used to assert propositions which are true if and only if either something is-*f* or something is not-*f*, this insight could not be generalized. My argument was this. Introduce the predicate 'is tove', and give it the same sense as 'has the property last mentioned by John and which is and isn't red'. Now of course there is no such property as being tove. To claim that there is, is to assert a proposition which entails a contradiction. So I said that 'is tove' is true of nothing. I also said, though, that 'is not tove' is true of everything, (and that there is the property of not being tove). But if the criterion cited above were in general acceptable, we would be committed to holding that there is the property of being tove also—an absurdity.

But consider some sentence '*a* is not tove'. This can be used to assert two very different propositions. One is the proposition that there is the property of being tove and *a* lacks it. But that proposition is false, not matter what *a* is. Accordingly, 'is not tove' thus construed is true of nothing, as indeed 'is tove' is true of nothing. But the sentence may also be used to assert that it is not the case that *a* is tove. And that proposition is true. But then 'is not tove' has the same sense as does the predicate, 'it is not the case that ... is tove' (*not* the same sense as 'lacks the property of being tove'). And *that* predicate can harmlessly be viewed as standing for the property of *being such that it is not the case that it is tove*. There *is* such a property. Likewise there is a complement to it.

And so I think no absurdities follow from my declaration that I shall in general use sentences of the form 'There is such a predicable as *f*-ness' to assert propositions which are true if and only if either something is-*f* or something is not-*f*.

that which something is an example of is always a kind. (The relation is intransitive, non-symmetrical, and irreflexive.)

First, the concept of a possible kind:

Def. 1: K is a *possible* kind =df it is possible that there should be something which is an example of K.

Correspondingly, the concept of an *impossible* kind:

Def. 2: K is an *impossible* kind =df it is impossible that there should be something which is an example of K.

The concept of a possible kind, be it noted, is not the concept of a kind which can *exist*, but of a kind which can have an example; and that of an impossible kind is not that of a kind which can not exist, but of one which can not have an example. And now for the concept of a necessary kind:

Def. 3: K is a *necessary* kind =df it is impossible that there be something which is *not* an example of K.

We can then introduce the important concept of a property *being essential within* a kind:

Def. 4: (Having) the property P is *essential within* K =df P and K are such that necessarily if something is an example of K then it has P.

It is of crucial importance to notice the difference between a property being essential within a certain kind, and its being a property *of* that kind. The property of *being a physical object* is essential within the kind: Chair In This Room; there couldn't be something which was an example of that kind while lacking that property. But it is not a property *of* that kind. For neither this kind, nor any other is a physical object. Rather, this kind has the property of *having essential within it the property of being a physical object*.

Next, let us introduce the concept of two kinds *coinciding* at a certain time:

Def. 5: K *coincides with* K' at time t =df at t there is nothing which is an example of K which is not also an example of K and vice versa.

Thus, if this room now had only chairs as items of furniture, the kind: Item Of Furniture In This Room, would at present coincide with the kind: Chair In This Room.

Next, we shall need the concept of one kind *including* another:

Def. 6: K includes K' =df K and K' are such that necessarily
   if something is an example of K' then it is an example
   of K.

Thus the kind: Domestic Cat, includes the kind: Domesticated
Siamese Cat.

Given these definitions, we can affirm this truth: if K includes
K', and if the property P is essential within K, then P is also
essential within K'. And also this: if it is essential to x that it is an
example of K, and if the property P is essential within K, then P
is an essential property of x.[13] And this: if P is essential within k,
then the property of having-P- essential-within-it is an essential
property of K.

It will also be useful to have the concept of one kind being a
species of another—*ursus horribilis* being a species of *ursus*,
Bachelor being a species of Male Human Being, etc. Now it
might be thought that K is a species of K' just in case K'
includes K. But for one thing, an impossible kind is included
within every kind, and accordingly would be a species of every
kind—surely an absurdity. (Also a necessary kind includes
every kind, and thus would have every kind as a species—also
an absurdity.) Further, consider the two kinds: Right-Angled
Figure With Equal Length Sides, and Right-Angled Figure
Whose Diagonals Are At Right Angles To Each Other. These
include each other, and thus would be species of each other.
But that too seems not right. For reasons such as these, the
concept of a species will have to be defined somewhat more
circuitously than might at first be supposed. Let us first say that

Def. 7: P is a *conjunctive property of* properties *being-f* and *being-g*
   =df *being-f* and *being-g* are distinct properties, and P=the
   property of *being-f* & *being-g*.

Then let us formulate the concept of a conjunctive analysis of a
property:

Def. 8: The non-null set α of properties is a *conjunctive analysis* of
   property P=df The conjunctive property of the members
   of α is identical with P.

[13] P is an *essential* property of x =df there is no possible world in which x exists and
lacks P.

Later it will be helpful to have the concept of a property being *analytic within* a kind, a concept that can now be explained thus:

Def. 9: Property P is *analytic within* kind K =df P is a member of some conjunctive-analysis of K's property associate (viz., *being a k*).

And lastly, let us define 'species' thus:

Def. 10: K is a *species* of K' =df Every property which is a member of some conjunctive analysis of *being a k'*. (viz., the property-associate of K') is also a member of some conjunctive analysis of *being a k* (viz., the property-associate of K'), but not vice versa.

The kind: Bachelor, is by this criterion a species of the kind: Male Human Being. And notice that it is also included within the kind: Male Human Being. *Being included within* and *being a species of* do not always go hand in glove like this, however. For though an impossible kind is included within every kind, it is certainly not true that it is a species of every kind. And though a necessary kind includes every kind, it is not true that every kind is a species of it. Moreover, consider the kind: Closed Straight-Sided Figure Whose Interior Angles Are All Right Angles, and the kind. Closed Straight-Sided Figure Whose Diagonals Are Of Equal Length And At Right Angles. The latter is included within the former. There couldn't be an example of it which is not an example of the former (and not so vice versa). However, the latter is not a species of the former. For in some conjunctive analysis of the property-associate of the former there will appear the property of having all its interior angles right angles. But that property will not appear in any conjunctive analysis of the property-associate of the latter.

One more concept concerning kinds, of great importance to our subsequent purposes, must be introduced. Many, though not all, kinds are such that it is possible for them to have properly formed and also possible for them to have improperly formed examples. Let us call such kinds, *norm*-kinds. The Lion is obviously a norm-kind. The kind: Red Thing, however, seems not to be. For there can be no such entity as an improperly red thing, a malformedly red thing. So too the kind:

Properly Formed Orchid and the kind: Malformed Orchid, are not norm-kinds.

Now in the case of norm-kinds we have application for the concept of some property *being normative within* a certain kind.

Def. 11: The property P is *normative within* the norm-kind K =df K is a norm-kind, and it is impossible that there be something which is a properly-formed example of K and lacks P.

The properties of a species which the botanical or zoological taxonomist cites are, for the most part, properties normative within, but not essential within, the species. (Notice that any property essential within a norm-kind will also be normative within it; but not so vice versa.)[14]

Having presented the rudiments of a theory of kinds, my suggestion now is this: occurrence-works and object-works are *kinds*—kinds whose examples are the occurrences or objects of those works. An occurrence-work is an occurrence-kind of a

---

[14] In his article 'The Concept of a Kind' (in *Philosophical Studies*, xxix (1976), pp.53–61) Michael Loux attempts to pick out from the set of all kinds those which fit the Aristotelian concept of a kind. His proposal is as follows. Suppose that by calling a kind 'extendible' we mean that it could have more examples than it does have. And suppose that by saying that a kind K 'properly includes' a kind K^* we mean that K includes K^* and it is impossible that there be something which is an example of K and not of K^*. Let us then say that a kind K is a 'candidate for an Aristotelian kind' (a 'CA-kind') if and only if (i) K is a possible kind, (ii) K is an extendible kind, and (iii) whatever has the property of being an example of K, has that property essentially. Loux's proposal then is that a kind K is an *infima species* if it is a CA-kind such that there is no kind K^* which is a CA-kind and which K properly includes.

Loux himself observes that on Aristotle's view, only men are capable of laughter (risible) and every man has risibility essentially. And so, given other obvious premisses, it turns out that the kind: Object That Is Risible, is an *infima species*. Accordingly, given Aristotle's thoughts about men and their properties, Man, and Object That Is Risible, are *infimae species* that necessarily coincide in their exampleships. Loux suggests that this is quite satisfactory; because, he asserts, these are in fact one and the same kind. And the criterion of kind-identity that he offers is just the one which we earlier considered and rejected. But given the unacceptability of this criterion, and given the criterion which we have put in its place, we get the unsatisfactory result (unsatisfactory certainly to Aristotle) that Man and Object that is Risible are *distinct infimae species* that necessarily coincide in their exampleships.

Further, consider the following: it is impossible (I think) that I or any of my readers be a Pharoah in the Third Dynasty. But then consider the kind: Human Incapable of Being A Pharoah In The Third Dynasty. This is a CA-kind. For it is possible, it is extendible, and it is (I think) essential to each of us who are examples of it that we be examples of it. But this kind is properly included within the kind: Man. Accordingly Man is not an *infima species*. And that too is out of accord with the results desired.

certain sort, an object-work is an object-kind of a certain sort. More specifically, art works are *norm*-kinds. A symphony can have incorrect as well as correct performances. A poem, incorrect as well as correct copies.

The plausibility of this thesis will have to rest in its illuminating power. But at once we can see that it passes muster on the points where the theory that art works are sets failed. Just as an art work might have had different and more or fewer occurrences or objects than it does have, so too the kind: Man, might have had different and more or fewer examples than it does have. If Napoleon had not existed it would not then have been the case that Man did not exist. Rather, Man would then have lacked one of the examples which in fact it had. And secondly, just as there may be two distinct unperformed symphonies, so too there may be two distinct unexemplified kinds—e.g., the Unicorn, and the Hippogriff.

V. *A Doctrine of Analogy*

We left the phenomenon of the massive sharing of predicates between art works and their examples at the point where it had put us on the track of an ontological affinity between art works and natural kinds. We must now return to that phenomenon, since for our subsequent purposes it will be important to spy some of the *pattern* of that sharing, and even more important to determine whether the sharing of a predicate between an art work and some one or more of its examples is normally grounded in the sharing of some *property* for which the predicate stands. If it is, then the predicate is used *univocally*. On the other hand, if the predicate stands for two different properties with some systematic relation between them, then the predicate is used *analogically*. If not even that is true, the predicate is used *equivocally*.

From the start one feels that there is some connection, more than coincidental, between a predicate's being true of the examples of an art work and its being true of the work. Can this feeling be substantiated? What might the connection be?

One of the examples we have already used provides us with evidence for concluding that the following formula will not do: a predicate 'is-f' is true of some art work W if 'is-f' is true of every example of W. For 'is a performance' is true of all the examples of many if not all occurrence-works but cannot be true, in its normal sense, of any of these art works themselves.

So suppose that from here on we discard from consideration those predicates which are true of one or more of the examples of some art work but which, in their normal meaning, *cannot* be true of the work itself. (When a predicate used with normal meaning cannot be true of W, it will be said to be *excluded by W*. Likewise when a property cannot be possessed by W, it will be said to be *excluded by W*.) What then of the formula: for any predicate 'is-f' which is not excluded by W, 'is-f' is true of W if 'is-f' is true of every example of W? One objection to this formula is that it is far more constricted in its application than what we were looking for. 'Has a G sharp in its seventh measure' may be true of Bartok's First Quartet even though of many of its performances it is not true. Indeed, it may be true of none of its performances.

A clue to a better formula can be discovered by looking more closely at this example. Is it not the case that 'has a G sharp in its seventh measure' is true of Bartok's First Quartet when it is impossible for there to be a *correct* example of Bartok's First which lacks the property of having a G sharp in its seventh measure? And consider another of the examples we have offered. Is it not the case that 'has "no" as its third word' is true of 'Sailing to Byzantium' when it is impossible for there to be a *correct* example of 'Sailing to Byzantium' which lacks the property of having 'no' as its third word?

These examples naturally suggest to us the following formula: for any predicate 'is-f' which is not excluded by W, if there is some property *being-f* which 'is-f' stands for in normal usage and which is such that it is impossible for there to be something which is a correct example of W and lack *being-f*, then 'is-f' is true of W.

But to this general formula as well there are counter-examples. Consider, for instance, the predicate 'is a perform-ance or was highly thought of by Beethoven'. There will be many works from which this predicate (used in its normal sense) will not be excluded. Likewise, it is impossible for there to be something which is a correct *example* of some such work and lack the property of *being either a performance or highly thought of by Beethoven*. For it is impossible for the example to lack the property of being a performance. Yet the predicate in question may very well not be true of the *work*. For the work cannot be a performance, and it may not have been highly thought of by Beethoven.[15]

The essence of the difficulty here seems to be that some predicates stand for properties such that it is impossible for there to be something which is an example of *W* at all, correct or incorrect, and lack the property. Now such properties fit exactly our definition of properties *essential within* the kind *W*. If we would eliminate from consideration predicates standing for such properties, then counterexamples of the sort suggested will be forestalled. So given some work *W*, consider any predicate 'is-*f*' which is neither excluded by *W* nor stands for some property essential within *W*. If there is some property *being-f* which 'is-*f*' stands for in normal usage and which is such that something could not be a correct example of *W* and lack *being-f*, then 'is-*f*' is true of *W*. (It should be noticed that the claim here is not *if and only if*, but just *if*.)

If we express this formula by using our concept of a property's *being normative within* a kind, it then comes to this: For any predicate 'is-*f*' which is neither excluded by *W* nor stands for a property essential within *W*, if there is some property *being-f* which 'is-*f*' stands for in normal usage and which is normative within *W*, then 'is-*f*' is true of *W*.

The core feature of this proposal is the suggestion that what is required for something to be a correct example of an art work plays a decisive role in determining what can be predicated truly of the work. Or to put it yet more indefinitely, the core feature is the suggestion that the concept of an art work is intimately connected with the concept of a correct example of the work.

Perhaps if we considered the matter in detail we would find still more pattern to the sharing of predicates between art works

[15] In general, take a predicate of the form 'is either *A* or anti-*W*', where 'is anti-*W*' represents a predicate such that (i) it is excluded by *W* and (ii) when predicated of examples of *W* it stands for a property such that necessarily if something is an example of *W* then it has that property, and where 'is *A*' represents any predicate whatsoever which is not excluded by *W*. Then the 'disjunctive predicate' represented by 'is either *A* or anti-*W*' is itself not excluded by *W* and is itself such that when predicated of some example of *W* it stands for a property such that something would not be a correct example of *W* if it lacked it. Yet obviously the predicate may very well not be true of *W*.

and their examples than what we have thus far uncovered. But enough has been discovered for our subsequent purposes. So let us now move from the level of language to the level of ontology and consider whether, when predicates are shared according to the general pattern uncovered, there is also a sharing of properties designated by those predicates.

One is naturally inclined to think that there is. Our dictionaries do not, after all, tell us that a certain word standardly means one thing when truly predicated of an art work and something else when truly predicated of an example of the work. Yet I think that we must in fact come to the conclusion that predicates shared between art works and their examples do not function univocally when the sharing follows the general pattern we have uncovered. For what one means, in correctly predicating 'has "no" as its third word' of some copy of 'Sailing to Byzantium', is that the third word-*occurrence* is 'no'. But when one correctly predicates 'has "no" as its third word' of 'Sailing to Byzantium' itself, one cannot mean this. For the poem does not consist of word-occurrences (and neither does its artefactual component). Similarly, what one means in correctly predicating 'has a G sharp in its seventh measure' of some performance of Bartok's Fifth is that in its seventh measure there was an *occurrence* of the G sharp pitch. But the quartet itself does not consist of sound-occurrences. So I think it must be admitted·that we have not discovered a systematic identity but only a systematic relation between the property designated by some predicate when it is correctly predicated of some art examples and the property designated by that same predicate when truly predicated of the art work. Our conclusion must be that the sharing of predicates between art works and their examples pervasively exhibits *analogical* predication.

The situation is as follows. Suppose that 'is-*f*' is a predicate which can be shared between an art work W and its examples, and suppose further that a property for which 'is-*f*' stands when truly predicated of examples of W is *being-f*. Then for those cases in which the sharing of 'is-*f*' fits the general pattern which we formulated, 'is-*f*' when truly predicated of W stands for the property of *being such that something cannot be a correct example of it without having the property of being-f*. Or in other words, it stands for the property of *having the property of being-f normative within it.* If *having a G sharp in its seventh measure* is a property that a sound-sequence-occurrence can have, then to predicate 'has a G sharp in its seventh measure' of Bartok's Fifth Quartet is not to claim of Bartok's Fifth that it *has* that property. It is rather to claim that that property is *normative within* Bartok's Fifth.

VI. *What Is It to Compose?*

I have suggested that an art work is a *kind* whose examples are the occurrences or objects of the work; and more specifically, that it is a norm-kind, capable of having both correct and incorrect examples. Now these schematic suggestions must be worked out in detail. For the sake of convenience I shall conduct the discussion by referring exclusively to music and then, in conclusion, briefly indicate how the points made can be applied in arts other than music.

What must one do to compose a musical work? The beginning of the answer is clear: one must select a certain set of properties which sound-sequence-occurrences can exemplify—the property of being a piano sound of F pitch, the property of being a piano sound of A pitch, etc.[16]

But there's more to it than this. For whenever one selects things, one selects them *as* the ones which are so-and-so. One selects them *for* such-and-such purpose. And in principle the very same things which one selects *as* the ones which are so-and-so or *for* such-and-such purpose can also be selected as, or for, something else. Now merely selecting *as* or *for* something or other is not sufficient for composing. A composer might select a set of sound-sequence-occurrences as ones that he never wants to hear again. He would not then have composed. We must ask, then, what purpose lies behind the composer's selections.

The clue is to be found in our conclusion that a musical work is a norm-kind. The composer selects properties of sounds for the purpose of their serving as criteria for judging correctness of occurrence. By reference to his selected set, we can judge sound-sequence-occurrences as correct or incorrect. And when

---

[16] One can also compose by building and programming a machine, and letting the machine make the actual selections. This qualifying addition should be understood in all that follows.

we *do* so use his selection, we are using it as he intended. At the end of the composer's activity, sound-sequence-occurrences can be correct or incorrect by reference to that just-selected set of criteria for correctness.

In selecting a set of properties required for correctness, the composer composes a work—that one, namely, which has exactly those properties (plus any others presupposed by them) as normative within it. And any particular sound-sequence-occurrence which is correct by reference to that particular set of requirements for correctness will be a correct occurrence *of* the work composed.

Over the past quarter century analogies to games have played so prominent a part in philosophical discussion that to draw such an analogy once more is to risk ennui or nausea. But the inventing of a game does provide a genuinely illuminating analogy to the composing of a musical work. The inventor of a game selects certain properties which action-sequence-occurrences can exemplify; and therein he makes a game—that one, namely, which has exactly those properties (and any others presupposed by them) as normative within it. Specifically, he selects those properties as a set of criteria for correctness in occurrence.

The work of the taxonomist, though he too deals with norm-kinds, is significantly different from the work of both the composer and the game-inventor. The taxonomist has a certain species in mind and attempts to discover and state some of the properties normative within it. In so doing he makes claims. What he says is true or false of the species in question. You and I, talking now about one of Bartok's works, may do the same. But that is not what Bartok did in composing. In selecting a set of properties as criteria for correctness of occurrence he was not describing a work. He was bringing it about that there was such-and-such a work—the one which has the properties thus selected (and their prerequisites) as normative within it.

To get the nature of composing yet more clearly before us, glance once again at games. The inventor of a game, in addition to selecting a set of properties as criteria for correctness, may also have views as to what a *well-played* occurrence of his game would be like, and views as to how best to win at his game. Such views are matters of judgement and opinion on his part. They are true or false. Accordingly, his holding of such views is fundamentally different from his selection of a set of properties as criteria for correctness of occurrence. For in this latter there is nothing either true or false. His holding of views as to what would constitute a well-played occurrence of his game, or as to the best strategies for winning at his game, has nothing at all to do with his invention of it.

So too, a composer may have views as to what an aesthetically excellent occurrence of his work would be like, and views as to how best to achieve such an occurrence. He may think a certain tempo would give the best performance, or a certain registration on the organ. But if he does not lay these down as requirements for correctness they remain as matters of opinion and judgement on his part. As such, they are true or false. And his holding of such true/false views has nothing to do with his act of composing. Of course it's not always clear, at every point, whether the composer selected a set of criteria for correctness of occurrence or whether he expressed his views as to how correct occurrences of the work composed can also be made aesthetically excellent.

A corollary to this understanding of the nature of composing is that to improvise is not to compose. That corollary is clearly correct. Suppose that someone has improvised on the organ. And suppose that he then goes home and scores a work of such a sort that his improvisation, judged by the requirements for correctness specified in the score, is at all points correct. In spite of that, the composer did not compose his work *in* performing his improvisation. In all likelihood, he did not even compose it *while* improvising. For in all likelihood he did not, during his improvising, finish selecting that particular set of requirements for correctness of occurrence to be found in his score. Suppose, for example, that at a certain point in his improvisation he introduced a bit of rubato, with full consciousness of doing so. In so doing he has not yet decided whether to select rubato at that point as required for correctness of occurrence. One cannot uniquely extract a work from a performance.

I said that in selecting a set of properties as criteria for correctness of occurrence the composer composes a work. And the work composed, I said, is that one which has exactly those properties and their prerequisites as normative within it. The reason for adding 'and their prerequisites' is that it will usually if not always be the case that certain properties which the composer did not select will also be required for correctness—even ones which are not essential within the work. For something cannot have the ones he did select without having others.[17] So, by the definition of 'normative within', those others will also be normative within the work. We can say this: in selecting a set of properties as criteria for correctness of occurrence, the composer has composed that work which requires for correctness in its occurrences all and only those properties that he has thus selected along with whatever others an occurrence would have to have if it had those.

But is it true that there is exactly one such work? And if it *is* true, *why* is it true? *Why* is it true that a musical work is uniquely determined by the properties normative within it? A work, we said, is a norm-kind whose examples are the occurrences of the work. But can there not be a number of distinct norm-kinds which have the same properties normative within them? Let us see.

Suppose that two possible, non-necessary, kinds, *the K* and *the K**, have the same set of properties normative within them. Call that set, κ. In other words, suppose that though *the K* is not identical with *the K**, yet it is impossible that something should be a correct example of *the K* and lack any of κ, and also impossible that something should be a correct example of *the K** and lack any of κ.

That could come about in just one way: some of the properties essential within (and thus normative within) one of the kinds are only normative, not essential, within the other. Is that in fact a real possibility? Can there in fact be a pair of norm-kinds related in that fashion? How about these: The Siamese Cat, and The Properly-Formed Siamese Cat? All the properties normative within the former are essential within the latter, but not vice versa. But of course the latter is not a norm-kind; and our suggestion has been that art works are norm-kinds, capable of having both correct and incorrect examples.

---

[17] Perhaps something could not have some at least of those others without also having some at least of the ones he singled out. So in principle it is possible for the composer to make a different selection of properties and yet to compose the very same work.

So consider *this* pair of kinds: Performance Of Bartok's Fifth Quartet, and Performance Of Bartok's Fifth Quartet Which Is Correct In Its First Ten Measures. These are clearly distinct kinds. There could be something which is an example of the former and not of the latter. And they are both norm-kinds. Further, they are wholly alike with respect to the set of properties normative within them. However, some of the properties which are merely normative within the former are essential within the latter. And in particular that is true for the property of *being a performance of Bartok's Fifth Quartet which is correct in its first ten measures*. It is for that reason that there can be performances which are examples (incorrect ones of course) of the former which are not examples of the latter.

We seem to have found the refutation of our claim. The work composed, we said, was that work which requires for correctness in its occurrences all and only those properties that the composer has selected as criteria for correctness, along with whatever others an occurrence would have to have if it had these. Now it seems that in general there will be no one such work. It seems that there will be a number of such works. But if that is really a consequence of our theory, the theory is reduced to absurdity. For surely if there is no ambiguity as to which properties the composer selected, then also there is none as to which work he composed. Are we on the wrong track in our whole theory?

Not at all. But an explanation is in order. The kind: Performance Of Bartok's Fifth Quarter Which Is Correct In Its First Ten Measures, is not the work Bartok composed. The musical work determined by Bartok's selection of properties is one which can be incorrect in its first ten measures as well as in any of its other measures. In general, take the set of properties that some composer selected as required for correctness of occurrence plus any others presupposed by these. If there is some pair of norm-kinds such that both members have that set of properties normative within them, but such that a member of that set of properties is essential within one of those kinds and not essential within the other, then the former is not the work the composer composed. And the work he did compose is just that norm-kind which, by this test, proves never to have the property of *not being the musical work he composed*. The work he composed is that norm-kind—of all those which have the selected properties and their prerequisites as normative within them—which is maximally generous in the policy of preferring to have an occurrence as *incorrect* example rather than as *no* example at all.

In focusing on composing we must not overlook the fact that there are musical works which were probably never composed. There are works of indigenous folk music such that probably no one ever singled out the requisite properties in the requisite way for composing the work. The work just emerged from performances. But though there may be no one who selected in the requisite way (enough of) the properties normative within the work so as therein to compose it, there will certainly be people who *use* those properties either as guidelines for performing or as criteria for criticizing occurrences with respect to correctness. And given a set of properties thus used, there will be a unique determination of a work which has exactly those properties (and their prerequisites) as normative within it. But it will be the work of those practitioners, not the work of some composer.

In one or the other of these two somewhat different ways —the way of the composer and the way of the practitioners—a work is always a work *of* somebody. Nothing is ever a work of music without, in one or the other of these two ways, being the work of some person or persons. Every musical work can in principle be identified as the so-and-so work of composer C, or as the so-and-so work of practitioners P.

I have tacitly assumed that the composer can make the selections whereby he composes 'in his head'. Mozart said that he composed whole symphonies in his head. Perhaps he was speaking the truth. But whether or not some composer composes a work entirely 'in his head', normally he indicates for the rest of us what his work is like. And thereupon the work enters into, or becomes available for entering into, human culture. Thereupon the set of properties selected as required for correctness can be used by the rest of us as guidelines for performing. Thereupon the set of properties selected can be used by the rest of us as criteria for criticizing occurrences with respect to correctness. Thereupon the set of properties selected can even be used by the rest of us as guidelines for *imagining* an occurrence.[18] What should be added is that most composers do most of their composing for such functions as these. They have such purposes in mind.

But to understand what the composer *characteristically* does when indicating to us his set of requirements, we must not picture him as completing in his head the selection of that set and then merely *reporting* his selections to us. I now can report what some composed work is like. I can do so by inscribing a score. And if the score is wholly accurate, I would then have spoken truly at all points. By inscribing the score I would have made true claims. But that is not characteristically what the composer does. He might do that. Then by means of his score he would make true/false claims about a work already composed. But more characteristically, he makes his selections *in* putting down his inscriptions. Selecting properties is something that one can do in one's head. But also it is something that one can do by inscribing perceptible signs; then one selects by signifying. And that is what the composer *characteristically* does when he scores his work. By inscribing such-and-such signs in such-and-such manner and circumstance he selects a set of properties as required for correctness of occurrence. That is what his inscribing counts as.

Now in selecting by signifying, the composer may make mistakes—not the mistake of falsely reporting what he had already selected, but the mistake of selecting what he did not intend to select. His setting down of various notations may count as his selecting a middle C at a certain point, when he never intended to select middle C. His selection of middle C may have been done inadvertently. He may have misspoken himself and in that way produced an incorrect score. One's use of a notation system acquires a life of its own.

In such cases, what should we take to be the work composed? I have said that the work composed is uniquely determined by the properties selected as required for correctness of occurrence. But that is not, in practice, how our music publishing houses operate. When they receive a score they *correct its mistakes*—changing a C natural to a C sharp in a certain measure,

---

[18] It's possible that the composer might have composed purely conceptual music which, though some of us can imagine what an occurrence would be like, can in fact not be performed because of the limitations of instruments or performers.

etc. They try to revise the autograph score received from the composer in such a way that it signifies what the composer *would* have signified, had he made no mistakes in his use of the notation. The resultant score is what they regard as specifying the work composed. I shall follow them in that practice. Often one can distinguish between the properties that the composer *did* select, and the properties that he *would* have selected had he used his notation system correctly (if he used one at all). It is the latter that I shall regard as determining the composer's work. For surely we want to take the composer's mistakes for what they are—mistakes, which generosity requires us to correct.

But in following this policy are we not appealing to the composer's intentions? And haven't our twentieth-century critics warned us against ever doing any such thing? Indeed they have. And concerning some appeals to intention, the warning is very much in place. But I am suggesting an appeal to the composer's intentions only in a minimal and innocuous way. I am suggesting that if the composer made mistakes in scoring, then we should regard the work composed as determined by what he *would* have signified had he *not* made any mistakes. And that is no more questionable an appeal to intention than what takes place when a publisher corrects the mistakes in the manuscript that a critic submits. Apart from correcting errors in notation, we appeal to what *in fact* the composer selected when we wish to determine the nature of the work he composed. We do not appeal to what he *intended* to select. We appeal to what he *did* select.

I have described the composer as one who selects, as criteria for correctness of occurrence, a set of properties which sound-occurrences can possess. On hearing this, one is naturally disposed to assume that these are all *acoustic* properties of sounds. But not so. The composer can also lay down as a condition for correctness that the sounds have the property of being produced in such-and-such fashion on such-and-such instruments. Such a property can conveniently be called an *instrumental* property. Composers can and often do include instrumental properties among their selections.

The traditional composer–scorer in the West over the past 200 years offers an interesting blend of properties signified. In part he signifies purely acoustic properties of sounds: the property of *being middle C in pitch*, the property of *being a quarter note long in 4/4 time at andante tempo*, the property of *being forte in volume*, etc. But in addition he tells us, say, that the composition is for violin. He does not go on to tell us how those instruments called 'violins' are to be constructed, nor does he tell us how he wants them played. He *presupposes* the existence of musical instruments of the species: Violin, and of a practice tradition for playing instruments of that species; and he *takes for granted* that some of his readers will know which instruments those are and what that practice tradition is.

One way to depart from this mainline tradition is to make a composition for such-and-such instruments played in such-and-such fashion, but then not to presuppose the existence of such instruments, or of practice traditions for playing them. For example, one might compose a work for prepared piano; and then tell how the piano is to be prepared. Or one might compose a work for ordinary piano but then give instruction for playing it in a non-ordinary way: plucking its strings, rapping its sounding-board. Or one might do as Harry Partch did: invent and construct a new instrument called 'cloud-chamber bowls', devise standard ways of playing it, and then compose a work for that hitherto non-existent instrument.

At a deeper level, however, these various possibilities are only variants on the mainline tradition. The composer follows the tradition in signifying certain purely acoustic properties and then, in addition, making clear to us that the composition is for such-and-such an instrument played in such-and-such a fashion. Whether he remains with the traditional instruments and the conventional practice traditions, or whether he devises new ones, makes no great difference when we see that it is possible for the composer to depart from this deeper-lying mainline tradition. He can do so in either of two directions. He can signify no acoustic properties whatsoever, confining himself to telling us that his composition is for such-and-such instruments played in such-and-such a way. John Cage does that with his *Radio Music* (1956). Alternatively, he can confine himself to signifying purely acoustic properties, in no way telling us that the composition is for such-and-such instruments played in such-and-such a way. J. S. Bach did that with his *Art of the Fugue*.

As one might expect, sometimes it's not decisively clear whether the composer has specified that the sounds have certain instrumental properties or whether, instead, he has only specified that the sounds have the acoustic property of *sounding as if they were produced in such-and-such fashion on such-and-such an instrument*—a *mixed*-acoustic property, we might call it. Suppose, for example, that a composer tells us that his work is *for* pipe organ; and that it is clear that he means it to be played in conventional fashion. Then to be a correct occurrence of this composition an occurrence must have the mixed-acoustic property of *sounding as if it were produced by playing a pipe organ in the conventional manner*. But is the instrumental property of *being produced by playing a pipe organ in the conventional manner* also required for correctness?

Until the advent of electronics this particular issue was never concretely presented to anyone. Pipe-organish sounds were produced only by pipe organs. So the answer for traditional composers is not decisively clear. We seem, in fact, to take ambivalent stands on the matter. Almost all of us assume that it is possible to produce a correct performance of one of Bach's works for pipe organ on an electronic organ. Yet I dare say that few of us would regard a sound-sequence-occurrence produced by playing a keyboard to be a correct performance of some work for violin. Perhaps it is the radical difference in means of performance that is decisive for us.

But whatever we decide concerning Bach's works for organ, a knowledge of pipe organs of the sort that Bach was acquainted with, and of the practice traditions that he presupposed, is none the less important; for only by reference to these do we know what is that mixed-acoustic property of *sounding pipe-organish* which is normative within Bach's works for pipe organ. The history of music is inseparable from a history of instruments and of practice traditions for playing them.

Having analysed the nature of composing we can now profitably deal with a question alluded to in Section I of this Part: why can paintings and sculptures not be viewed as single-exampled kinds rather than as physical objects, thereby giving us a 'unified theory' of works of art? P. F. Strawson, after saying that 'in a certain sense, paintings and works of sculpture' are types, adds this footnote:

The mention of paintings and works of sculpture may seem absurd. Are they not particulars? But this is a superficial point. The things the dealers buy and sell are particulars. But it is only because of the empirical deficiencies of reproductive techniques that we identify these with the works of art. Were it not for these deficiencies, the original of a painting would have only the interest which belongs to the original manuscript of a poem. Different people could look at exactly the same painting in different places at the same time, just as different people can listen to exactly the same quartet at different times in the same place.[19]

Strawson's point here is that though, as a matter of fact, in the field of painting it is the particular paintings which are (or, are regarded as) the works of art, this is quite coincidental. If the technology of reproduction were more advanced, there would be kinds which would be (would be regarded as) works of art, and the particular painting which the artist painted would have no more status than that of the first example of the work. In short, if reproductive techniques were more advanced, the situation for painting would be as it already is for graphic art.

About this, several remarks. In the first place, Strawson evidently agrees that *as things are* in the field of painting, it is the particular paintings which are the works of art. So as a matter of fact we cannot form a unified theory of the ontology of art artefacts.

But secondly, Strawson mislocates the reason for this phenomenon. He attributes it to inadequacy of reproductive techniques. But in music we do not demand that the various occurrences of a single work all sound similar to the point of indiscernibility. We allow wide variation. The reason that painting is different is that the painter, in creating his painting, does not select a set of properties as criteria for correctness of occurrence. Accordingly, he does not uniquely determine some norm-kind. No requirements for something's being a correct object of something are selected in creating *The Odalisque*. If there were, we could determine whether *The Odalisque* is a correct or incorrect object of the composed art work, just as we can determine whether the author's manuscript copy of his poem is or is not a correct copy. In fact, nothing of the sort can be done for *The Odalisque*.

[19] P. F. Strawson, *Individuals* (Methuen & Co.: London, 1959), p. 231.

Of course, one can pick out things which to a certain degree of closeness *resemble* this painting, in one or another respect. There is a kind associated with the property of resembling *The Odalisque* in such-and-such respects to such-and-such a degree. *The Odalisque* is itself an example of the kind. It is not a norm-kind, however; and none of our names of paintings are names of such entities.

But *could* we somehow, in the field of painting, compose norm-kinds? Certainly. If, instead of applying paint to canvas, the artist would draw up a set of specifications for paintings, then he would compose a norm-kind. He might also, if he wished, paint a painting in accord with the specifications. But that would be quite incidental. In fact, this phenomenon already exists in the field of painting. One finds it in the 'paint by number' sets for children.

In conclusion it should be noted that our analysis of what it is to compose holds as much for aleatory music, in which chance plays a significant role, as it does for non-aleatory. Chance can play a role in the process of composing. John Cage tells of his idea of letting the specks on the paper one is using determine one's selections. Using chance in this manner does not alter the fact that in composing one selects a set of properties by which to judge correctness of occurrence. More customarily, however, chance is allowed or required to play a role in performance. Composers sometimes stipulate, for example, that sections of the work are to be played in randomly determined sequence. Obviously requirements for correctness still enter in such cases. They enter at two different points. It is required that the *sequence* of sections be randomly determined. And *within* the sections it is required that such-and-such acoustic and instrumental properties occur. So it is for aleatory works in general. Aleatoriness is itself required at certain points if the work is to be performed correctly; all the members of the choir singing on a single pitch, when what is asked is that they make random noise, would result in an incorrect performance. But then secondly, there will always be points where certain definite acoustic or instrumental properties are required if the performance is to be correct.

VII. *What Is It to Perform a Musical Work?*

Having looked at things from the side of the composer let me
now shift focus and look at them from the side of the performer,
asking: 'What is it to perform a musical work?' For the sake of
clarity I shall remain true to my earlier resolution to use the
word 'performance' exclusively for a sound-sequence-
occurrence of a certain sort, namely, one brought about by
performing; and not to use it for instances (cases) of the *action* of
performing.

There can be performances which are not performances of
works. In the case of complete improvisation, for example,
there is no performance of a *work*. Yet there is a performance—an occurrence of a sound-sequence which is brought
about by an instance of the intentional action of performing.
However, let us set aside this sort of performance and this sort
of instance of performing and concentrate wholly on performances of works.

A point to be kept in mind is that a sound-sequence-
occurrence which was not produced by an intentional act of
performing may yet have all the acoustic properties normative
within some musical work. The wind's blowing through the
rocks, someone's doodling on a piano, or an electronic organ's
going berserk, might produce a sound-sequence-occurrence
which sounds just like a correct performance of 'Greensleeves'.
A performance of the work W is something more than an
occurrence having all the acoustic properties normative within
W.

A more subtle point is this: suppose that someone, not believing that he is performing a work, improvises a sound-
sequence-occurrence. And suppose that every acoustic
property normative within some work W is one that he by intent
exemplified in the occurrence he brought about. He neither
knows nor believes that all those properties are normative
within some work or other. But they do all happen to be
normative within W. Has he then performed W? What he has
done is to produce an occurrence which by intent has all the
acoustic properties which are in fact normative within some
work. But he has not produced an occurrence which by intent
has all the properties which he *believes* to be normative within

some work. Is the former ever sufficient for performing that work? I am going to assume, in my analysis, that it is not. I am going to assume that one cannot, in that way, inadvertently perform a work. One performs a work only if one *believes* that one is performing a work.

On the other hand, one may perform that which is the such-and-such work of composer C, or the such-and-such work of practitioner P, without knowing that one has done so, and without believing that one has done so—even believing that one has *not* done so. Suppose I believe of some work of J. S. Bach that it was composed by one of his sons. I may none the less perform that work. One's misattribution of a work does not prevent one from performing it. To take account of the fact that what one believes to be the work W may not in fact be the work W, I shall henceforth put our question this way: What is it to perform that which one believes to be the work W?

An answer which comes to mind at once is that it consists of producing a sound-sequence-occurrence by (intentionally) following the specifications for correct occurrence that the composer gave in the score associated with that work. But several objections can be raised, to the effect that the following of the score for that which one believes to be the work W is neither sufficient nor necessary for performing that work.

For one thing, one might in every detail follow the specifications for correct occurrence found in (some correct copy of) the score for a work and yet not perform the work. For often the specifications for correct occurrence that composers give in scores are incomplete for ensuring that those who follow them will produce occurrences, let alone correct occurrences, of the work. Scores originated in the Western world in medieval times, when they functioned as devices to remind performers of what they had learned apart from the score. By gradually acquiring greater specificity they gained the function of serving to inform people as to what is required for correct occurrence. But even so, many things go presupposed rather than specified. As we saw in our preceding section, the composer often presupposes the existence in his society of certain kinds of instruments and of practice traditions for performing on the specified instruments. Thus it is that a performer might follow all the specifications for correct occurrence given in some (correct copy of) a score and yet fail to perform the associated work. His performance may be too far off target to count as an occurrence of the work.

On the other hand, it is not necessary that one follow *all* the specifications found in a score in order to perform the work associated with that score. Indeed, one can perform some work without *at all* following the specifications for correct occurrence given in the score for that work. For there may at the time be no score, or one may be unaware of it. If Beethoven had completely composed his Opus 111 'in his head' and only scored it later, it would have been possible for him in the interim to have performed the work even though there was as yet no score. That is, it would have been possible for him not merely to produce a sound-sequence-occurrence having the acoustic properties required for something to be a performance of Opus 111, but actually to perform Opus 111. That is of course only a hypothetical case. But in fact the vast bulk of indigenous folk music has always been unscored; so of course one cannot follow the specifications for correct occurrence given in the scores for those works. Yet those works can be performed.

It is true indeed that specification of the properties required for a work's correct occurrence can be communicated to performers by means other than scores, and by people other than composers. The performer of indigenous folk music can be told verbally how some passage must sound. Or the correct rhythm can be stomped out for him by foot. But quite clearly it is no significant improvement over our first thought to say that to perform a work *W* is to produce a sound-sequence-occurrence by (intentionally) following *whatever* specifications for correct occurrence of *W* have been given to one. For not only is it not necessary that there *be* any such specifications but also, conversely, in many cases one might follow *all* the specifications ever given to one, those expressed in score notation and otherwise, and still not produce an occurrence of the work. Bartok in his early career set about scoring various Hungarian folk songs. His project did not consist of taking the specifications that the Hungarians were expressing in something other than the Western scoring system and expressing them in score notation. It consisted rather of providing those works, for the first time in their careers, with anything near full specifications of the acoustic properties required for correct occurrence. So it must be said that performing a work W does not consist of intentionally following all the specifications ever given one of properties required for a correct occurrence of W.

The specifications of which we have been speaking are specifications of the *properties* a sound-sequence-occurrence must have if it is to be a correct occurrence of the work in question. Being reminded of this we are naturally led onto the thought that the phenomenon of performing is attached to those properties themselves, not to specifications thereof. I think this is correct. But several complications present themselves on the road to a satisfactory analysis.

In the first place, what a person *believes* to be the properties normative within that work which he believes to be W can be more close or less close to what in fact are those properties. And I take it as true that a person can perform that work even though not all the properties normative within the work (or required by those) are believed to be such by him. He may be uncertain or ignorant or mistaken on some points and yet perform the work. Noah Greenberg and his New York Pro Musica group may very well have performed the medieval work *Play of Herod*, even though by Greenberg's own acknowledgement they were uncertain at many points of the properties normative within the work. On the other hand it is surely true that one's uncertainty, ignorance, or error as to the properties normative within some work can be so severe that in exemplifying what one believes to be those properties one does not perform the work. One performs no work at all.

Secondly, a person can try to exemplify with greater or less exactness what he believes to be the properties normative within that work which he believes to be W. And I take it as true that a person need not try to exemplify *exactly* what he believes to be those properties if he is in fact to perform that work which he believes to be W. Performers, knowing well the properties normative within some work, often deliberately depart from them in the belief that the resulting performance will be better—or sometimes in the knowledge that they are incapable of executing the passage correctly. In spite of that the performer may well have performed the very work from whose normative properties he believed he was departing. On the other hand, one can intentionally depart so far from what one knows or believes to be the properties normative within some work that the result does not count as a performance of that work.

Thirdly, a person can be more successful or less successful in his attempt to exemplify what he believes to be the properties normative within that work which he believes to be W. And I take it as true that a person need not be wholly successful in order to perform that work. He may unintentionally strike what he knows to be the wrong note and yet perform the work. On the other hand, one can fail so abjectly in one's attempt to exemplify what one believes to be the properties normative within some work that one has not performed the work at all—has indeed not succeeded in performing *any* work.

So there are three fundamentally different reasons for the phenomenon of someone producing an incorrect performance of that work which he believes to be W. The performer may be unsuccessful in trying to exemplify what he believes to be the properties normative within that which he believes to be W, the performer may deliberately depart from what he believes to be those properties, and the performer may be uncertain or mistaken or ignorant as to what are those properties. Likewise there are three fundamentally different reasons for the phenomenon of someone not even producing an incorrect performance of that work which he believes to be W, even though he meant to produce a performance thereof.

Given these complications, how are we to frame a concept of *performing*? Well, first this: in thinking of a *performance* of a work (not just of a *correct* performance) we all operate with the notion of an occurrence of a sound-sequence being closer or less close in its acoustic and instrumental properties to what a *correct* performance of the work would be like. Such relative closeness is by no means merely a matter of the *quantity* of the departures—if indeed departures can be counted. (Suppose one transposes an entire piece into a different key; how many changes is that? One? Or one for each of the sounds played at a different pitch?) It is also a matter of the *scale* of the departures. A reversal of the order of the movements in a quartet would yield a performance farther from a correct performance than would an omission of a quarter note in some rather shapeless transition passage. In a similar way, we operate with the notion of that which one believes to be the properties normative within some work being closer or less close to the properties which are actually normative within that work. These two notions, it seems to me, go into our concept of performing a work.

One or two other complications must still be mentioned. But first let us have before us a preliminary formulation of our analysis. In the light of what I have said so far I suggest this:

One performs that work which one believes to be W if and only if one brings about a sound-sequence-occurrence which comes fairly close to exemplifying the acoustic and instrumental properties normative within what work, and one does so:

 (i) by having beliefs which come fairly close to being correct and complete as to what are the acoustic and instrumental properties normative within the work;

 (ii) by aiming to produce a sound-sequence-occurrence such that for most of the properties about which one has those beliefs, one tries to make the occurrence exemplify them, and for at best a few, one does not try to make it exemplify them; and

 (iii) by coming fairly close to succeeding in that attempt on one's part to produce a sound-sequence-occurrence which, for most of those properties, will exemplify them.

And now for some of the additional complications. Suppose, knowing well some musical work, one plays a record (of a recording) of it; and in that way produces a sound-sequence-occurrence. By these preliminary formulations one would have performed the work. Yet of course one has not. What takes place is not a performance, but a *reproduction* of a performance, of the work. So we must exclude the bringing about of sound-sequence-occurrences which are reproductions of occurrences which took place earlier.

Another range of phenomena is somewhat less easily dealt with. Suppose that some musical composition has been put on a player piano roll. And now suppose that one puts one of the rolls on a player piano, and then pumps the piano so that it is played at desired speed and volume. Has one thereby performed the composition? I think that our ordinary concept of *performing* does not yield a decisive 'Yes' or 'No' answer to this question. But now suppose, alternatively, that some composer has composed directly on tape, and that one now puts the tape in one's own tape machine and plays it. Has one thereby performed the composition? In this case it is quite clear that one has *not* done so. Performing disappears from sight for such music. Notice that neither in this case, nor in the player piano case, is the resultant sound-sequence-occurrence a reproduction of another occurrence which took place earlier.

We can visualize an ordered sequence starting from someone performing a composition by playing a piano, through the ambiguous case of someone operating a player piano, on to the case of someone producing an occurrence but not a performance of a composition for tape by putting the tape on a machine, setting the dials, and letting it play. But what is the principle of ordering in this sequence? *This*, I think: as we move along the series, there is less and less *feedback* from what the operator of the instrument *discerns* to be the acoustic properties of the sound-sequence-occurrence produced, to what he actually does with his instrument subsequently; as indeed there is less and less *adjustment* of what he does to his instrument in the light of what he *anticipates* will be the results if he does this or that to his instrument. In the case of the pianist the feedback and adjustment is enormous, of a complexity that defies description, and requiring years of practice. In the case of the operator of the player piano there is some significant feedback and adjustment, mainly pertaining to volume and tempo, though obviously feedback and adjustment have been reduced greatly. In the case of the operator of the tape machine the adjustment and feedback are at a minimum.

If this analysis of the sequence is correct, then what can be said is that one *performs* a musical composition on an instrument only if there is a significant amount of adjustment and feedback which goes into one's production of a sound-sequence-occurrence. In the case of putting on the tape and operating the tape machine, these are comparatively insignificant, though not wholly missing. In the case of playing the piano, these are highly significant. In the case of operating the player piano, they are somewhere in between.

Here then is our completed analysis of what it is to perform:

One performs that work which one believes to be *W* if and only if one brings about a sound-sequence-occurrence which is not a reproduction of any other occurrence, and which comes fairly close to exemplifying the acoustic and instrumental properties normative within that work which one believes to be *W*, and one does so:

(i) by operating the instrument(s) from which the sound is produced in such a way that there is a relatively large amount of *adjustment* in how one handles the instrument(s) in light of what one anticipates will be the acoustic properties of the resultant sound-sequence-occurrence if one does this or that to the instrument, and a relatively large amount of *feedback* from what one discerns to be the acoustic properties of the resultant sound-sequence-occurrences to what one does subsequently with the instrument(s); and

(i) by having beliefs which come fairly close to being correct and complete as to what are the acoustic and instrumental properties normative within the work; and

(iii) by aiming to produce a sound-sequence-occurrence such that, for most of the properties about which one has those beliefs, one tries to make the occurrence exemplify them, and, for at best a few, one does not try to make it exemplify them; and

(iv) by coming fairly close to succeeding in that attempt on one's part to produce a sound-sequence-occurrence which, for most of those properties, will exemplify them.

When one thus brings about a sound-sequence-occurrence, let us say that one is *guided by* the properties normative within the work that one believes to be *S*.

One implication of this formulation should be highlighted. Suppose that some pianist has composed a slight variation on some composer's work. And suppose that he now performs his own variant rather than the original. I do not think it true that he has therein also performed the original. And I do not think he would therein have performed the original even if the acoustic and instrumental properties of the sound-sequence-occurrence that he produces are such that *exactly* those properties might be exemplified in a performance of the original work. It is our stipulation (iii) that prevents the undesired result. For suppose, to simplify the case, that there is no mis-attribution involved. And suppose that the pianist knows fully the properties normative within the original, and also those normative within his own variant. It would not have been his aim to produce a sound-sequence-occurrence exemplifying the acoustic and instrumental properties that he believes to be normative within the original. It would rather have been his aim to produce one exemplifying the acoustic and instru-mental properties that he believes to be normative within his variant.

Perhaps it is worth noting that sometimes a performer's goal of producing a performance as aesthetically excellent as poss-ible of the work he is performing may require him to perform the work incorrectly at certain points. The composer perhaps thought otherwise at the time of composition, and possibly continued to do so. That was in part his reason for making those points matters of correctness. But he may just have been mis-taken. Correct performances might well be better if something else had been made the correct thing at that point—which is to say, might well have been better if a slightly different work had been composed.

Then, also, the attempt to produce a performance as aesthet-ically excellent as possible will inevitably require the performer to make decisions on all sorts of matters where correctness is not even at issue. On some of such matters the composer may very well have had an opinion. He may even have expressed it. He may expressly have intended that his work be performed thus and thus because he thought that that would yield the best performances. But once again, he may have been mistaken.

How do we find out which properties the composer has selected for judging correctness in occurrence by? How do we find out which norm-kind he has singled out? How do we find out which properties are normative within the work composed? How do we find out what the work is like that he has composed? It should be evident by now that these four questions, though distinct, are inextricably related.

We go by the best evidence we have. In the first place we try to discover the relevant parts of the practice tradition that the composer took for granted. Then, secondly, if the composer made, or authorized the making of, a score we begin by trying to find out what the autograph score-copy was like in the relevant respects. But a precise knowledge of the practice tradition may have been lost. And there may never have been a score. Or if there was, we may no longer have the autograph copy nor any reliable evidence as to what it was like in certain relevant respects. Or we may have several differing copies from the composer's hand and not know which he authenticated. Or we may have the original authenticated copy but it may contain what we recognize to be slips on the part of the composer-scorer, and we may find it impossible to determine what a correct copy would be like. Or we may have an original, authenticated, and correct copy but no longer know how to interpret all the symbols. And then there is the peculiar case of Anton Bruckner's symphonies, in which the extent of Bruckner's authorization of his editor's massive revisions is thoroughly obscure. In all such cases and many others we simply have to acknowledge that we are to some extent uncertain as to which properties the composer selected for judging correctness of occurrence by. In being thus ignorant, we are also ignorant as to precisely which norm-kind the composer singled out. And so we are ignorant as to the precise nature of the work he composed. Yet it is clear what we are looking for: the properties that the composer selected for judging correctness of sound-occurrences by. And often, of course, we have very good evidence as to what those properties are.

The situation for those works which are the works of a group—for example, indigenous folk music—is not substantially different. The group in question will use a certain set of properties for judging correctness of occurrence. That then determines the properties normative within the associated work. So that is what we try to discover. Usually a group operates in such matters by acknowledging certain of its members as authorities: a certain group of the old men in a society are acknowledged as knowing how the music should go. So we consult them. And if they differ on some point, then on that point the group has no criterion for correctness. On disputed points they will always agree, though, that everything falling outside a certain rather limited range of possibilities is incorrect. As it were, they have criteria for incorrectness. Though there may have been disagreement as to how some of the Hungarian folk songs that Bartok scored should go at some points, at no point do they go as the beginning of Penderecki's *Resurrection*.

VIII. *What Kind of Kind is a Musical Work?*

A musical work is a norm-kind whose examples, if any, are sound-sequence-occurrences. But now, more specifically, with which of such kinds are musical works to be identified? Sound-sequence-occurrences come in many kinds. Which of these many kinds is identical with Beethoven's Opus 111?

What particularly forces this question on our attention is the distinction made in the preceding section between those sound-sequence-occurrences which are *performances* of some musical work *W* and those which, though not performances of *W*, yet possess all the acoustic and instrumental properties necessary for being occurrences of *W* (excluding here from instrumental properties the property of *being a performance*). The question which this distinction brings to mind is this: are the examples of a musical work confined to performances of the work? That is to say, is it the case, for any musical work *W*, that the property of *being a performance of W* is essential within *W*? The wind blowing through the rocks cannot produce a performance of 'Greensleeves'. Might it none the less produce an example of it? Or is that impossible?

Our discussion concerning the nature of performing not only brings this question to mind. It quickly furnishes an answer. When one plays a tape, of a composition for tape, one produces an example of the composition. One does not, though, produce a performance; for no one *performs* the composition.[20]

Of course it might not be the case, for *every* musical work *W*, that the property of *being a performance of W* is essential within it, while yet it is the case, for *some* work *W*, that the property of being a performance is essential within it. The phenomenon of the player piano makes this look dubious, however. Consider

---

[20] There is also the possibility that the property of *being a performance*, though not essential within works of music, is yet normative within them. However, the existence of compositions for tape surely refutes that view as well. Naturally this still leaves open the possibility that this property is normative within *some*, though *not all*, compositions.

any work for piano which can be put on player piano rolls. We saw that it is not clear that what one produces, when a roll for that work is put in a piano and the piano is pumped, is a performance of the work. Surely, though, it is an example, an occurrence, of the work. After all, one hears the work in hearing the sound-sequence-occurrence produced in that particular playing of it. And in general, it would seem that if one hears work W in hearing some particular sound-sequence-occurrence, then that occurrence should be regarded as an occurrence of work W.

So it is not necessary, if something is to be an example of Beethoven's Opus 111, that it be a performance—that it be a sound-sequence-occurrence produced by someone performing the work. A possibility to be considered, though, is that it is necessary that the occurrence be produced *either* by someone performing it *or* by someone playing it, as on a player piano or on a record player. So too, of compositions for tape it is obviously not required that their occurrence be produced by performing. Possibly, though, it *is* required that the composition be played by someone who uses an appropriately derived tape. Perhaps it is the case that no example of the work has been produced if all that happens is that some electronic organ goes berserk and produces a sound-sequence-occurrence having all the acoustic properties normative within the composition.

Playing, as we are thinking of it here, involves either the reproduction of a performance (as in the playing of a work by putting on a record), or the use of some appropriately derived artefact in the production of the sounds (as a roll for a player piano, or a copy of the tape that the composer made of a composition for tape). Perhaps what is necessary for a musical work to be exampled is that it be *either* performed *or* played. Let us consider that possibility.

Suppose that something could be an occurrence of a musical work without being either a performance or a playing of the work. How then would we pick out the examples of some work W? Well, any sound-sequence-occurrence which has *all* the properties *normative* within W will of course be an example of the work. But those would all be correct occurrences. What on this view would be an *incorrect* occurrence? Presumably it would be any sound-sequence-occurrence which still comes fairly close to exemplifying the properties normative within W. Thus on this view a property essential within the work would be: *coming fairly close to exemplifying the properties normative within W.*

Our question, then, is whether there is any absurdity in either of these views—the one, the view that essential *within* musical work W is the property of *being a sound-sequence-occurrence brought about by performing or playing W*; the other, the view that that property is not essential within the work, but that instead a property essential within the work is that of *coming fairly close to exemplifying the properties normative within W*? Let us call these views, A and B respectively. On A, musical work W is identical with the kind: Sound-Sequence-Occurrence Produced By Performing Or Playing W. On B, musical work W is identical with the kind: Sound-Sequence-Occurrence Coming Fairly Close To One Exemplifying The Properties Normative Within W. Of course, anything which is an example of the former kind will be an example of the latter. Thus the former is included within the latter. And accordingly, the property of *coming fairly close to exemplifying the properties normative within W* is as much essential within the former kind as within the latter.

I see no reason to doubt that there are kinds of these sorts, and that they are indeed distinct. So our question comes down to this: are musical works always of the former kind, the A-view sort, or are some at least of the B-view sort? Let us sharpen the issue by drawing out some of the implications of each view.

On B, an occurrence of 'Greensleeves' might be brought about by the wind whistling through the rocks of Bryce Canyon; and as a corollary, a person might hear 'Greensleeves' without the occurrence that he hears being produced by performing or playing. Furthermore, *in* hearing a performance or a playing (correct or incorrect) of a work W, one could hear an occurrence of a distinct work W^* which is neither a performance nor a playing of W^*. For on B, a given sound-sequence-occurrence may be an example of two (or more) distinct works such that the occurrence is a performance or playing of one work and neither a performance nor playing of the other(s). Thus on B one can hear several distinct musical works in listening to a performance or playing of just one work. On A, however, none of these results obtains. For on A, the only examples of a musical work are performances or playings of that work.

As just remarked, on B it is possible for two distinct works to share some of their examples. Indeed, it is possible for them to share all their examples. This is so because a sound-sequence-occurrence which has enough of the properties required for a correct (or indeed incorrect) occurrence of work W might also have enough to be an occurrence of a distinct work W^*. Counter to what one might expect, however, it is also true on A that two distinct works can share examples. For suppose that one work W is normatively included with another W^*, in the sense that all the properties normative within W^* are also normative within W. Where the one allows some latitude with respect to correctness in a cadenza, let us say, the other does not. Then all performances and playings of the included work W will be performances or playings of the normatively inclusive work W^*. However, it is *only* when one work is normatively included within the other that, on A, two works can share any examples. And in that respect, view A gives different results from view B.

Furthermore, if it be true that a work cannot be performed or played until it has been composed, then on A there can be no occurrence of the work before its composition—that is, before that kind which *is* the work has become a musical work by virtue of the composer's activity. Not so on B, however.

So there are indeed significant differences between the sort of kind which, on A, is to be identified with a work of music and the sort of kind which, on B, is thus to be identified. It would seem, however, that none of the differences we have thus far singled out gives a decisive advantage to either view A or view B. Of course the implications of these two views diverge on more issues than those we have thus far noted. Yet also in those additional, undiscussed divergences I see no *decisive* reason for preferring the one view to the other. The kinds with which these two views propose to identify a given musical work are existent, and are clearly distinct from each other. Yet neither view seems to yield a decisive absurdity.

The situation, I think, is this. When we refer to and speak about what we regard as musical works we do not, with definiteness, pick out entities of either sort as opposed to those of the other. That is no doubt because in most respects entities of these two sorts do not differ.[21] And the points where they do differ are so far on the edge of our normal concerns in the arts that we never have to make up our minds one way or the other as to which of these sorts of entities we intend to be dealing with. It is possible, of course, that future developments in the arts will force us to make up our minds; and it may just be that different developments will force us to move in different directions to cope with different phenomena. But though future developments in music might confront us with works for some of which A is decisively correct and for others of which B is, that does not settle the issue for the mass of musical works now extant. For them, we have no decisive reason for preferring either of A or B to the other.

It does seem to me, though, that on most matters view A provides us with a more *natural* understanding. Neither view yields any decisive absurdities. Yet fewer of A's consequences diverge from the ways in which we normally think of musical works. It's possible, of course, that we are mistaken at crucial junctures in how we normally think of musical works. Yet in the absence of any decisive reason for thinking so, I shall henceforth speak of musical works as if they were all of the kind specified in view A. I shall speak of them as if they were, all of them, kinds of performances or of playings.

What is worth noting here, before we leave the matter, is that if the ontological principles in accord with which we have been conducting our investigations are correct, then no kinds come into or go out of existence. Accordingly, on neither view A nor view B do musical works come into or go out of existence. A kind exists just in case its property-associate exists. And we said that for any property, *being-f*, there is that property if and only if either something is-*f* or something is not-*f*. (We added certain qualifications which need not be repeated here.) Quite obviously a consequence of this is that properties, and so too then *kinds*, do not become or perish. So on both view A and view B, a composer does not bring that which is his work into existence. Musical works exist everlastingly. What the composer does

[21] For example, we think of musical works as capable of existing unperformed—witness the common lament of the contemporary composer that he cannot get his works performed. Likewise we think of them, once they exist, as existing at a certain time whether or not an example is occurring at that time. We do not think of them as existing intermittently. Each of these is a straightforward consequence of *both* A and B.

must be understood as consisting in bringing it about that a preexistent kind becomes *a work*—specifically, a *work of his*. To compose is not to bring into existence what one composes. It is to bring it about that something becomes a work. And the composer does that by selecting certain properties as criteria for correctness in occurrence. Though a composer may be eminently creative in his selection, he is not a creator. The only thing a composer normally brings into existence is a copy, a token, of his score. In music, creation is normally token creation.

A final query which comes to mind concerning the nature of those kinds which are works of music is whether they can change with respect to the properties normative or essential within them. Can a work thus change? Or is it in that respect immutable, and is the phenomenon that we might ordinarily describe as a single work changing, actually a temporally successive series of slightly different works? Can a composer change his mind with respect, say, to the instrument assigned to play the theme at a certain point in his composition, and still have the identical work? Can a work of folk music change over time?

The most efficient way to approach this question is to determine whether it is essential to a work W that it have essential or normative *within* it whatever properties it *does* so have. For if it is essential to it, then W cannot change in that respect, and cannot have been different from how it is in that respect. On the other hand, if it is not essential, then we will have to consider whether there is something else which prevents its changing.

So suppose that at a certain time t the property P is essential within W. We want to know whether it is possible that at some other time, P may not be essential within W (and whether even at t it is possible for P not to be essential within W). Now to suppose that at t the property P is essential within W, is just to suppose that at t it is impossible that something should be an example of W and lack P. But in general, if a proposition is impossible at any time it is impossible at all times, and necessarily so. Thus, if P is essential within W at *any* time, it is that at all times. Accordingly, those kinds which are works of music are immutable with respect to the properties essential within them, for they cannot be different in this respect from how they are.

What, then, about change with respect to properties normative within musical works? Well, to suppose that at t the
property P is normative within W is to suppose that at t it is
impossible for there to be something which is a correct example
of W and lack P. But once again, if a proposition is impossible at
any time it is impossible at all times, and necessarily so. Thus
those kinds which are works of music are also immutable with
respect to the properties normative within them; for they cannot even in this respect be different from how they are.

IX. *Applications to Arts other than Music*

In developing our theory as to the nature of the artefacts of art
we have used music as our principal example. Let us now
briefly consider how the theory applies to arts other than music.
It will be helpful to begin by highlighting a few matters concerning music, which thus far in our discussion have received
only minor attention.

As already remarked, many occurrences of musical works
take place by way of someone playing a record of some recording of one of those works' performances. I put a tape in my tape
machine, and there in my living room takes place an occurrence
of Mahler's *Symphony of a Thousand*. Now even if the performance
recorded was wholly correct, still the occurrence produced by
my playing of the tape may be an incorrect example of the
work—by virtue of some defect in the equipment used along the
way, or by virtue of some defect in how someone used the
equipment. So the work's requirements for correctness have
independent application to that occurrence which takes place
in my living room. But they do not serve to guide me in my
production of the occurrence. Accordingly, what takes place in
my living room is not—by our analysis of *performance* of a
work—a performance of Mahler's symphony. What takes
place is only a reproduction of a performance, and so only a
playing of the work.

We also took notice of the fact that it is possible to compose
directly onto magnetic tape, thus producing a tape without
recording some sound-sequence-occurrence. In such a case,
occurrences of the work are brought about by someone's playing the original tape or a copy derived therefrom. What results

from so doing is genuinely an occurrence of the work, though not a performance of it. It too is only a *playing* of the work.

Three things are worth noting about this latter sort of case. In the first place the composer, though certainly he selects properties as required for correctness in occurrence, does not *signify* those properties. He does not use symbols to stand for those properties. Still, he does want his work to be available to the public for producing occurrences. So he produces an artefact such that it and copies derived therefrom can be used in the very process of producing occurrences of the work, without at all serving to give *instructions* for producing such occurrences. And if the (corrected) prototype tape or a copy thereof is used properly in the process of producing an occurrence, then a correct occurrence of the work will ensue.

Secondly, the composer need say nothing, or virtually nothing, as to how to use his tape so as to give rise to a correct occurrence of his work. He can simply presuppose properly functioning tape machines, standard ways of operating those machines, and standard settings for those machines; and the only instruction he need give, even tacitly, is this: Use the tape in a properly functioning machine in the standard way. But these very same instructions for proper use of his production-artefact are given no matter what the composition. Thus the instructions are wholly general, wholly non-specific to any particular composition.

Thirdly, not only are the instructions that the composer gives or presupposes for the use of his tape wholly non-specific to his own particular composition. In the 'practice tradition' for tape machines which he presupposes everything has been made routine. Adjustment and feedback are at a minimum. Great knowledge and skill go into the making of tape machines and the making of the tapes. But the knowledge and skill required for properly using a tape is minimal.

Notice how different it is for scored music of the traditional sort. There too the composer presupposes properly functioning instruments of a certain sort; and there too he presupposes a practice tradition for playing those instruments. But playing the instrument in accord with the practice tradition requires enormous amounts of adjustment and feedback on the part of performers. Secondly, the composer must give detailed instructions specific to his own particular composition as to what those skilled in the practice tradition should do with their instruments so as to give rise to a correct occurrence of the work. Lastly, the artefact that the composer produces—his autograph score—is not a production-artefact. It is not actually used to make sounds of the desired sorts. Violins are so used, and violin bows. But not scores.

All these differences are of course the result of the fact that the artefact which the composer of music for tape makes is not a sequence of symbols giving instructions for producing correct occurrences of his work, but rather an artefact to be used in the production process itself—that, plus the fact that tapes and tape machines are such that whatever variations in sound the composer desires can be achieved by using the machine in the standard way and then building the variations into the tapes themselves.

Cinematic works have both interesting similarities to, and interesting differences from, musical works for tape. Here too there can be both correct and incorrect examples—which shows that once again we are dealing with requirements for correctness. But more specifically, cinematic works are like compositions for tape in that associated with the work is an artefact to be used in the production-process itself. All decisions as to properties normative within the work must ultimately be made by reference to what a showing cannot fail to be like when the (corrected) prototype film is properly used. Further, instructions as to proper use of the relevant instruments—projectors—are wholly non-specific to any particular cinematic work. And the use of those instruments in accord with the 'practice tradition' is wholly routine.

What makes cinematic works interestingly different, though, is that characteristically two different people are responsible for the work. Two different people select requirements for correctness in occurrence. Further, they make their selections in two very different ways. Let us simplify the situation somewhat by treating cinema as if it were a purely visual art.

In the typical case, the process of making a cinematic work begins with a *script* produced by a screen writer. The screen writer selects certain properties of illuminated colour-pattern-sequence-occurrences; and in his script he gives instructions to directors for producing a prototype film (i.e., strip of celluloid) such that, when used in the standard way in properly functioning projectors, showings will ensue which exhibit the properties selected. The director is then the one whose task it is actually to produce a film, thereby to bring a cinematic work into existence. There is no cinematic work, but only a project for one, until someone has brought into existence a strip of celluloid of the appropriate sort. Accordingly, the screen writer must be understood as selecting properties that he *would like to see* become normative within some work. His selections have the nature of proposals. In his selection of properties he does not actually compose a work which *has* those properties as normative within it.

The film that the director produces, like the tape in a musical composition for tape, is a production-artefact. In producing this film the director follows, with more or less fidelity, the instructions of the screen writer. But he himself must make a great many selections of properties as required for correctness in showing. It would be impossible for him not to go beyond the instructions of the screen writer in specificity. Where the screen writer specifies certain colours, the director must select specific shades of those colours.

The result of bringing about a work in this fashion is that there are two sets of criteria for correctness of occurrence —one, the proposals of the screen writer, the other, the actual selections of the director. As we have just seen, the selections of the director will necessarily be more detailed than the proposals of the screen writer. Accordingly, if the director faithfully follows the instructions of the screen writer, the set of correctness-requirements proposed by the writer will be a subset of those selected by the director. But of course they may conflict, with the result that a showing of the film is correct, judged by reference to the director's selections, and incorrect, judged by reference to the writer's proposals.

That does not mean, however, that we have two different cinematic works on our hands. The properties normative within a cinematic work are just those which a showing cannot lack if it is produced by using the corrected authorized prototype film in the standard way in a properly functioning projector. And the director is the one who makes, or supervises the making, of that film. He is responsible. In making and supervising the making of the film he may faithfully follow the instructions of the screen writer. But even if he does not, the fact that showings of the work do not fit what the writer proposed does not make them incorrect occurrences of the writer's cinematic work. There is no such work. It is the authorized corrected prototype film, coupled with properly functioning projectors and standard ways of using them, that 'fixes' the work. There can indeed be incorrect occurrences of the work. But those will come about by way of using improperly functioning projectors, or running the film through projectors in other than the standard way, or using defective copies of the prototype film.

Quite obviously this implies that a screen writer's script may be used in the production of many distinct works of cinematic art. It may in fact be *faithfully followed* in the production of many distinct cinematic works. To re-shoot a script is not to bring about a distinct production of the same work. It is to produce a distinct work. The difference between cinematic works and dramatic works on this point should be obvious.

We should take note of one other ontologically significant feature of cinematic works. In very many cases the prototype film is made by having actors play roles and then 'shooting'. But what takes place at a given showing of the cinematic work is *not* an instance of role-playing. A showing of a cinematic work consists not of instances of role-playing but rather of an occurrence of a sequence of illuminated colour-patterns (counting black and white as colours). These colour-patterns may be used to *represent* someone, and may be photographically derived from instances of role-playing. But role-playing itself does not occur there in the cinema. Actors function in the compositional process of bringing a cinematic work into existence. But in occurrences of the work they make no appearance. In drama, by contrast, actors have no function in the compositional process of bringing the work into existence. Rather, they are needed for occurrences of the work.

The fact that role-playing may enter into the making of a film but does not enter into its showing makes the showing of cinematic works quite different from the playing of a tape or record of a recording of some musical performance. A performance which is recorded actually *consists* in an occurrence of certain sounds, and one's playing of a tape or record of a recording of some performance *results* in an occurrence of certain sounds.

In graphic art, too, the artist prepares an artefact—his plate—to be used within the process of producing examples. And the properties normative within the work are whatever properties an impression would have if a sheet of the proper sort of paper were pulled in the proper way through a properly inked and properly functioning press in which the artist's plate served as the printing plate. In this case, however, no *copies* of the production-artefact are permissible; that is to say, the plate that the artist produces is not allowed to serve as the prototype for other plates. And what constitutes the proper sort of paper, being pulled in the proper way, and being properly inked, are by no means determined simply by the 'practice tradition' for printing presses. Rather, quite independently of the production of his plate the artist must determine the kind of paper and ink to be used; and in many cases he must determine just how the impressions are to be pulled. Thus the proper use of his plate is highly specific to the work associated with the plate. Further, there is only a moderate amount of routine in the use of his plate so as to produce correct examples. Especially in the inking of the plate there is considerable room for adjustment and feedback—considerable room for skill. It is interesting to note that graphic art in the twentieth century has, if anything, retreated from routine in the production of impressions. There was more routine in the pulling of Dürer's prints than there is in the pulling of William S. Hayter's prints.

In the respects under discussion architectural works are wholly analogous to musical works; so let us not tarry. The artefact that the architect produces—his architectural drawings—is a set of symbols which indicates many at least of the properties required for correctness in examples. Many others are presupposed as known from the practice tradition within which the architect is working. At the same time, the architectural drawings serve as instructions for the production of correct examples.

Drama deserves more consideration; for it confronts us with phenomena different from any we have yet considered. At the heart of drama lies the phenomenon of role-playing. A dramatic work, on its artefactual side, consists of a sequence of role-playings. And a correct example of it consists of an *occurrence* of that sequence. A dramatic work is composed, then, by someone's selecting a certain set of properties as required for correctness in an occurrence of a sequence of role-playing. Normally the selection of such properties is made, or the properties already selected are signified, by the composition of a script which then not only serves to signify the properties selected but also to give instructions to directors and actors.

Unlike cinematic works, the instructions that the script provides are not instructions for the creation of a production-artefact upon the completion of which the work comes into existence. In the field of drama neither authors nor directors create any production-artefact. (An exception, of sorts, will be mentioned shortly.) And in the field of drama the writer of the script has already brought the dramatic work into existence. Nothing more needs doing for that to take place. Rather, the dramatic script gives instructions for the composition of a *production*. Now a production of a dramatic work can itself have many performances. It is, accordingly, itself an occurrence-kind, as is the dramatic work itself. And it is the director who fixes the requirements for something's being a correct occurrence of his production. So in drama, as in cinema, we have two sets of correctness requirements; one, that of the scriptwriter, the other, that of the director. But the selection by the author is not merely the selection of properties that he *proposes* become normative within some work. He selects them in such a way that thereby he has *composed* a work within which they *are normative*. Likewise, however, the director selects properties as required for correctness. If the actors stray from his requirements in some performance, then his production has been incorrectly performed.

In the case of a dramatic performance, then, we can best view ourselves as dealing with *two* distinct works, each with its own requirements for correctness. One is the dramatic work, composed by the author. The other is the dramatic-production work, composed by the director.

If the director of a dramatic work has not in all respects followed the instructions of the author, then there is conflict between that work and the production work. Something cannot be a correct example of both. Otherwise the production work will be normatively included within the dramatic work. For the production work will always be much more detailed than the dramatic work. The director must settle all sorts of issues which the dramatist leaves open. The road to a correct performance of the production work is more straight and narrow than is the road to a correct performance of the dramatic work. But in any case, a dramatic performance, being an occurrence of two different works, can be judged with respect to correctness by reference to two different sets of criteria: those of the author's dramatic work, and those of the director's production work.

The authors of dramatic works put into their scripts staging instructions, costuming instructions, casting instructions, etc. Yet in most dramatic works, most of the instructions are specifications of what the actors are to *say* in playing the characters. In effect, the words specified constitute production-artefacts. They are to be used in the process of producing an occurrence of the work. Yet a great deal more is required for the correct performance of a dramatic work than just what results directly from directors and actors following the explicit instructions and uttering the specified words. There is all the rest that the actor must do if he is to 'play his character'. This is to be arrived at by a sensitive consideration of what properties a person would have and what actions he would perform if he uttered (outside of role-playing) such words as the ones specified. *Those* are the properties the actor must represent someone as performing. And a correct dramatic performance must have whatever properties are necessary for such representations to occur, as well as for the explicit instructions of the author to be followed.

Literary works remain. What is new here is that the author, in order to indicate his criteria for correctness, neither offers instructions for producing correct examples nor produces an artefact to be used in the production-process. Rather, he produces a prototype example: an actual copy or actual utterance of the work. If the example is to function as a prototype for the production of other examples we must know which of its properties are to function prototypically and which not. The remarkable thing is that normally this is wholly unambiguous.

In most cases it takes virtually no sensitivity whatsoever, given the poet's or the novelist's autograph copy, to know how to go about determining whether something is an accurate replica of the copy, and thus, to determine whether something is a correct copy of the work.

X. *The Goodman Alternative*

To conclude this Part of our discussion I propose to scrutinize the theory of the nature of art works developed by Nelson Goodman in his *Languages of Art*.[22] Between these two theories, his and mine, there is at many points a head-on clash—or certainly what appears on first reading to be a head-on clash. Accordingly, a consideration of the Goodman alternative will serve to highlight the significance of various facets of my own theory.

The most obvious and striking point of contrast between my theory and Goodman's arises on the issue of whether a work of music can have an incorrect performance: Goodman holds that it cannot, I have contended that it can. A good way to get into Goodman's theory as a whole will be to follow the trail that leads him to his conclusion.

A thesis around which very much of Goodman's book pivots is stated in these words:

A score, whether or not ever used as a guide for a performance, has as a primary function the authoritative identification of a work from performance to performance.[23]

What Goodman has in mind by this thesis is spelled out just a few paragraphs later:

Scores and performances must be so related that in every chain where each step is either from score to compliant performance or from performance to covering score or from one copy of a score to another correct copy of it, all performances belong to the same work and all copies of scores define the same class of performances. Otherwise, the requisite identification of a work from performance to performance would not be guaranteed; we might pass from a performance to another that is not of the same work, or from a score to another that determines a different—even an entirely disjoint—class of perform-

---

[22] Bobbs-Merrill: New York, 1968.
[23] Ibid., p. 128.

ances. Not only must a score uniquely determine the class of performances belonging to the work, but the score (as a class of copies or inscriptions that so define the work) must be uniquely determined, given a performance and the notational system.

This double demand is indeed a strong one. Its motivation and consequences, and the results of weakening it in various ways, need to be carefully considered. We may begin by asking what the properties are that scores, and the notational systems in which scores are written, must have in order to meet this basic requirement.[24]

What Goodman visualizes here is a zig-zag process from performance to score-copy with which the performance complies, to performance complying with the score-copy, to score-copy with which the performance complies, etc., with optional sideways moves from one score-copy to another score-copy, this whole ballet being such that in performing it we never move from a performance of one work to a performance of a distinct work. He then asks what works and scores must be like for this ballet to take place. Concerning scores, his conclusion is that they must be *notational*; and he proceeds to explain what he means by that.

In trying to understand just what it is that Goodman has in mind in posing and answering the above question, it is important to realize, as he himself makes clear, that he is not using 'score' in the usual sense. Many things that we would normally call a score do not fit the concept of a score that he is working with; and conversely, many things that do not fit our ordinary concept of a score do fit his. He defines 'a score' as 'a character in a notational system'.[25] He explicitly says that he has 'broadened the application of "score" to embrace characters of the sort described in any notational system, not merely in musical notation'.[26] And on pp. 179–92 he points out many ways in which what we ordinarily call scores do not satisfy his criterion for being a score. Indeed, what can be said is this: a Goodman-score, in music, is just whatever sort of symbol is necessary for guaranteeing identity-preservation in performing the zig-zag ballet. And so in asking what a score must be like if it is to function in the prescribed way in the identity-preserving

[24] Ibid., pp. 129–30. See also p. 178.
[25] Ibid., p. 177.
[26] Ibid.

zig-zag ballet, Goodman is just asking what a symbol must be like thus to function. Though he thinks we have some symbols that do thus function, the defence of that claim is not at all central in Goodman's discussion. At its centre is just the theoretical question: What would symbols have to be like if they were thus to function?

Now for each score there is the class—possibly empty—of those things that comply with the score. Call that, *the compliance-class* of the score. Goodman's doctrine is that if there is a work associated with a given score, that work will be the compliance-class of the score. That, at least, is how he states his doctrine. He also makes clear, though, that in his view there are no classes, and so no works. There are only performances compliant to scores, not classes of performances compliant to scores. Whenever we use a sentence in which we apparently commit ourselves to classes we are, if not just speaking falsely, then describing in a misleading way a reality devoid of classes. Having said this, however, Goodman proceeds to use the 'vulgar' language of classes without doing anything by way of showing us how to speak better. We as his readers have no choice, then, but to take him as holding that works of music are classes. For there is no other theory to be found in Goodman. He proposes no theory of which his 'class language' can be viewed as a convenient, albeit misleading, expression.

Already in section II of this Part we saw, though, that works of music are not classes; and in our own theory we developed the alternative view that they are *kinds*. It may be helpful briefly to recapitulate the considerations we brought against the class (set) theory of works of art. For one thing, on this view all works which lack performances would be identical with each other. There would be only one such work, because there is only one null-class. Obviously, though, there are *many* unperformed works. Secondly, a work of music can have had more or fewer or different performances than in fact it does have; it does not have its performances essentially. A set, however, has its membership essentially. And thirdly, given that a set exists only when its members exist, there is no such entity as the set of all and only those things which are ever performances of Beethoven's First. At any given time the expression 'the set of all and only those entities which are (presently) performances of

Beethoven's First' will pick out a set. But the set it picks out will vary from time to time, depending on the performances which are taking place at that time. Throughout such flux of sets, however, Beethoven's First endures.

To these objections Goodman might of course reply that when he speaks of works of music he is not using the ordinary concept of *work of music* but is simply applying the phrase 'work of music' to a compliance-class of a notational symbol of a certain sort. If that were the case, then to avoid confusion we would have to speak of 'Goodman-works' as well as of 'Goodman-scores'. However, I know of no passage which suggests that Goodman would in fact take this line of response. To do so would make his enterprise even more hypothetical than already it is. We would then not have a theory as to the nature of works of art. We would only have a theory as to what compliance-classes must be like and what symbols must be like if identity is to be preserved in performing the zig-zag ballet.

Goodman's reason for refusing to allow that works of music can have incorrect performances is that, if they could, identity-preservation in performing the zig-zag ballet would no longer be guaranteed. Let us see how he argues the case. 'The constitutive properties demanded of a performance of the symphony are those *prescribed in* the score,' he says.[27] And then he goes on to say that 'a performance, whatever its interpretative fidelity and independent merit, has or has not all the constitutive properties of a given work, and is or is not strictly a performance of that work, according as it does or does not pass this test.'[28] A bit later he says that 'an incorrect performance, though therefore not strictly an instance of a given quartet at all, may nevertheless ... be better than a correct performance.'[29] And yet later, 'a score must define a work, marking off the performances that belong to the work from those that do not ... What is required is that all and only performances that comply with the score be performances of the work.'[30]

Suppose that at this point someone replies that Goodman is simply mistaken in the assumption he is making. There can be,

[27] Ibid., p. 117.
[28] Ibid., pp. 117–18.
[29] Ibid., pp. 119–20.
[30] Ibid., p. 128.

and there are, incorrect performances of musical works. If a
theory leads to the denial of this fact, why, then so much the
worse for the theory. Goodman knows of course that such an
objection will be forthcoming. In a footnote to one of the
passages quoted above he says:

Of course, I am not saying that a correct(ly spelled) performance is
correct in any of a number of other usual senses. Nevertheless, the
composer or musician is likely to protest indignantly at refusal to
accept a performance with a few wrong notes as an instance of a work;
and he surely has ordinary usage on his side. But ordinary usage here
points the way to disaster for the theory (see V, 2).[31]

The later passage to which Goodman alludes in this footnote
then runs as follows:

Since complete compliance with the score is the only requirement for
a genuine instance of a work, the most miserable performance without
actual mistakes does count as such an instance, while the most
brilliant performance with a single wrong note does not. Could we not
bring our theoretical vocabulary into better agreement with common
practice and common sense by allowing some limited degree of deviation in performances admitted as instances of a work? The practising
musician or composer usually bristles at the idea that a performance
with one wrong note is not a performance of the given work at all; and
ordinary usage surely sanctions overlooking a few wrong notes. But
this is one of those cases where ordinary usage gets us quickly into
trouble. The innocent-seeming principle that performances differing
by just one note are instances of the same work risks the consequence—in view of the transitivity of identity—that all performances
whatsoever are of the same work. If we allow the least deviation, all
assurance of work-preservation and score-preservation is lost; for by a
series of one-note errors of omission, addition, and modification, we
can go all the way from Beethoven's *Fifth Symphony* to *Three Blind Mice*.
Thus while a score may leave unspecified many features of a performance, and allow for considerable variation in others within prescribed
limits, full compliance with the specifications given is categorically
required. This is not to say that the exigencies that dictate our
technical discourse need govern our everyday speech. I am no more
recommending that in ordinary discourse we refuse to say that a
pianist who misses a note has performed a Chopin Polonaise than that
we refuse to call the whale a fish, the earth spherical, or a grayish-pink
human white.

[31] Ibid., p. 120 n.

In those concluding lines Goodman seems to be saying that our customary allowance for incorrect performances is false. In ordinary life this falsehood is best overlooked; it is not only innocent but tolerable. There is no point in eradicating it. There may be some point in keeping it. But in theory, not so.

Why is it that Goodman thinks it false that a work can have incorrect performances? Well, keep in mind the law of the transitivity of identity, says Goodman. In general, if $A = B$ and $B = C$, then $A = C$. Now if we allow incorrect performances to count as performances, then starting at any musical work we could, if we performed the zig-zag long enough, arrive at every other work whatsoever (or at least, at a great many others). The conclusion would have to be then that there is just one work. But that is absurd. So we must allow that works cannot have incorrect performances.

What Goodman is assuming here is that if from work A one could arrive by the zig-zag process at work B, then $A = B$; and if from B one could arrive by that process at C, then $B = C$. And then, with that as background, he reminds us of the implications of the law of the transitivity of identity. But if this is indeed the argument, there is something very peculiar about it. Goodman has been asking what scores and works would have to be like if, in the performance of the zig-zag, we were never to move from one work to another. He observes that scores would have to be notational and that works would have to be incapable of having incorrect performances. Let us suppose him to be correct on both counts. It doesn't follow that works *in fact* are incapable of having incorrect performances. All that follows is that, if they are capable of having incorrect performances, the zig-zag won't necessarily keep us within the confines of one single work. If one has laid the correct stipulations on what works and scores must be like if, in following the zig-zag, we are never to move from one work to another, then indeed if we follow the zig-zag from A to B and tolerate only the right kinds of works and scores, A will be identical with B. But that scarcely points to some 'disaster for theory' which ensues if we hold that works can have incorrect performances.

So the crucial question becomes this: is there some necessity in being able to perform the zig-zag in identity-preserving fashion? Is there some absurdity which ensues if we are not able to do this—if we don't have the right kinds of scores around and cannot be dislodged from our common-sense conviction that one can perform a work incorrectly? The whole Goodman theory pivots on the answer to this question.

Strangely, it's not clear that Goodman himself thinks there is any absurdity. For he holds that works may antedate scores; and obviously if some extant work lacks a score it lacks a notational score. Further, he holds that our extant scores are not fully notational, and accordingly that they do not satisfy the requirement. We have already heard him make the latter point. Let us look at a passage in which he makes the former.

Where the works are transitory, as in singing and reciting, or require many persons for their production, as in architecture and symphonic music, a notation may be devised in order to transcend the limitations of time and the individual. This involves establishing a distinction between the constitutive and the contingent properties of a work ... Of course, the notation does not dictate the distinction arbitrarily, but must follow generally—even though it may amend—lines antecedently drawn by the informal classification of performances into works and by practical decisions as to what is prescribed and what is optional ...

Where there is a theoretically decisive test for determining that an object has all the constitutive properties of the work in question without determining how or by whom the object was produced, there is no requisite history of production and hence no forgery of any given work. Such a test is provided by a suitable notational system with an articulate set of characters and of relative positions for them ... Authority for a notation must be found in an antecedent classification of objects or events into works that cuts across, or admits of a legitimate projection that cuts across, classification by history of production; but definitive identification of works, fully freed from history of production, is achieved only when a notation is established.[32]

Goodman's claim, in short, is that identity-preservation in the zig-zag process is necessary if we are to have 'definitive identification of works fully freed from history of production'. He observes that before the advent of scores this condition was not satisfied; he observes that now, after the advent of scores, it is still not fully satisfied. He agrees, however, that in spite of this past and present lack, musical culture goes on—works get

[32] Ibid., p. 122. Cf. pp. 196-7.

composed, get performed, get listened to. In short, the absurdity ensuing when we do not have the equipment for guaranteeing that the zig-zag ballet will be performed in identity-preserving fashion is mild indeed. Goodman has provided us with no reason for changing our views that works can have incorrect examples.

In fact, in his pursuit of a kind of work and a kind of score which will guarantee the preservation of identity in the performance of the zig-zag ballet, Goodman is pursuing a will-o'-the-wisp. There are no musical works which cannot be performed incorrectly. And also there is no hope of definitively recovering score and work from performance. Consider once again our example of the improvisation. And now suppose that we know *exactly* what the performer has in his arsenal of symbols. Suppose further that his symbolism is fully notational. Can we now unambiguously derive from his performance a work and a score for that work? Certainly not. For we do not yet know what in the performance is to be optional with respect to correctness and what is to be required. Suppose a trill occurs at a certain point, and suppose that the performer has the symbolic equipment for scoring the trill and doing so notationally. Can we then unambiguously derive a work such that a trill belongs at that point to the work? No, we cannot. For the trill may occur in a correct performance of a work in which the trill is optional. Equally it may occur in a correct performance of a work in which it is required for correctness. But those would be distinct works.[33]

---

[33] One other consequence of Goodman's theory is worth taking note of. He says that 'the verbal language of tempos is not notational. The tempo words cannot be integral parts of a score insofar as the score serves the function of identifying a work from performance to performance. No departure from the indicated tempo disqualifies a performance as an instance—however wretched—of the work defined by the score' (p. 185). I should have thought that this implication of his theory which Goodman with honesty draws out is in fact false, and thus a refutation of the theory.

PART THREE

Worlds

I. *Preliminaries*

A charge against the writer and teller of fiction which has flitted in and out of Western history is that he is a liar—one who says what is false knowing it to be false. David Hume's words are characteristic: 'Poets themselves, tho' liars by profession, always endeavour to give an air of truth to their fictions...'[1] In a well-known passage from his *Apology for Poetry* Sir Philip Sydney replied to this old charge in the following words:

> Now for the poet, he nothing affirms, and therefore never lieth. For, as I take it, to lie is to affirm that to be true which is false... But the poet (as I said before) never affirmeth... And therefore, though he recount things not true, yet because he telleth them not for true, he lieth not—without we will say that Nathan lied in his speech before-alleged to David; which as a wicked man durst scarce say, so think I none so simple would say that Aesop lied in the tales of his beasts; for who thinks that Aesop writ it for actually true were well worthy to have his name chronicled among the beasts he writeth of.

In this passage Sydney repudiates what might be called an *assertionist* view of fiction. His answer to the charge that the writer of fiction asserts what he knows to be false is that the writer, *qua* writer of fiction, does not assert anything at all, and hence nothing false. As to what he does if not assert, Sydney does not say.

No doubt the assertionist is not totally without defences. Yet I think those defences must ultimately crumble.[2] And rather than joining the attack on the view that to compose a work of fiction is to make claims about our actual world, I wish to develop the thesis that to do so is to fictionally project a world distinct from our actual world. In this Part of our discussion I

---

[1] *Treatise concerning Human Nature*, I. iii. 10.
[2] Cf. Alvin Plantinga, *The Nature of Necessity (Clarendon Press: Oxford, 1974), pp. 153—9.*

shall explore the nature of the world projected. In the next, the
nature of the action of projecting.

Though the fictional projection of a world is an activity
distinct from that of making claims about our actual world, yet
one can make a claim about our actual world by fictionally
projecting a work's world. Think, for example, of Aesop's tale
'The Ass and the Grasshopper'. In telling this tale Aesop was
not claiming that our actual world contains talking animals.
Yet by way of fictionally projecting a world containing talking
animals he asserted that 'One man's meat is another man's
poison'. In effect Aesop made his point twice over: first by
telling his tale, then by appending his metaphorically expressed
moral. Similarly the prophet Nathan, by the telling of his story
about the rich man seizing the lamb of the poor man in order to
entertain a traveller, accused King David of thievery. And
Chaucer's Pardonner asserted by the telling of his tale that *radix
malorum cupiditas est*. So even though telling a tale is not to be
identified with making a claim, yet one can make a claim *by*
telling a tale. One can make a point by telling a story.

Worlds are not projected only in fiction. But whether projected in the fictional mode or in some other, they are the same.
Accordingly it makes no difference to our theory of worlds
whether we approach it from the side of fictional projection, or
assertive projection, or whatever. Yet there is advantage in
making fiction our ingress. Any theory as to the nature of the
worlds of works of art must take account of the fact that most of
them are merely possibilities, some even impossibilities—very
few in their entirety are actualities. Now the fictioneer is one
who deals pervasively with what are merely possibilities, sometimes even impossibilities. Seldom does he deal exclusively with
actualities. Accordingly, by approaching worlds from the side
of fiction we will avoid getting hung up on actuality.

Our exploration of worlds will be conducted by attending
rather exclusively to novels and dramas. But fictional and other
projection in the arts is no more confined to the media of novels
and dramas than is world projection confined to the mode of
fictional projection. So this too is a self-imposed restriction,
gaining for us the virtues of a less diffused discussion. Here and
there I shall indicate how the points made can be applied to
non-novelistic and non-dramatic fiction. But throughout it

must be remembered that language and role-playing are but two among the many media whereby world projection can be accomplished.

In taking as basic the distinction between a world projected and the action of projecting a world, we are adopting an approach which is similar to, and even a generalized version of, the structuralist approach to narrative literature. That approach is nicely summarized by Seymour Chatman as follows:

The elements of the formalist-structuralist theory of narrative . . . can be epitomized as follows. Each narrative has two parts: a *story* (*histoire*), consisting of the content, the chain of events (actions and happenings), and what may be called the existents (characters and settings), the objects and persons performing, undergoing, or acting as a background for them; and a *discourse* (*discours*), that is, the expression, the means by which the content is communicated, the set of actual narrative 'statements'.[3]

What the structuralists call the *story* of a narrative is one species of what I call the *world* of a work. The genus as a whole includes as well the worlds of such non-narrative works as individual representational paintings, dramatic performances, and passages of prose and verse consisting wholly of state descriptions and including no indication of happenings. I intend what I say about the worlds of works of art to be as applicable to these as to stories.

Since the concept of world of a work includes but is broader than the concept of story of a narrative, so too our correlative concept of *world projection* must be broader than the structuralist concept of *discourse*. It is broader both because it includes *media* of projection other than just the medium of word-utterings and word-inscribings, and because it includes *modes* of projection other than just fictional projection.

II. *In and Out of Worlds*

If we are to attain clarity on the nature of the worlds that are fictionally projected we must distinguish clearly between the action of fictionally projecting a world, on the one hand, and the

[3] 'Towards a Theory of Narrative' in *New Literary History*, vi, No. 2 (Winter, 1975), pp. 295–318.

action of describing the contents of an already projected world, on the other. That *describing* the world of a work is fundamentally different from *fictionally projecting* that world can be seen at once by noticing that we cannot evaluate the action of fictional projection by reference to the truth and falsehood of what was claimed. For nothing was claimed. On the other hand, when we *describe* the world of a work and its contents we make claims. Hence our action can be evaluated by reference to the truth or falsehood of what was claimed.

What makes it easy to overlook this crucial distinction between projecting a world and describing a world already projected is that both actions are customarily performed by uttering or inscribing sentences—and often the same sentences at that. Near the beginning of the Guerney translation of Gogol's *Dead Souls* one finds, for example, this sentence: 'While the server was still spelling out the note, Pavel Ivanovich Chichikov himself set out to look the town over and, it would seem, was quite satisfied with it.' In putting down the Russian original of that sentence Gogol was engaged in the action of fictionally projecting a world. Accordingly, it would have made no sense for him to blot out the sentence on the ground that what he had asserted by inscribing it was false. There are plenty of reasons he might have had for blotting out the sentence; that is not one of them. But if *I* now assertively utter, speaking about the world of *Dead Souls*, 'While the server was still spelling out the note Chichikov set out to look the town over,' I am not fictionally projecting a world but rather making a claim, and a true one at that.[4]

Though the action of fictionally projecting a world cannot be evaluated by reference to the truth or falsehood of what was claimed, yet it can of course be evaluated. And one can make mistakes in performing it. In one's projecting of a world one may have intended to tell the 'Rumpelstiltskin' story. But one may have got it wrong somewhere. Then too, the author of a story, by way of the sentences he actually puts down, may project a world somewhat different from the one he intended to project, and in that way make a mistake.

---

[4] Eventually we shall see that the state of affairs that Gogol fictionally projected with these words is distinct from that which I assert with these words. Thus the difference does not lie merely in the difference between fictionalizing and asserting.

Not only is it important, if we are to attain clarity on the concept of the world of a work, to distinguish between projecting a world and describing a world already projected. We must also have a sharp sense for the difference between a state of affairs' being true in some projected world and its being true in our actual world. On this matter too we are prone to fall into confusion. To diminish the possibilities of such confusion in our own discussion I shall henceforth not even speak of a state of affairs as *true in* some work's world, but only as *included within* it.

Take that familiar example of the philosophers, the proposition (state of affairs), 'Pegasus is a winged horse.' Most assuredly this is included within the world of the Greek myth. But that very same proposition is true in the actual world. It's true in the actual world that if there were an example of the Pegasus-character it would be a winged horse. Not so, however, for that other familiar example, 'Pegasus never existed.' It is indeed true in the actual world that no example of the Pegasus-character has ever existed. Most emphatically, however, what is included in the world of the myth is not that, but rather 'Pegasus exists.' In order for that world to occur there must exist an example of the Pegasus-character. Or take, 'A melancholy disposition is caused by an excess of bile.' Probably this is not true in the actual world. It seems quite clearly, though, to have been included in the world of certain of Shakespeare's plays.

We dig yet deeper into the matter if we consider propositions in which we are confronted with a 'crossover' between some fictitious character and some actual, concrete entity. For example, 'Gogol created the character Chichikov in the late 1830s or early 1840s.' Apparently this is true in the actual world. But it is not included in the world of *Dead Souls*. For in that world Gogol nowhere puts in an appearance. He is not to be found among the *fictionis personae*. And so, of course, his creating that character is not included within that world. Or suppose that one of the incidents in *Dead Souls* had been Chichikov drinking vodka with Tsar Nicholas I. Then included within the world of *Dead Souls* would have been the state of affairs of someone named 'Pavel Ivanovich Chichikov' drinking vodka with Tsar Nicholas. But now suppose that I am writing a biography of Nicholas I, an exhaustive biography, if you will.

Am I then to write down, 'On one occasion, at least, someone named 'Pavel Ivanovich Chichikov' drank vodka with Tsar Nicholas'? Probably not. And *certainly* not on account of Gogol's tale. The most accurate and exhaustive account of Nicholas's appointments would reveal no such encounter. What *could* correctly be written down about the Tsar was that he was portrayed by Gogol in *Dead Souls* as drinking vodka with someone named 'Pavel Ivanovich Chichikov'. That is true in the actual world. But then, in turn, it would not be the case that included in the world of *Dead Souls* was the Tsar's being portrayed by Gogol in *Dead Souls* as drinking vodka with someone named 'Chichikov'.

When we move to drama the distinction between what is included in some projected world and what is true in our actual world becomes even more subtle to make out and fascinating to observe. Suppose that I have gone to see a performance of *Hedda Gabler*. And suppose that I remark afterwards to someone that it was staged in such a way as to allow us to see Hedda shoot herself. How are we to understand this? Surely in some rather straightforward sense of the words one *can* see Hedda shoot herself. But suppose that I go again the next night, and again am observant. Then again I will see Hedda shoot herself. How odd. Did she not kill herself with that shot I saw her fire the night before? How does she come by these marvellous resuscitative powers? How often does Hedda shoot herself? How often has she shot herself in the world's history? But I—how could *I* see Hedda shoot herself? George could have seen her. And Lövborg. But I? Am I among the *dramatis personae* of Ibsen's play?

If we keep clear the distinction between the world of Ibsen's play and our actual world—and correspondingly the distinction between what is included in the former and what is true in the latter—then we are well on the way to unravelling this snarl. If the discussion concerns what is included in the world of the drama, then certainly it is not the case that I saw Hedda shoot herself, since 'I exist' isn't even included in that world. And what's included in that world is that Hedda shot herself just once. What I can see is someone playing the role of Hedda. That is, true in the actual world is my seeing someone playing the role of Hedda, though that's not included in the world of

Hedda Gabler. But of course those who play the role of Hedda do not customarily shoot themselves while so doing. Speaking strictly, I did not see anyone shoot herself. What I saw was someone playing the role of someone who shoots herself. By a sort of elision we speak of, say, Maggie Smith as Hedda, and then ascribe to this dual 'person' attributes belonging to the two different members of the duality.

In performances of the drama *MacBird* one of the actors impersonated Lyndon B. Johnson. Now suppose Johnson had gone to a performance of *MacBird.* Would he then have been watching himself? Could he thus, for example, observe himself dying? Can one, in the theatre, observe one's own funeral? Evidently not. And though this situation is more subtle than the one we have just analysed concerning Hedda Gabler, the way to unravel it is the same. In the actual world Johnson would not have observed himself from a distance but rather would have observed an *actor* from a distance.[5]

But what are we to say about a character that realizes its own fictionality? A state of affairs of this sort is included in the world of Pirandello's *Six Characters in Search of an Author.* But obviously it is not true in our actual world nor in any other possible world. Likewise, it isn't true in any possible world that a *person* realizes his fictionality. By contrast, a state of affairs consisting of a person's realizing his fictionality *is* included in the world of John Barth's 'Life Story'.[6]

In a passage in Brecht's *Messingkauf Dialogues* the following bit of dialogue occurs:

THE DRAMATURG: What about the fourth wall?
THE PHILOSOPHER: What's that?
THE DRAMATURG: Plays are usually acted as if the stage had four
    walls, not three; the fourth being where the audience is sitting. The
    impression given and maintained is that what happens on the stage
    is a genuine incident from real life, which of course doesn't have an
    audience. Acting with a fourth wall, in other words, means acting
    as if there wasn't an audience.

[5] A slightly different situation would be that which would obtain if Brecht had seen Günther Grass's *The Plebeians Stage an Uprising.* Grass insisted that the actor playing the playwright would not be impersonating Brecht. Maybe so. But there can hardly be any doubt that Brecht was Grass's *model* for the playwright-character in his play.

[6] In John Barth, *Lost in the Funhouse* (Doubleday: New York, 1969). The example was pointed out to me by Kendall Walton.

THE ACTOR: You get the idea? The audience sees quite intimate
episodes without itself being seen. It's just like somebody looking
through a keyhole and seeing a scene involving people who've no
idea they are not alone.[7]

In objection to this fourth-wall theory of drama the
Philosopher, who is probably Brecht's spokesman in the
dialogue, says that few people labour under the illusion which
the theory suggests they do, and that it would be a mistake for
anyone at all to do so. Surely the Philosopher is right in thus
rejecting the illusionist theory of theatre, so popular among
realists earlier in our century. Yet the defect in the fourth-wall
theory is deep and is not dispelled by the Philosopher's anti-
illusionist comments. For the theory regards *us* as watching the
dramatis personae. Thus in subtle fashion it confuses what is
included in the world of the drama with what is true in our
actual world. What we actually see when we go to a dramatic
performance are some real life persons—the actors. What we
also sometimes see is three rather flimsy walls. But what is
represented is a room of four walls; and it is not the case that the
room represented is something we see. Likewise what the actors
represent is the various *dramatis personae*; and it is not the case that
the *dramatis personae* are people we see. Of course it is possible to
include in the world of a drama some people observing others
by looking through a keyhole. And it is even possible in the
actual world for us, who bought our tickets expecting to be an
audience, to be placed in a situation where we are playing the
role of someone looking into a room spying on someone. But to
regard *us* as watching the *dramatis personae*—that is just confusion.

It must not be concluded that the differentiation between
what is included in the world of a dramatic performance and
what is true in the actual world can always be clearly made out;
nor must it be concluded that it *should* always be something that
can be clearly made out. On the contrary: many important and
subtle dramatic effects depend on allowing actors to slip in and
out of roles, on allowing it to remain ambiguous in certain
passages whether actors are in or out of roles, and thus on

[7] p. 51 in *The Messingkauf Dialogues*, transl. by J. Willett (Methuen & Co.: London,
1965).

obscuring the distinction between what is true in our actual world and what is included in some projected world. Most of the 'asides' in Elizabethan drama are probably best interpreted straightforwardly as consisting of the actor slipping out of character and talking directly to the audience (either that, or as belonging to a residual play outside the play). But consider the part of the Stage Manager in Thornton Wilder's *Our Town*. The person who plays this part begins by not playing a role, talking instead directly to the audience. His opening lines are these:

This play is called 'Our Town.' It was written by Thornton Wilder; produced and directed by A... (or: produced by A...; directed by B...). In it you will see Miss C...; Miss D...; Miss E...; and Mrs. F...; Mr. G...; Mr. H...; and many others.

But then shortly and almost indiscernibly the actor has slipped into playing a role, the role of a guide to Grover's Corners. We find him saying such things as these:

The sky is beginning to show some streaks of light over in the East there, behind our mount'in.

And

We've got a factory in our town, too,—hear it? Makes blankets.

What makes this structure especially fascinating is that when the actor playing the part of the Stage Manager slips into the role of town guide, then we the audience slip into the role of town observers. For example, when the person playing the Stage Manager says:

Here comes Howie Newsome delivering the milk,

then he is playing the role of a town guide addressing his tour members—*we* playing the role of the tour members. It must be conceded that the tourists we represent are of a rather god-like sort so far as their observational capacities are concerned. They are able to see and hear what goes on in the town without anyone in the town, other than the guide, being aware that they are doing so. But they are tourists none the less; and it is we the audience who play them.

Obviously this whole area constitutes a fascinating field for exploration—both artistically and theoretically. It would be interesting, for example, to consider those cases of one dramatic world nested within another which occur when there is a play within a play, and then to look for cases in which it remains ambiguous as to what is included in which of the two dramatic worlds. That fascinating Elizabethan play *The Knight of the Burning Pestle* (Beaumont and Fletcher) would be interesting to analyse with this in mind, as would Macleish's *J.B.* and Pirandello's *Six Characters*. The dazzler, though, is Tom Stoppard's *The Real Inspector Hound*.

III. Elucidation and Extrapolation

Which states of affairs are to be reckoned as included within the world of a given work of art?

In pursuing the answer to this question I shall be looking for a general rule, a principle. The search will not be guided simply by testing one and another proposed rule against the set of those things which satisfy the ordinary concept of the *story* or the *world* of a work of art. This would leave too many unresolved cases. Rather, I shall try to formulate a rule which in addition avoids various absurdities and conforms to the strategies of interpretation followed by reputable critics. A consequence of this procedure is that by the end of our discussion we will have *refined* rather than analysed the ordinary rough concept of the *story* or the *world* of a work.

The world which an author projects by way of his text certainly includes the states of affairs which he explicitly *mentions*. It includes as well those which he *suggests* with more or less indirectness. Narrations are never wholly explicit. Good ones are far from that. Consider the concluding paragraph of Jorge Borges's story 'The Streetcorner Man':

Nice and easy, I walked the two or three blocks back to my shack. A candle was burning in the window, then all at once went out. Let me tell you, I hurried when I saw that. Then, Borges, I put my hand inside my vest—here by the left armpit where I always carry it—and took my knife out again. I turned the blade over, real slow. It was as good as new, innocent-looking, and you couldn't see the slightest trace of blood on it.[8]

[8] In J. Borges, *The Aleph*, transl. by N. T. diGiovanni (Bantam Books. New York, 1971).

Borges explicitly mentions here such states of affairs as *someone's reporting that he walked the two or three blocks back to his room, someone's reporting that he put his hand inside this vest*, etc. What in context he also unmistakably suggests without ever mentioning is *someone's having stabbed a bully named 'Francisco Real'*.

If some state of affairs is either explicitly mentioned by the author or suggested by what he says, let us say that the author has *indicated* that state of affairs.[9] And let us call the activity of discovering what it is that an author has indicated, *elucidation*. Elucidation is often a difficult and complicated procedure. We have to discern the presence and force of irony, the meaning of metaphors, the suggestions borne by emphasis, the presence of ambiguity (*double entendre*). And sometimes elucidation is stymied. Try as we may we cannot discern what an author mentioned in a certain passage or what he suggested.

But on anyone's practice, the world projected by way of a text almost invariably includes more than what the author indicated by way of the text—more than what he mentions or suggests. For the sake of convenience let us call the activity of determining what is included in the projected world beyond what the author indicated, *extrapolation*. Often elucidation and extrapolation are both called *interpretation*. But it should be clear that they are decidedly distinct activities. Of course there is no sharp line between cases of them. Yet quite obviously the question as to whether in *The Turn of the Screw* Miles and Flora saw apparitions of Peter Quint and Miss Jessel is a question of extrapolation, not of elucidation.[10]

Now suppose that among the things some author indicates is the state of affairs of *a person named 'John''s being exactly 6 foot tall*. We naturally conclude that the world also includes the state of affairs of *a 6 foot tall person named 'John''s not being 7 foot tall*. And an obvious suggestion as to the principle tacitly at work here is that we must reckon as included within the world projected by way of some text not only what the author indicates but also whatever is required (entailed) by that which he indicates.

[9] *Indication* is a species of what later I will call 'introduction'. See Part Four, section VI. What is nowadays called 'hermeneutics' is the science which deals with the principles of what I call elucidation.

[10] Still another activity sometimes called 'interpretation' is that of giving an account of why the author wrote what he did—as in Marxist and Freudian criticism.

But this principle has some rather surprising and unsettling consequences. For one thing, by this principle every world of a work will include all necessary states of affairs—that is, all states of affairs which cannot fail to occur. For (to shift over to the language of propositions) a necessary truth is entailed by every proposition whatsoever. Thus by this criterion the most exotic truths of logic and mathematics are included in every work's world. If necessary we could no doubt live with such a consequence, reflecting that there is no reason why the scope of a work's world should not extend vastly beyond what a critic's or an author's purposes lead him to be interested in. But another consequence of the principle cannot be viewed with such equanimity. Sometimes that which an author indicates is impossible of occurring. Now an impossible state of affairs requires (entails) every state of affairs whatsoever. So when an author indicates what is impossible the principle cited has as its consequence that every state of affairs whatsoever is included within the world of the work. But that makes the concept of *world of the work* trivial and useless for such cases. Extrapolation becomes an idle activity.

Sometimes the impossibility of what an author indicates is due to a slip on his part. For example, he may at some point have indicated something which he did not intend to indicate. Then the fair thing to do is to revise the text to accord with his intent and extrapolate from that. So henceforth when I speak of the world projected by way of a text I shall mean the world which is or would have been projected by way of a *correct* copy of the text. But there are other cases in which the author at all points indicated what he intended to indicate, but failed to notice that he had thereby contradicted himself. He failed to notice, say, that he had ascribed two different birth dates to his hero. In such cases it is possible to compose alternative minimal revisions of the text, each of which indicates a self-consistent set of states of affairs. Then without anything being lost we could allow the concept of *the world projected by means of the text* to be applied only to these text-revisions and not to the offending text itself.

But sometimes the composition of such revisions would require massive labour. And more importantly, sometimes the impossibility of what an author indicates is not at all due to a slip on his part. Pirandello's already mentioned *Six Characters in Search of an Author* is a superb example. For in *Six Characters*, six characters—not six actors but six characters—walk onto a stage begging for some actors to play them. That could not happen. Yet for such cases too we want a concept of world of the work that applies, and applies without triviality. For it is clear that even for such cases we 'flesh out' the world beyond what the author indicates. Accordingly, when an author's having indicated something impossible is not the result of inadvertence on his part, there is no alternative but to introduce some refinement into the principle formulated. (Some of the prints of M. C. Escher confront us with the same issue in the realm of visual arts.)

One strategy that comes to mind at this point is to work with the concept of a 'strand': assemble what the author has indicated into conjunctions each of which is possible of occurring and each of which is as comprehensive as any such. Conjoin with each such conjunction whatever is required by it. Call the result a 'strand'. Extrapolation would then be based on these strands. And the world projected by way of a text could be conceived as including what the author has indicated, plus the strands derived from that.

But quite clearly this would not be satisfactory.[11] For suppose that the following sentence occurred in the text of some novel: 'Houdini succeeded in escaping from the box which had been submerged in the Cuyahoga. While resting on the bank and doodling on a piece of bark with a pencil lying about he saw, to his amazement, that he had drawn a square circle.' By the criterion offered, all the states of affairs indicated with these sentences would be included in the world of the work. By the same token, however, that state of affairs indicated with the words 'He saw, to his amazement, that he had drawn a square circle' would not be found within any strand which grounds extrapolation. For of course that state of affairs is impossible of occurring. Yet do we not in fact wish to have it available for grounding extrapolation? On the basis of what is indicated with that sentence do we not wish to say, for example, that included within the world of the work is *Houdini's being amazed, Houdini's drawing a mathematical figure*, etc.? Evidently we must in some

---

[11] The point that follows was first made to me by Robert Howell.

way unravel this impossible state of affairs itself, so as to make
what is 'contained within' it available for grounding extrapolation.

So consider some such impossible state of affairs S. In all or
most cases there will be a set of distinct states of affairs, $\langle s, \ldots,$
$s_n \rangle$, such that the conjunction of the members of the set is a state
of affairs identical with S. Call that a *conjunctive analysis* of S. Let
us now expand the strands which ground extrapolation to
include, beyond those indicated states of affairs which are
possible of occurring, those possible states of affairs which are
members of some conjunctive analysis of those indicated states
of affairs which are impossible. We can then say, as before, that
the world of the work includes what is indicated, plus the
strands derived from that.

For example, the state of affairs of *Houdini's seeing with amazement that he had squared the circle*, is identical with this: *Houdini's
having drawn a circle & Houdini's having drawn a square figure &
Houdini's circle being the same as his square figure & Houdini's having
been amazed & Houdini's having seen that he had drawn a circle which
was a square figure & Houdini's having been amazed over what he saw.*
Thus *Houdini's having been amazed* is a member of a conjunctive
analysis of *Houdini's having seen with amazement that he had squared
the circle*. Accordingly it is included in a strand derived from
what was indicated. Likewise *Houdini's having drawn a circle* is a
member of a strand. And since this requires *Houdini's having
drawn a mathematical figure*, both of these states of affairs are also
included in a strand derived from what was indicated. (If an
indicated state of affairs is impossible, then it may be that some
members of a conjunctive analysis of it will also be impossible.
But those will not be included in any strand derived from what
was indicated.)

However, on anybody's practice the world projected by way
of a text includes more than can be got by following this
principle. Consider, for example, the sentence already quoted
from Gogol's *Dead Souls*: 'While the server was still spelling out
the note, Pavel Ivanovich Chichikov himself set out to look the
town over...' Neither here nor elsewhere does Gogol indicate
the state of affairs of *the servant of a man named 'Chichikov''s being
able to see well enough to read*. Nor is this required by what he
indicates; for it is logically possible to spell out a note by

extra-sensory perception. Yet we can surely conclude from what Gogol indicates that that state of affairs is included in the world of *Dead Souls*.

How do we arrive at the conclusion that the *servant of a man named 'Chichikov''s being able to see well enough to read* is included in the world projected by way of the text of *Dead Souls*? Perhaps we do so by tacitly appealing to some such (contingent) subjunctive conditional as this: if some strand derived in the way suggested from what is indicated by Gogol would occur, then *the servant of a man named 'Chichikov''s being able to see well enough to read* would occur. But to which contingent subjunctive conditionals are we entitled to appeal, so as to ground our extrapolation? Are we entitled to appeal to any true ones whatsoever which have this same antecedent, concluding that their consequents are included in the world projected by way of the text of the work? And is the world projected by way of a text to be understood as including what the author indicates by way of that text, plus the impossible members of every conjunctive analysis of what he indicates, plus the strands derived in the way suggested from what he indicates, along with whatever else would contingently occur if some strand occurred?

To help us decide whether this general principle of world-inclusion—call it the α-principle—is acceptable, let us try to find a controversial application of it. Suppose it is true that if two boys were to exhibit a relationship to each other of the sort delineated by Mark Twain for the characters Huckleberry Finn and Nigger Jim, then there would be a homosexual relationship between them. Are we then to conclude with Leslie Fiedler[12] that *two boys named 'Huck' and 'Jim' having a homosexual relationship* is included in the world projected by way of the text of *Huckleberry Finn*?

A somewhat similar question concerning Shakespeare's *Hamlet* has an unproblematic answer. Those who believe in the substantial truth of Freudian psychological theory have argued that if someone behaved as does Hamlet in *Hamlet*, that behaviour would be due to his having an Oedipus complex. Now Shakespeare himself probably had a theory as to the cause of Hamlet's sort of behaviour; such as, that it was due to an

---

[12] '"Come Back to the Raft Ag'in, Huck, Honey"' in Fiedler, *An End to Innocence* (Beacon Press: Boston, 1966).

excess of bile. At various points in his works he suggests that the humours theory current in his day applies to the characters in his works, and most likely this is what the humours theory would say about a Hamlet-like melancholy. To avoid complicating the example let us suppose that in the text of this very play *Hamlet* Shakespeare clearly suggests that the humours theory holds for the characters in this drama. Now the humours theory is incompatible with the Freudian theory. And since on our supposition Shakespeare indicates the humours theory with his text, that rules out the use of those conflicting parts of Freudian theory in determining what is included in the world of the *Hamlet* text. In particular, *a person named 'Hamlet''s having an Oedipus complex* would not be included in that world, at least not if the only ground for thinking it would be is the (supposed) truth of the subjunctive conditional that if someone behaved as does Hamlet in *Hamlet* his behaviour would be due to an Oedipus complex. For even if this subjunctive conditional were true, it would still not be the case that if an *entire* strand, derived in the way suggested from what is indicated by Shakespeare with the *Hamlet* text, would occur, then there would be a person named 'Hamlet' whose behaviour was due to an Oedipus complex. In conducting our extrapolations we must consider *complete* strands derived from what is indicated, not just some fragments thereof. And that means that if the entirety of what is indicated is possible, then that single strand derived from the entirety of what is indicated must ground our extrapolation.

But this point does not help us to deal with the homosexual extrapolation from what is indicated with the text of *Huckleberry Finn*. We have learned that we must not ask whether, if two boys exhibited a relationship of the sort delineated for the characters Huck and Jim, there would then be a homosexual relationship between them. Rather (assuming that the entirety of what Twain indicates is possible), we must ask whether, if the whole of what Twain indicated occurred, there would then be a homosexual relationship between two boys named 'Huck' and 'Jim'. But so far as I know, the answer to this latter question is the same as that to the former. Twain, so far as I can tell, indicates no explanatory theory conflicting with the homosexual theory.

So there is no way of avoiding the issue: are Huck and Jim to be acknowledged as having a homosexual relationship in the world of *Huckleberry Finn*, on the ground that if what Twain indicates occurred, the state of affairs of *two boys named 'Huck' and 'Jim' having a homosexual relationship* would occur? I am sure that many critics would resist drawing this conclusion, and that they would resist drawing it even if they acknowledged that the ground cited was true. By thus resisting they would indicate that they were working with a different principle of world inclusion from the α-principle. What might that different principle be?

Think of this question along the following lines. For any strand Q derived in the way suggested from what is indicated with some text T, there will be an associated set of contingent subjunctive conditionals each of the form: If strand Q occurred, then state of affairs S would occur. Let us call that, the *conditional set associated with* the strand Q. Earlier we more or less took for granted that a certain subset of the conditional set associated with strand Q is such that the consequents of the members of that subset are included in the world projected by way of T. Our question then was: which subset? An answer which sprang naturally to mind was this: the subset consisting of all those members of the conditional set associated with Q which are *true*. But applying this principle to the *Huckleberry Finn* situation brought out that the principle has consequences not acceptable to all critics. The question as to why they are not acceptable was not raised. But probably most critics who dislike the α-principle do so because on this principle all sorts of new discoveries, no matter how unexpected or astonishing or shocking to the author, can be used to ground extrapolation—psychological discoveries, historical discoveries, geographical discoveries. The author, once having put some words down, is henceforth irrelevant to his work. At any rate, we are left looking for that subset of a strand's associated conditional set on which those who do not accept the α-principle might base their extrapolation.

When an author composes a narrative with the intent of making it available to others he writes with a certain audience in mind. Much of what he says and how he says it is conditioned by what he assumes to be true of that audience. In particular, much of it is conditioned by what he assumes the bulk of that audience to believe. What he assumes they believe constitutes the context within which he does his writing. Specifically, it constitutes the basis of the extrapolation which he expects them to perform. Gogol, for example, writes in the expectation that the world he projects by way of the text of *Dead Souls* will be fleshed out by means of the beliefs that he assumes to be *au courant* in his intended audience, beliefs as to what would occur if that which he indicates occurred.

I suggest that many of us do our extrapolating along the lines of what we take to be those expectations of authors. To flesh out the world of a text beyond what an author indicates with the text we appeal to what we think the author assumes the bulk of his intended audience believes would occur if a strand derived in the way suggested from what he indicates occurred. Sometimes, of course, we have virtually no thoughts of the requisite sort. Particularly is that the case for fantasy. If the states of affairs indicated by Lewis Carroll in *Alice in Wonderland* occurred, what others would occur? Probably Carroll assumed virtually no beliefs on that matter whatsoever. For such works little extrapolation is possible. But to return to our earlier example: quite likely Twain did not assume the belief to be *au courant* in his intended audience that if what he indicated occurred, then *two boys named 'Huck' and 'Jim' having a homosexual relationship* would occur. Consequently, by the principle cited, this latter state of affairs, the consequent of the conditional, is not included in the world projected by way of the text of *Huckleberry Finn*.

From within the conditional set associated with some strand we were looking for that subset which might be used for grounding extrapolation by those among us who reject the α-principle. I suggest that often that subset consists of those conditionals which are assumed by the author of the work to be believed by the bulk of his intended audience. And here then is a principle of world-inclusion alternative to the α-principle—call it the β-principle: The world projected by way of some text T includes what the author indicates by way of T, plus the impossible members of every conjunctive analysis of what he indicates, plus the strands derived in the way suggested from what he indicates, plus what he assumes the bulk of his intended audience believes would occur if some strand derived from what he indicates occurred.[13]

I suggested a reason that some critics might offer for rejecting the α-principle and preferring the β-principle, or something like it. I think that many of those whose response is the opposite would object to the β-principle on the ground that an author's assumptions and beliefs are irrelevant to what is included within his work's world, and to our activity of extrapolation. Once he has inscribed the words of his text, his work is out of his hands; and he must live with the consequences of his inscriptions whether he likes them or not. If I am correct in suggesting these as the reasons for the conflicting handling of the *Huckleberry Finn* case, then of course similar conflicts would arise on very many other cases as well. And then in raising the question as to what is to be reckoned as included in a work's world we are touching on fundamental questions, highly controversial in the twentieth century, concerning the relation of an author to his work and concerning the relation of an author to the public's interpretation of his work. The resolution of those issues would require an investigation of a very different sort from that of the following pages. Further, almost all that I shall say will be true no matter which principle is accepted. So let us drop our inquiry into the principle of world-inclusion at the point of having uncovered two conflicting principles, each with its devotees. A modicum of industry would uncover other such principles as well.[14]

In the preceding, when I have spoken with full explicitness I have spoken not of the world *of*, or *associated with*, some text, but rather of the world that some author used some text to project; and so also, not of the states of affairs indicated by some text,

[13] It may sometimes be that this last taken as a whole, is itself an impossible state of affairs. If so, then a strand-analysis should be performed on it. I shall not go into the details, since they would follow exactly the strategy proposed for dealing with those cases in which what is indicated is impossible. A few of the formulations that follow, to be fully accurate, would have to be slightly revised to take care of this sort of case.

[14] For example, one might allow the aesthetic excellence of the resultant worlds to enter into the decision as to whether some state of affairs is or is not to be reckoned as included within the world of a text. Cf. Charles Stevenson, 'Interpretation and Evaluation in Aesthetics', reprinted in M. Weitz, *Problems in Aesthetics* (Macmillan: New York, 1970). And then too, as a variant on the β-principle one might suggest that the relevant matter is not what an author assumes his intended audience to believe, but rather what his intended audience would naturally take *him* to believe. (This particular possibility was pointed out to me by Kendall Walton.)

but rather of the states of affairs that some author used some text to indicate. That is partly because I wished to keep before us the *action* of world projection. But there was a second reason as well: it is possible for two people to use the same text to indicate different states of affairs, thus to project different worlds. The world indicated is not, in general, determined merely by the text. It is determined by text plus context, *given* an act of using the text to project a world.

What comes to mind here is Jorge Borges's fascinating story, 'Pierre Menard, Author of Don Quixote'. The story is about an obscure twentieth-century French writer who undertook to write *Don Quixote—the Don Quixote*. 'It is unnecessary', says the narrator, 'to add that his aim was never to produce a mechanical transcription of the original; he did not propose to copy it. His admirable ambition was to produce pages which would coincide—word for word and line for line—with those of Miguel de Cervantes,' and to do so by continuing to 'be Pierre Menard and to arrive at *Don Quixote* through the experiences of Pierre Menard.' His strategy was, in Menard's own words, this:

My solitary game is governed by two polar laws. The first permits me to attempt variants of a formal and psychological nature; the second obliges me to sacrifice them to the 'original' text and irrefutably to rationalize this annihilation ... To these artificial obstacles one must add another congenital one. To compose *Don Quixote* at the beginning of the seventeenth century was a reasonable, necessary and perhaps inevitable undertaking; at the beginning of the twentieth century it is almost impossible. It is not in vain that three hundred years have passed, charged with the most complex happenings—among them, to mention only one, that same *Don Quixote*.

The narrator of the story nicely describes the difference between one of the passages from the *Don Quixote* of Cervantes and the corresponding passage from the *Don Quixote* of Pierre Menard:

The text of Cervantes and that of Menard are verbally identical, but the second is almost infinitely richer. (More ambiguous, his detractors will say; but ambiguity is a richness.) It is a revelation to compare the *Don Quixote* of Menard with that of Cervantes. The latter, for instance, wrote '... truth, whose mother is history, who is the rival of time, depository of deeds, witness of the past, example and lesson to the present, and warning to the future.' Written in the seventeenth century, written by the 'ingenious layman' Cervantes, this enumeration is a mere rhetorical eulogy of history. Menard, on the other hand, writes: '... truth, whose mother is history, who is the rival of time, depository of deeds, witness of the past, example and lesson to the present, and warning to the future.' History, *mother* of truth; the idea is astounding. Menard, a contemporary of William James, does not define history as an investigation of reality, but as its origin. Historical truth, for him, is not what took place; it is what we think took place. The final clauses—*example and lesson to the present, and warning to the future*—are shamelessly pragmatic.[15]

Our world has seen few experiments of the Pierre Menard sort. Accordingly confusion will rarely arise if usually we speak simply of the world of some text, rather than of the world that some author used some text to project.

IV. *A Work's World is a State of Affairs*

It is time to advance to a consideration of the ontological status of worlds of works of art. A guiding consideration will be that one cannot project, single out, refer to, mention, what does not exist. For I hold it as a fundamental ontological principle that something cannot have a property at a certain time unless it exists at that time. But if one could refer to something at a time at which it does not exist, then that to which one referred would have the property of being referred to at a time at which it does not exist—in violation of our ontological principle.

I furthermore assume that there exist *propositions*, by which I mean entities capable of being asserted and of being believed to be true, and that these are distinct from sentences; for I do not know how either assertion or belief could be understood without this assumption. You and I can assert *the same thing*; but that seems to me not capable of being true unless *there is* something

---

[15] The final paragraph of the story is worth quoting for the delight it gives: 'Menard (perhaps without wishing to) has enriched, by means of a new technique, the hesitant and rudimentary art of reading: the technique is one of deliberate anachronism and erroneous attributions. This technique, with its infinite applications, urges us to run through the *Odyssey* as if it were written after the *Aeneid*, and to read *Le jardin du Centaure* by Madam Henri Bachelier as if it were by Madam Henri Bachelier. This technique would fill the dullest books with adventure. Would not the attributing of *The Imitation of Christ* to Louis Ferdinand Celine or James Joyce be a sufficient renovation of its tenuous spiritual counsels?'

that we both asserted. And we can assert the same thing with two different sentences; but that seems to me not capable of being true unless sentences and propositions are distinct entities.[16] Further, I hold that propositions and states of affairs are just the very same entities—that the proposition that Carter is from Georgia is identical with the state of affairs of *Carter being from Georgia*.

So let us begin our scrutiny of the ontological status of worlds of works of art with some brief comments concerning the ontology of states of affairs—entities such as *Napoleon invading Russia*, and *Rockefeller being Vice-President of the United States*. With respect to such entities it is crucial to distinguish between *existing* and *occurring* (or *obtaining*, if one prefers). Though there exists such a state of affairs as *Napoleon invading Russia* (since it's possible that there is someone who believes that Napoleon is invading Russia), that state of affairs is not now occurring—though indeed it did once occur. On the other hand, *Rockefeller being Vice-President* both exists and is occurring (now in 1976). There exist other states of affairs which do not at any time occur, such as *Napoleon invading Ethiopia* and *Rockefeller being a life long Democrat*. And of these, some *could not* at any time occur. For example, *me being married to someone who lacks a spouse*.

It will be convenient to have some terminology for these distinctions among states of affairs. Let us call a state of affairs which can at some time occur, a *possible* state of affairs. And let us call one which cannot at any time occur, an *impossible* state of affairs. It is important to be clear on the fact that a possible state of affairs is not one which could exist. It is one which, existing, *could occur*. And an impossible state of affairs is not one which could not exist. It is one which, existing, *could not occur*. Further, it makes no difference to some state of affairs' being possible whether it does or does not occur. All that matters is whether it can occur or could have occurred.

My suggestion now is that the world projected by way of an artefact of art not only includes certain states of affairs but is itself a state of affairs. By way of his artefact the artist projects a possible or impossible state of affairs. That is the reality with which he deals. It need not be actuality. The state of affairs

---

[16] For further discussion of the matter see my *On Universals*, Chap. I.

which he projects may never occur. It may in fact be impossible of occurring.

But *which* state of affairs is the one that is to be identified with the world projected with some artefact of art? One wants to say: 'Whichever one includes all and only those states of affairs which are to be reckoned as included within the world of the work.' Yes indeed. But what are we to understand by this locution that we have been using so freely, 'included within'? And then, too, we must not so soon forget that we were left with two conflicting principles of world-inclusion.

Let us try to arrive at our destination by setting out first toward a more precise articulation of the concept of *strands* than that offered thus far. I begin with a definition of 'requires': a state of affairs S *requires* a state of affairs S^* just in case it is impossible that S occur at some time and S^* not occur at some time or other. For example, *my (presently) blotting out a line I wrote* requires *my having written a line*. Since we shall need it shortly let us also have a definition of 'prohibits': a state of affairs S *prohibits* a state of affairs S^* just in case it is impossible that S occur at a certain time and S^* also occur at some time.

Next let us pick out from the possible states of affairs projected by some author A with some artefact T, those which are as inclusive as any thus projected. A possible state of affairs S projected by A with T is *as inclusive* as any thus projected if:

 (i) S is a conjunction of states of affairs each of which is a possible state of affairs indicated by A with T, or a possible state of affairs which is a member of a conjunctive analysis of what is indicated, or a state of affairs required by any of these; and

 (ii) S is possible; and

 (iii) every state of affairs S^* which is indicated, or is a member of a conjunctive analysis of what is indicated, by A with T, and which is not required by S, is such that $(S \ \& \ S^*)$ is impossible.

In order now to define 'strand' we must differentiate between the concept relevant to the α-principle and that relevant to the β-principle. What we may call an α-strand of what is projected by A with some artefact T is a conjunction of:

   (i)   a possible state of affairs which is as inclusive as any projected by A with T, and of

  (ii) whatever contingent states of affairs would occur if that one occurred, and of

 (iii) whatever is required by the conjunction of these.

Similarly, a *β-strand* of what is projected by A with some artefact T is a conjunction of:

   (i)   a possible state of affairs which is as inclusive as any projected by A with T, and of

  (ii) whatever contingent states of affairs A assumes the bulk of his intended audience believes would occur if that one occurred,[17] and of

 (iii) whatever is required by the conjunction of these.

Then the *α-world projected by author* A with artefact T is the conjunction of what A indicates with T, and of the impossible members of the conjunctive analyses of what he indicates, and of all the α-strands of what A projects with T. Likewise, the *β-world* projected by A with T is the conjunction of what A indicates with T, and of the impossible members of the conjunctive analyses of what he indicates, and of all the β-strands of what A projects with T.

Finally, a state of affairs S is *included within* the α-world projected by A with T if and only if S is indicated by A with T, or is a member of a conjunctive analysis of what is indicated, or is required by one of the α-strands of what A projected with T. And so, similarly, for the definition of 'S is included within the β-world projected by A with T'.

Throughout my discussion up to this point I have spoken of *the* world of a work of art. It is now clear that, strictly speaking, there is no such entity as *the* world of art (at least if we confine the phrase 'world of a work' to the concept of *an α-world or a β-world*). Rather, if a work has any world it will normally have both an α-world and a β-world. Nevertheless, for convenience sake I shall continue sometimes to speak, inaccurately, of *the* world of a work of art.

It will not have escaped the notice of the reflective reader that if this theory as to the nature of the world associated with some

---

[17] For this, and (iii) immediately following, see p. 124, n. 13.

artefact of art is correct, then this world is not something that the artist brings into existence. Neither is it something that the artist makes occur. The world of *Dead Souls* existed apart from Gogol's activity as writer; and neither he nor anyone else has made it occur. The artist's activity consists in projecting an already existent but normally non-occurrent state of affairs by way of indicating certain states of affairs. Of course that state of affairs which the artist projected was not the world associated with his artefact until he composed that artefact and thereby projected the world. Yet all the while that conjunctive state of affairs which is in fact the world associated with the text of *Dead Souls* existed, awaiting Gogol's selection, waiting to become the world of his work. The text is made and associated with the world rather than the world made and associated with the text. World projection is a mode of selection, not a mode of creation.

Of course there is room for creativity. The creativity of the artist with respect to the worlds associated with his artefact consists in his ability to envisage states of affairs distinct from any that he believes ever to have occurred or been indicated by anyone else. It consists in his ability to envisage states of affairs distinct from any which he believes his experience to have acquainted him with. We as human beings are created with the marvellous capacity to envisage states of affairs which never occur, even states of affairs which could not occur. It is that capacity for envisagement which makes for creativity in fiction. Of course it may happen that all the states of affairs a fictioneer indicates have in fact occurred or have in fact been indicated, unbeknownst to him. On the other hand, it never happens that all the states of affairs which the artist indicates are such that he does not believe them to have occurred or been indicated. The projecting of worlds is never wholly creative.

In conclusion, it is worth remarking that there is no particular connection between the aesthetic excellence of a work of fiction and the degree to which the projection of its world was creative. The incidents in Thomas Wolfe's *Look Homeward Angel* seem to have been taken in good measure from his own experience. If so, his projection of the world associated with the text was not creative to any significant degree. Yet the novel may well be a great work of art. It is doubtful that, in general, aesthetic excellence requires creativity. But even if it does, artistic creativity comprises more than creativity with respect to world projection.

V. *The Non-Comprehensiveness of a Work's Worlds*

The worlds of a work of art may be aesthetically complete, finished, rounded off, with a genuine beginning and a genuine ending. Yet ontologically each strand thereof, and so an entire world when as a whole it constitutes a strand, is almost never fully or maximally comprehensive. To see in what sense that is true let us have before us the concept of a maximally comprehensive state of affairs:

A state of affairs S is *maximally comprehensive* =df for every state of affairs S^*, S either requires or prohibits S^*·

Any state of affairs which is not maximally comprehensive may be said to be *non-comprehensive*. A *possible world* may then be thought of as a possible state of affairs which is maximally comprehensive.[18] That which is *the actual world at a given time t* may be thought of as that possible world which occurs at t. And for a state of affairs to be *true in* a possible world is for it to be required by that world.

Now rarely will a strand of a work's world be a possible world. No matter how voluminous it may be, rarely will it be a possible state of affairs which prohibits or requires every state of affairs whatsoever. Those possible states of affairs which are strands of the worlds of *War and Peace* are vast indeed. Yet they do not, for example, either prohibit or require *Jimmy Carter being elected President in 1980.* Rather than themselves being possible

---

[18] I hold that there are both tensed and tense-indifferent states of affair—a distinction to be explained in the next section—and that some at least of the former vary across time in their truth-value. However, most of our contemporary possible-worlds theorists tacitly assume that propositions cannot vary across time in their truth-value. Accordingly, what they take to be a possible world is what I would describe as a truth-value invariable state of affairs which, for every truth-value invariable state of affairs, either requires or prohibits it. (One might call that an *everlasting* possible world, in contrast to a *temporal* possible world.) The corresponding concept of *actual world* is naturally also different from that above. For these points, see my 'Can Ontology Do Without Events?'

worlds they are *required* by *infinitely many* possible worlds. In that sense they are *segments* of possible worlds.[19]

The non-comprehensiveness of the strands of a work's worlds accounts for some phenomena which are at first sight paradoxical. Consider, for example, that old chestnut of the critics: how many children had Lady Macbeth? In Act I Lady Macbeth says:

> I have given suck, and
> How tender 'tis to love the babe that milks me ... [I. vii. 54–5.]

On the basis of this evidence surely both the α-principle and the β-principle yield the conclusion that Lady Macbeth had a child. Accordingly, included within the worlds of *Macbeth* and thus required by them is the state of affairs of *someone named 'Lady Macbeth' having given birth to a child*. But those worlds (assuming they are possible) do not include and thus do not require the state of affairs of *someone named 'Lady Macbeth' having given birth to exactly one child*, since there is no evidence at all from which we can infer on either principle of inclusion that Lady Macbeth had just one child. But neither do they include nor require the state of affairs of *someone named 'Lady Macbeth' having given birth to exactly two children*, for the same reason. And so forth, for all other numbers. Yet, to say it once again, they do require, because they include, the state of affairs of *someone named 'Lady Macbeth' having given birth to a child*.

Possible worlds, being maximally comprehensive, are different. There is no possible world which requires *someone named 'Lady Macbeth' having given birth to a child* which does not also require some state of affairs of the form *someone named 'Lady Macbeth' having given birth to exactly n children* (*n* being equal to or greater than 0).

Consider the Law that if a state of affairs of the (particular) form $(\exists x)\,(Fx)$ obtains, then some state of affairs of the corresponding (singular) form, Fa, obtains. Call that, the Particu-

---

[19] Perhaps there is an exception. Suppose that all the states of affairs indicated by way of some text are included in the actual world. And suppose that the analysis that David Lewis provides of counterfactuals is correct, and that the analysis also applies to those subjunctive conditionals whose antecedents are true. Then the world of the work will be the actual world. And that of course is fully comprehensive. See D. Lewis, *Counterfactuals* (Harvard University Press: Cambridge, Mass., 1973), pp. 26–31. (I was reminded of this feature of Lewis's analysis by Alvin Plantinga and Kendall Walton.)

lar/Singular Law. This Law is true. Likewise it is true in every possible world; that is, it is required by every possible world. It is a necessary state of affairs. It is on that account also included within every *work's* world. But this is not in conflict with the fact that a work's world may include a proposition of the form $(\exists x)$ (Fx) while including no corresponding one of the form Fa.

Again, surely the worlds of *Macbeth* include, and thus require, the state of affairs of

(1) someone named 'Lady Macbeth' having red hair or it not being the case that someone named 'Lady Macbeth' has red hair.

But they do not include, and thus do not require, the state of affairs of

(2) someone named 'Lady Macbeth' having red hair,

and neither do they include nor require the state of affairs of

(3) it not being the case that someone named 'Lady Macbeth' has red hair.

The worlds of the work could occur without (2) occurring, but so too they could occur without (3) occurring. They could not occur, though, without (1) occurring. And this all comes about because of the non-comprehensiveness of the worlds of *Macbeth*.

Possible worlds, being maximally comprehensive, are once again different. No possible world could require (1) without also requiring one or the other of its disjuncts, (2) or (3). In general, any possible world which requires a state of affairs of the form $p \vee q$ also either requires p or requires q. Hence what we might call the Disjunction/Bivalence Law, that a state of affairs of the form $p \vee q$ entails that either p is true or q is true, is included within, and hence required by, all works' worlds. For it is a necessary truth, and hence required by every strand. Nevertheless, the non-comprehensiveness of works' worlds yields the result that a given such world may require $p \vee q$ and require neither p nor q.

So we shall never know how many children Lady Macbeth had in the worlds of *Macbeth*. That is not because to know this would require a knowledge beyond the capacity of human beings. It is because there is nothing of the sort to know.

Likewise, as he himself saw, there are not and never will be any answers to the questions Keats put to the worlds projected by way of a Grecian urn:

> Who are these coming to the sacrifice?
>   To what green altar, O mysterious priest,
> Leads't thou that heifer lowing at the skies,
>   And all her silken flanks with garlands drest?
> What little town by river or sea shore,
>   Or mountain-built with peaceful citadel,
>   Is emptied of this folk, this pious morn?
> And, little town, thy streets for evermore
>   Will silent be; and not a soul to tell
>   Why thou art desolate, can e'er return.

In conclusion, it should be observed that we have been using and will continue to use the word 'world' with two rather different senses. Though a possible world and a work's world are both states of affairs, they are very different sorts of states of affairs. The requirement which a state of affairs must satisfy to be a possible world—namely, that of being a possible state of affairs which is maximally comprehensive—is a requirement (almost) never satisfied by worlds of works. Of these latter, some are impossible. And of those which are possible, rare is the one which is maximally comprehensive. Corresponding to these two different concepts of world are the two distinct concepts of *being true in* (some possible world) and *being included within* (some work's world).

VI. *Characters*

Earlier we discussed the opening sentence of Gogol's *Dead Souls*: 'A rather handsome, light travelling carriage on springs rolled into the gates of an inn in a certain provincial capital ...'. It's not hard to grasp which state of affairs Gogol indicated by inscribing this sentence, thus to bring about its inclusion within the world of his work. But now consider the sentence, from later in the same novel, which begins thus: 'While the server was still spelling out the note, Chichikov set out to look the town over ...'. What state of affairs did Gogol indicate by his use of *this* sentence? The correct answer to that question seems to me by no means evident. So to track it down will be our project in this section. If we are to catch our quarry, we shall have to develop a theory of fictional characters, supplemented with a theory as to how those characters' names function, within the telling of fiction but then also outside.[20]

Some readers, approaching the matter with what John Woods in his recent book, *The Logic of Fiction*,[21] calls the 'naïve theory of fiction', will perhaps think it evident which state of affairs Gogol indicated when he wrote, '. . . Chichikov set out to look the town over . . .'. Let me follow Woods in sketching the main features of this theory. As I do so, I shall also follow him in taking Sherlock Holmes as my principal example of a fictional character.

The character Sherlock Holmes was created by Conan Doyle. In writing his fiction Doyle did not *describe* Holmes. He *created* him. But of course even when Doyle was finished with his creating, Holmes did not exist. He remained merely fictional. None the less, there now *is* this character, Sherlock Holmes. Accordingly we must acknowledge that *there are* things that *don't exist*—fictional characters among them.

Though Holmes did not and does not exist, he none the less has properties. (Or if one insists on a more sparse ontology at this point, there are predicates true of him.) He lived on Baker Street. He did not live on Charing Cross Road. He was a person. He was a man. He was British. He had a body.

How do we tell which properties Holmes does in fact have (which predicates are in fact true of him)? For a very broad range of cases we do so by appealing to what Woods calls the 'sayso' of Conan Doyle, along with legitimate inferences therefrom. For remember: *Conan Doyle* created Holmes. And he did so by inscribing the words he did. So it seems appropriate to appeal to Conan Doyle's sayso in determining what Holmes is actually like.

[20] An incomparably perceptive treatment of the nature of characters is to be found in Luigi Pirandello's *Six Characters in Search of an Author*, and in his comments on the play. Both can be found in *Naked Masks: Five Plays* by Luigi Pirandello (E. P. Dutton: New York, 1952). L. C. Knights's famous 'How Many Children Had Lady Macbeth', in his *Explorations* (G. W. Stewart: New York, 1947), details some of the misuses, among critics, of the search for characters. Knights's hostility to these misuses leads him into a position which, if it does not quite repudiate all consideration of characters, certainly puts this far down on the list of what critics should do.

[21] Mouton: The Hague, 1974.

Further, Woods claims that on the naïve view Holmes is an *impossible* being, in the sense that he couldn't possibly come into existence. He is confined forever to that twilight zone which is the realm of mere being, lying between sheer nothingness and full-bodied existence.

There is another sense, though, in which Holmes is not an impossible being but in which certain other fictional characters *are*. Some characters are created so as to have properties and perform actions that an existent person *could not possibly* have or perform. For example, Lewis Carroll might so have created one of his characters that he squared the circle—a feat which no existent person could possibly bring off.

Lastly, all characters, or certainly *almost* all characters, are *incomplete*, in the sense that there are some properties that the character neither has nor lacks. Woods's own example is that of having a mole on one's back. Did Holmes have that property? On the basis of Conan Doyle's say so and what can legitimately be inferred therefrom we cannot say that he did. But likewise we cannot say that he did not. So with respect to this property Holmes is incomplete.

Something like that, says Woods, is the naïve theory of fiction; and having stated the theory he goes on to explore what a semantics for it might look like.

To return then to our point of entry into this presentation of the naïve theory: someone who held this theory might think it evident that when Gogol wrote, '... Chichikov set out to look the town over ...', he was indicating that state of affairs which consists in the real but non-existent person Chichikov having the property of setting out to look the town over, and that he was doing so by referring to that non-existent person with the name 'Chichikov' and predicating that property of him.

In fact, however, it is far from evident on the naïve theory that this is what Gogol was doing with this sentence and with the name 'Chichikov'. The theory holds that *once Chichikov has been created*, then he can be referred to, can have properties predicated of him, etc. But it is far from evident that *Gogol* in the telling of his story can refer to Chichikov. Presumably Gogol cannot refer to Chichikov before he has created him. So does he then create and refer to him in the very same breath?

And does he indicate the state of affairs of Chichikov having the property of setting out to look the town over, with the very same sentence-inscribings by which he creates Chichikov? Surely the answers that the naïve theory ought to give to such questions are far from evident.

However, I myself in pursuing the answer to our opening question in this section will not presuppose the truth of the naïve theory. For the theory seems to be definitely mistaken. I shall not underatke to give a full-scale critique of the theory. Rather I shall content myself with exposing to the light some fundamental ontological principles on whose denial the theory is founded. Since the principles to be cited will be ones that I myself accept, they will serve to govern the development of my own theory as to the nature of characters and the function of their names (as indeed they have governed our discussion up to this point!)

Consider then the following ontological principle, call it the

Principle of Exemplification: Everything x is such that for every property P and every time t, x has P at t only if x exists at t.

This principle seems to me to be true. It seems to me a principle that we ought to keep in mind in all our construction of theories. And notice that one of its implications is that we cannot refer to what does not exist. For if I have referred to x, then x has the property of having been referred to by me; and the Principle tells us that nothing can ever have a property unless, when it has that property, it exists. It's obvious, though, that to accept the naïve theory is to commit oneself to the denial of this Principle. For the naïve theorist holds that characters have the properties of being born, of dying, of thinking, all without ever existing.

There are several different ways in which the naïve theorist can develop his denial of the Principle of Exemplification. One is just to hold that every property whatsoever is such that something can have the property without existing. (A necessary corollary would be that 'exists', 'is real', etc., do not express properties.) But a more interesting way of denying the Principle can be opened up by asking what *is* this property expressed by the predicate 'thinking' which supposedly

Holmes has without existing? Surely it cannot be the property
which we ordinarily predicate of someone when we say of him
that he is thinking. For that property is one that something
cannot have without existing. If one had powers of extra-
sensory perception, and even beyond that, could discern
without fail where the activity of *thinking* was being performed,
never would one find some non-existent person performing it.
And necessarily so. Accordingly, the fundamental peculiarity
of characters is not that they have all the ordinary properties
but have them without existing. Rather it is that they have
their own peculiar range of properties, properties that ordinary things cannot have. Where you and I have the property
of *thinking*, they do not have that property but rather what may
be called the property of *thinking without existing*; where we have
the property of *having been born*, they instead have the property of
having been born without ever existing. Thus many at least of our
predicates are systematically ambiguous, typically expressing
one property when predicated of existent entities and another,
though related, property when predicated of characters. And
with respect to each such pair the Principle of Exemplification
is true for the former member and false for the latter.

A full elaboration of this particular way of denying the Principle of Exemplification would have to go well beyond holding
that there is a range of properties which something can have
without itself existing. For many properties are such that something cannot have them without standing in relation to various
other contingently existing entities as well. And many if not all
such properties would also have to be repudiated as holding of
characters. Surely it is true, for example, that Holmes had a
body taking up space in London. But now suppose that we
scrutinize London around the turn of the century as closely as
we can. We will find there no body, identical with Holmes's
body, which stands to space and to London in the relation of
taking up some of the former in the latter. The response,
however, is that the property which we truly predicate of
Holmes when we say of him that he had a body taking up space
in London is one which something can have without there
existing a body, London, and space, such that that is the
person's body and it takes up space in London. Accordingly it's
quite beside the point for you and me to scrutinize the existent

bodies occupying existent space in existent London to determine whether it's true that Holmes had a body occupying space
in London.

An interesting way of developing the theory further would be
to hold that some of the properties that non-existent entities
can have are ones that existent entities can also have, so that
for them there is no pair of the sort $\langle\phi$-ing, ϕ-ing-
without-existing$\rangle$. For example, when first reflecting on
these matters many of us have the feeling that though the
ordinary property of thinking is such that something cannot
have it without existing, the ordinary properties of *being referred
to* and of *having a property* are different. These do not require that
their exemplifiers exist, though on the other hand they *permit*
them to exist. The theory we are imagining could easily
accommodate this conviction. Further, it would naturally hold
that some of our *ordinary* properties are ones that only non-
existent entities can have and for which there are no counterparts for existing entities—*being a character*, for example. This
just is the property of *being a character without existing*; and for it
there is no counterpart exemplifiable property of *being a character
with existing*. All this would give us a way of understanding how
something could both be a character and be of woman born: the
entity in question would have the *ordinary* property of being a
character and the *extraordinary* property of *being of woman born
without existing.*[22] But let us halt. For my purpose here is certainly not to develop the naïve theory.

A virtue of the particular version of the naïve theory just
sketched is its concession that, for many predicates, the
properties ordinarily expressed by those predicates are such
that something cannot have them without itself, and in many
cases other (contingent) things as well, existing. Yet in spite of
this virtue I adhere to the Principle of Exemplification. For I do
not believe that anything has such properties as this theory
postulates. Nothing has the property of *thinking without existing*.
Nothing has the property of *drinking tea with Gladstone without
oneself, tea, and Gladstone existing.*

Consider now a second ontological principle, call it the

---

[22] Notice that an implication of the theory sketched above is that all fictional
characters, no matter how realistic they may seem, have properties that no existent
person could possibly have. Thus all are radically impossible.

Principle of Completeness: For everything x and every property P, x either has P or lacks P.

This seems to me a true principle, and accordingly one that we ought to respect in our construction of theories. But as already seen acceptance of the naïve theory commits one to its denial. In turn, denial of the Principle requires that one also deny certain of the laws (theorems) of first-order logic. One such law is what in the preceding section we called the Disjunction/Bivalence Law: a disjunction, *either p or q*, is not true unless either p is true or q is true. Yet, as often observed, the naïve theory requires the denial of this law. It does so because it holds that there are incomplete entities. (On the naïve theory it's not true that Holmes had a mole on his back, and also not true that Holmes did not have a mole on his back. Yet it's true that Holmes had a mole on his back or Holmes did not have a mole on his back. Holmes is not so bizarre a character that this last is not true!)

So also, the Particular/Singular Law is a law of first-order logic: an existential generalization, $\exists x(Fx)$, is not true unless some instantiation thereof, Fa, is true. But this too fails for characters, again because of the denial of the Principle of Completeness. (On the naïve theory there is a number greater than 0 such that that is the number of children Lady Macbeth gave birth to. Yet it's not the case that 1 is the number of children Lady Macbeth gave birth to, nor is it the case that 2 is the number, and so on for all the numbers.)

And then it must not be forgotten that, as we have already seen, the naïve theory requires the denial of the law of non-contradiction. Some characters are such that there is a property which the character both has and lacks.

Chichikov will be our own principal example of a character. But before getting to Chichikov, let us speak of Russia's role in the world of *Dead Souls*. A page or two into *Dead Souls* we find these words: 'Even as in enlightened Europe, so in enlightened Russia as well there are at present rather many worthy persons who never dine in a tavern without having a chat with the waiter...'. I think it clear that by his use of this sentence (strictly, its Russian original) Gogol was referring to Russia with the proper name 'Russia', and posing of it that it has rather many worthy persons who never dine in a tavern without chatting with the waiter.[23] Furthermore, by thus referring to Russia and posing of it what he did, Gogol indicated the state of affairs of *Russia having rather many worthy persons who never dine in a tavern without chatting with the waiter*. Accordingly, that state of affairs is included within the world of *Dead Souls*.

Furthermore, that indicated state of affairs, and so the world of *Dead Souls*, is *anchored to* Russia. By that I mean this:

Definition 1: A work's world *WW* is *anchored to x* = df there is a strand *S* of *WW* which is necessarily such that if *S* occurs at some time then *x* exists at some time.

The worlds of works of art are characteristically anchored not only to such necessarily existing entities as properties and states of affairs, but also to such contingently existing entities as cities, countries, persons, oceans, and so forth. Thus the entities to be found 'in' the worlds of works of art are not all fictitious entities.

By no means all the entities to which a work's world is anchored are referred to by the author. For a work's world is anchored to all necessarily existing entities, and obviously not all of those are referred to. Somewhat more surprisingly, not all the entities to which an author refers are entities to which the world of his work is anchored. Suppose, for example, that Gogol had written: 'The country whose sovereign is Nicholas I I has rather many chatty persons.' Now as a matter of fact, the country whose sovereign was Nicholas I I at the time Gogol was writing was Russia. So by inscribing that sentence, Gogol would have been (or at least, might have been) referring to Russia. Yet the world of his work would not, on account of his use of this sentence, have been anchored to Russia. For Nicholas I I might have been sovereign of some other country, and Russia might not have existed. Accordingly, the state of

[23] If it were not that the word 'predicating' carries the strong connotation that in predicating one *asserts*, we could speak of Gogol *predicating*. We need a broader concept, however. Gogol did not predicate of Russia that it has rather many . . . For he did not assert that of Russia. Yet obviously he did something closely analogous to predicating it of Russia. I shall speak of him as *posing* it of Russia—understanding posing as an action just like predicating except that it is not confined in its occurrence to contexts of assertion. A fuller explanation of *posing* will be given in Part Four.

affairs indicated by this sentence might have occurred without Russia ever existing.

The situation is this: if an author refers to something with what Kripke has called a *rigid designator*—an expression which, remaining the expression it is in our actual language, never designates something in one possible world distinct from what it designates in another—then the world of his work is anchored to that entity referred to. However, if an author refers to some entity with a non-rigid designator, then the world of his work is not anchored to that entity—provided the entity exists contingently. (The worlds of works are anchored to necessarily existing entities whether or not they are referred to in those works.)

Now on first glance the situation for Chichikov looks parallel to that for Russia. It looks as if by writing 'Chichikov set out to look the town over', Gogol was (rigidly) referring to some person Chichikov, and posing of him that he set out to look the town over. It looks as if therein Gogol was indicating the state of affairs of *Chichikov setting out to look the town over*. And it looks as if, on account of this state of affairs being included in the world of *Dead Souls*, the world of that work is anchored to some person Chichikov as well as to the country Russia.

But almost certainly Gogol was not referring to anyone with his use of this name. An implication of our two ontological principles is that there was no non-existent person to whom he was referring; for they imply that there are no non-existent entities. But also it seems unlikely that there existed some person to whom Gogol referred with 'Chichikov'. Chichikov is a fictitious entity.

It is of prime importance to see that though Gogol in using 'Chichikov' did not refer to some person of whom he then posed various things, yet it is certainly true that in the world of *Dead Souls* people do this. They address someone as 'Pavel Ivanovich Chichikov'; they refer to him, and predicate things of him. It is clear, I trust, how we should understand this. If that state of affairs which is the world of *Dead Souls* is to occur, there must be someone named 'Chichikov', he must on various occasions be addressed as 'Chichikov', he must on various occasions be referred to, he must be characterized in certain specified ways, etc. All this and more must happen if that which is the world of

Dead Souls is to occur. And all this is of course compatible with our insistence that Gogol in writing *Dead Souls* did not refer to anyone with 'Chichikov'.

But what then was Gogol doing with 'Chichikov' if not using it to refer to someone? Well, let us look once more at the role of Russia in Gogol's tale. In the course of referring to and posing things of Russia, Gogol performed other actions as well, among them that of (partially) delineating a kind, a type, a sort—a kind of country, a country-kind. Specifically, one of the kinds which Gogol (partially) delineated in the course of referring to and posing things of Russia is such that to be an example of it an entity must be a country, must be named 'Russia', must have rather many persons who always chat with the waiter when dining out in a tavern, and so forth for all the properties which Gogol posed of Russia. Of course, it may well be that Russia itself never was in all respects an example of that particular kind of country (partially) delineated by Gogol—the Russian-in-*Dead Souls* kind of country. None the less, that kind is what I shall call a *component in* the world of *Dead Souls*, meaning by that this:

Definition 2: A kind K is *a component of* a state of affairs S =df S is necessarily such that if S occurs, then an example of K exists at some time.

On the concept of *world of the work* that we formulated in section IV of this Part, there are many more states of affairs belonging to the world of *Dead Souls* than just those that Gogol indicates. In addition there are all those capable of being appropriately extrapolated from those. An implication of this is that many of the kinds which are components of the world of *Dead Souls* are only *partially* delineated by Gogol. Another of its implications is that some of the kinds which are components of his work's world are not even partially delineated.

Back then to Chichikov. We have seen that a *kind* of country may be (partially) delineated in the course of referring to and posing things about some country. It is possible, however, to delineate a kind of country without doing so in the course of referring to and posing things about some country. Indeed, it is possible to delineate a kind of country without referring to anything at all. Consider, for example, the opening sentence of

Dead Souls which begins thus: 'A rather handsome, light travel-ling carriage on springs rolled into the gates of an inn in a certain provincial capital...' In using this sentence (more accurately, its Russian original), Gogol was not referring to some carriage of which he was then predicating that it rolled into the gates of an inn in a certain provincial capital. For a condition of (non-mistakenly) referring to some entity x with some expression E in assertively uttering some sentence S, so it seems to me, is that in all possible worlds in which E is true of x, the proposition expressed with S is true if and only if the attribute predicated of x is exemplified by x. On this condition, nothing is (normally) referred to with the expression 'A rather ... carriage on springs'.[24] Yet Gogol, in his inscribing of this sentence, did none the less (partially) delineate for us a type of carriage.

And that, I suggest, is like what Gogol was doing with the name 'Chichikov'. Without using this name to refer to anyone, he was none the less, by his particular way of using it, (par-tially) delineating for us a certain kind of person, that is, not a *person* of a certain kind but a certain *person-kind*—the Chichikov-in-*Dead-Souls* kind. There never was any person to whom Gogol referred with 'Chichikov'; neither was there a person Chichikov to whom the world of Dead Souls is anchored. Rather, there is a person-kind—the Chichikov-in-*Dead Souls* kind—which was partially delineated by Gogol and which is a component of the world of *Dead Souls*.

Having come thus far, I see no reason to resist taking the last step of concluding that what we customarily call the *characters* in the world of a work of art (when that world is possible) are certain kinds of persons which are components in that world—not persons of a certain kind, but certain person-kinds.

If characters are person-kinds, then they *do* exist. There exists that person-kind which is a component of the world of *Dead Souls* and has essential within it the property of being named 'Chichikov'. But the author did not bring that kind into existence. He selected it, and so presented it to us for our attention. Perhaps, though, a person-kind is not properly called a 'character' until some work has been composed of whose

---

[24] A mistaken reference to x, is a case of referring to x as so-and-so when x is not so-and-so.

world it is a component. Then it would be a mistake to think of *characters* as awaiting selection by some author. That would be true only of person-kinds. And then what could be said of the fictioneer is that he brings it about that what are not characters become such.

In so far as the kinds an author delineates are different from any which he believes to be or have been exampled or delineated, we may say that he has been *creative* in his delineation of that character. But to be thus creative is not to bring the character into existence. It is not to create it. Neither is it to bring it about that the character has an example. From the infinitude of person-kinds the author selects one. His creativity lies in the freshness, the imaginativeness, the originality, of his selection, rather than in his bringing into existence what did not before exist.

I suggested that a character in a work's world—when that world is possible—is a person-kind which is a component of that work's world. (And let us continue, until Section V I I I, to speak only of those works' worlds which are possible.) But not every such distinct person-kind which is a component of a work's world should be regarded as a distinct character of that world. Rather, the characters are those person-kinds which are what I shall call the *maximal* components of the world. To see the basic idea, go back to the opening sentence of *Dead Souls*: 'A rather handsome, light travelling carriage on springs...' By virtue of the state of affairs here indicated, a component of the world of *Dead Souls* is the kind: Carriage On Springs. Another is the kind: Light Travelling Carriage On Springs. Yet another is the kind: Rather Handsome Light Travelling Carriage On Springs. In this succession we have a succession in the direction of a kind which is a maximal component within the world of *Dead Souls*.

As a first attempt at formulating this concept of *maximal component* we can say this: The kind K is a maximal component in a work's world if and only if K is a component in that world, and there is no other component K^* of that world such that every property essential within K is essential within K^*, but some property essential within K^* is not so within K. As it stands, however, this will not quite do. For it might just happen that there are two distinct characters in some world, so related that the one just happens to be wholly included within the other. To take account of this possibility, let us frame our definition thus:

Definition 3: K is a *maximal* component in a work's world WW =df K is a component in WW and is such that, if there is any other component K^* of WW such that every property essential within K is essential within K^* but some property essential within K^* is not so within K, then if WW were to occur there would have to be an example of the K distinct from an example of K^*.[25]

Now whenever I use the phrase 'the Chichikov-in-*Dead Souls* character', what I mean to refer to thereby is that maximal component in the world of *Dead Souls* which has the property of being-called-'Chichikov' essential within it. (I assume that the world of *Dead Souls* is possible.)

Characters of course have properties. Indeed, for them our ontological Principle of Completeness holds, as for everything else. But of more interest for our purposes than the properties *of* characters are the properties *essential within* characters. And when we look at these, we catch sight of the phenomenon that the naïve theorist of fiction was groping toward when he held that characters are incomplete.

A work's world contains a great many more states of affairs than the author indicates. Accordingly, the characters which are components of a work's world characteristically have a great many more properties essential within them than are actually cited by the author. By virtue of extrapolating on the states of affairs indicated, we flesh out the characters. Yet none of the characters which is a component in some work's world is such that for every property, either having it or lacking it is essential within the character. (Unless it should so happen that the work's world itself is a possible world.) In that way, every (possible) character is what might be called *non-determinate*.

Definition 4: K is determinate =df K is such that for every property P, either having P or lacking P is essential within K.

[25] Sometimes one speaks of a work's world as containing two (or more) characters 'just alike'. If they really are 'just alike', we should construe such a claim as the claim that if the world were to occur, there would have to be two (or more) examples of that one person-kind.

And of course, if a possible kind K is not determinate, then it will be said to be *non-determinate*. If K is non-determinate, then there is some property P such that neither having P nor lacking P is essential within K.

Now you and I—and indeed everything else that exists—each exemplify at every time in our existence a determinate kind. For concerning every property whatsoever, at every time I exist either I possess it or I lack it (our Principle of Completeness). And the determinate kind which I exemplify at a given time is just that possible kind which has essential within it the having of all the properties that I then possess and the lacking of all others. Of course very many of the properties which I possess (or lack) I do not possess (or lack) essentially; whereas whatever is essential within a kind is such necessarily. But any appearance of incompatibility between these facts is dissipated by noting that I might very well have been an example of a determinate kind different from that of which I am in fact an example. (Everything that exists is, at any time at which it exists, an example of exactly one determinate kind.)

For example, that determinate kind of which I am now an example has essential within it either having the property of *having had a toothache when four years old* or lacking it. And that is because *I* now either have that property or lack it. But the character Chichikov is different. Essential within Chichikov is the property of *either having had or not having had a toothache when four years old*. But the property of *having had a toothache when four years old* is not essential within it, and neither is the property of *not having had a toothache when four years old*. For something could be an example of the Chichikov-in-*Dead Souls* character without having the former property. But so too, something could be an example of that character without having the latter property.

Thus we see one of the principal advantages of construing characters as kinds: kinds themselves are complete entities. But at the same time, many of the possible ones are non-determinate, and almost all of those possible ones which are *characters* are non-determinate. The intuitions of the naïve theorist are accommodated without our ontological principles being violated.

Could the Chichikov-in-*Dead Souls* character have been more determinate, having more properties essential within it? Or less determinate, having fewer? Or could the character have been developed somewhat differently by Gogol, so that it would have had different properties essential within it than it does in fact have?

Gogol could of course have written a text in which he expanded his tale about a confidence trickster named 'Chichikov', still calling his tale *Dead Souls*. Or he could have written a text in which he abbreviated the tale, eliminating some episodes. Or he could have written a text in which some episodes were somewhat different. But if he had written a text different in any of these ways, the world associated with his text would have been distinct from the one associated with what is in fact his text. And for many of those alternative worlds, that character which would be the maximal component having the property of *being called 'Chichikov'* essential within it, would be distinct from what is in fact the Chichikov-in-*Dead Souls* character. Indeed, if those other characters differed from this last with respect to *any* of the properties essential within it, then they would not be identical with it. That is what then would be the case, rather than that that kind which is in fact the Chichikov-in-*Dead Souls* character would then have been somewhat different. It belongs to the essence of a kind to have essential within it the properties that it does so have.

Yet surely Gogol could have developed the character Chichikov differently—more expansively, less expansively, in alternative ways. It's not just that he could have written a different text, with a world whose maximal component having the property of being called 'Chichikov' essential within it was different. He could have represented, or portrayed, Chichikov differently. So too, having written one book, Conan Doyle offered the *further* adventures of Sherlock Holmes. And then there is the related phenomenon of different writers telling the story of Hercules, of Hamlet, of Don Juan, of Faust—telling it differently. Faust is portrayed very differently indeed by Marlowe and by Goethe.

To understand this last phenomenon we must distinguish the Faust character *simpliciter* from the Faust-in-Goethe's-*Faust* character, and also from the Faust-in-Marlowe's-*Dr. Faustus* character. In the Western literary and folk tradition there is the concept of a character which has essential within it such properties as *being called 'Faust', striking a pact with the devil*, etc. We may call that, *the Faust character*. Given that character, one may then write a work whose world has that character as a component. But it may well be that the Faust character is then not a maximal component within one's work's world but instead includes another which *is* a maximal component. Should I write such a work, the Faust character would include the Faust-in-my-*Faust* character. To write such a work is what it is to develop the Faust character. That's what it is to portray Faust as so-and-so, to represent Faust as so-and-so—when the property of *being so-and-so* is not one which is essential within the Faust character itself. And obviously, on this explanation, the Faust character can be developed differently by different writers.

The situation for Chichikov—and Sherlock Holmes—is not substantially different. To the best of my knowledge there is no concept of the Chichikov character embedded in literary or folk tradition. But given the Chichikov-in-*Dead Souls* character, one might distinguish, in a rough and ready way, between the properties central within the character and the ones incidental. We do, in fact, all do this intuitively. Central within the Chichikov-in-*Dead Souls* character are such properties as *being a confidence trickster, being a denizen of Russia, being called 'Chichikov'*, etc. One may then form the concept of a character which has just those central, core properties essential within it. One might call that character simply 'the Chichikov character'. It is a component within the world of *Dead Souls*. But it is not a maximal component within it. Rather, it includes that maximal component which is the Chichikov-in-*Dead Souls* character. Obviously the Chichikov character, thus conceived, could have been developed differently by Gogol. It could today, in fact, be developed differently by someone else.

VII. *Proper Names in Fiction*

A good deal of what we have said in the preceding section applies, without qualification, only to those works' worlds which are possible, and correspondingly, only to those characters which are possible. To introduce the qualifications

necessary to give the theory application to possible and impossible works and characters alike, it will prove necessary to have
in hand an understanding of how proper names function in the
writing and telling of fiction. So that is what we turn to next. Of
course such an understanding is necessary, in any case, as a
complement to a theory of characters.

I see no reason to doubt that sometimes proper names in
fiction are used to refer—as 'Russia' in *Dead Souls*. However, I
shall set this use off to the side. For though there are a great
many problems surrounding the referential function of proper
names, this is just their central function in our language. It has
nothing in particular to do with fiction. Such functioning as
that of 'Chichikov' in *Dead Souls* is what I shall attend to. For I
have already concluded that Gogol was not using this to refer.

I think it best to attack the problem a bit circuitously. Suppose I am telling a tale and that my opening two sentences are
these:

(i) A man slunk into a room. He was dark and stooped.

I think it must be admitted that (normally) in thus using 'a
man' one is not using the expression to stand for, or refer to,
anything—for the reason offered in the preceding section.
Normally, by assertively uttering that sentence one indicates,
without referring to anything, that general state of affairs which
could also be indicated with the existentially quantified sentence, 'There exists something such that it is a man and it slunk
into a room.'

But if 'a man' in the first sentence of (i) is not used to stand for
anything, how then does 'he' in 'He was dark and stooped'
function? Obviously it does not function as standing for that for
which 'a man' also stands, since 'a man' is not used to stand for
anything. And if by saying that a pronoun has a certain noun as
its *antecedent*, we mean that it is governed by that noun in such a
way that it stands for what the noun stands for, then 'he' does
not have 'a man' as antecedent. But neither of course does 'he'
stand for the general term 'a man'. I am not predicating of this
term that it was dark and stooped.

Yet in some way or other 'he' is governed in its function by
the general term 'a man'. It is, one might say, *cross-indexical* in its
function. And what it is indexed to, specifically, is 'a man'

rather than 'a room'. For what I said was (i), and not instead the absurdity, 'A man slunk into a room. It was dark and stooped.' By means of using the pronoun in this non-referential but cross-indexical fashion I am able to indicate the state of affairs of *a man, who was dark and stooped, slinking into a room*; and of differentiating it from the state of affairs of *a man slinking into a room, which was dark and stooped*. Of course, the way in which I have just indicated these two states of affairs again incorporates pronouns used in non-referential cross-indexical fashion—the pronouns 'who' and 'which'. And if I indicate my original state of affairs with the existentially quantified sentence,

(ii) There is something such that it is a man and it walked into a room and it is dark and stooped,

then I once again use pronouns with a non-referential, cross-indexical function. This time, though, I have not only changed the pronoun from 'he' to 'it'. I have also changed the governing general term from 'a man' to 'something'.

Seeing this, one naturally wonders whether it is possible to indicate this state of affairs with a sentence in which there is no longer a pronoun functioning non-referentially and cross-indexically. The answer is 'Yes,' thus:

(iii) A dark and stooped man slunk into a room.

Now in the existentially quantified sentence (ii), the 'it' is of course customarily said to be functioning as a *variable*. Accordingly, when a noun or pronoun functions non-referentially and cross-indexically in the fashion indicated, whether in a quantificational sentence or not, let us say that it is functioning as a variable.

To attain the next stage in our attempt to understand the function of names in fiction, we must observe that not only pronouns but proper names can function as variables. Suppose, for example, that my tale had opened thus:

(iv) A man named 'George' slunk into a room. The man was dark and stooped,

or thus:

(v) A man named 'George' slunk into a room. George was dark and stooped.

It seems clear that in (iv), 'the man', and in (v), 'George' in the second sentence, are functioning exactly as did 'he' in (i). They are not being used to refer. Rather, they too have a cross-indexical but non-referential function. Accordingly, the name 'George' in the second sentence of (v) is functioning as a variable. However, the general term to which it, and 'he' in (iv), are indexed has changed. Now it is not 'a man' but rather 'a man named "George"'.

But why, one might ask, would the fictioneer want to use proper names as variables? Why not stick with pronouns as variables, along with common nouns prefaced with definite articles, such as 'the man' in (iv)?

One obvious purpose served by the use of proper names as one's variables is the rhetorical purpose of heightening the vividness of the narration. This is what Sydney in his *Apology for Poetry* took to be the purpose of introducing proper names into fiction. He says:

But hereto is replied that the poets give names to men they write of, which argueth a conceit of an actual truth, and so, not being true, proves a falsehood. And doth the lawyer lie then, when under the names of 'John a Stile' and 'John a Noakes' he puts his case? But that is easily answered. Their naming of men is but to make their picture more lively, and not to build any history; painting men, they cannot leave men nameless.

But the rhetorical purpose served by the use of proper names in the telling of fiction is typically deeper than just the increase of vividness. It also enables the cross-indexing function to be carried out with clarity and elegance. This is clear if we consider a tale opening with such a sentence as this: 'A certain provincial capital was located 25 miles from the nearest capital but 200 miles from the next nearest.' It is clear that as the teller of this tale proceeds he is going to have difficulty in making clear which of these cities he is speaking of on a given occasion. An obvious way of solving the problem is to use the phrases 'the first of these cities', 'the second of these cities', 'the third of these cities'. But the obviousness of this solution is outweighed by its stiltedness. For the purposes of his narration, the use of three proper names has the virtue of combining clarity of cross-indexing with elegance.

We noticed that in (v), the proper name 'George' functions as a variable, as does 'the man' in (iv). Furthermore, we saw that the variable is indexed back to the same expression in the two cases—to 'a man named "George"'. Now in using this latter expression, the speaker refers to the name 'George' by displaying it within quotation marks. And to refer to a name is of course neither to use it to refer nor to use it as a variable. So here is a third distinct way in which proper names put in their appearance within fiction. But in the referring to names which occurs in fiction there is nothing *peculiar* to fiction. So we need not linger here.

It is worth noting, somewhat parenthetically, that in both (iv) and (v), the state of affairs indicated by the speaker is one that cannot occur unless a man named 'George' slunk into a room and was dark and stooped. Thus, essential within the character (partially) delineated is the property of *being named* '*George*'. In this regard an interesting variant on (iv) and (v) is the following:

(vi) A man—I shall call him 'George'—slunk into a room. George was dark and stooped.

Here the state of affairs toward which a fictional stance is taken is exactly the same as in part of (iv) and (v). But parenthetically another state of affairs is indicated, that of *the speaker being about to call him 'George'*. Toward this state of affairs the speaker does not adopt a fictional stance but instead an assertive, or maybe a 'resolutive' stance. He avoids indicating that *being named* '*George*' is essential within the character, instead weakly suggesting that it is not, but says that he is going to use the name 'George' to tell his story. And indeed, there is no necessity in a narrator's projecting a world by using the names which people bear within that world. The narrator might in fact go on from (vi) to make it perfectly clear that there is this discrepancy, explaining that he is not going to specify a name for his character, or that he will do so but not himself use the name in his telling of the tale. In that way he would be driving a wedge between the rhetoric and the world of his tale. He would be using 'George' as a variable in the telling of his tale even though *being named* '*George*' is not essential within the character (partially) delineated.

Another, slightly different, variant on (v) is this:

(vii) A man slunk into a room. George was dark and stooped.

Here again it is not indicated that *being named 'George'* is essential within the character. But neither does the speaker say that he is going to call him 'George'. The name is just inserted and we are left to gather the significance this might have for what is included within the world.

This in fact is how the name 'Chichikov' initially occurs in *Dead Souls*. Suddenly the name is used as a variable governed by 'a man''. We are given no clue as to whether *being named 'Chichikov'* is essential within the character, or whether the name is introduced solely to be used as a variable by the narrator. Soon, though, the uncertainty is dissipated. For people in the world call him 'Chichikov'. And that is clear indication that *being named 'Chichikov'* is essential within the character.

Let us return from these parenthetical remarks to our main topic, the function of proper names in the fictional narration. Suppose, lastly, that my tale had opened thus:

(viii) George slunk into a room. He was dark and stooped.

How does 'George' function here? Evidently it does not function as a variable, for there is no general term to govern its use. But also it is not used to refer. And neither is it being referred to by being displayed. I think there is only one alternative available: 'George' functions here as itself a general term governing the functioning of subsequent variables. More specifically, it functions either as would the general term 'a man called "George"', or as would the general term 'a man whom I shall call "George"'. In most cases I think it functions in the former way. But once again, only the remainder of the tale will make it decisively clear. If people in the world of the work call someone 'George', that of course confirms that 'George' in its initial use was used by the writer in the same way that 'a man called "George"' would be. But if somehow or other it is made clear that in the world of the work he is not called 'George', then the alternative interpretation is confirmed.

We have covered, I think, the range of functions which

proper names play in fiction. A sort of limiting case occurs when a proper name is referred to by displaying it, so as to be able to say something about it. Apart from this, proper names in fiction are sometimes used to stand for things. Sometimes they function as variables. And sometimes they function as general terms, either like ones of the form 'a K called "N"' or like ones of the form 'a K which I shall call "N"'. And as to the names of (fictitious) characters, it should be obvious that their function is confined to that of variables and general terms. (Except in those cases in which the characters which are components of some work's world have essential within them the property of *referring to* some fictitious entity by name.)

A final point. The states of affairs indicated by our openings, (i) to (viii), are all general ones. They can all be indicated by quantificational sentences beginning, 'There exists something such that it is a man and...' So it turns out that in this and the preceding section we have arrived at positions very close to Aristotle's central point when he said:

the poet's function is to describe, not the thing that has happened, but a kind of thing that might happen... The distinction between historian and poet consists really in this, that the one describes the thing that has been, and the other a kind of thing that might be... Hence [poetry's]... statements are of the nature rather of universals, whereas those of history are singulars. By a universal statement I mean a statement of what such or such a kind of man will probably or necessarily say or do—which is the aim of poetry, though it affixes proper names to the characters...

VIII. *Putting a Character Together Again*

If a work's world is possible, then a character in such a world is a person-kind which is a maximal component of that world. And if a work's world is impossible, then what might be called *a character in some strand S* of that world is a person-kind which is a maximal component of the strand S. But a character in some strand of a work's world, where that world is impossible, may not yet be a character of that work's *world*. For it may just be that the whole of some character in that work's world is never to be found within any single strand, but is on the contrary divided up among several strands. Our problem now is to put such a character together again. For of course, when the work's world is not itself a strand, our interest is not in those entities which are characters in some strand of the work's world but in those entities which are characters *in the world*.

Let us go back to that short of beginning of a tale from our last section, expanding it just slightly:

> (i.a) A middle-aged man slunk into the room. He was dark and stooped.

One of the maximal components of the world here projected has essential within it the properties of *being a man*, of *being middle-aged*, and of *being dark and stooped*. How do I tell this? How do I tell that there is a maximal component which has essential within it not only the property of *being a man*, but also that of *being middle-aged*, that of *slinking into the room*, and that of *being dark and stooped*? Quite obviously I do so by noticing that the property of *being middle-aged* is designated by the adjective '*middle-aged*' and that this adjective qualifies an occurrence of the term 'man'; that the property of *slinking into the room* is designated by the phrase 'slunk into the room' and that this phrase is attached to the very same occurrence of the term 'man'; and that the property of *being dark and stooped* is designated by the phrase 'was dark and stooped' and that this phrase is indirectly attached to that very same occurrence of the term 'man', by virtue of the fact that the grammatical subject 'he' to which it is directly attached is cross-indexed to that same occurrence of the term 'man'.

It is by following up such modifiers, and such direct and indirect verbal attachments, to the same occurrence of the same term, that we are convinced it is one single maximal kind that we are dealing with. And that, basically, is how it always goes. We draw lines of dependency, attachment, and governance from modifiers, verbs, and quantifiers, watching to see whether we do or do not wind up ultimately at the same occurrence of the same term.

Let us now expand our tale just a bit more:

> (i.b) A middle-aged man slunk into the room. He was dark and stooped. He was fair of complexion.

Quite obviously we have here an impossible world projected. Someone cannot be both dark and fair of complexion. Accordingly we must think of this world as split up into at least two strands, each having a certain person-kind as maximal component. Properties essential within one will be those of *being a man*, *being middle-aged*, *slinking into the room*, *being dark*, and *being stooped*. Properties essential within an other will be these very same ones, except that instead of the property of *being dark* there will be the property of *being fair of complexion*.

That, I say, is what we will find if we look into the strands of this work's world. Yet it is obvious that above and beyond these maximal components of the strands there is an impossible character in this world. And somehow both the property of *being dark* and the property of *being fair of complexion*, though they fall into different strands, go into the make-up of this single character. Our knowledge that that is so based on the fact that the variable to which the verb 'was fair of complexion' is attached is cross-indexed to that very same occurrence of 'man' to which all the other verbs are attached, directly or indirectly, and that the adjective modifies. Following out the various lines of modification, attachment, and governance, we wind up at the same place.

We saw that the world projected with (i.b) has at least two strands, each containing a person-kind as maximal component. For simplicity's sake suppose that it has *exactly* two. Give the name D to that person-kind which has essential within it the property of *being dark*, and the name F to that one which has essential within it the property of being fair of complexion. Correspondingly, call the property-associate of the former, *being a thing which is-d*; and call that of the latter, *being a thing which is-f*. Now *being a thing which is-d & (being) a thing which is-f* will also be a property. Further, there will be for it a kind-associate. And it is *that* kind, that impossible kind, which is the character of the work's world—not D, and not F. The character of the work's world will be a species of D, and also a species of F. But D and F are not themselves characters of the work's world, the reason being that they have, as a species of themselves, that other kind which is related to them in the way indicated. (For the concept of *species*, see Part Two, Section IV.)

We have taken a simplified situation in which there were just two distinct person-kinds which were maximal components in strands of the work's world. But now that we have seen the structure of this simplified case, composing a completely general formulation is not difficult. No additional illumination would be gained by doing so, however. We have seen what is important; namely, the basic strategy to be followed in putting characters together again, once they have been split up across distinct strands. Just one thing should be added. What is included in a work's world, when that world is impossible, is not just the content of the various strands. What is also included is whatever impossible states of affairs the author has indicated, plus those impossible states of affairs which are members of conjunctive analyses of what he has indicated. And it may well be that from these we will come up with additional properties which are members of conjunctive analyses of the property-associate of some impossible kind which is a character within the work's world. (These will be properties impossible of exemplification.) The way to tell is fundamentally the same as that which we have already canvassed: one follows up lines of modification, attachment, and governance.

That now completes our theory of characters. We have spoken solely of those fictitious entities which are characters—person-kinds. Obviously fiction deals with many other sorts of fictitious entities as well: fictitious countries, cities, dogs, carriages, etc. However, our limitation to characters was wholly a matter of convenience. Nothing in our theory of characters limits it to characters. What we have offered is a theory of fictitious entities.

I close by recalling the words that Pirandello gave to the Father in his *Six Characters in Search of an Author*: ' . . . one is born to live in many forms, in many shapes, as tree, or as stone, as water, as butterfly, or as woman. So one may also be born a character in a play.' [Act 1.] And 'as I say, sir, that which is a game of art for you is our sole reality.' [Act 3.]

IX. *Proper Names from Fiction out of Fiction*

Suppose that someone assertively utters 'Hamlet was neurotic', it being understood that the character in question is the Hamlet-in-Shakespeare's-*Hamlet* character. Then 'Hamlet' stands for the character Hamlet—that is, for the particular person-kind. And the proposition that would (normally) be asserted is true[26] just in case the property expressed by the predicate—namely, being neurotic—is *analytic within* what the subject 'Hamlet' stands for. (For the concept of *analytic within*, see Part Two, Section IV.) Or if Hamlet is a possible character, we can also say this: The proposition is true just in case the property expressed by the predicate is *essential within* what the subject 'Hamlet' stands for. What is most emphatically not the case is that the proposition is true just in case that for which the subject stands *has* the property that the predicate expresses. Very many other examples follow this same pattern—for example, 'Chichikov was a confidence trickster' and 'Sherlock Holmes was a detective.' In such cases we are using the name to refer to a character; and our assertion is true just in case the property that the predicate expresses is analytic (or essential) within that entity for which the name stands.

Furthermore, for all sentences and propositions which fit this pattern, if the proposition is true, then it is *essential* to the kind for which the subject stands that it have the property of having analytic (or essential) within it the property expressed by the predicate. Accordingly, if the subject is functioning as a rigid designator, then the proposition asserted is necessarily true—since kinds exist necessarily. Suppose, however, that 'Chichikov' in 'Chichikov was a confidence trickster' is not functioning as a rigid designator but as short for 'the character in *Dead Souls* which has the property of being called "Chichikov" essential within it'. Then the proposition expressed by the sentence is only contingently true. For the person-kind in question might never have been made into a character, and *Dead Souls* might never have existed (though the *world* of *Dead Souls* could not have failed to exist).

There are, though, sentences containing names of fictional characters and propositions asserted with these sentences that do not fit the above pattern. Consider these, for example: 'Hamlet has proved endlessly fascinating to psychoanalysts' and 'Hedda was portrayed last night as shooting herself out of sight of everyone.' The proposition (normally) asserted

---

[26] That is, true *in the actual world*, though indeed it is also *included within* the world of *Hamlet*.

with the former is not true just in case the Hamlet-in-*Hamlet* character has analytic or essential within it the property of proving endlessly fascinating to psychoanalysts; nor is the proposition (normally) asserted with the latter true just in case the Hedda-in-*Hedda Gabler* character has analytic or essential within it the property of having been portrayed last night as shooting herself out of sight of everyone. Rather, in these cases the proposition asserted is true[27] just in case that entity for which the subject stands *has* the property expressed by the predicate. Further, in both these cases, the property expressed by the predicate is not essential to that kind which is the character in question. However, that will not always be true for sentences and propositions that fit this pattern. It would not be true, for example, if one assertively uttered 'Hedda is a person-type.'

It is easy to see how 'Sherlock Holmes was created by an author' and 'Sherlock Holmes was born of woman' can both be used to assert what is true. The proposition (normally) asserted with the former is one which is true just in case that entity for which 'Sherlock Holmes' stands has the property expressed by the predicate. The proposition (normally) expressed by the latter is true just in case that entity for which 'Sherlock Holmes' stands has essential or analytic within it the property expressed by the predicate.

Perhaps it's worth seeing briefly how these analyses work out when a sentence susceptible of a relational analysis is employed to assert a proposition—say the sentence '*a* lived in *b*.'

Consider first the situation in which both '*a*' and '*b*' stand for fictional entities—as with 'Flem Snopes lived in Yokapatawpha County.' The proposition asserted with '*a* lived in *b*' is then true if and only if essential within *a* is bearing to *b* the relation of living in an example of it. (Equivalently, if and only if essential within *b* is bearing to *a* the relation of being lived in by an example of it.)

Secondly, consider the situation in which '*a*' stands for a fictional entity and '*b*' for a non-type—as with 'Chichikov lived in Russia.' The proposition asserted with '*a* lived in *b*' is then true if and only if essential within *a* is bearing to *b* the relation of living in it (conversely and equivalently, if and only if *b* bears to

[27] True, once again, in the *actual* world.

a the relation of being what something must live in if that thing is to be an example of *a*.)

Thirdly, consider the situation in which '*a*' stands for a non-type and '*b*' for a fictional entity. The propostion asserted with '*a* lived in *b*' is then true if and only if essential within *b* is bearing to *a* the relation of being lived in by *a* (conversely and equivalently, if and only if *a* bears to *b* the relation of its being impossible that something should be an example of *b* and not have *a* living in it).

The two patterns we have unearthed cover the vast majority of cases in which we use the names of characters outside the telling of fiction, in our making of assertions. But not quite all such uses fit under either of these patterns. For on either of these patterns, I would be speaking truth if I assertively uttered 'Chichikov exists.' The Chichikov -in-*Dead Souls* character *does* have the property of existing. And also it is the case that that property is essential (and analytic) within that character. Yet, using our words with normal meaning, one would speak truth if one assertively uttered, 'Chichikov does not and never did exist.'

One thing that might be claimed, by assertively uttering this latter sentence with normal sense, is that the character *has* the property of never having been exemplified. If so, that fits our second pattern. But perhaps one might also, speaking thus, be claiming that Gogol was not referring to anyone when he used the name 'Chichikov' in *Dead Souls*. Or that there never was anyone to whom the world of *Dead Souls* is anchored and to whom Gogol referred with 'Chichikov'. If so, what one asserted would be true. But it would fit neither of the patterns we have elicited.

Still, the presence of such cases must not be allowed to obscure the main point. Take those cases in which we assertively utter a simple subject/predicate sentence containing a proper name used to stand for some character. Sometimes the proposition asserted is true if and only if the property expressed by the predicate is analytic (or essential) within that entity for which the name stands. In the vast majority of other cases, it is true if and only if that entity for which the name stands *has* the property expressed by the predicate.

It's worth noticing that the claim that Gogol was not

referring to anyone when he used the name 'Chichikov' in *Dead Souls* might be true in two quite different ways. For one thing, it may be that Gogol never intended to refer to anyone with the name 'Chichikov'. In such a case, let us say that the Chichikov-character occurs *fictionally* in Gogol's *Dead Souls*. But it could also be that Gogol intended to refer to someone with 'Chichikov', but for whatever reasons did not succeed in doing so. In such a case, let us say that the Chichikov-character occurs *mythically* in *Dead Souls*. By contrast, if Gogol had intended to refer to someone with 'Chichikov', and had succeeded, let us say that the Chichikov-character occurs *historically* in *Dead Souls*. The Napoleon-character probably occurs historically in Tolstoy's *War and Peace*, whereas it seems likely that in the early tellings of the Greek myths the various god-characters occurred mythically. In all likelihood the tellers intended to refer to something with 'Zeus', but failed, since the requisite thing did not exist. Perhaps, by contrast, the Pegasus-character occurred historically in the original Pegasus stories. For perhaps those stories were embellishments about an actual horse. After all, the properties that one poses about something to which one refers need not all be properties that the thing has, and need not even all be properties that one *thinks* it has.

A character which occurs one way in one telling of a story may occur another way in a later telling of the story. I do not believe that I can refer to Venus. Accordingly the Venus-character, though it probably occurred mythically in the original telling of the Venus tales, would occur fictionally in my discourse if I now narrated them. And if someone thought that the St Nicholas-character was occurring historically in a telling of one of the traditional stories about St Nicholas when actually it was occurring fictionally, and went on to retell the story, the character might occur mythically in his own telling. It could even happen that a character which occurs fictionally in one telling of a story occurs historically in a later. For example, I might refer to some contemporary sleuth and tell about him one of the Sherlock Holmes stories. I can do so even though the person in question does not fit the Sherlock Holmes-character and even though I do not think he fits it. One can knowingly fictionalize about the existent.

Whether a character which occurs historically in one telling of a story can occur mythically in a later telling seems to me problematic—except just in the rather uninteresting way that in the interim the entity in question may have gone out of existence. What certainly can happen though is that stories in which, say, the Pegasus-character occurs historically may later, by virtue of embellishments, be superseded by stories in which the Pegasus-character occurs mythically. But then we are not dealing with the same story but rather with an interrelated sequence of stories. And then the Pegasus-character in story A of the series is not identical with the Pegasus-character in, say, story L of the series.

Though the Napoleon-character occurs historically in *War and Peace*, it is still the case that what we have said about the structure of claims concerning fictionally or mythically occurring characters holds for such historically occurring characters as well. The fact that they occur historically makes no difference to that. Very many of such claims are true just in case such-and-such property is analytic or essential within the character. Many others are true just in case the character *has* or *possesses* such-and-such a property. If, referring to the Napoleon-in-*War and Peace* character, one assertively utters 'Napoleon was the unwitting victim of irresistible impersonal forces', we would have an example of the former. And if, referring to the same character, one assertively uttered 'Tolstoy never succeeded in developing Napoleon in his story', we would have an example of the latter.

X. *Narrating Characters, Authorial Narrators, and Speakers*

The words of a novel are the words of its author. He it is who puts them down and projects a world thereby.

Yet, look at the opening sentences of Dickens's *David Copperfield*:

Whether I shall turn out to be the hero of my own life, or whether that station will be held by anybody else, these pages must show. To begin my life with the beginning of my life, I record that I was born (as I have been informed and believe) on a Friday, at twelve o'clock at night. It was remarked that the clock began to strike, and I began to cry, simultaneously.

The *form* of these words is such that they might well function as the opening of an autobiography. And given that they were put down by Dickens, if they were functioning as autobiography it would be the autobiography of Dickens. Dickens would be using the 'I' to refer to himself. But surely that is not how they are functioning. The autobiographer uses his words to assert. *David Copperfield*, however, is a work of fiction; and we have agreed with Sydney that the fictioneer 'nothing affirmeth'.

How then are these words functioning? Well, even if we agree that Dickens in *David Copperfield* is not engaged in telling his autobiography but rather in fictionally projecting a world, still it is coherent to suppose that he is using the 'I' to refer to himself. For with the text that follows he may be putting forth an elaborate fiction about himself. Certainly there is nothing impossible in that. So is that how these words are functioning? If so, then of course Dickens must exist if the world of the work is to occur.

Take another example, Anthony Burgess's novel *A Clockwork Orange*. The novel opens thus:

There was me, that is Alex, and my three droogs, that is Pete, Georgie, and Dim, Dim being really dim, and we sat in the Korova Milkbar making up our rassodocks what to do with the evening, a flip dark chill winter bastard though dry. The Korova Milkbar was a milk-plus mesto, and you may, O my brothers ...

It is coherent to hold that Burgess was referring to himself with the occurrence of the pronoun 'me', and that the whole story is a fiction about himself. If that's how these words are in fact functioning, then Burgess would have to exist if the fictionally projected world of *Clockwork Orange* were to occur.

But though it is coherent thus to understand *David Copperfield* and *Clockwork Orange*, I think that this understanding is mistaken. It is not at all likely that Dickens was referring to himself with those several occurrences of 'I', nor that Burgess was referring to himself with that occurrence of 'me'.

Let us unravel these situations a bit. Earlier in our discussion I introduced the concept of a strand of some work's world *being anchored to* some entity. That consists in the strand's being such that it could not occur unless that entity exists. Now suppose that some projected world is a strand and is such that it could not occur unless that person who is the author existed. The world would then be anchored to the author. The world of an autobiography is like that. And we have just seen that, in principle, the world of a novel may also be like that. Perhaps Sylvia Plath's *Bell Jar* is in fact like that. Perhaps it is a fiction about herself. It's clear at any rate that Borges' story 'The Streetcorner Man' is anchored to himself, Borges. Here once again is how the story ends:

Nice and easy, I walked the two or three blocks back to my shack. A candle was burning in the window, then all at once went out. Let me tell you, I hurried when I saw that. Then, Borges, I put my hand inside my vest—here by the left armpit where I always carry it—and took my knife out again. I turned the blade over, real slow. It was as good as new, innocent-looking, and you couldn't see the slightest trace of blood on it.

The sly inclusion of the name 'Borges' in the second from last sentence is the clue that the world of this work is anchored to its author, Borges.

If *David Copperfield* and *Clockwork Orange* are not to be interpreted as anchored to their authors, each of them being a fiction about its author, how then are they to be interpreted? From our preceding discussion we also have in hand the concept of a character's being *a component* of a projected world. Now one of the characters in Dickens's novel is the David Copperfield-in-*David Copperfield* character. And I suggest that the most plausible way of interpreting the novel is to construe the *character* David Copperfield as speaking those opening words, indeed, as speaking all the words that follow in the text. These words do not give us what Dickens says about himself, assertively or fictionally. They give us what David says. It is David's autobiography that we read, not Dickens's. Or to speak with more explicitness: the character David Copperfield is such that essential within it is the property of uttering all the words of the text of *David Copperfield*, thereby performing whatever speech actions the world of the work requires that he thereby perform. Accordingly I shall call the David Copperfield character, the *narrating character* of the novel *David Copperfield*. Dickens projects a world by using the David-character as the narrating character of his work.

From here we must proceed to a general definition of 'narrating character'. But to get to that destination a few complications must be noted. In the first place, the text of the novel may include, in addition to sentences that the author uses to fictionally project a world, sentences that he uses to make assertions about our actual world. *War and Peace* is an obvious example. Accordingly, we had better speak about a narrating character of a *passage* of a literary text, rather than of a text as a whole.[28]

Secondly, distinct passages of a text may have distinct narrating characters. Two splendid examples of this are A. E. Housman's poem 'Is My Team Ploughing?' and W. H. Auden's ballad 'O What is that Sound which so Thrills the Ear'. Let me quote the first two stanzas of the former:

> 'Is my team ploughing,
>   That I was used to drive
> And hear the harness jingle
>   When I was a man alive?'
>
> Ay, the horses trample,
>   The harness jingles now;
> No change though you lie under
>   The land you used to plough.

The narrating character of the first stanza is the dead man; that of the second stanza his yet-living friend.

A third complication is this: one character may faithfully quote the words of another, so that if the world of the work is to occur, there must be an example of the second character who utters the words quoted as well as the first who utters those very same words in quoting them. Here is an example from *David Copperfield*, with David speaking:

(1) 'Mrs. David Copperfield, I *think*,' said Miss Betsey; the emphasis referring, perhaps, to my mother's mourning weeds, and her condition.

Miss Betsey must instantiate the words, 'Mrs. David Copperfield, I *think*,' but so must David.

Perhaps there are various ways to cope with this last compli-

---

[28] Words which occur twice or more in a text—for example, 'then I went home', constitute two different passages. The text itself is to be thought of as a sequence of words, and a passage of the text as a sub-sequence.

cation, so as to yield the result that David is the narrating character of (1), and indeed of the totality of the text of *David Copperfield*. The strategy I propose to follow is that of regarding *both* David and Miss Betsey as narrating characters of the passage,

> (2) Mrs. David Copperfield, I *think*,

and only David as the narrating character of the more inclusive passage, (1), and indeed of

> (3) 'Mrs. David Copperfield, I *think*,' said Miss Betsey.

The rationale for this strategy is that if the world of the work is to occur, an example of the David character and an example of the Miss Betsey character would each have to utter or inscribe (1), whereas only an example of the David character would have to utter or inscribe the more inclusive (1) and (3). Thus, what makes David the sole narrating character of *David Copperfield* is not that no passage within the text has anyone other than David as a narrating character, but rather that the whole text is such that someone must utter that entire passage if the world of the work is to occur, and David alone is a narrating character thereof.

With these points in mind we can frame the definition of 'narrating character' as follows:[29]

Def. 1: Character C is a *narrating character* of passage P of work W =df C is a character in the world WW projected by W; and C is such that for WW to occur, an example of C must utter or inscribe the totality of P (or its equivalent in some other language) and thereby perform whatever actions an example of C would thereby have to perform if WW were to occur.

We can also now define the concept of an *exclusively narrative passage* as follows:

Def. 2: Passage P is an *exclusively narrative* passage =df the world of the work to which P belongs is such that for

---

[29] The following definitions are framed so that they are fully satisfactory only for those worlds which are strands. Having shown, in the preceding, how to deal with impossible worlds, I shall here set those off to the side. They introduce complications irrelevant to the points at issue here.

every passage of *P* there are one or more characters in the work's world which are narrating characters of that passage.

On these definitions, the text of Housman's 'Is My Team Ploughing?' is an exclusively narrative passage. Yet there is no character which is the narrating character of the entire passage. Rather, the first stanza has a narrating character, the second has a different narrating character, etc. By contrast the text of *War and Peace* is not an exclusively narrative passage, since Tolstoy's lengthy interpolations on historical destiny are not narrative. For the world of the work to occur, no one need utter those passages. But even those parts of *War and Peace* in which philosophical speculation does not take place do not constitute an exclusively narrative passage. For Tolstoy's novel is structured as third-person narration, and is filled with *he said's* and *she said's* which are not to be attributed to any character belonging to the work's world. By contrast, the text of *David Copperfield* is both an exclusively narrative passage, and is such that there is for it, in its totality, a single narrating character.

Earlier I suggested the possibility that Sylvia Plath's *The Bell Jar* is a fiction about herself, constructed in such a way that the 'I' refers to herself. But whether Plath was or was not referring to herself with the 'I' in the novel, none the less she does delineate a certain character—call it the 'I'-character—in the novel. This 'I'-character must be distinguished from Plath herself. Plath after all is not a person-type but a person. And probably she herself was not in all respects an example of the 'I'-character. Probably what she fictionalized about herself diverged here and there from what she was actually like. The text of *The Bell Jar* is, as a whole, an exclusively narrative passage; and for that passage as a whole, there is just one narrating character. The conceptual framework developed applies nicely to *The Bell Jar*.

But on the assumption that this work is in fact a fiction about its author, there is another, closely related, concept which can be formulated and also applied to cases such as this. It is the concept of a *person*—not a character, but a person—being what I shall call the *speaker* of a passage. We may define this concept of a speaker of a passage as follows:

Def. 3: Person *Pr* is a *speaker* of passage *P* of work *W*=df the world *WW* projected by *W* is anchored to *Pr*; and if *WW* is to occur, *Pr* must utter or inscribe *P* (or its equivalent in some other language) and thereby perform whatever actions *Pr* would thereby have to perform if *WW* were to occur.

Since the latter part of the nineteenth century many fictioneers have been attracted to the device of constructing their works of fiction in such a way that the text as a whole is exclusively narrative, so that for every passage thereof there is a narrating character. No doubt many have been attracted to this device by the easily achieved unity, and the immediacy of effect. In the structure of such narration there is nothing between us and one (or more) of the characters of the world. All that stands in the text is what some one (or more) of the characters said. The author has disappeared from view.

However, this unity and immediacy are bought at the price of severe constrictions on the nature of the world projected. Consider a novel or story whose text is exclusively narrative and whose world contains a character which is the narrating character of the whole of the text; and imagine the world of such a work obtaining. In the case of *David Copperfield* we are to imagine a person named 'David Copperfield' as uttering all those words to be found in the text of Dickens's novel. Now under what circumstances would someone pour forth such a lengthy stream of words? He might do so if he were making a record of his life and experience; that is quite clearly the situation envisaged both for *David Copperfield* and *A Clockwork Orange*. Or he might do so if he were pouring forth a lengthy soliloquy (Poe's 'The Cask of Amontillado') or a monologue to some audience which either never interrupts or whose interruptions are known are known to us only through the narrating character's reports of them (Poe's 'The Tell-Tale Heart'). But apart from such situations there seems nothing else. So to compose an exclusively narrative text with a single narrating character is perforce to limit oneself to indicating states of affairs which wholly consist of someone, in a record or soliloquy or monologue, pouring out a lengthy stream of words. Such situations obviously constitute an exceedingly minor part of human life.

Of course the world of the work thus constructed is by no

means confined to the states of affairs indicated. Dickens indicates the state of affairs of someone pouring out in his diary the stream of words to be found in the text of *David Copperfield*; and on the basis of this we extrapolate, fleshing out the world of the work far beyond what is indicated. It remains true, though, that what is indicated is just the writing of a lengthy autobiography.

While still making do with narrating characters and with an exclusively narrative text, thus while still maintaining a structure which excludes the author, the constrictions pointed to above can to a great extent be overcome if there are two or more narrating characters instead of just one, these engaging in dialogue with each other. In such a case what the author indicates is still confined to a situation consisting of someone speaking. But there are a great many more situations in which lengthy dialogue takes place than there are situations in which lengthy monologue takes place. The poems of Housman and Auden already referred to are good examples of this strategy. Of course a serious problem in the use of this strategy is making clear to the reader which character is speaking which passage. The problem is solved in these two cases by giving the characters alternating verses of equal length. (In addition, Housman puts the speeches of the dead man in quotation marks.) Such a fictional device brings us very close to a text suitable for dramatic performance. In fact, all that separates it from a standard text of that sort is the absence of marginal indications as to which character has which lines, and the absence of performance indications.

In developing my concept of a *narrating character* I have had my eye on a relatively limited range of literary fiction—by and large, on fiction told in the first person. I have suggested that the projected world of such first-person works as *David Copperfield* and *A Clockwork Orange* has, as its basic structure, that of someone narrating something. But the question then arises: how are we to analyse those works which do not have the narrating-character structure?

Prominent among the canonical theses of contemporary literary theory is the thesis that there are no such works. Every work of literary fiction, so goes the orthodox view, presents to us for our consideration a complex situation whose fundamental structure is that of someone narrating something to someone.

Twist and turn as he may, never can the writer of fiction give to his tale a structure other than that of narrator to narratee. ('Narrator' and 'narratee' are the words customarily used by critics.) Like Chinese boxes—box within box—that's fiction.

The specific manner in which this canonical thesis is developed varies from writer to writer. Beardsley allows for the possibility that sometimes the narrator should be identified with the author. Seymour Chatman, in his recent book, *Story and Discourse*, will have none of that. He says, 'it is quite clear (well established in theory and criticism) that we must distinguish between the narrator, or speaker, the one currently "telling" the story, and the author, the ultimate designer of the fable ...'[30] And again, this time explicitly pitting himself against Beardsley, he says: 'That it is essential not to confuse author and narrator has become a commonplace of literary theory. As Monroe Beardsley argues, "the speaker of a literary work cannot be identified with the author—and therefore the character and condition of the speaker can be known by internal evidence alone—unless the author has provided a pragmatic context, or a claim of one, that connects the speaker with himself." But even in such a context, the speaker is not the author, but the "author" (quotation marks of "as if") ...'[31] Thus Beardsley and Chatman disagree on whether the author can ever be the narrator. What both assume, however, is that every story has the fundamental structure of narrator narrating to narratee.

In his discussion of narrative structure, Chatman then constructs a taxonomy based on the relative prominence of the ever-present narrator. 'The teller', he says, 'is best accounted for, as a spectrum of possibilities, going from narrators who are least audible to those who are most so. The label affixed to the negative pole of narratorhood is less important than its reality in the spectrum. I say "nonnarrated': the reader may prefer "minimally narrated," but the existence of this kind of transmission is well attested.'[32]

[30] Seymour Chatman, *Story and Discourse* (Cornell Univ. Press: Ithaca, N.Y., 1978), p. 33.
[31] Ibid., pp. 147–8.
[32] Ibid., pp. 146–7.

On first hearing, this is a most surprising thesis—that the fundamental structure of all stories is that of someone narrating something to someone. Presumably not all human narration consists of narrating what someone narrated. Why then must fictional narration have this structure? Why can't the novelist just straightforwardly tell us a tale of love and death, birth and war, jealousy and endeavour? Why must his tale always be the tale of a *narration* of love and death, birth and war, jealousy and endeavour?

Well, I think it can be. And I wish to show that the arguments offered in favor of the canonical thesis come far short of establishing it. But before we look at those arguments, it may be helpful to have before us an example of the sort of passage on which I disagree with the canonical view. Here is one such, from Henry James's 'The Beast in the Jungle':

'Well,' she quickly replied, 'I myself have never spoken. I've never, never repeated of you what you told me.' She looked at him so that he perfectly believed her.

To passages of this linguistic form Chatman gives the nice appellation, 'direct speech/tagged style'—*direct speech*, because it records what someone said in the mode of direct rather than indirect speech, and *tagged*, because attached to the direct speech quotation is the tag, 'she quickly replied'.

It is my contention that for the world of James's story to occur, it is not necessary that someone utter all the words of this passage. Specifically, it can occur without anyone uttering,

(1) she looked at him so that he perfectly believed her.

Likewise, it can occur without anyone uttering,

(2) she quickly replied.

It cannot occur, though, without someone uttering the word

(3) Well.

Nor can it occur without someone uttering the words,

(4) I myself have never spoken. I've never, never repeated of you what you told me.

It would be agreed by all parties that the world of this passage can occur without any example of one of the *explicitly delineated characters* uttering (1) or (2). But my contention is stronger. It is my contention that the world of this work can occur without *anyone at all* uttering those words. In writing the passage quoted Henry James set down some words, and thereby projected a world. But the world he projected does not have as its fundamental structure that of someone in turn uttering all those words.

But here the battle is joined. For the canonical thesis holds that for this direct speech/tagged style passage from Henry James there is a narrating character. Those who hold this thesis would admit that the presence of this character as a component of the world projected by this passage must be inferred. It is not one of the 'up-front' characters. None the less, it is held that if the world of this passage is to occur, there must be someone who utters all of (1)–(4). It is held not to be sufficient that a woman have looked at a man so that he perfectly believed her. What is necessary is that someone utter the words, 'She looked at him so that he perfectly believed her.'

Fiction, on this view, is not usually the tale of a tale—that is, the fictional telling of a *fictional* telling. Always, though, it is the fictional telling of *some* mode of telling. The teller, the narrating character, may and usually does remain nameless. The other characters of the work's world may never acknowledge his presence. He may be all but invisible. Yet there he is.

What are the reasons for this extraordinary view? Why this doubling of tellings? Usually no reason is offered. The canonical thesis is assumed, rather than argued for. None the less, I think we can see, in a general way, what it is that has led literary theorists to hold the thesis.

Perhaps the best place to begin is by looking at a passage which is often cited as offering a reason for the view in question—namely, a passage from Monroe Beardsley's *Aesthetics*. The passage is cited, for example, by Chatman. 'In every literary work', says Beardsley, 'there is first of all an implicit *speaker*, or voice: he whose words the work purports to be.' And then he goes on to say:

The speaker is not to be identified with the author of the work, nor can we learn more of the speaker than he reveals in the poem, say by studying the life of the author. It is not Housman whose heart 'with rue ... is laden,' or Frost who has 'miles to go before I sleep;' ... We have no more justification for identifying the author with the speaker than with any other character in the work...[33]

Beardsley goes on to qualify slightly this extreme position. He says:

The temptation to confuse the speaker with the writer is the greatest with lyric poetry, which almost always contains personal pronouns. Ordinarily, however, we have no reason to regard the 'I' of the poem as the writer, just as we have no reason to regard the 'you,' if there is one, as the reader. The 'I,' like the 'you,' is, in one sense, simply one of the characters in the work, perhaps the only one. Of course the speaker is a rather special, or privileged, character, since it is from his point of view that everything is seen, and in some lyric poems all that happens is what happens in his mind. Now, in some writings, e.g., autobiography, we must take the personal pronoun to refer to the writer. Is there not then ever any good reason for taking a poem as, in the same sense, autobiographical?[34]

Beardsley answers his question by saying that there are a few cases, rare, he suggests, in which the work should be taken as autobiographical:

But a narrative work in the first person, in which the speaker has the name of the author, and is known to resemble him in certain important respects—especially, to clinch the matter, if it is subtitled 'An Autobiography' or 'A Memoir'—*is* a work in which the author speaks for himself.[35]

Beardsley's whole view then is this:

In general, the correct principle seems to be that the speaker of a literary work cannot be identified with the author—and therefore the character and condition of the speaker can be known by internal evidence alone—unless the author has provided a pragmatic context, or a claim of one, that connects the speaker with himself. But we must grant that what constitutes a pragmatic context is not always certain.[36]

---

[33] Monroe Beardsley, *Aesthetics* (Harcourt, Brace: New York, 1958), p. 238.
[34] Ibid., pp. 238–9.
[35] Ibid., p. 239.
[36] Ibid., p. 240.

As a preface to my critique of this view, a word must be said about Beardsley's use of the term 'speaker'. If one took at face value the use of the term in the passages quoted, Beardsley would be committed to the view that for every literary work *there is some person* who is what I have called the *speaker* of the text. And the question he would then be discussing is whether the speakers of literary works are ever identical with their authors. But quite clearly that is not Beardsley's view, nor his question. He does not think that, for each literary work, we can pick out some person who is its speaker. In one of the passages quoted he speaks of 'the speaker' as a *character*. And that is the clue: what Beardsley calls *the speaker* of a literary work is what I have called the *narrating character* of a literary work. But if so, then there is little point in asking whether the narrating character of a work is ever identical with the author of a work. For it is *impossible* that they should *ever* be identical. Authors are persons. Characters are not and cannot possibly be persons. They are person-types. The relevant question is not whether the narrating character of a work is ever identical with its author. The relevant question is whether every work has a narrating character—and whether some works have speakers identical with their authors. Beardsley's answers to these questions, as I understand him, are that all literary works have narrating characters, and that a few, though only a *very* few, have speakers identical with their authors.

Our principal concern, here, is with the tenability of the former of these two claims. It will be instructive, though, first to appraise the latter. Just why it is that Beardsley holds that only a very few works have speakers identical with their authors? Well, he remarks that Housman's heart was not laden with rue, even though the 'I' of the text says that his heart 'with rue . . . is laden'. And from this he concludes that the author is not the speaker. But how does this conclusion follow from the facts cited? For if we allow, as surely we must, that a person can fictionalize about himself, then it is clear that Housman may not have had a rue-laden heart, may even have *known* that he did not, and yet fictionally projected a world such that if it is to occur, he, Housman, must have a rue-laden heart. Surprisingly, it looks as if Beardsley is tacitly holding the principle that the author of a work cannot fictionally entertain about himself things which are not true of himself. But the truth is that just as we can assert of ourselves what is not true, so too we can fictionalize of ourselves what is not true.

None the less, I agree that most first-person narrations should not be construed as passages having a person as speaker, with the author as that person. Earlier I suggested that *David Copperfield* should probably not be construed thus, nor *Clockwork Orange*, though perhaps *The Bell Jar* should be so construed. The way to tell—and sometimes we cannot tell decisively—is to appeal to what Beardsley calls 'the pragmatic context'.

However, for our understanding of the structure of fiction generally this issue is really of only secondary importance. For the vast bulk of works clearly do not have speakers. At best they have narrating characters. Accordingly, the primary question is not whether all works have speakers but whether all works have narrating characters, as Beardsley contends they do. Let us turn, then, to an appraisal of this claim.

Just why is it that Beardsley thinks that every work of literary fiction has a narrating character? Why, in his own words, does he hold that 'in every literary work there is first of all an implicit *speaker*, or voice: he whose words the work purports to be'? Strikingly, he doesn't say. He *announces* that for every literary work there is a narrator; and he then *goes on* to discuss whether that narrator can ever be identified with the author. But for the major thesis, that every work has a narrator, he gives no reason at all. But neither, to the best of my knowledge, does anyone else explicitly offer a reason for the canonical view.

It is possible, however, to *surmise* the considerations which have led contemporary literary theorists and critics to assume that the fundamental structure of the world of a literary work is always that of a narrator narrating to a narratee. What I have emphasized thus far is that the writer of fiction projects a world for our consideration. But there is something else which he does, something of great importance for the reader with literary intentions to notice. To see what this something else is, let me cite a passage from Balzac's *Gambara* which Emile Benveniste cites, and which Jonathan Culler in turn cites in his book, *Structuralist Poetics*:

After a turn in the arcades, the young man looked at the sky and then at his watch, made an impatient gesture, entered a tobacco shop, lit a cigar, placed himself before a mirror, and glanced at his clothes, somewhat more elaborate than the laws of taste in France permit. He adjusted his collar and his black velvet waistcoat, which was criss-crossed by one of those large golden chains made in Genoa; then, throwing his velvet-lined coat onto his left shoulder with a single movement and letting it hang there in elegant folds, he continued his walk, without allowing himself to be distracted by the leers of passers-by. When the lights in shops began to go on and the night seemed to him sufficiently dark, he made his way towards the square of the Palais Royal like a man who was afraid of being recognized, for he kept to the side of the square until the fountain so as to enter the rue Froidmanteau screened from the hackney cabs.

About this passage Culler then says this:

... the reader of literature will have recognized a narrative voice: 'one of those large golden chains made in Genoa' implies a relation of complicity and shared knowledge between narrator and reader; 'like a man who was afraid of being recognized, *for*...' gives us a narrator who infers a state of mind from an action and presumes that the reader will accept the connection as he describes it. If we were to separate the story from all marks of a personal narrator we would have to exclude ... even the slightest general observation or evaluative adjective, the most discreet comparison, the most modest 'perhaps', the most inoffensive logical connection, all of which partake of *discours* rather than *histoire*.[37]

In this passage we have a sample of the consideration which has been decisive in leading twentieth-century theorists and critics to adopt the canonical thesis. It seems impossible to construe all the words in a literary text as picking out states of affairs included in the explicitly projected world. Some of them can only be viewed as revealing or expressing various things about the teller of the tale, revealing, perhaps, various opinions and attitudes of his about the actual world, or about the tale he is telling and the narratee to whom he is telling it. Literary *discourse* cannot be viewed solely as telling a *story*. *Discourse* has significance independent of story. It is to account for this independent significance of discourse that the theorist postulates a narrator for each story—and a narratee.

Now I think that these observations about the significance of

[37] Jonathan Culler, *Structuralist Poetics* (Cornell Univ. Press: Ithaca, N.Y., 1975), p. 198.

discourse beyond story are true, and profoundly important. But just why do they force us to postulate a narrating character for each work? Why not say that it was the author, Balzac, who implied with his words, or *presented* himself as implying, 'a relation of complicity and shared knowledge' with his contemporary French audience? Why not hold that it was the author, Balzac, who observed about the character he was developing, or *presented* himself as observing, that he acted 'like a man who was afraid of being recognized'?

I think the answer that the theorist would give at this point is like the answer that Beardsley gave at a similar point. He would say that the author Balzac, for all we know, might not in fact have thought that a person who behaved thus was acting like someone afraid of being recognized. And he would say that the author Balzac, for all we know, might not have believed that his audience knew anything at all about large chains made in Genoa. And these observations are correct. But the observations do not justify the conclusion, for a reason adduced earlier. Authors like the rest of us can pretend, and they like the rest of us can fictionalize about themselves and about other existent entities. They can put on a *persona*; and part of that *persona* may consist in pretending various things about their audience. Of course—and this is crucial—for the person who is reading with literary intent, it makes no difference whatsoever where the *persona* blends with the author's face and where it diverges, where pretending and fictionalizing ends and where fidelity to self begins. What the reader with literary intent notices is just that Balzac *implied or pretended to imply . . ., observed or fictionalized about himself that he observed . . .*, etc. The reader with literary intent, confronted with fiction which is not exclusively narrative in structure, cares only about how the author *presents* himself. If he presents himself as having an attitude of scornful superiority, that is what counts. It matters not whether in fact he has a deep inferiority complex.

Accordingly, to understand that component in the significance of literary discourse which is independent of the explicit story, it is not necessary to postulate an embracing implicit story. All that is necessary is that we recognize clearly that authors can pretend to be what they are not, and can pretend to be doing what in fact they are not doing. (Furthermore, it is ironic that those who wish to account for that significance of *discourse* which is independent of *story* should do so by postulating an additional, embracing *story*!)

It may be added that not only is the postulation of a narrating character for every passage of literary fiction not necessary. It is useless. A commonplace of contemporary criticism is that narrators are not always reliable. But if the 'unreliability' of authors leads us to postulate narrators, then the unreliability of narrators must, by the same considerations, lead us to postulate narrators behind narrators, etc., to the point of dizziness or exhaustion.

So in summary, where the canonical twentieth-century view sees uniformity, I see a divide. The canonical view holds that every work of literary fiction has a narrating character, these narrating characters varying with respect to their obtrusiveness. I, on the contrary, hold that some literary works and passages of literary works have narrating characters, while others do not. In getting clear on the issues here, the decisive question to ask is always: what would things have to be like if the world of the work were to occur? Would there have to be someone speaking or inscribing all the words of the text, or would there not have to be such a person? And in arriving at the answer to this question we must keep firmly in mind that authors, like the rest of us, can pretend to be what they are not and do what they don't, and that they can fictionalize concerning themselves.

We have before us a convenient name for the structure of those pasages of fiction for which there is a narrating character. We can say that they have a *narrating-character structure*. It will be convenient to have a counterpart name for those passages of fiction for which there is no narrating character. Let us say that they have an *authorial-narrator structure*. And let us, along the same line, say that for a passage of fiction such as the one quoted from Henry James, there is a *narrator*. The narrator is the author. Henry James is the narrator of the passage quoted. He is not, though, the *speaker*, in the sense defined earlier, since for the world of the work to occur it is not necessary that James exist.

XI. *Point of View*

In the preceding section we saw that the significance of fictional discourse goes beyond story. In literary fiction there is always more to the workings and significance of the author's use of his words than just that thereby he projects a world. Consequently an adequate reading or analysis of fiction cannot concern itself solely with the projected world, nor just with the projected world plus the sounds of the words. For one thing, fictional discourse does not merely give us the story but it gives us the story *in a certain way*. But secondly, often there are dimensions to the significance of fictional discourse which even go beyond the fact that it gives us the story in a certain way.

I wish to look at a few of the more important dimensions of this supra-story significance of fictional discourse. Perhaps it is worth noting first, however, that the phenomenon to be analysed is customarily called 'point of view' by literary critics and theorists. One can see why it is thus called if it is remembered that the canonical way of construing the significance of fictional discourse beyond story is to attribute all such significance to the 'implied narrator' and his narratings. The phenomenon of discourse's supra-story significance is then understood simply as the narrator's point of view—his point of view *on* the projected world. Indeed, Percy Lubbock in his classic book, *The Craft of Fiction*, defines 'point of view' thus when he says, 'The whole intricate question of method, in the craft of fiction, I take to be governed by the question of the point of view—the question of the relation in which the narrator stands to the story.'[38]

Though I think it misleading to give the name 'point of view' to the phenomenon of discourse's supra-story significance, I shall none the less follow the tradition and speak thus on occasion. The phrase is misleading in two ways. For one thing, back of the phrase lies a certain way of construing the phenomenon of discourse's supra-story significance. And that construal of the phenomenon I regard as mistaken. But secondly, often the very words which serve to fictionally project a world also give expression to certain beliefs and attitudes concerning the *actual* world; and that, of course, is not to be

[38] Percy Lubbock, *The Craft of Fiction* (New York: Viking Press, 1957), p. 251.

fitted within the standard idea, formulated by Lubbock, that point of view concerns the narrator's relation to the story. I trust that, with these warnings before us, no harm will result from now and then conforming to standard parlance and using the phrase, 'point of view'. I mean by it simply, the supra-story significance and workings of fictional discourse.

So once again, what are some of the important dimensions of point of view? And here it won't be necessary to distinguish fiction of the narrating-character structure from the fiction of the authorial-narrator structure. Just as the author's discourse, in the authorial-narrator structure, has significance beyond story, so too the narrating character's discourse, in the narrating-character structure, has significance beyond that of serving to project a world. And a certain dimension to the significance of the one will always have its counterpart in the other. Of course, throughout it should be remembered that, for the authorial-narrator structure, we are concerned solely with how the author *presents* himself in the course of his narration.

(1) A point often made by the contemporary critic is that a world can be projected with varying degrees of reliability and unreliability. Our entire access to the world of the work is through the words of the authorial narrator or the narrating character. We flesh out the world by drawing conclusions about decisive events, about the psychological make-up of various characters, about features of the countryside in which the story is set, etc.; and all our extrapolations are based on the authorial narrator's or the narrating character's discourse. But how precarious the extrapolations sometimes are. The words of the narrating character, or of the author as he presents himself, may make it clear to us that he is demented, or neurotic, or a lying braggart, or unduly infected by eighteenth-century optimism, or trying desperately to block out some unpleasant reality; and all of that must be taken into account as we try to find our way into the world of the work.

(2) The particular way in which discourse projects a world for us often has a *temporal dimension* worth taking note of. In turn, this temporal dimension has a number of different facets. For one thing, narrations vary with respect to their *pacing*. Sometimes, as in Proust, the story is narrated with expansive leisureliness. Sometimes, as in Hemingway, with abrupt briskness.

Secondly, the events belonging to the projected world will always be narrated in a certain order—call it the *narrative temporal order*. And this order must be distinguished from the order in which they occur in the projected world—call that, the *worldly temporal order*. These two orders may nicely stay in phase. But then again, they may not. Something that happened earlier may be narrated later; that would be a flashback. And something that happened later may be narrated earlier; that would be a flash-forward. By combining the narrative and worldly temporal orders in different ways, a variety of different aesthetic effects are possible.

Thirdly, in the case of fiction of the narrating-character structure, there will be temporal order-relations of succession and simultaneity between the acts of narrating and the occurrences of the states of affairs indicated. Typically the states of affairs indicated will have occurred *before* the indicating of them—and the tense, accordingly, will be the past tense. But they may occur simultaneously, and then the tense will be the present tense. Further, it may be that the states of affairs indicated must have occurred at such-and-such a *distance* of time before the actions of indicating took place. David Copperfield's birth occurred at a more or less definite distance of time before his narrating of his birth.

(3) An important facet of a narrating character's or authorial narrator's point of view is that he exhibits knowledge of just certain sorts of states of affairs in his projected world, while of others he exhibits ignorance. Further, the narrating character will often exhibit the fact that he acquired the knowledge he does have in some particular way, of various alternative ways. Thus the point of view will have what I shall call a *knowledge/ignorance contour*.

For example, unless one ascribes to one's narrating character exceptional powers of extra-sensory perception, of his own inner life he will have direct knowledge but of the inner life of others he will either have no knowledge or only knowledge indirectly acquired. Further, if he is an adult and the fiction is realistic he will know things which a child typically does not know, and no doubt fail to perceive things which a child typically perceives. If he is a child, on the other hand, there will be characteristic lacunae in his knowledge (provided the fiction is realistic). And so forth. In these and other ways the knowledge and ignorance of the narrating character will be significantly different from that of the other characters. On this fact are grounded many of the striking effects, ironies, and surprising turns, of fiction.

On this matter of the knowledge/ignorance contour of point of view, it will be worth explicitly comparing the situation for authorial narrators to that for narrating characters. In authorial-narrator fiction of the old fashioned sort, the knowledge/ignorance contour of the point of view is not *particularized* to any of the characters in the world of the work. The authorial narrator in Fielding's novels, for example, exhibits *direct* knowledge of the inner life of all his characters. In the twentieth century, however, beginning especially with Henry James, authors have explored the possibility of telling the tale from the 'point of view'—i.e., with the knowledge/ignorance contour—of *one* of the characters, without making that character the *narrating* character, preserving instead the structure of authorial narrator. In this way the extreme constrictions of the narrating character device, of which I took note earlier, are skirted, while yet the tale is told with the knowledge/ignorance contour of one of the characters. Thus one of the considerable advantages of the narrating character device is preserved—namely, that of securing unity by telling all from the perspective of one of the characters. In the words of Henry James, one of the characters is chosen as the *centre* or the *reflector*; and then all is reported as he perceives and knows it.[39] With the reflector's inner life, for example, the authorial narrator has unmediated acquaintance; but everyone else is described as perceived and known from the outside, as the reflector with all his idiosyncrasies and limitations perceives and knows them. Of course it is possible to take yet one step beyond the single reflector device, and to describe *everyone* 'from the outside.' This would yield yet a different knowledge/ignorance contour.

(4) Another important facet of a narrating character's or authorial narrator's point of view is what might be called *focus*. He dwells on, stresses, focuses on, certain sorts of things and phenomena in the world of his work, and allows others to pass

[39] See Henry James's 'Preface to *The Wings of the Dove*,' in his *The Art of the Novel* (New York: C. Scribner's Sons, 1934).

unnoticed or unremarked. In dealing with people he focuses, say, on their psychological dynamics; in dealing with physical objects he focuses on their colours or their shapes; in dealing with political matters he focuses on the ethical dimensions; etc. A striking feature of André Bresson's films is his habit of often focusing on tiny physical details of the world of the work.

(5) A narrating character or authorial narrator will often evaluate, and exhibit an attitude towards, the characters, countries, events, etc., in his world. He may exhibit fondness or revulsion, admiration or disdain, for one of the characters. He may condemn, or he may approve, the structure of the society. If he sees God as underlying the reality of the projected world, he may urge obedience, or quest, or indifference, or defiance. If there is violence in his world, he may delight or grieve therein, approve or condemn. Probably no writer has ever been so explicit in his evaluation of characters and incidents in his projected world as Thackeray. And deliberately and intentionally so. Here is how Thackeray speaks of his intentions at the beginning of Chapter VIII of *Vanity Fair*:

And, as we bring our characters forward, I will ask leave, as a man and a brother, not only to introduce them, but occasionally to step down from the platform, and talk to them: if they are good and kindly, to love them and shake them by the hand: if they are silly, to laugh at them confidentially in the reader's sleeve: if they are wicked and heartless, to abuse them in the strongest terms which politeness admits of.

(6) Over and over the discourse of narrating character, and even more often, of authorial narrator, will function symbolically, or allusively, without anyone in the projected world taking something as symbolic or allusive. Literature is filled with characters who function in the discourse as Christ-figures, without anyone in the projected world taking them as such. And the banquet scene in Bunuel's film *Viridiana* is clearly presented in such a way as to allude to Leonardo's painting of the Last Supper. Nobody in the projected world, however, catches any such allusion.

(7) Lastly, the discourse of narrating character or authorial narrator often serves to express various beliefs and attitudes concerning the *actual world*. That became clear in Culler's

analysis of the Balzac passage. With the very words whereby he projects a world Balzac also presents himself as expressing the belief that certain large golden chains are made in Genoa.

XII. *The Temporality and Historicity of Worlds*

Time enters in various ways into the structure of the worlds of works of art; and those worlds themselves are in various ways tied down to the history of our actual world. Let us look briefly at this temporality and historicity of worlds of works of art.

States of affairs differ among themselves with respect to what might be called the *temporal modalities* of past, present, and future. Consider, for example, these states of affairs: *Rockefeller (presently) being Vice-President of the United States*, *Rockefeller having been Vice-President* and *Rockefeller going to be Vice-President*. The first of these occurs at some time if and only if at that time it *is* the case that Rockefeller is Vice-President. The second occurs at some time if and only if at that time it *was* the case that Rockefeller is Vice-President. The third occurs at some time if and only if at that time it *will be* the case that Rockefeller is Vice-President. *Present-tensed*, *past-tensed*, and *future-tensed* states of affairs we might call such as these.[40]

Not every state of affairs specified by using a participle in the present tense should be assumed to be a present-tensed state of affairs. *Napoleon (presently) invading Russia* is a present-tensed one. *Napoleon (sometime) invading Russia* is not. It may be called a *tense-indifferent* state of affairs. For it is necessarily true that it occurs at some time if and only if at that time it either *is or was or will be* the case that Napoleon is invading Russia.[41]

---

[40] For a detailed defence of the view that there are tensed states of affairs, see my essay 'God Everlasting' in *God and the Good*, edited by Orlebeke and Smedes (Eerdmans Publishing Co.: Grand Rapids, 1975). There the argument is conducted by using the language of propositions rather than that of states of affairs.

[41] Perhaps it's worth observing that on this criterion, all states of affairs which are *impossible* of *ever* occurring are tense-indifferent.

If a tense-indifferent states of affairs occurs at any time it occurs at all times; and conversely, if it fails to occur at any time it fails to occur at all times. For example, *Rockefeller (sometime) being Vice-President* occurs at all times or at no times. If at some time it is or was or will be the case that Rockefeller is Vice-President, then at all times that is the case. Whereas if at some time it neither is nor was nor will be the case that Rockefeller is Vice-President, then at no time is or was or will it be the case that he is. In fact, of course, *Rockefeller (sometime) being Vice-President* occurs at all times. What follows from this temporal-invariability of tense-indifferent states of affairs is that they cannot

Given these concepts we can now ask this question: does the basic structure of the world associated with some artefact of art consist exclusively of tense-indifferent states of affairs, or does it sometimes consist of, or include, tensed ones as well?

Consider once again our now familiar sentence from *Dead Souls*: 'While the server was still spelling out the note, Chichikov set out to look the town over.' One facet of the grammar of this sentence is that the verb is in the past tense. Keeping this in mind, let us ask: what state of affairs is Gogol with his sentence inviting us to consider? That a person named 'Chichikov' *sometime* sets out to look the town over? Surely not. What Gogol said is that Chichikov *set* out. What he thereby invited us to consider is not Chichikov's *sometime* setting out but Chichikov's *having set out*. The sentence quoted is wholly typical of the basic grammatical structure of *Dead Souls*. Accordingly the basic structure of the world of *Dead Souls* is in the temporal modality of the past. Gogol casts some of what he has his characters *say* into other tenses. But the encompassing framework of what he indicates consists entirely of past-tensed states of affairs. In that way, temporal modality is inherent in the basic structure of the world of his artefact.

---

recur—that is, they cannot occur at some time and then at some later time not occur and then at some yet later time again occur.

If we wish to find states of affairs which at some times are occurring and at other times are not, we shall have to look to tensed states of affairs. *Rockefeller's (presently) being Vice-President* is occurring (1975). But two years ago it was not occurring; and no doubt ten years hence it will not be occurring. Likewise *Rockefeller's having been Vice-President* was not occurring a year ago but now is occurring (understanding the claim that it is occurring in such a way that the claim is true if and only if at any time in the past 'Rockefeller is Vice-President' was true). And *Rockefeller's going to be Vice-President* will not be occurring ten years hence but now is (understanding the claim that it will be occurring in such a way that the claim is true if and only if at any time in the future 'Rockefeller is Vice-President' will be true). But though it is among tensed states of affairs that we shall have to look if we are to find ones which vary across time as to their occurrence, it is not the case that all tensed ones do thus vary. For example, the present-tensed state of affairs, *7's (presently) being prime*, does not.

Because the present-tensed state of affairs of *7's (presently) being prime* cannot vary across time as to its occurrence, it cannot recur. On the other hand, it is only among present-tensed states of affairs that we will find ones which are capable of recurring. A past-tensed state of affairs such as *Napoleon's having invaded Russia* occurs for the first time at a certain point in time and then inescapably occurs at all times thereafter. And a future-tensed state of affairs such as *Napoleon's going to invade Russia* occurs at all times until at a certain point Napoleon is for the last time invading Russia and then it never again occurs. But *Napoleon's (presently) invading Russia* can occur for a while, cease to occur, and then once again take up occurring.

The worlds of dramatic performances are similar in that their basic structure also consists of tensed states of affairs. There is this difference, though: the world projected by a dramatic performance is always, in its basic structure, in the modality of the *present*. What we are invited to consider is various present-tensed states of affairs. The reason lies in the intrinsic nature of the medium. The medium of the dramatic performance is role-playing. The actor plays the role of a certain character, thereby delineating that character. It is exclusively by virtue of the actor's *doing* and *being* various things in the course of the performance—not by virtue of his *having* done or been various things previously, or *going to* do or be various things in the future—that the character he plays is delineated as doing and being various things.[42] And the character he plays is delineated as *doing* and *being* those things—not as having done and been them, nor as going to do and be them. It is by virtue of Maggie Smith at some time during the performance pretending to shoot herself that the work's world thereby projected includes the state of affairs of *someone named 'Hedda Gabler' (presently) shooting herself*. Of course, Maggie Smith may represent Hedda Gabler as reporting that so-and-so *has* occurred. And then, if Hedda is to be taken as speaking the truth, the world of the work will include a certain past-tense state of affairs. None the less, Maggie Smith will *now* do something which represents Hedda as *presently* saying that. The worlds projected by dramatic performances are intrinsically contemporaneous in their basic structure.

We saw that the world of *Dead Souls* is retrospective in its basic structure. But is that always true of literary fiction? Is literary fiction, in contrast to drama, intrinsically retrospective? No. Here, for example, is the opening of the story 'Four Summers' by Joyce Carol Oates:

It is some kind of special day. 'Where's Sissie?' Ma says. Her face gets sharp, she is frightened. When I run around her chair she laughs and hugs me. She is pretty when she laughs. Her hair is long and pretty.

We are sitting at the best table of all, out near the water. The sun is warm and the air smells nice. Daddy is coming back from the building

---

[42] This is not fully accurate. Strictly, it is not true that the *character* is delineated as doing or being those things. The character is delineated as having those actions and those properties *essential within* it (or, *analytic within* it).

with some glasses of beer, held in his arms. He makes a grunting noise when he sits down.

'Is the lake deep?' I ask them.

The story continues in this fashion, with the basic verbs all in the present tense. Accordingly we have here a piece of literary fiction the basic structure of whose world is in the temporal modality of the present. I know of no examples whose basic structure is in the temporal modality of the future. But that too is surely possible. Nothing in the *structure* of literary fiction confines the basic structure of the worlds projected to the temporal modality of past or present.

We can note much more briefly two other ways in which temporality enters into the structure of the world of works. The world of a work may—as we say—'cover a certain length of time'. It may have a certain temporal duration intrinsic to it. It is not hard to see what that comes to: the *duration* of a work's world (where that is a strand) is the length of time it would take for the world of the work to occur. Secondly, as we saw already in the preceding section, the world of a work may have temporal *succession* intrinsic to it. That is to say, among the states of affairs included in the world of the work there may be pairs such that one member of the pair must occur before the other if the work's world is to occur.[43]

We have seen the various ways in which temporality enters into the structure of works' worlds. Let us now move outside that internal structure. Characteristically the fictioneer does not allow his projected world to flutter loose from the events of our actual history. Not only are temporal modality, duration,

---

[43] Here is the place to note that there are two other ways in which temporal succession enters importantly into the arts. Certain artefacts of art are such that they have temporal parts; and if so, there will be succession among the parts. Performances of musical works are like that. The proof that a performance has temporal parts is that it is half over at a certain time. Accordingly, its second half succeeds its first half. The text of a literary work is different. And then also the fact that our apprehension of the works and worlds of art is usually (if not always) achieved by a succession of acts of noticing is a third way in which succession enters into the arts. Thus we *successively* peruse the pages of a novel's text which itself exists *non-successively*, and thereby we become acquainted with the novel's world which has *succession* intrinsic to it.

When people speak of 'the temporal arts', it seems to be usually those arts whose artefacts have temporal parts that they have in mind. Of course, certain arts like literature are such that one category of their artefacts (e.g., texts) do not have temporal parts and another category of their artefacts (reading aloud of texts) do have temporal parts.

and succession often intrinsic to the world of his work. The
world as a whole is often tied down to actual history, and that in
two ways. It may be *anchored to certain events* of history, and it may
be *set within* a certain stretch of history. Let us look into these
two phenomena, beginning with anchoring.

Neither duration nor succession is intrinsic to what is indicated by Piero's *Flagellation of Christ*. For this painting, like all
paintings, presents us directly only with a momentary look of
things; it is from this that we must do our extrapolating. (Of
course the entire world of this painting, including as it does
states of affairs beyond those directly indicated, most certainly
does have duration and succession intrinsic to it.) None the less,
this world is anchored to the historical event of Christ's flagellation. It could not occur without that event which was Christ's
flagellation taking place (existing). By contrast, modality,
duration, and succession are surely all intrinsic to what is
indicated by Tolstoy's *War and Peace*. And in addition to such
internal, intrinsic temporality, the world of the work is
anchored to various of the events of history—pre-eminently of
course to Napoleon's invasion of Russia. The world of the work
could not occur without that historical event having taken
place. For instance, in the world of the work is Pierre's fleeing
Leningrad on account of Napoleon's attack on the city. And
that state of affairs could not occur without there having been
that event of Napoleon's attack on Leningrad. In that way the
world of *War and Peace* is anchored to the wartime events of
Napoleon's invasion.

Those were comments on the phenomenon of a work's world
being anchored to the events of our world's history. To see, by
contrast, what constitutes the *setting* of a work's world, let us
again take an actual example, the setting of Thomas Mann's
story *Death in Venice*. We can gather what the setting is from the
fact that the story is dated 1911, and from the fact that its
opening sentences are these:

Gustave Aschenbach—or von Aschenbach, as he had been known
officially since his fiftieth birthday—had set out alone from his house
in Prince Regent Street, Munich, for an extended walk. It was a
spring afternoon in that year of grace 19—, when Europe sat upon the
anxious seat beneath a menace that hung over its head for months.

From these two facts and from what follows in the story we know that Mann set his story in the opening decade of our century. The simplest and most natural way to understand this is to understand it as consisting in the fact that if the world of this work were to occur, it would have to occur (would have to have occurred) in the first decade of our century. In general we can say this: a strand of a work's world is *set within* the time-stretch bounded by times t_1 and t_2 just in case if the world of the work were to occur, it would have to occur in the time-stretch bounded by t_1 and t_2.

Sometimes an author indicates—mentions or suggests—the setting of his work's world. But often he does not. And then we must arrive at a knowledge of the setting by the process of extrapolation. On the basis of the clothes that the author indicates his characters as wearing, the things he indicates them as knowing, etc., we extrapolate to the story's setting.

The events to which some work's world is anchored need not take place within the setting of that work's world. From Renaissance times we have many representations of Christ's birth which, while anchored to that event, are set within a stretch of time roughly simultaneous with the time of the artist's life. Furthermore, the temporal modality of a work is independent both of its anchoring and of its setting. A world may be projected whose temporal mode is that of contemporaneity, which is set wholly within a stretch of time future with respect to the act of projecting, and which is anchored to events of the past. A 1975 performance of a stage adaptation of *1984* would be an example. In such combinations there are, of course, a variety of temporal impossibilities.

XIII. *Postlude*

I have followed the lead of fiction in exploring the nature of a work's world. And within the genus fiction I have mainly followed the lead of novelistic fiction. But lest anyone draw mistaken conclusions as to the significance of our discussion thus far, let it be noted that an understanding of a fictional work's world leaves us short of an understanding of the nature of fiction. For the concept of a work's world can be applied not only to works of fiction but also, say, to works of history. William Shirer, by way of his *Rise and Fall of the Third Reich*, projected a world. The world he projected includes those states of affairs which he indicated plus those which can be extrapolated therefrom. Works of fiction are not unique in having worlds.

Nor are they unique in that their worlds are selected creatively. The responsible historian does indeed confine himself, in what he indicates, to what he believes has occurred. Not so the liar. The liar in what he indicates is as creative as the fictioneer. Indeed, we speak of a lie as 'a fiction'. Yet the fictioneer is not a liar. For he, unlike the liar, 'nothing affirmeth'.

So we have returned to our beginning. The historian and the liar are similar to the writer and teller of fiction in that they too indicate states of affairs, thereby projecting a world. They are different in that they something affirm. But what then does the fictioneer do if he 'nothing affirmeth'? The answer is that he *fictionally*, rather than assertively, projects a world. But this is uninformative. For we do not yet know what it is to use an artefact to fictionally project a world. Our understanding of the nature of fiction hangs on that. Until we understand that we will not understand what Gogol was doing with the text of *Dead Souls*. Neither will we understand what Botticelli was doing with the picture *Birth of Venus*. For Botticelli with a picture, like Gogol with sentences, fictionally projected a world.

XIV *Appendix: Ontology Consolidated*

In our discussion in this Part, a somewhat elaborate ontological theory has been presupposed. In closing out this phase of our discussion I propose to elucidate the general structure of this background theory.

I have assumed, throughout, that there are states of affairs. Furthermore, I have assumed that states of affairs are identical with propositions. If this latter assumption is indeed true, then it is not difficult to formulate a criterion for the identity of states of affairs. It will of course be the same as a criterion for the identity of propositions.

What comes to mind first of all as a criterion for the identity of propositions is that P and P^* are identical just in case it is impossible that one of them be true and the other false. But this, quite obviously, does not differentiate propositions finely enough. For a consequence of the criterion is that there is just one necessarily true proposition and just one necessarily false one.

Now propositions can be picked out from other entities as those capable of being asserted. And by presupposing this fact, a better criterion can be formulated thus:

P is identical with P^* just in case it is impossible that someone should assert P and not thereby have asserted P^*, and conversely.

For example, it is impossible that someone should assert that Socrates is wise, and not thereby have asserted that wisdom is a characteristic of Socrates. To assert these is to make the very same claim on actuality. Accordingly these are identical propositions. And on the assumption that the state of affairs of *Socrates being wise* is identical with the proposition that Socrates is wise, and that the state of affairs of *wisdom being a characteristic of Socrates* is identical with the proposition that wisdom is a characteristic of Socrates, it follows of course that these states of affairs are also identical.

In the case of states of affairs it is important to distinguish between their existing and their occurring. If a state of affairs exists at all, it exists necessarily and everlastingly. But of those that exist, some are capable of occurring and some not; some do occur and some do not; and some occur necessarily and some contingently.

Now in the preceding discussion I have assumed not only that there are states of affairs. I have also assumed that there are *occurrences* of states of affairs. And, stretching the sense of the word 'event', I have called all occurrences of states of affairs, *events*. I sneeze at a certain time. In doing so, the state of affairs of me (presently) sneezing occurs. But in doing so, what also happens is that a particular sneeze, an occurrence of the state of affairs of me (presently) sneezing, comes into existence (i.e., takes place), consisting in my actually performing the action of sneezing. Again, Napoleon invaded Russia. In his doing so, the state of affairs of Napoleon (presently) invading Russia occurred. But in his doing so what also happened was that a particular invasion, an occurrence of the state of affairs of Napoleon (presently) invading Russia, took place, consisting in Napoleon's actually performing the action of invading Russia.

Sneezes, invasions, blottings of lines, flagellations, cases of being Vice-President, all are events.

For events there is no distinction similar to that between the occurring and the existing of states of affairs. An event takes place (exists) at or within a certain time, and that is the end of the matter. Consequently events are neither possible nor impossible in any way similar to that in which states of affairs are possible and impossible—i.e., possible *of occurring* and impossible *of occurring*. Of course, for some descriptions it is possible that there *be* events of those descriptions; and for other descriptions, it is impossible that there *be* events of those descriptions. And then too, there is a distinction to be made between those events which exist everlastingly and necessarily—an occurrence of 3 being prime would be an example—and those which exist only temporarily and contingently—an occurrence of Carter being President would be an example.

An event consists of (i.e., *is*) an entity's *actually having* a certain property, or one or more entities' *actually standing in* a certain relation. In that way, too, events differ from states of affairs. The state of affairs of Rockefeller being President does not consist of Rockefeller *actually having* the property of being President; for it exists whether or not Rockefeller ever actually has that property. But if there had been an occurrence of that state of affairs, the event constituting that occurrence, viz., Rockefeller being President, would have consisted of Rockefeller actually having the property of being President.

Naturally one is suspicious of an ontology which includes both states of affairs and events. If we allow the state of affairs of John running, is it not sufficient to hold that this occurs at certain times? Why hold that at or within the time of its occurring there *is* in addition an occurrence of it—a particular concrete event consisting of John's actually running? Or if we hold that there are such concrete events as John's actually running, taking place at or within certain times, why hold that there is in addition the everlastingly existing state of affairs of John running? If we hold that there are concrete events, why not make do without states of affairs for them to be occurrences of?

To the latter question—why not make do without states of affairs—my answer is that I would not know how even *to begin* explicating the concept of the world of a work of art without appealing to states of affairs. To the former question—why not make do without events if one has states of affairs in one's ontology—my answer is less decisive. In my paper, 'Can Ontology Do Without Events?'[44] I discuss Roderick Chisholm's claim that an ontology which includes states of affairs can do without events—that is, without occurrences of those states of affairs. In that paper I do not profess to *show* that such an ontology is untenable. Rather I claim to show that, at this point in the progress of philosophical discussion, we have no good reason to think that it *is* tenable—no good reason to think that an ontology which includes states of affairs will be adequate if it excludes occurrences of those states of affairs; and *some* reason to think it will not be adequate. So it is more for the sake of convenience than for the sake of settled philosophical conviction that, in the foregoing, I have assumed the existence of events.

The concept of a kind, or type, of which I made extensive use in Part One, can be put to use here in giving us a unified theory of predicables and primitive states of affairs. All such entities, it seems to me, are kinds—kinds of events. Not, that is, events of certain kinds but rather certain *event-kinds*. Specifically, a state of affairs is a kind whose examples are or would be events which are occurrences of that state of affairs. And likewise a predicable is a kind whose examples are or would be events which are instances of that predicable. This needs, of course, a bit of explaining.

Begin with events. An event consisting of my actually sneezing took place yesterday. Another event consisting of my actually sneezing took place today. Both are occurrences of the state of affairs of *me (presently) sneezing*. And my proposal is that this state of affairs is identical with the kind: *occurrence of me (presently) sneezing*.

This particular state of affairs does in fact have occurrences. Others of course do not; and of these, some could not. But both these facts are compatible with the claim that a state of affairs is identical with the kind whose examples would be occurrences of that state of affairs. For as we saw in Part One, there are impossible kinds—ones incapable of being exampled. And

[44] In *Essays on the Philosophy of Roderick M. Chisholm*, edited by Ernest Sosa (Rodopi: Amsterdam, 1979), pp. 177–205.

there are kinds which as a matter of contingent fact go forever unexampled. In the other direction, many of those states of affairs which could have occurrences could have multiple occurrences. Such might be called *universals*.

Now consider, in addition to the two events of my actually sneezing, one of which took place yesterday and the other today, the event of Kit's actually sneezing, which took place yesterday. This is an occurrence of the state of affairs, *Kit (presently) sneezing*. And all three of these sneezings are instances of the attribute *sneezing*. My proposal is that this attribute is identical with the kind: Instance Of *Sneezing*. This particular attribute actually has instances. Others, though, do not, and some of them could not have instances. Of those which could have instances, many could have multiple instances. These may accordingly be called *universals*.

If these proposals are correct, then attributes and states of affairs are alike in being event-kinds. But there is this obvious difference between them. An event which is an instance of some attribute at a certain time consists, by virtue of that, in some things actually having that property or performing that action at that time. Or as I shall say, by virtue of that it consists of some thing's actually *exemplifying* that attribute at that time. That is not the case for states of affairs. Things do not have or perform them. The attribute of *sneezing* has, as it were, a 'gap' in it. That 'gap' is filled by me in the case of the state of affairs of *me sneezing*, by Kit in the case of the state of affairs of *Kit sneezing*, etc. Let us, to capture this difference, say that states of affairs are 0-degree event-kinds and that attributes are 1-degree event-kinds. Further, let us say that the unit-set of that thing which, for a given instance of an attribute A, exemplifies the attribute, is *the exemplification set for that instance of the attribute A*.

Relations are also event-kinds. But they are multiple-degree kinds. To see in what sense this is true, consider any relation R. If some event were an instance of R it would, by virtue of that, consist in some entity x_1 bearing R to entities $x_2 \ldots x_n$. R is then an event-kind of whatever degree is n. Take, for example, the relation *being father of*. An event which is an instance of this consists, by virtue of that, in some entity x_1 bearing the relation of *being father of* to some entity x_2. The relation is accordingly a 2-degree event-kind. By contrast, the relational property of *me being father of* is a 1-degree event-kind; and the state of affairs of *me being father of Kit* is a 0-degree event-kind.

Now consider any event which is an instance of some relation *R*. That event will, by virtue of that, consist in some entities bearing *R* to each other. Let us, in an obvious analogue to what we said about attributes, call the set of those entities, *the exemplification set for that instance of R*. The exemplification sets for instances of *being father of* will always have two distinct entities as members. That for every instance of *being identical with* will have just one entity as member.

Some of these event-kinds which are predicables are capable of having multiple exemplification sets for their instances (or, to put it more simply but less explicitly, some are capable of being multiply exemplified). Some are not. *Sneezing* is, so is *kicking*. *Being sole survivor of the first and only sinking of the 'Titanic'* is not. One might call those event-kinds which are capable of having multiple exemplification sets for their instances, *universals*. This is, in fact, the traditional concept of a universal: a universal is what is capable of being predicated truly of many. But then it must be clearly noticed that this is a different concept of a universal from that introduced earlier. On the concept earlier introduced, something is a universal just in case it is an event-kind capable of having multiple occurrences. On this concept, something is a universal just in case it is an event-kind capable of having multiple exemplification sets for its instances.

Let us return to the 1-degree event-kind, *sneezing*. Not only do various *events* bear to this the relation of being instances of it. Also the various primitive states of affairs of the form *x* sneezing—for example, *me sneezing* and *Kit sneezing*—bear some relation to it. Let us say that each of these states of affairs is a *completion* of sneezing. And, more generally, for every event-kind of degree $n + 1$, there is a set of event-kinds of degree n whose members are completions of that event-kind. For some property, *being ϕ*, the set consists of all states of affairs of the form *x being ϕ*. For some 2-degree relation *R*, it consists of all 1-degree properties of the form *x having R to* or *having R to y*, etc. Properties and relations do not vary across time as to the set of their completions. In particular, they do not vary in this respect depending on whether their completions have occurrences and instances or not.

What must above all be allowed to emerge from this discussion is that the relations *being an occurrence of, being an instance of, exemplifying,* and *being a completion of,* are intimately connected, yet distinct. Both the intimacy and the distinctness must be respected if ontological clarity is to be attained.

The events which are the occurrences of states of affairs are of course the very same events which are the instances of predicables. Thus certain states of affairs will bear to certain attributes the relation of being included within them. The relation was defined already in Part One: one kind *K* is included within another *K** if and only if it is impossible that something should be an example of *K* and not of *K**. Thus the state of affairs of *me sneezing* is included within the property of *sneezing*. What must be clearly seen, if this relationship of inclusion is to be understood, is that *me sneezing* is not included within *sneezing* because the former is an instance of the latter, but because nothing could be an example of the former which is not also an example of the latter. For the state of affairs of *me sneezing* is not an instance of *sneezing*. It is a completion of it.

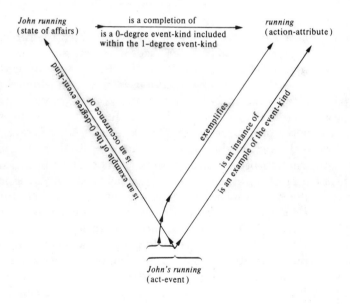

PART FOUR

Projection of Worlds with Works

I. *Preliminaries*

Our main aim in this essay is to understand the nature of world projection as it occurs in the arts. We have looked at the nature of the artefacts by the use of which this action takes place. We have looked at the nature of the worlds projected. We are ready now to explore the nature of the action itself—*projection*.

Our aim will be to construct a theory of world projection which is fully general in two different directions. In the first place, since this action occurs in all the arts, the theory of world projection to be proposed must apply to all cases of world projection *no matter what the artistic medium* in which the projection takes place—be it painting, sculpture, music, dramatic role-playing, or whatever. Secondly, the theory must apply to all cases of world projection *no matter what the mood* in which that projection takes place. The theory must apply to *fictional* world projection, as in Gogol's *Dead Souls*. But equally it must apply to *assertive* world projection, as in John Donne's *Divine Sonnets*.

Here at the very beginning we face a choice fundamental for the construction of our theory. Shall we choose as our basic concept that of an artist producing or using an *artefact which projects* some world, or shall we choose as our basic concept that of an *artist projecting* some world by producing or using an artefact? That is, shall the basic concept of world-projection be that of a relational property belonging to artefacts, these artefacts being the object of some action on the part of the artist; or shall it be that of an action on the part of artists, who perform it by way of performing some other action on the artefact?

To simplify the consideration of this choice, let us for the moment confine our attention to literary artefacts. Suppose we chose the former strategy. Then a first attempt to find a form of sentence satisfactory for describing specific cases of world-projection in the arts might look like this:

(1) Artist A produced (or used) text T which in language L projects the world W.

To see that this will not do, however, notice that in general there *is no* world uniquely related to a text as that world which the text projects. The situation which confronts us is not that of a sequence of words which, in a given language, uniquely projects a world. At best it is that of a sequence of words which, in a given language, is capable of being used on various occasions in such a way that, on one such, it projects *one* world, and on another such, another. World-projection, if ascribed to words, is not just language-relative but occasion-relative as well.

There are ways in which one can attempt to cope with this fact, without deserting this strategy and taking as basic the concept of the *artist* projecting a world. One such way would be to hold that that which projects a world is not a sequence of words but rather some inscription or utterance of a sequence of words—some *token* of that *type* which is a word-sequence. The thought is that such entities are as occasion-specific in their existence as world-projection is occasion-relative.

Now one might well wonder how we are to think of *a language*, if it is to consist of such perishing entities as word-utterances. But let us here forgo pressing this ontological difficulty, to observe that in fact one does not in this manner secure unique specification. For consider some inscription of a word-sequence, an inscription which supposedly uniquely projects world W in language L. The fact that this inscription exists at some time, and uniquely projects W in L, does not yet uniquely determine W as what on that occasion is projected. What must be added is that L is *the language used* on that occasion. Which language is in use itself varies from occasion to occasion.

I think it must be concluded that the person who wishes to take as basic for his theory the phenomenon of artefacts projecting worlds, rather than that of artists projecting worlds, should cease to think of projection as a three-term relation holding between artefact and world, relative to a language, and should instead think of it as a multi-term relation, relative as well to various ways and circumstances of using artefacts (usages). Relative to some specific usage U, text T in language L projects world W; whereas relative to some other usage U^*, text T in language L projects W^*. Our (1) then becomes this:

(1*) Artist A performed U on text T when language L was in effect for him; and text T with respect to U and L, when L is in effect for the one who produces T, projects world W.

But this still will not do as the basic form of sentences describing cases of world-projection. For what must now be observed is that worlds are projected with different *stances*, in different *moods*: a world can be *assertively* projected; that is, the various states of affairs indicated can be asserted. Likewise, a world can be *fictionally* projected. And so on. But how can this fact be acknowledged by those who wish to treat projection as fundamentally a relation of artefact to world (relative to language and usage)? For the basic concept of assertion is surely that of an action performed by a human being. No doubt one can establish a derivative sense for 'assert', such that sentences assert. But that would be parasitic on the phenomenon of human beings asserting. Words can stand for, signify, refer, denote. What they cannot do, in any basic sense, is assert.

Accordingly I shall take as my basic concept of world-projection that of an action performed by human beings, an action performed always by way of performing some other action. To describe a specific case of world-projection in the arts we can always use a sentence of the form:

(2) Artist A projects world W by performing action ϕ.

Thus the theory that I shall develop is, at bottom, a theory of actions rather than a theory of symbols (signs). It stands more in the twentieth-century tradition of theories of speech actions (Austin, Searle, *et al.*) than in the twentieth-century tradition of semiotic theories of art (Langer, Goodman, *et al.*).

As preliminary to presenting my formal theory, let me sketch out, in an informal way, the line of thought to be followed. Suppose I assert that the door is closed, and that I do so by uttering, in appropriate manner and circumstance, the English sentence 'The door is closed.' I would then have performed two distinct actions, the action of asserting that the door is closed and the action of uttering the English sentence 'The door is closed.'

That these are distinct actions is proved by the fact that one can be performed without performing the other—indeed, each can be performed without the other. One can utter those English words without making that assertion. One might, for instance, offer them as an example of some point about the English language. But equally one can make that assertion by uttering other English words—or by uttering words from some other language.

In addition to observing the distinctness of these actions we must observe their connection in this case. *By* my performance of the action of uttering I perform the action of asserting. The mode of connection is *count*-generation. My uttering those words counts as my making that assertion.

Once we see that asserting that the door is closed is an action which can be count-generated by many different sentence-utterings, then it is but a small step to the realization that it can be performed without the use of words at all. One can make assertions with semaphores, with smoke-signals, with winks, with gestures—and with works of art.

Let us go back once more to that action of asserting that the door is closed. In addition to asserting that the door is closed I can ask whether the door is closed, I can command that the door be closed, etc.; and all of such actions can be performed by the utterings of sentences. In each such case I would be dealing with the same state of affairs—the door's being closed. But I would be dealing with it in different ways. I would be taking up toward it various different stances. What Sidney said, in effect, was that the poet (fictioneer) does not take up an assertive stance toward the states of affairs with which he deals.

Now in the preceding paragraph we saw that one can take up an assertive stance toward some state of affairs not only by uttering some bit of language but by other means as well. So, too, however, one can take up some *non*-assertive stance toward some state of affairs by means other than uttering some bit of language. In particular, by showing a picture of a closed door to someone, in the appropriate manner and circumstance, one can issue the command to close the door.

Those are the clues that I shall be following out. World-projection is an action. And language and art alike can be used to perform this action. This implies, in terms of Sassure's famous distinction, that it is language as *parole* rather than language as *langue* that is basic for our theory. Correspondingly, it implies that our *use* of art works rather than those works *as such* is basic.

II. *One Act Counting as Another*

By inscribing words on paper and thus composing the text of *Dead Souls* Gogol performed the action of fictionally projecting a world. Likewise, by applying paint to canvas and thus creating his *Birth of Venus* Botticelli performed the action of fictionally projecting a world. Those are two occurrences of the action I wish to explore. *Fictional* projection, though, is but one of many modes of world projection that occur in the arts; and it is with world projection in general that we are concerned.

Always one projects a world by doing something else: by inscribing words on paper, by applying paint to canvas, or whatever. An occurrence of world projection is never a foundational but always a generated act. Further, it is always an act which is *count*-generated. So it is with an analysis of this species of act-generation that I begin.

A review of a few of the points made in the Part One will be helpful. I defined 'to generate' in such a way that the claim that an act of x's ϕing generated an act of x's ψ-ing is equivalent to the claim that x ψ-ed by ϕ-ing. And I differentiated various species of act-generation. One of these I called 'count-generation'. I said that an agent P *count*-generates ψ-ing by ϕ-ing at t if and only if:

(i) P generates ψ-ing by ϕ-ing at t, and
(ii) P's act of performing the action of ϕ-ing counts as an act of P's ψ-ing.

From there I went on to explain the count-generation of *acts* (as opposed to actions) thus: If P count-generates ψ-ing by ϕ-ing at t, then the act of P's ϕ-ing at t count-generates an act of

P's ψ-ing. But I left the matter at this point. I offered no analysis of what it is for P's act of performing the action of ϕ-ing to count as an act of his ψ-ing. That is what needs doing now.

What is it for P's act of performing the action of ϕ-ing to *count as* an act of P's ψ-ing? Specifically, what is it for my act of uttering the English sentence 'would you open the door?' to *count as* my issuing the request to open the door? What is it for one's performance of one action to *count as* one's performance of another?

Before we begin, it would be well to observe that the English phrase 'counts as' is also used in a sense quite different from that with which I am here working. For example, we might say of someone going through certain motions that what he is doing counts as dancing a jig. In such a case, we are not claiming that two distinct actions stand in the relation of someone performing the one by performing the other. Rather we are claiming that that which he is doing, that *act*, that *event*, is an instance of the *action* of dancing a jig. Somewhat similarly, one might say of some living thing of a primitive sort that it counts as an animal. In doing so, one would be claiming that it is an example of animal life, that it is an example of an animal, or in short, that it is an animal. Our concern in this section is exclusively with counting-as construed as action-generation (and act-generation) of a certain sort.

The conventional wisdom as to the nature of count-generation—if a pun will be pardoned—is that this relation depends essentially on the existence of *conventions*. That, for example, is the view of Alvin Goldman. That species of act- and action-generation which I call count-generation, Goldman chooses to call *conventional* generation. And then he goes on to say this: 'Conventional generation is characterized by the existence of rules, conventions, or social practices in virtue of which an Act A' can be ascribed to an agent S, given his performance of another act, A.' As examples of conventional generation Goldman then gives these, among others: S's signalling for a turn by S's extending his arm out the car window; and S's checkmating his opponent by S's moving his queen to king's knight 7. And then he continues: 'In each of these cases there is a rule, R, according to which S's performance of A justifies the further ascription of A' to S. In the first example there is the rule, "extending one's arm out the car window while driving counts as signalling for a turn." ' And then he concludes, 'With these examples in mind, we can state the following condition for conventional generation. Act-token A of agent S conventionally generates act-token A' of agent S only if the performance of A in circumstances C (possibly null), together with a rule R saying that A done in C counts as A', guarantees the performance of A'.'[1]

It will be noticed that this passage in Goldman cannot be viewed as *explaining* what it is for an act A to count as an act B. Viewed thus, what is said is circular. Rather, the passage simply puts forth the thesis that an act A will count as an act B only if there is a rule to the effect that if some action of which A is an instance is performed in such-and-such a circumstance, then that act will count as an instance of a certain other action. And *rules* Goldman seems to regard as identical with conventions, or as he also calls them, social practices.

One finds a similar claim in John Searle's book, *Speech Acts*. Searle says this, for example, 'Such facts as are recorded in my above group of statements I propose to call *institutional facts* ... [T]heir existence ... presupposes the existence of certain human institutions. It is only given the institution of marriage that certain forms of behaviour constitute Mr Smith's marrying Miss Jones. Similarly, it is only given the institution of baseball that certain movements by certain men constitute the Dodgers beating the Giants 3 to 2 in eleven innings ... These "institutions" are systems of constitutive rules. Every institutional fact is underlain by a (system of) rule(s) of the form "X counts as Y in context C".'[2] Here too it will be noticed that we are not provided with an *analysis* of what it is for act A to count as act B. Rather we are presented with the thesis that a person's performance of action X *does* count as his performance of action Y only if there is a rule to the effect that when someone performs X in circumstances of sort C, then that *counts as* his performance of B.

I think it is not the case that an act A does count as an act B only if there is some rule, or convention, of the indicated sort in effect. But rather than attacking directly that thesis of Goldman and of Searle, I shall let my view on the matter emerge as a

[1] Goldman, *A Theory of Human Action*, pp. 25–6.
[2] John Searle, *Speech Acts* (Cambridge University Press: Cambridge, 1970), pp. 51–2.

consequence of my general analysis of count-generation. Let us turn then to that.

Perhaps it will help the reader follow the drift of the discussion if I state in advance, in preliminary and unqualified fashion, my main thesis. It is this: For someone to count-generate ψ-ing by ϕ-ing is for that person to acquire, upon performing the action of ϕ-ing, the rights and responsibilities connected with the action of ψ-ing. My proposal will be that at the centre of the phenomenon of act A counting as act B is not the existence of rules and conventions, also not the existence of intentions, but rather the acquisition of rights and responsibilities. What I shall offer, in short, is a *normative* analysis of count-generation. Convention and intention do indeed play a role, and we shall see what that role is. But they are not at the centre.

Before we set foot on the path of our analysis, it will be helpful to have in hand a few examples.

(1) I and my wife sign our names to the completed Internal Revenue Service form. Our doing so counts as our declaring that the statements made therein are true, complete, and correct to the best of our knowledge and belief.

(2) Pete, who is the coach, touches his left hand to his tongue. His doing so counts as his commanding the batter to bunt.[3]

(3) Rich switches on the left side blinkers. His doing so counts as his signalling that he is going to turn left.

(4) Michael reaches the opposite side first. His doing so counts as his winning the game.

Begin by looking at the second of these examples, that in which Pete's touching left hand to tongue counts as his commanding the batter to bunt. The action of commanding a batter to bunt has certain prima facie rights and responsibilities attached thereto. For example, nothing contravening, it ought to be brought about only if the signaller has been paying reasonably close attention to the game and genuinely believes that the best strategy at this point would be for the batter to bunt. And now, if at

---

[3] For those among my readers who are not well acquainted with baseball, I should explain that for a batter to bunt is to deliberately hit the ball so that it will go only a short distance from home plate, but within bounds.

some time Pete's performing the action of touching left hand to tongue would count as his performing the action of instructing the batter to bunt, then the prima facie rights and responsibilities which someone would have if he performed the latter action would accrue to Pete if he performed the former. Then at the time in question (nothing contravening) Pete ought to touch left hand to tongue only if he has been paying reasonably close attention to the game and genuinely believes that the best strategy at this point would be for the batter to bunt. What otherwise would be an utterly innocuous act, Pete's touching his left hand to his tongue, would become loaded with all the significance borne by instructing the batter to bunt.

Again, suppose that on some occasion my performing the action of uttering the sounds 'Winter is over' counts as my performing the action of asserting that winter is over. One of the prima facie responsibilities attached to the action of asserting that winter is over is that one ought to perform it only if one believes that winter is over. Thus, given the counting-as situation which holds, I ought (nothing contravening) to perform the action of making the sounds 'Winter is over' only if I believe that winter is over.

The point can be generalized. But first it should be noted that a sentence of the form 'an act of x's ϕ-ing would count as an act of x's ψ-ing' may express a true proposition at some times and a false one at others. For example, when Pete is driving home after the game, then it is no longer true that his touching left hand to tongue would count as an act of his instructing the batter to bunt.

The generalization then is this:

Thesis I: If at t an act of x's ϕ-ing would count as an act of x's ψ-ing, then the prima facie rights and responsibilities of someone who performs the action of ψ-ing would accrue to x if he performed the action of ϕ-ing.

But this is only a necessary condition for its being true that an instance of one action would count as an instance of another. To see why it is not more than this, why it is not also a sufficient condition, suppose it to be true on a given occasion that by pulling the trigger Joe causally generates an act of his killing the horse. Suppose further that he knew this would happen. If so, then probably whatever prima facie rights and responsibilities are attached to the action of killing the horse would on this occasion accrue to Joe if he pulled the trigger.

To have a sufficient as well as necessary condition for count-generation we shall have to dig deeper, trying to discover *why* it is true in the case of count-generation, that the prima facie rights and duties which are attached to one action would accrue to someone if he performed another. Quite clearly this happens by virtue of what human beings do. It does not happen, say, by virtue of the causal texture of nature. But what is it that someone must do, so as to bring it about that this happens?

Well, consider our second case. Suppose that when the player came up to bat Pete had conferred with him and told him that if he wanted him to bunt, he would give instructions to do so by touching his left hand to his tongue. That would bring it about that while the batter is up, the prima facie rights and duties which are attached to instructing the batter to bunt would accrue to Pete if he touched left hand to tongue. But just what is it, in what Pete did, that brought about this result? This, I think: Pete has intentionally induced the belief in the batter that (nothing contravening) he would perform the action of touching left hand to tongue if those conditions are satisfied such that a coach *has* a prima facie responsibility to instruct someone to bunt if they *are* satisfied, and that he would do so only if those conditions are satisfied such that a coach has a prima facie responsibility *not* to instruct someone to bunt *unless* they are satisfied. Pete has intentionally induced a certain trust in the batter—the trust, for example, that while the batter is up (and nothing contravening), he will touch his left hand to his tongue only if he believes that the bunt is the best strategy. Now if one intentionally induces a certain trust in someone, then one acquires the prima facie responsibility of acting in a manner faithful to that trust. Accordingly Pete now has a prima facie responsibility not to touch left hand to tongue unless those conditions are satisfied such that one has a prima facie responsibility not to instruct a batter to bunt unless they are satisfied, and a prima facie responsibility *to do so* if the relevant conditions *are* satisfied. It is for that reason that, while the batter is up, whatever prima facie rights and responsibilities are attached to the action of instructing to bunt accrue to Pete if he touches left hand to tongue. For example, if Pete now touches left hand to tongue without believing that the best strategy at this point is to bunt, then he has violated a prima facie responsibility which he assumed by intentionally inducing the trust that (nothing contravening) he would instruct to bunt only if that condition (along with others) was satisfied.

One additional point must be made. Suppose that Pete intentionally *tries* to induce the relevant belief in the batter, but fails. The batter is thinking about something else, perhaps, and not listening. Is it then true that the prima facie rights and duties attached to the action of commanding the batter to bunt would accrue to Pete if he touched left hand to tongue? Yes, I think so, *provided that* the batter is responsible for not having acquired the relevant belief in response to whatever it is that Pete did to try to induce it. Then if Pete would touch left hand to tongue, he would have acquired the prima facie rights and responsibilities of one who commands to bunt.

To see how things work in a somewhat different case, let us flesh out our third example a bit. Suppose the situation is that there is a convention in effect, so that the other drivers on the road believe that a driver will switch on his left side blinkers only if those conditions are satisfied such that one has a prima facie responsibility not to signal that one is going to make a left turn unless they are satisfied, and so that they believe that if the conditions for being responsible *to* signal *are* satisfied, he *will* switch them on. One such condition is, of course, that of intending to make a left turn imminently. Further, suppose that Rich *believes* that they believe thus, and has not intentionally done anything which would make them responsible for surrendering their belief with respect to himself. Then Rich has a prima facie responsibility to act consistently with what they trust, and with what he *believes* they trust, him to do. Accordingly, he now has a prima facie responsibility not to switch on the left side blinkers unless conditions for signalling that one is going to make a left turn are satisfied, and to switch them on if the conditions for signalling *are* satisfied.

On the other hand, suppose again that there is this convention and that Rich knows about it, but that he has intentionally done something of such a sort that the other drivers are now responsible for believing that he will not be acting in accord with the convention. Then it is not true that whatever the prima facie rights and responsibilities attached to an action of signalling that one is going to turn left, are ones that would accrue to Rich if he turned on the left side blinkers.

Let us vary the case a bit. As constructed above, the case is one in which there is a certain convention in effect, so that the other drivers believe p and Rich believes that they believe p. Revise it so that they believe p but Rich does not believe that they believe p. Suppose that Rich has just entered our society and lacks the belief that the other drivers on the road believe that a driver will switch on his left side blinkers only if those conditions hold such that one has a prima facie responsibility not to signal that one is going to make a left turn unless they hold. Is it then true that whatever prima facie rights and responsibilities are attached to an action of signalling a left turn would accrue to his switching on his left side blinkers? I think not, *unless* Rich is responsible for his ignorance. Unbeknownst to him, Rich by switching on his left side blinkers *can* gather to himself the prima facie rights and responsibilities attached to an action of signalling that one is going to make a left turn, but only if he *should have known* the convention. In the absence of that, if Rich switches on the left side blinkers because he rather enjoys the blinking light and the clicking sound, he would not thereby have acquired the prima facie rights and responsibilities of one who has signalled; and accordingly, what he has done would not *count as* his signalling that he is going to turn left. So too, if a person who doesn't know German just happens when in Germany to make the sounds of some German sentence, his act of so doing would not count as an act of his asserting something. But if a person who knows that sales at auctions are consummated by innocent-seeming gestures unwittingly makes the buying gesture while attending an auction, that perhaps counts as agreement to buy. (Of course the seller may sympathize with his plight and cancel the agreement.)

Let us vary the example yet once more, this time to make it a case in which the other drivers do not believe p, whereas Rich believes that they do believe p. He believes that they have a certain convention, but they do not have that convention. Perhaps he believes that among them a driver signals a left turn by extending his left arm straight out the driver's window. In fact, they have no such convention. Is it then true that if Rich would extend his left arm straight out his window, he would gather to himself whatever prima facie rights and responsibilities belong to the action of signalling that one is going to turn left? I think so, *provided that* the other drivers are responsible for knowing what Rich *thinks* the convention to be.

I think that that covers the spectrum of cases of accrual of rights and responsibilities which differ in relevant ways. However, before we can use these insights to propose an analysis of count-generation, two other important matters must be mentioned. In the first case we discussed, it was clearly important what beliefs Pete intentionally induced, or tried to induce, in the batter. But suppose he had told his young son, before the game, that he would never give orders to bunt by touching his left hand to his tongue, because that is a sign too easily picked off. Quite clearly, in spite of this, if Pete would touch left hand to tongue the act of his doing so would count as an act of his commanding the batter to bunt. For the batter is an 'interested party' as the son is not. What Pete induced or tried to induce the batter to believe is relevant to the rights and responsibilities that would actually accrue to him upon touching left hand to tongue. What he got or tried to get his son to believe is irrelevant. I shall, in our general formula, use this concept of *interested party*, trusting that from this example it is clear enough for our purposes what I have in mind. But what if there are several interested parties, and the agent intentionally induces conflicting beliefs in different ones? Then I think we must simply allow that it is ambiguous as to whether some act on his part would or would not count as so-and-so.

Secondly, an act of x's ϕ-ing counts as an act of x's ψ-ing only if x performs the action of ϕ-ing freely (i.e., could have refrained, and did not act under compulsion). If the millionaire did not sign his name freely, then his signing his name does not count as disposing of his wealth in accord with the stipulations of the will. Also the agent must be *compos mentis* at the time, and above a certain minimum of intellectual comprehension. Tiny children, morons, those no longer in possession of their mental faculties, cannot dispose of their wealth by signing their names to documents. But presumably this condition is already taken care of by our stipulation that when count-generation is accomplished by virtue of acting in accord with some conventional practice which is in effect, the agent must *believe* that that practice is in effect (or, be responsible for not believing it). The moron, the child, and the person who is not *compos mentis*, lack the intellectual comprehension necessary for having such a belief. They 'would not realize' what they were doing if they signed their names.

We are ready now to propose our analysis of count-generation.

Thesis II: An act of x's ϕ-ing performed at t counts as an act of x's ψ-ing if and only if:

  (i) x generates ψ-ing by ϕ-ing at t;

 (ii) x performed the action of ϕ-ing freely;[4]

(iii) the prima facie rights and responsibilities of someone who performs the action of ψ-ing have accrued to x at t by virtue of his ϕ-ing; and

(iv) (iii) is true either because:

    (a) x has intentionally induced the belief in interested parties, or x has tried to induce the belief in them and they are responsible for not having acquired it, or the interested parties *should have* the belief, that for any condition C such that x has a prima facie responsibility not to perform ψ-ing unless C holds, x would not perform ϕ-ing at t (nothing in his judgement contravening) unless C holds, and for any condition C such that x has a prima facie responsibility *to* perform ψ-ing if C holds, he would perform ϕ-ing at t (nothing in his judgement contravening) if C holds; or

    (b) x believes or is responsible for his not believing that

---

[4] One qualification on (ii) is perhaps necessary. Suppose someone wishes to express his anger to someone, but finds the prospect of doing so distasteful, and accordingly resolves to get drunk and utter the anger-expressing words then. I take it that he might indeed express his anger by uttering those words. In such a case, the person freely and in sound mind makes the decision to perform the generating act, but he does not perform the generating act when he is acting freely and is in sound mind. So (ii) should have this clause attached: 'or acted freely and was of sound mind when he resolves to perform ϕ-ing at some later time when he would not be acting freely and be in sound mind.'

the interested parties already have the belief, and he has not intentionally done anything which would make them responsible for surrendering it, that for any C such that x has a prima facie responsibility not to perform ψ-ing unless C holds, x would not perform ϕ-ing at t (nothing in his judgement contravening) unless C holds, and for any C such that x has a prima facie responsibility *to* perform ψ-ing if C holds, x would perform ϕ-ing at t (nothing in his judgement contravening) if C holds.

To avoid overburdening an analysis already heavily burdened, I have refrained from inserting a qualification which is necessary for its full truth. It should at this point be mentioned, however. Suppose that in our case of the coach and the batter, the batter comes to bat believing that if the coach wants him to bunt, he will rub his neck. For that is the sign agreed to before the game began. And suppose that Pete knows that the batter comes to bat believing that. But suppose that Pete wishes, for whatever reason, to change the bunt sign, for this particular batter on this occasion, to touching left hand to tongue. And suppose that he accordingly tries to communicate to the batter that this is the new sign, with the result that the batter is now responsible if he does not believe that this is the sign that the coach will use if he wants him to bunt. But suppose that the batter in fact does not acquire this belief. Perhaps he is so busy thinking about whether his annual salary is best invested in real estate or in computer stock that he scarcely hears what the coach says. Suppose that the coach, seeing that he is not getting through to the batter, eventually in frustrated annoyance gives up trying. And now suppose that shortly thereafter, wanting the batter to bunt, he rubs his neck, whereupon the batter bunts. I think that the coach's acting thus would in fact count as his giving the order to bunt. He has simply reverted to acting in accord with what he knows the batter believes, instead of acting in accord with what he tried to get the batter to believe and what the batter should in fact believe. Accordingly a qualification allowing for cases of this sort should be inserted in (iv.b).

That completes my proposed analysis of what it is for an act

A to count as an act B. In conclusion, a few comments explanatory of the analysis should be made.

In the first place, on this analysis of *counting as*, one act may count as another even though no one counts it as the other. That is to say, act A may count as act B even though the agent does not in fact act in accordance with the prima facie responsibilities which have accrued to him from B, and even though no one does in fact accord him the prima facie rights which have accrued to him from B. Counting-as is a matter of prima facie rights and responsibilities, not a matter of *according* and *acting in accord with* rights and responsibilities.

Secondly, on this analysis it may be true that, at time t, an act of x's ϕ-ing counts as an act of x's ψ-ing even though it was never an intention on x's part to perform the act of ϕ-ing only if (nothing contravening) the prima facie responsibility conditions for performing ψ-ing held. What counts is what the agent intentionally tried to lead people to believe, or what he allowed them to believe and did not try to shake them out of believing, not what his own intentions for acting were. The con artist never intends to act in the way in which he gets, or tries to get, people to believe he will. So too, if a person responds to the judge with the words 'I do', he cannot, by having 'mental reservations', prevent that from counting as his promising to tell the whole truth.

Closely related is this point: suppose it is true, at a certain time, that if x would perform ϕ-ing, the act of his doing so would count as an act of his ψ-ing. And suppose he does then perform ϕ-ing. Then whether or not he *intended* to perform ψ-ing, he has done so. As long as a counting-as arrangement is in effect, things are, as it were, out of his hands. If the coach absentmindedly, thus unintentionally, touches left hand to tongue when the arrangement for instructing to bunt is in effect, he has none the less given orders to bunt. However, it is essential that Pete's touching left hand to tongue have been done freely and that he be of sound mind at the time. Otherwise his act will not count as an act of instructing to bunt.

Fourth, in the preceding discussion I have persistently spoken of *prima facie* rights and responsibilities, tacitly distinguishing them from the rights and responsibilities actually pertaining to a concrete act. It may be, in a certain situation, that one has a prima facie responsibility not to touch left hand to tongue unless one believes that the best strategy is to bunt. However, in spite of this it may *in fact* be true that one ought to touch one's left hand to one's tongue even though one does not believe that bunting would be the best strategy. For it may be that the totality of one's prima facie responsibilities in this situation make it in fact obligatory to touch one's left hand to one's tongue. One's doing so, however, would none the less count as one's commanding the batter to bunt. Sometimes one is in fact obliged to mislead people—though there is no prima facie responsibility to mislead people.

Fifth, in my discussion I have spoken hardly at all of the prima facie *rights* that an agent acquires by doing so-and-so—that is, the prima facie responsibilities that he imposes on others. But prima facie rights as well as responsibilities accrue to us upon the performance of count-generating actions. Not only do I (nothing contravening) have a responsibility not to assert p unless I believe p; also, if I assert p I have (nothing contravening) the right to be believed. By making the sounds 'the bridge is washed out' I impose on others the prima facie responsibility to believe that the bridge is washed out.

Sixth, though I have confined my analysis of the performance of one action counting as the performance of another to the situation in which the agent of the two performings is a single person, as I noted earlier in section I of Part One, not all such cases are in fact of that sort. We saw, for example, that a team can do one thing by doing another, and that an organization can do something by way of some official of the organization doing something. So too, one person can do something by way of someone else doing something 'on his behalf'—as when someone acts as proxy for another, or exercises power of attorney for another, or acts in the capacity of guardian for another, or just simply speaks on behalf of another. If one were going to construct a full analysis of count-generation, the full range of such diverse cases would have to be taken into account.

Lastly, if this normative analysis of count-generation is at all on the right track, then we can also see why our generating acts, in themselves, are typically so innocuous—things like making certain fairly quiet noises, inscribing certain marks, etc. For if there was much in the way of prima facie rights and responsibilities attached to the generating actions themselves, that would over and over contravene a person's prima facie responsibility to perform or refrain from performing the generated action. It's because in itself it makes no difference one way or the other whether Pete touches his left hand to his tongue that that action serves so nicely as a signal in baseball. Pete can then concentrate all his attention on whether he should or should not instruct the batter to bunt. He needn't reflect on whether, independently of its being a signal, he should or should not touch left hand to tongue.

III. *Arrangements and Systems for Acting*

There are many other arrangements that the government could have chosen for my wife and me to declare that what stands in our Internal Revenue Service form is correct, many other arrangements that the coach could have chosen for instructing the batter to bunt, many other arrangements that Rich could have chosen for signalling that he was going to make a left turn. So it always is. Any act which is count-generated in one way could have been count-generated in a multiplicity of other ways as well.

How can we best conceive of what I have just now been calling *arrangements*? As ordered pairs, I think. An arrangement for ϕ-ing is an ordered pair of actions, $\langle \phi\text{-ing}, \psi\text{-ing} \rangle$, such that someone by performing ϕ-ing could count-generate an act of his ψ-ing. Thus, $\langle$Touching left hand to tongue, Instructing a batter to bunt$\rangle$, is an arrangement for instructing a batter to bunt. And every such ordered pair of actions is *an* arrangement for acting.

If we do think of arrangements for acting along these lines, then it becomes easy to say what it is for such an arrangement to be *in effect* for certain people at a certain time; and secondly, what it is for it to be *used* by a certain person at a certain time. A given arrangement for acting, $\langle \phi\text{-ing}, \psi\text{-ing} \rangle$, is *in effect for* person P at time t just in case, if P would perform the action of ϕ-ing at t, the act of his doing so would count as an act of his ψ-ing. And a given arrangement for acting, $\langle \phi\text{-ing}, \psi\text{-ing} \rangle$, is *used by* P at t just in case P at t performs the action of ϕ-ing, and the act of his doing so count-generates an act of his ψ-ing. It may be noted here that very often the generating actions in arrangements for acting which are in effect for a person involve some *intention* on the part of the agent.

The interesting question which this explication of what it is for an arrangement for acting to be in effect at a certain time for a certain group of people is of course this: How do such arrangements *come* into effect? What brings it about that one arrangement for signalling to bunt rather than another is in effect for a coach and batter at a certain time? Along the course of our analysis I have said a number of things relevant to answering this question. But let me here answer it in systematic fashion.

For one thing, a given arrangement for acting, $\langle \phi$-ing, ψ-ing$\rangle$, may be in effect for P at t by virtue of someone having stipulated that, at t, a person of P's sort shall perform the action of ϕ-ing if and only if the prima facie responsibility conditions for ψ-ing are satisfied, and by virtue of this stipulation having been assented to. It may be P himself who does the stipulating. But it need not be. Someone else may make the stipulation; and if P knows about it and does not dissent, and if the interested parties know about it, that will do as well. So sometimes an arrangement for acting is in effect because of the making and assenting to a certain stipulation.

Secondly, it may be a *convention* (i.e., a practice) among a certain group G of people for a person of P's sort to perform the action of ϕ-ing if and only if (nothing judged contravening) the prima facie responsibility conditions for ψ-ing are satisfied. If P knows this, if his performing ϕ-ing at t would have the members of a subset of G as interested parties, and if he has done nothing which dissociates his action from the convention, then the arrangement $\langle \phi$-ing, ψ-ing$\rangle$, is in effect for him. Thus, sometimes an arrangement for acting is in effect because of the existence and knowing acquiescence in a certain convention.

But thirdly, there are stranger cases than either of these. Sometimes an arrangement for acting is in effect because of what (following David K. Lewis in his *Convention*) I shall call 'salience'. A person may gesture in a certain fashion in a certain situation; and his doing so may count as his signalling for help. He may take onto himself all the rights and responsibilities of having signalled. But there may be no convention concerning the significance of the gestures he uses. And there may have been no stipulation concerning their significance. It may just be that salient features of the situation and the gesturing are such that if he would perform those gestures in that situation, the act of his doing so would count as an act of his signalling for help. So too, it is now something of a convention, when a person is backing up a truck, for someone behind but off to the side of the vehicle to hold his hands a certain distance apart in view of the driver and thus to tell the driver how much farther he can go back. If he holds them three feet apart when there is only an inch left to go, he has lied. But once upon a time there was no such convention. Yet this very same arrangement might then have been in effect. If so, it was in effect by virtue of salience.

In short, it is by virtue of stipulations, conventions, and saliences that arrangements for acting are in effect, with the result that our performance of one action counts as our performance of another—so that, for example, a soft-voiced utterance of the innocuous sound GUILTY may acquire the shattering significance of a man thereby being condemned to death.

Normally we do not operate in the piece-meal fashion which our discussion thus far might suggest. Rather, the coach has a whole system for giving orders to batters. And drivers have available to them a whole system for signalling to others what they are going to do. How may such systems be thought of?

Consider the set σ of all actions by the performance of which some action or other can be count-generated. There are various functions from subsets of this set into subsets of the set γ of all actions which can be count-generated. Among them are functions such that every ordered pair consisting of some member of that function's domain, plus the value of that function for that argument, is an arrangement for acting. Call these functions, *functions-for-acting*. Then any ordered pair $\langle \{s_1, \ldots, s_n\}, f \rangle$, consisting of the domain of some function-for-acting plus that function itself, is a *system for acting*.

Take, for example, the two actions of *switching on one's left side blinkers while driving*, and *switching on one's right side blinkers while driving*. Call these, SL and SR respectively. And consider some function F which assigns to SL the action of *signalling that one is going to turn left*, and to SR the action of *signalling that one is going to turn right*. Then the ordered pair, $\langle \{SL, SR\}, F \rangle$ is a system for acting.

Let us call the domain of that function-for-acting which is the function-member of some system S for acting, the *stock* of S. Thus a system for acting has as members the set of its stock along with its particular function-for-acting. Also, let us call the range of that particular function-for-acting which is the function-member of some system for acting, the *scope* of the system.

Perhaps a diagram will help. Suppose that some function, F, looks like this:

$$\text{domain} \quad \left\{ \begin{array}{l} s_1 \longrightarrow g_1 \\ s_2 \longrightarrow g_2 \\ s_3 \longrightarrow g_3 \end{array} \right\} \quad \text{range}$$

In usual fashion we can think of the function F *as itself* the set whose members are the ordered pairs $\langle s_1, g_1 \rangle$, $\langle s_2, g_2 \rangle$, $\langle s_3, g_3 \rangle$. Now the system S will just be the ordered pair whose first member is the domain of F—that is $\langle s_1, s_2, s_3 \rangle$; and whose second member is F itself. And the stock and scope of S will be as follows:

$$S = \left\{ \langle s_1, s_2, s_3 \rangle, F \right\}$$

$$\text{stock} \quad \left\{ \begin{array}{ll} s_1 & g_1 \\ s_2 & g_2 \\ s_3 & g_3 \end{array} \right\} \quad \text{scope}$$

A system $S = \langle \sigma, F \rangle$ for acting is *in effect for* P at time t just in case, for any member s of the stock of S, if P would perform s at t, the act of his doing so would count as an act of his performing the action $F(s)$.

A system S is *used by* P on a given occasion just in case S is then in effect for P and P performs an action which is a member of the stock of S.[5]

---

[5] We are now in a position to understand the structure of an exception I cited to a point made earlier (Part One, section I). I said that every pair of actions, $\langle \phi$-ing, ψ-ing$\rangle$, such that ψ-ing can be generated by ϕ-ing, is such that someone could perform

IV. *Illocutionary Actions*

From among the actions which are susceptible of being count-generated we can single out those which I shall call *illocutionary actions*. I call them that on the ground that the set of these actions probably comes close to coinciding with that of those that Austin had in mind when he introduced the term 'illocutionary action'.

Suppose that on a certain occasion a speaker issues the command to close a certain door, and that he does so by uttering in a certain manner and circumstance the English words 'Close the door'. In such a case he has generated one action by another: he has generated the action of issuing that particular command by performing the action of uttering those particular words. And the specific mode of generation is count-generation. His uttering generates his commanding because at the time it was true that if he would perform the act of uttering in that particular fashion the words 'Close the door', his act of doing so would count as an act of issuing the command to close that door.

Some special terminology will be helpful. Let me stretch the sense of the word 'uttering', and call both an action of inscribing a sentence (from some language), and an action of pronouncing aloud a sentence (from some language), an uttering of that sentence. Then any action which consists of uttering some sentence in a certain manner and circumstance will be called a *language action*. And any action which can be purely count-generated by performing some language action, I shall call an *illocutionary action*.[6] It should be evident that illocutionary actions are a highly diversified lot. They include such actions as asserting, promising, christening, and making a parliamentary motion.

ϕ-ing and not thereby perform ψ-ing. An exception I cited was this: ⟨Checkmating one's opponent's king in chess, Winning at chess⟩. The exception arises of course because the actions cited are ones which can only be performed by *using* a specific *system* for action, that of chess. And of course the various arrangements going to make up that system which is chess are *essential to* the identity of that system. A system for winning in which 'checkmating the king' did not count as winning would not be chess (and that is so even if 'checkmating the king' were done in the same way as in chess). There are, of course, a multitude of exceptions having a similar structure.

[6] I shall say that *P purely* count-generated ψ-ing by ϕ-ing just in case *P* count-generates and does not *causally* generate ψ-ing by ϕ-ing.

Though illocutionary actions are actions which can be purely count-generated by performing some language action, it will be immensely important for our subsequent discussion to notice that they can be generated by actions of other sorts as well. The illocutionary action of issuing the command to close the door can be performed by the use of 'sign' language, by the use of smoke signals, by the arranging of objects in a certain fashion, by the use of gestures, etc. But of course an illocutionary action can be made to occur *only* by someone performing some action which generates it. That too will be immensely important to keep in mind. The mere *existence* of something—whether sentence, or picture, or semaphore flag, or, indeed, action—will not do so.

It will be important to differentiate illocutionary actions from actions which one can *causally* generate by language actions. For example, the action of x informing y that x wants the door to be closed, is not an illocutionary action. To see this, suppose that an act of Sebastian's uttering the words 'Close the door' generates an act of Sebastian's informing somebody that he wants the door to be closed. This latter act is identical with Sebastian's bringing about the event of someone's being informed that Sebastian wants the door to be closed. And this event is *caused by* the act of Sebastian's uttering the words 'Close the door'. Thus the act of Sebastian's informing somebody that he wants the door to be closed is causally generated. And accordingly, the action of x informing y that x wants the door to be closed is, in this circumstance, causally generated by Sebastian. But so it always is: whenever this action is generated, it is *causally* generated. And it can never be performed without being generated. Other examples of actions which can be causally but not count-generated by the performance of language actions are the action of x communicating y to z, and the action of x evoking emotion y in z.

In the preceding section I talked about *arrangements for acting*, where an arrangement for acting is an ordered pair of actions such that someone can count-generate the second by the first. From the set of all such arrangements for acting, I shall be limiting our attention in what follows to those whose generable member is an illocutionary action. *Arrangements for illocutionary action*, we may call them.

Illocutionary actions are—all of them—actions which can be count-generated. And if our analysis of count-generation is correct, only a being which has rights and responsibilities can count-generate. Now I hold that animals do not have rights and responsibilities. So also I hold that animals do not perform illocutionary actions. Behaviourist accounts of language can be seen as attempts to account for language wholly in terms of causal generation, not at all in terms of count-generation. Thus the behaviourist account of language is an account which attempts to set off to the side, or ignore, the moral dimension of man, and focus only on that which we have in common with animals.

V. *Statal Actions*

Illocutionary actions, to say it once again, are a highly diversified lot. Any action which one can purely count-generate by uttering a sentence of some language in some manner and circumstance, is an illocutionary action. Let me now single out, from the set of all illocutionary actions, those that I shall call *statal actions*.

Consider the following illocutionary actions:

(1) asserting that my study door will be closed,
(2) commanding that my study door (will) be closed,
(3) asking whether my study door will be closed,
(4) expressing the wish that my study door (will) be closed, and
(5) promising that my study door will be closed.

The first could be performed by uttering in a certain manner and circumstance the sentence 'The door will be closed.' The second could be performed by uttering in a certain manner and circumstance the sentence 'Close the door.' The third could be performed by uttering in a certain manner and circumstance the sentence 'Will the door be closed?' The fourth, by uttering in a certain manner and circumstance the sentence 'Would that the door would be closed.' And the fifth, by uttering in a certain manner and circumstance the sentence 'I promise that the door will be closed.'

Now consider (1)–(5). Each is a 1-degree action which takes

a person as agent. But also, each is a *completion of* a 2-degree action which takes a person as agent and a state of affairs (or if one prefers, a proposition) as object. For example, the 2-degree action of *asserting* takes persons as agents and states of affairs as objects. It cannot be exemplified except by a pair whose members are a person and a state of affairs. And the 1-degree action (1) is a completion of this 2-degree action of asserting.

Let us call any 2-degree action which can be exemplified only by ordered pairs, the first of whose members is a person and the second a state of affairs, a *2-degree statal action*. And let us call any 1-degree action which is a completion of a 2-degree statal action, and is such that it can be exemplified only by a person, a *1-degree statal action*. *Asserting* is a 2-degree statal action. *Asserting that snow is cold* is a 1-degree statal action which is a completion of the 2-degree action, asserting.

Given any 1-degree statal action A, there is an ordered pair whose second member is a 2-degree statal action A^* of which A is a completion, and whose first member is a state of affairs S such that a person P performs A^* on S if and only if P exemplifies A. Let us call that, a *state/action pair associated with A*. Thus a state/action pair associated with the 1-degree statal action of *promising that my study door will be closed* is the pair $\langle$*My study door being closed*, Promising that x will be brought about$\rangle$.[7]

And now we can say this: world-projection as such is a 2-degree statal action; and an action consisting in the projecting of some specific world, for example, the action of projecting the world of *Dead Souls*, is a 1-degree statal action. Correspondingly, systems for world-projection are systems for the performance of statal actions.

VI. *Mood-Actions and Mood-Action Systems*

Lastly, from among the set of all statal actions I wish now to single out a special group which I shall call *mood-actions*, examples being asserting, commanding, and asking.

[7] Because of the interactions of tenses, a 1-degree statal action may have more than one state/action pair associated with it. Take, for example, the 1-degree action of asking whether the door will be closed. The pair $\langle$*The door (presently) being closed*, Asking whether x will occur$\rangle$, is a state/action pair associated with this 1-degree action. But the pair $\langle$*The door going to be closed*, Asking whether x is occurring$\rangle$, is another.

Consider the four English sentences:

   (i) 'The door will be closed.'
  (ii) 'Close the door.'
 (iii) 'Will the door be closed?'
  (iv) 'Would that the door would be closed.'

These sentences bear an obvious similarity to each other. There is provision in normal English for uttering each in such a manner and circumstance that though one will thereby have performed four different 2-degree statal actions, there is some single state of affairs on which all four actions are performed. Specifically, one possibility for such a common state of affairs is *my study door (presently) being closed.* I can utter the first in such fashion as thereby to assert that *my study door being closed* will occur. I can utter the second in such fashion as thereby to command that *my study door being closed* be brought about. I can utter the third in such fashion as to ask whether *my study door being closed* will occur. And I can utter the fourth in such fashion as thereby to express the wish that *my study door being closed* will occur.

But the sentences (i)–(iv) also differ in a significant way. They differ with respect to what grammarians call *mood.* The first is in the indicative mood, the second in the imperative, the third in the interrogative, the fourth in the optative. In the present context it is easy to see the significance of these moods. If one wants to *claim* that some state of affairs is occurring, the appropriate mood to use is the indicative. If one wants to *command* that some state of affairs be made to occur, the appropriate mood to use is either the indicative (uttered with 'imperative' inflection), or the imperative. If one wants to *ask* whether some state of affairs is occurring, the appropriate mood to use is either the indicative (uttered with 'interrogative' inflection) or the interrogative. If one wants to *express the wish* that some state of affairs will occur, the appropriate mood to use is the optative.

The fact that there are distinct moods for such statal actions as asserting, asking, commanding, and expressing the wish that, leads one to wonder what would be yielded by singling out those 2-degree statal actions for which there is, in some extant language or other, an appropriate mood. Would this yield us a

set of actions bearing a significant analogy to each other? And if
so, would it also yield us *all* the actions bearing that particular
analogy to each other?

Certainly we have no right to expect such a result. Language,
after all, is filled with fortuitous features. Why should mood not
be one of them? One's suspicion of danger is confirmed by the
fact that (to the best of my knowledge) *promising that* does not
have a special mood in any language. Yet does not promising
bear a deep analogy to these other actions? In the performance
of any one of them one does not merely single out some state of
affairs but takes up what one feels to be a special kind of stance
toward that state of affairs. Promising is like that too. In
promising to bring about some state of affairs one takes up a
stance toward it. And does not that stance seem very much
analogous to that of asserting, commanding, etc.? Grammatical
mood can be for us no more than a suggestive clue.

Let us explore the hint that asserting, asking, commanding,
and expressing the wish that, along with promising, involve
taking up a special sort of stance toward some state of affairs. In
standard English, in order to claim that *my study door (presently)
being closed* will occur I can utter indicative mood (i) with
characteristic inflection. But also I can utter this with characteristic inflection:

(a) 'I hereby assert that the door will be closed.'

To command that *my study door (presently) being closed* be made to
occur I can utter indicative-mood (i) with 'imperative' inflection or imperative-mood (ii) with characteristic inflection. But
also I can utter this with characteristic inflection:

(b) 'I hereby command that the door (will) be closed.'

To ask whether *my study door (presently) being closed* will occur I
can, instead of uttering indicative-mood (i) with interrogative
inflection or interrogative mood (iii) with characteristic inflection, utter this with characteristic inflection:

(c) 'I hereby ask whether the door will be closed.'

And lastly, to express the wish that *my study door (presently) being
closed* will occur I can, instead of uttering optative-mood (iv)
with characteristic inflection utter this with characteristic
inflection:

(d) 'I hereby express the wish that the door will be closed.'

And now, for promising that *my study door (presently) being closed* will occur, we have this available:

(e) 'I hereby promise that the door will be closed.'

So in (a)–(e) we have five different sentences of the form 'I hereby ϕ that the door will be closed.'

These sentences are peculiar. What is peculiar about them is this: If a person by uttering the sentence 'I hereby ϕ that the door will be closed' asserts that he thereby ϕ's that the door will be closed, then it *follows* that he has ϕ'd that the door will be closed.[8] For example, one can of course utter the sentence 'I hereby command that the door be closed' in all sorts of ways—dreamily, trying it out for sound, etc. But suppose that by uttering it one asserts that one thereby commands that the door be closed. Then it *follows* that one has commanded that the door be closed. On the other hand, I could utter 'I hereby wonder whether the door will be closed', and by doing so assert that I thereby wonder whether the door will be closed. But it does not follow that in fact I wondered whether the door will be closed. I may not have.[9]

Let us generalize, following the procedure of offering first a preliminary generalization and then introducing the necessary refinements.

Consider some English sentence of the form 'I hereby ϕ that p.' If, from the fact that a speaker by uttering this sentence

---

[8] A slight qualification will be introduced shortly when we introduce the concept of *a suitably competent speaker*.

[9] There is indeed an alternative construal of the situation. Perhaps when in normal usage we utter 'I hereby command that the door be closed', we do not *assert* that we thereby command that the door be closed while at the same time commanding that it be closed; but rather we command that the door be closed and at the same time *identify* what we are doing as commanding that the door be closed. Perhaps it is the presence of such identification, rather than the presence of assertion, that constitutes the difference between what we do when in normal usage we utter 'Close the door' and what we do when in normal usage we utter 'I hereby command that the door be closed'. I do not see any way of adjudicating between this identification construal of the situation and the assertion construal. But if some reader prefers the identification construal, the generalizations that I offer in the text can easily be revised accordingly. Where I say, 'from the fact that a speaker by uttering this sentence has asserted that he thereby ϕ's that p . . . ,' the alternative would be to say 'from the fact that a speaker by uttering this sentence has identified what he is doing as ϕ-ing that p . . . ,' etc.

has asserted that he thereby ϕ's that p, it follows that he *has* ϕ'd that p, then let us call ϕ-ing a *mood-action*.

Asserting, commanding, asking, expressing the wish, are by this criterion all mood-actions. And so too is promising.

How about the action of *stating in English*? Is that a mood-action? If S utters 'I hereby state in English that p' and by so doing asserts that he thereby states in English that p, does it follow that he has stated in English that p? Suppose that by 'state in English' is meant, *state by speaking English*. Then it seems it does not follow. He might utter that sentence and make that assertion and not be speaking English but some other language in which that same sentence is found. Suppose, alternatively, that by 'state in English' is meant, *state with a sentence to be found in English*. It still does not follow. It's possible that he should utter that sentence, and make that assertion; but that that sentence not be found in English. For that sentence *could* exist and be uttered and not have the property of being found in English. So whichever way we understand it, *stating in English* proves not to be a mood-action. Surely in that there is nothing unsatisfactory.

But then consider these:

(i) 'I hereby state with a twelve-word sentence that summer is over.'
(ii) 'I hereby state, therein contradicting myself, that some bachelors are married.'
(iii) 'I hereby state, taking some time to do so, that summer is over.'

In each of these cases there is the entailment in question. For example, if by uttering 'I hereby state with a twelve-word sentence that summer is over' someone asserts that he thereby states with a twelve-word sentence that summer is over, then it follows that he *did* assert with a twelve-word sentence that summer is over. So *stating with a twelve-word sentence* turns out, by the criterion offered, to be a mood-action. But now, suppose that instead of the words 'summer is over' there had been the words 'summer is not over'. Then the entailment would not be present. So then, by the criterion offered, *stating with a twelve-*

word sentence turns out not to be a mood-action. Obviously some repairs are in order.

The relevant peculiarity of (i) is that one can replace the words 'summer is over' with other words such that the result of so doing is that the entailment in question is *not* present. And so too for (ii). Let us then revise our preliminary generalization thus:

> Consider some English sentence of the form 'I hereby ϕ that p' If, for a given replacement for ϕ, all possible replacements for p are such that it follows, from the fact that a speaker by uttering this sentence has asserted that he thereby ϕ's that p, that he *has* ϕ'd that p, then let us call ϕ-ing a *mood action*.

By this criterion, *stating with a twelve-word sentence* and *contradicting oneself in stating* prove not to be mood-actions; whereas *taking some time to state* does prove to be a mood-action. This all seems satisfactory.

But there is another difficulty which must be met. Promising is the sort of action that we wish to turn out to be a mood-action, along with commanding, and so forth. But one cannot, in a given circumstance, promise anything whatsoever; nor can one, in a given circumstance, command anything whatsoever. If I have no daughter, then I cannot promise someone that he may date my daughter—though of course I can *mislead* him into *thinking* that I was promising him that. However, even in that circumstance it is perhaps the case that I can *assert* that I hereby promise that he may date my daughter by uttering 'I hereby promise that you may date my daughter.' So from the fact that I can assert this by uttering that, it does not follow that I have promised. Obviously the condition which must be attached is that the speaker be in a circumstance in which he *can* perform the action ϕ-ing that p.[10] Let us call such a speaker, a *suitably competent* speaker. This then is the finished generalization:

> Consider some English sentence of the form 'I hereby ϕ that p.' If, for a given replacement for ϕ, all possible replacements

---

[10] For some propositions p and some actions ϕ-ing, it is impossible for anyone ever to ϕ that p. For example, no one can promise that the door is shut. And I am inclined to think that one cannot promise someone that some punishment will befall him if he does so-and-so. One can threaten that, one can assure somebody of that, but not promise it.

for p are such that it follows, from the fact that a suitably competent speaker by uttering this sentence has asserted that he thereby ϕ's that p, that he *has* ϕ'd that p, then let us call ϕ-ing a *mood-action*.

Let us also call *mood-actions* those 1-degree statal actions which are completions of 2-degree mood-actions with respect to states of affairs (i.e., incomplete with respect to persons). Thus not only is *promising* a mood-action. So too is *promising that my study door will be closed*.

We can now easily form the concept of a *system for mood-action*. Such systems constitute a species of systems for acting. In particular a system for mood-action is a system for acting whose scope consists exclusively of 1-degree mood-actions. For example, the following is a system for mood-action. As members of the stock there are just two actions: (i) that of uttering aloud the words 'Close the door', and (ii) that of uttering aloud the words 'Was the door closed?' The function-for-acting F assigns the former action to the 1-degree action of issuing the command to close the door of my study, and assigns the latter to the 1-degree action of asking whether the door of my study is closed. The ordered pair $\langle\{$Uttering aloud the words 'Close the door', Uttering aloud the words 'Was the door closed?'$\}, F\rangle$ is then a particular system for mood-action. Further, one member of the scope has as an associated state/action pair the set $\langle My$ *study door being closed*, Commanding that p be brought about$\rangle$. The other has as an associated state/action pair the set $\langle My$ *study door having been closed*, Asking whether p is occurring$\rangle$.

If such a system as this last example were in effect, it might be by virtue of certain features of what is uttered and how it is uttered that some language act would generate an act of commanding rather than an act of asking, or an act of asking rather than an act of commanding. And it might be by virtue of certain other features of the utterance that a mood-stance would be taken up toward the past-tense state of affairs in question rather than the present-tense one, or vice versa. Let us generalize this idea.

Consider some system S for performing 1-degree mood-actions which are incomplete with respect to persons. From the system's scope, pick out some 1-degree mood-action, ψ-ing p.

Suppose that a state-action pair associated with ψ-ing p is $\langle p,$ ψ-ing$\rangle$. Suppose that the generating action assigned to ψ-ing p in S is ϕ-ing. And now suppose that S is in effect for a given person P at a time t. It may be by virtue of instances of ϕ-ing having the property of *being-f* that they would count-generate instances of ψ-ing p, instead of generating instances of some 1-degree mood-action (in the scope of the system) whose associated state/action pair[11] does not have p as a member but some other state of affairs instead. If so, call their having the property *being-f*, the *statal indicator* of the generating acts. Secondly, it may be by virtue of their having the property of *being-g* that instances of ϕ-ing would count-generate instances ϕ-ing p, instead of generating instances of some 1-degree mood-action (in the scope of the system) whose associated state/action pair does not have the 2-degree action of ϕ-ing as a member but some other mood-action instead. If so, call their having that property, the *stance indicator* of the generating acts. The point of making this distinction is, of course, that in a certain system the statal indicator of instances of some member of the stock may differ from the stance indicator thereof.

In our generation of mood-acts by the utterance of sentences from natural languages, the stance indicators of our acts are regularly distinct from the statal indicators. Standard English provides us with a way of uttering the sentence 'The door is closed' so as thereby to *assert* something. It also provides us with a way of uttering it so as thereby to *ask* something. The difference lies in whether one uses a falling or a rising inflection. In the former case, the stance indicator of the act would be that act's having the property of *being an uttering with falling inflection* of a sentence. In the latter case, it would be that act's having the property of *being an uttering with rising inflection* of a sentence. In effect, each of our natural languages makes certain properties which acts can have to serve in stance indicators, and certain other properties which acts can have to serve in statal indicators.

What is not the case, though, is that in our natural languages the sentences themselves can be divided up into two distinct

---

[11] For ease of formulation, I am speaking as if there is only one such pair. That may not be true. ψ-ing p may allow of alternative analyses into states of affairs and 2-degree actions.

series of words, with the statal indicator of some act being its having the property of being an uttering of the one series, and the stance indicator being its having the property of being an uttering of the other series. It is not at all difficult, however, to see how such a language might be constructed. As the counterpart to (i) one might have

(i') 'I assert (the door will be closed).'

As the counterpart to (ii),

(ii') 'I command (the door will be closed).'

As the counterpart to (iii),

(iii') 'I ask (the door will be closed).'

And as the counterpart to (iv),

(iv') 'I express the wish (the door will be closed).'

In such sentences, the burden of serving to indicate to which state of affairs a mood-stance is taken up is laid on the interior mood-neutral component of the sentence (call such components, 'radicals'). And the burden of serving to indicate which mood-stance is taken up, is laid on the prefix. In fact, of course, (i')–(iv') are strikingly like (a)–(d). The difference is that in uttering, for example, (b), one both commands and asserts that one is commanding. (ii'), however, is devoid of all assertive force.

It is worth noticing about a 'mood separation' language constructed on the model of (i')–(iv') that particular manner and circumstance of utterance remain relevant. The language could indeed be set up so that, no matter in what fashion I utter a well-formed sentence initiated with 'I assert', either I perform no speech action at all or I perform an action of asserting something. There would then be nothing like the sort of ambiguity which the indicative mood carries in English. But which particular state of affairs was signified with 'the door is closed' would still be determined not merely by the utterance of that series of words but by that utterance along with the particular manner and circumstance of uttering it. There would be more to the statal indicators than just the act's having the property of being the utterance of such-and-such words.

It will be convenient in what follows to have some brief

synonym for 'performed some mood-action on'. Accordingly I shall often, in place of those words, use the word 'introduced'. Thus some action of introducing state of affairs p, will always be some action of performing some mood-action on state of affairs p. The scope of a system for mood-action consists entirely of 1-degree actions of introducing a state of affairs.

And now we can say this: examples of world-projection are, all of them, mood-actions. And systems for world-projections are all systems for the performance of mood-actions.

VII. *The Fictive Stance*

And now at last we can come to grips with the difference between the fictioneer and the liar. Both take up a mood-stance toward certain states of affairs. The heart of the difference between them lies in the particular stance that each, in his 'capacity' of fictioneer or liar, takes up. The liar 'something affirmeth'. His is the assertive stance. The fictioneer—well, his is the *fictive* stance. But what is that? Let us approach the matter with novelistic fiction primarily in mind.

The novelist uses the very same sentences that we use in ordinary life. There is no peculiar language for fiction—other, perhaps, than such phrases as 'once upon a time' which the writer uses to indicate that he is engaging in fiction. Most of the sentences he utters are such that if we believed he was not fictionalizing we would take him as making assertions; others are such that if we believed he was not fictionalizing we would take him as expressing some wish; and so forth. But he isn't asserting, and he isn't expressing his wishes—not in his capacity of fictioneer.

Could it be that he is *pretending* to do so? Could it be that he is pretending to perform illocutionary actions which in fact he is not performing? Could it be that by uttering the sentences he does utter he is pretending to perform whatever illocutionary actions we would take him as performing if we believed that he was *not* pretending?[12] Or perhaps, whatever illocutionary actions would normally be performed by uttering those sentences?

[12] Cf. John Searle, 'The Logical Status of Fictional Discourse', in *New Literary History*, vi, No. 2 (Winter, 1975).

Sometimes the goal of pretence is deception: the confidence trickster who never graduated from college but pretends to be a physician with a medical degree does so with the aim of deceiving people into believing that he is a physician. But often pretence does not have deception as its goal. Children 'play school'. They *pretend* to be holding school. One of them plays the role of teacher; others play the role of students. But nowhere is deception in view. The pretence theory of what constitutes the fictional stance treats the fictioneer as one who plays a role. It should be no part of the theory to hold that, in general, the aim of this role-playing is deception. The novelist puts 'a novel' on his title-page. If anyone would otherwise have been deceived, that prevents it.

In order to judge the acceptability of the pretence theory, consider once more our familiar standby, 'Chichikov set out to look the town over.' On the pretence theory, Gogol by inscribing this sentence was pretending to assert some proposition. Likewise he was pretending to refer to someone and to predicate 'setting out to look the town over' of the person to whom he referred. But what proposition is it that he was pretending to assert? Earlier we concluded that the proposition which Gogol by means of these words introduced was a *general* proposition, perhaps 'that a person named "Chichikov" set out to look the town over'. But surely if pretending-to-assert is what Gogol was doing, *that* would not be the proposition that he pretended to assert. Gogol would be pretending to refer to some entity of which he pretended to predicate that he set out to look the town over; and so he would be pretending to assert a *singular* proposition. For if someone uttered those words in ordinary life we would normally believe that he had referred, and predicated, and asserted some singular proposition. But who might it be that Gogol pretended to refer to? Chichikov? Chichikov does not exist, and so is no more susceptible to pretended reference than to actual reference. And which singular proposition might it be that Gogol pretended to assert? The words 'Chichikov set out to look the town over', as they occur in *Dead Souls*, pick out no singular proposition, none anyway such that there is some person such that *he* must have set out to look the town over if the proposition is to be true.

To this it might be replied that Gogol pretended to refer

without there *being* anyone to whom he pretended to refer, and pretended to assert some singular proposition without there *being* any singular proposition that he pretended to assert. This reply saves the pretence theory against the objections lodged above. But it does so at the high cost of surrendering the view that the fictioneer introduces certain propositions and thereby projects a world. For on this view of fiction, the fictioneer does not take up the stance of pretence toward certain states of affairs, those .then being included in the world of the work. Rather, he just *pretends* to take up a stance toward some states of affairs, without there being any toward which he pretends to take up a stance. Of course, in so far as the fictioneer pretends to assert purely general states of affairs, or in so far as he actually refers to existent entities and then pretends to assert something about them, his pretence can still be viewed as having propositional content. But the point is that in so far as he deals with 'fictitious entities'—characters—we can only save the pretence theory by allowing the world of the work at that point to remain empty, void, blank. Surely that cannot be a satisfactory theory of fiction.

The better view is that the stance characteristic of the fictioneer is that of *presenting*. The fictive stance consists of *presenting*, of *offering for consideration*, certain states of affairs—for us to reflect on, to ponder over, to explore the implications of, to conduct strandwise extrapolation on. And he does this for our edification, for our delight, for our illumination, for our cathartic cleansing, and more besides. It's as if every work of fiction were prefaced with the words 'I hereby present that . . .' or 'I hereby invite you to consider that . . .' Of course all of us on occasion invite others to take up this stance toward some states of affairs. But most of us do so only incidentally. The novelist and the dramatist make a profession of what for the rest of us is only an incidental diversion. That is what makes them fictioneers.

The fictive stance, thus understood, is clearly a species of mood-action. For if Gogol utters 'I hereby present for consideration that while the server was still spelling out the note, Chichikov set out to look the town over', and if thereby he *asserts* that he thereby presents for consideration that while the server was still spelling out the note Chichikov set out to look the town over, then it *follows* that what Gogol said is true. He *did* present that for consideration.

On this theory, the essence of fiction consists not in the nature of the states of affairs indicated, nor in the truth or falsity of those states of affairs. It lies in the mood-stance taken up. The liar and the fictioneer may take up a stance toward the very same propositions, and they may each believe them to be false. The difference between them lies in the mood-stance taken up. So too, the historian and the fictioneer may take up a stance toward the very same propositions, and they may both believe them to be true. They may in fact *be* true. Yet there is a difference between them; and the difference lies in the mood-stance taken up. It is not necessary to a work of fiction that the states of affairs indicated be false, nor that the author believe them to be false. He may in fact believe them all to be true, and they may all *be* true. What makes him a fictioneer none the less is that he nothing affirmeth but something presenteth.

VIII. *Item/Usage Systems*

At this point we have in hand the conceptual equipment necessary for explaining what it is to use some art-artefact to project a world. Before offering the explanation, however, I wish to introduce various distinctions and concepts which will serve here to forestall certain misunderstandings and later will be used to explain how the workings of pictures differ from, yet also resemble, the workings of sentences.

The person who has engaged in a bit of reflection about language quite naturally thinks of a language, such as English, as consisting of *words*. And he thinks of words, in turn, as visual and auditory designs. One language he regards as consisting of one particular set of visual/auditory designs; another, of another such set.

The perspective of the present discussion is different. We are bringing into prominence the fact that languages are for doing things with. A language is for acting. More specifically, a language is for the count-generation of actions. A language is a *system for acting*. But it's only by an *action* that one can generate an action. And though a given language canonizes certain visual/auditory designs, it also canonizes certain *usages* of those visual/auditory designs. It's to the action of using a certain design in a certain fashion that English assigns the action, say, of asserting that snow is white.

But it's true that the actions which English canonizes are, all of them, actions of using certain visual/auditory designs in certain ways. More specifically, all of them are actions of *inscribing* certain visual designs or *uttering* certain auditory designs in certain manners and circumstances. And that's a point which hasn't yet been recognized in our theoretical framework. We haven't dug into, we haven't analysed, the actions constituting the stock of the systems and arrangements that we have been discussing. The reason we haven't, of course, is that the points we wanted to make didn't require us to do so. Now it's time we dug inside.

I shall not, however, confine our attention to those systems whose stock consists of actions of inscribing visual designs and actions of sounding out auditory designs. The sign 'language' of deaf mutes, the smoke 'language' of the American Indians, the semaphore 'language' of ships, require for their use that certain entities, certain objects, certain items, be used in certain ways. They do not, however, require that certain visual designs be inscribed in certain fashions nor that certain auditory designs be uttered. I wish then to form the concept of an *item/usage system* for illocutionary actions. Our natural languages will constitute a distinct species of such. And what in Part Six I shall call systems for picturing will constitute another.

Start with an example. Suppose that English is in effect for me at a certain time. Suppose that I then inscribe-in-manner-and-circumstances-U the design 'The door is closed'. Suppose that to this action English assigns the action of asserting that my study door is closed. Then I have count-generated an act of my asserting that my study door is closed.

This 1-degree action, of *inscribing in manner and circumstance U the design 'The door is closed'* (call it *I*), is a completion of the 2-degree action of ... *inscribing* ... *in manner and circumstance U*. It is that particular completion of it which is exemplified if and only if someone performs the 2-degree action on the design 'The door is closed'. (Of course there may be other 2-degree actions of which that 1-degree action is a completion.) We may call the

2-degree action, a *usage*, and we may call the design, an *item*. And we may speak of the 1-degree action I as *comprised of* the pair whose members are that usage and that item. (It may be comprised of other such pairs as well.)

In this example, both the usage and the item making up the pair of which I is comprised play a role in indicating which, of all the illocutionary actions belonging to the scope of English, would in fact be generated if I was performed when English is in effect. But that is not in general so. There are systems such that there is some one item which, for every member of the stock of the system, belongs to a pair of which that member of the stock is comprised. In such systems it's not the item but the usage which functions as indicating which member of the scope was generated on a specific occasion. But equally it's possible to have systems in which the opposite is true. Indeed, natural languages are frequently discussed as if they were like that—as if the sentences did all the indicating, and the particular usages of the sentence did none of it.

We are ready to form the idea of an *item/usage system*. Consider some system for illocutionary actions. Call it S. If each member of the stock of S is a 1-degree action which is a completion (incomplete with respect to agent) of a 2-degree action, let us call S an item/usage system. Further, suppose that some member ϕ-ing a of the stock of S is a 1-degree action which is a completion of the 2-degree action of ϕ-ing; and suppose that someone exemplifies the 1-degree action ϕ-ing a just in case he performs the 2-degree action of ϕ-ing on a. Then let us say that the pair, $\langle a, \phi\text{-ing} \rangle$, is an *item/usage pair associated with* ϕ-ing a. For example, the pair, $\langle$ the table, kicking $\rangle$, is associated with the 1-degree action of kicking the table. Let us also sometimes say that ϕ-ing a is *comprised of* the members of its associated item/usage pair.

Some particular dialect of the English language, at a particular time in the career of that dialect, is an item/usage system for the performance of illocutionary actions. More specifically, it is one each of the members of whose stock is comprised of a certain auditory-visual design plus a certain usage thereof. The dialect itself, since it can change, is a certain *kind* of item/usage system. (That is, not a system of a certain kind but a certain kind of a system.) And the English language as such is, in turn, a certain dialect-kind. What is said here of English is true of all other natural languages as well.

Sentences can in principle be used in countless different ways for the performing of illocutionary actions. What is striking about natural languages is that the usages of which the actions belonging to the stock of such systems are comprised are all species of *uttering* or *inscribing*. That is to say, they are all species of *producing an occurrence* of some sentence. All the usages are of that sort. But in no natural language is there just the one usage of producing an occurrence of a sentence in any manner and any circumstance. Rather, in every such language there are at least some sentences such that if someone produces an occurrence in one manner and circumstance, the act of his producing it counts as an act of his performing one illocutionary action; whereas if he or someone else produces an occurrence of the very same sentence in another manner or circumstance, he performs a different illocutionary action—or none at all. Indeed, the truth is probably this: for no natural language is there any illocutionary action S such that there is a sentence, of which some member of the language's stock consists, such that no matter what the manner or circumstance in which an occurrence of that sentence is produced, if the language is in effect when the occurrence is produced, then illocutionary action S is performed. Semantics requires pragmatics for its context.

But the items of which the members of the stock of some item/usage system are comprised certainly need not be sentences. They may be gestures of the sort to be found in the sign-language of deaf mutes. Neither need they be 0-degree occurrables like sentences and gestures. They can be concrete objects, such as pens. My picking up my pen can be made to count as my expressing the wish that I had a pencil. Or if they are 0-degree occurrables, the mode of usage need not be that of producing an occurrence in some manner and circumstance. The items in the standard semaphore system of ships are flags—i.e., flag-kinds. But to perform an illocutionary action in the system one does not produce an occurrence of a flag. Rather, one already has examples (occurrences) in one's possession. The mode of usage consists in moving them about and holding them out in certain fashions.

Consider now a system for illocutionary action such that

every member of the stock of the system is comprised of an item/usage pair such that the item is a type susceptible of having occurrences, and such that the usage is always the production of an occurrence of the item (in some manner and circumstance). Let us call such items, *signs*. Flags in semaphore systems are not signs. Words in English are.

IX. *World-Projection*

And now I can explain, with full generality, what it is to project a world by the use of some artefact of art.

Consider some 1-degree actions $a_1, \ldots, a_n$, having as associated item/usage pairs $\langle I_1, U_1 \rangle, \ldots, \langle I_n, U_n \rangle$. Suppose that by performing $a_1, \ldots, a_n$ some person P takes up mood-stances toward all and only the states of affairs $S_1, \ldots, S_n$. And suppose that WW is the world derivable by extrapolation from $S_1, \ldots, S_n$. Then WW is the world *associated with* $I_1, \ldots, I_n$ for that particular usage of these items. And P will be said to have *projected* WW by performing $a_1, \ldots, a_n$. Further, if toward all of $S_1, \ldots, S_n$, P has taken up a fictive stance, P will be said to have *fictively* projected WW. If, on the contrary, toward all of $S_1, \ldots, S_n$, P has taken up an assertive stance, P will be said to have *assertively* projected WW. And so forth for the other stances.

By inscribing in certain manners and circumstances the sentences in the text of *Dead Souls*, Gogol took up mood-stances toward certain states of affairs. The world to be derived by extrapolation from those states of affairs is the world associated with (Gogol's use of) the text of *Dead Souls*. And Gogol has projected that world by thus inscribing those sentences. So too Botticelli has projected a world with his painting *Birth of Venus*. And no doubt the mood of projection in this case too is fictive.

Probably it is seldom the case that the states of affairs toward which some author takes a stance by his use of some text are all ones toward which he takes a fictive stance. Much more commonly, to some he takes a fictive stance, to some an assertive stance, etc. Almost certainly, for example, Gogol *asserted* that Russia had rather many citizens who could not resist chatting with the waiter when dining out. Thus the cases in which the author fictively projects the entire world associated with a text on a given use are probably rare.

Normally the world of some work of art which is fictively projected will not as a whole obtain in our actual world. Thus a fictively projected world is normally not required by, but alternative to, our actual world. But as we saw before, this is not necessarily so. It is possible that, by coincidence, the total state of affairs constituting some fictively projected world should obtain in our actual world. Indeed, it is possible that this should be so by design.

'World projection' has been defined in such a way that the historian and the philosopher engage in world projection as well as the novelist. There is the world (associated with the text) of Descartes's *Meditations*, and there is the world (associated with the text) of William Shirer's *Rise and Fall of the Third Reich*.

X. *Mentioning and Suggesting*[13]

Let us have before us once more that final paragraph from Jorge Borges's story 'The Streetcorner Man' which we earlier cited as providing a good example of suggestion. And let us, to make things easier, suppose that Borges wrote the story in the English of the translation:

Nice and easy, I walked the two or three blocks back to my shack. A candle was burning in the window, then all at once went out. Let me tell you, I hurried when I saw that. Then, Borges, I put my hand inside my vest—here by the left armpit where I always carry it—and took my knife out again. I turned the blade over, real slow. It was as good as new, innocent-looking, and you couldn't see the slightest trace of blood on it.

About this we said that Borges here explicitly mentions such states of affairs as someone's having said that he walked the two or three blocks back to his room, someone's having said that he put his hand inside his vest, etc. What in context Borges unmistakably *suggests*, without ever mentioning, is the narrator's having stabbed a bully named Francisco Real. Not only does Borges suggest this state of affairs. Clearly he takes up a fictive stance toward it.

[13] The reader who is interested in the main lines of my theory and not in its fine points can, without loss of continuity, skip this section and the two following and pick the discussion up again in Section XIII.

What makes me think that Borges suggested this, that it belongs to the world of his work? Well, certainly a knowledge of English, and of the fact that English was in effect for Borges, will not by itself do it. From my knowledge of that I know that *someone's having said that he put his hand inside his vest* belongs to the world of the work. But I don't, from that, know that *the narrator's having stabbed a bully named Francisco Real* belongs to the world. Rather, I ask myself: Why else, if he did not want us to entertain the thought of the narrator's being the killer, would Borges have had the narrator remark that there wasn't a trace of blood on his knife? After reflecting on the matter I conclude that there is no other reason.

We have, here before us, an example of the difference between mentioning and suggesting. The root of the difference is this: mentioning is grounded in convention (or, now and then, in stipulation). Suggestion is grounded in salience.

Let me express the distinction a bit more carefully. Suppose that a certain system S for mood-action is in effect for a certain person by virtue of his not dissociating himself from a convention present among the people that he is addressing (the interested parties), or by virtue of stipulation. Suppose further that he performs various actions from the stock of the system, and thereby generates the mood-actions assigned in the system to those members of the stock. We may then say that he has *mentioned* those states of affairs which belong to the state/action pairs associated with the actions that he generated.

Now the function-member of a system S is of course nothing but a set of arrangements for acting, each arrangement being a pair of a member of S's stock and whatever member of S's scope is assigned in S to that member of its stock. So consider some such arrangement, $\langle \psi\text{-ing}, \phi\text{-ing} \rangle$, which belongs to S's function-member. Perhaps it is this: $\langle$Inscribing in manner-and-circumstance-U the sentence 'Chichikov set out to look the town over', Taking up a fictive stance toward Chichikov's setting out to look the town over$\rangle$. Now associated with any such arrangement $\langle \phi\text{-ing}, \psi\text{-ing} \rangle$, for acting, there will be the more complex action of *performing ϕ-ing by ψ-ing*. For example, associated with that arrangement cited just above is the action of *taking up a fictive stance toward Chichikov's setting out to look the town* *over by inscribing in manner-and-circumstance- the sentence 'Chichikov set out to look the town over.'*

So consider once again the person who uses our system *S* for mood action, a system in effect by virtue of convention or stipulation. In doing so, he performs the members of some arrangement $\langle \phi\text{-ing}, \psi\text{-ing} \rangle$ which belongs to the function-member of *S*. But then also he performs the action-associate of that arrangement, namely, the action of *ψ-ing by φ-ing*. Now by doing so, he may count-generate *another* mood-action, χ-ing. And if the system he uses, when he generates χ-ing by performing *ψ-ing by φ-ing*, is in effect for him by virtue of salience, then he will be said to have *suggested* the state of affairs belonging to the state/action pair associated with χ-ing.

Suggestion occurs when the use of a system which is in effect by virtue of salience is parasitic, in the way indicated, on the use of a system which is in effect by virtue of convention or stipulation. The stock of the salience-system consists of action-associates of the arrangements belonging to the function-member of the convention- or stipulation-system.

Mentioning and suggesting are then two different species of introduction. Mentioning occurs only when a system for mood-action is in effect by virtue of convention or stipulation. And suggesting occurs only when a system for mood-action is in effect by virtue of convention or stipulation and then *another* system, one in effect by virtue of salience, rides piggy-back on the first. If a mime makes no use of miming conventions, then neither mentioning nor suggesting takes place—though of course introducing does. And if, when picturing takes place, it is unclear just where convention leaves off and salience begins, then also it is unclear what is mentioned and what is merely introduced, and unclear what is suggested as opposed to mentioned. Obviously it is in the language arts that the concepts of mentioning and suggesting have their clearest and most frequent application. Furthermore, I think it is the case that in those arts which make use of language, what is mentioned according to the concept just defined is also mentioned according to the ordinary concept of *mentioning*; and what is suggested according to the concept just defined is also suggested according to the ordinary concept of *suggesting*.

It is by using our concept of suggesting that we can now also give a theoretical articulation of the point, made much earlier, that by telling a story one may make a point—that is, assert something about the actual world. That consists in the fact that by fictionally projecting a world, one may *suggest* various states of affairs toward which one takes up an assertive stance. Likewise we now have the theoretical equipment for explaining parables and allegories: in such cases too, by fictionally projecting a certain world one *suggests* a whole complex of states of affairs toward which one takes up one and another kind of mood-stance.

XI. *Signification-Systems and Denotation*

In my analysis of literary fiction I not only found it necessary to speak of the author as introducing certain states of affairs by indicating them, but also to speak of him as referring to something, and as posing something about that to which he referred. Let me now explain what I had in mind with this word 'posing', and make clear how referring and posing fit within our general theory—dealing in this section with reference and in the next with posing. I shall treat referring as a species of *signifying*.

Suppose that I utter-in-manner-and-circumstance-U the sentence 'The door is closed.' And suppose that the act of my so doing counts as an act of my asserting that the door of my study is closed. I have then signified my study's door with the words 'the door' (and specifically, I have *referred* to it with the words).

The action of signifying the door of my study with the words 'the door' is an illocutionary action, generated in this case by the item/usage action of uttering-in-manner-and-circumstance-U the words 'the door'. I could have generated this very same illocutionary action by some other action. And I could have generated a different illocutionary action by performing this very same item/usage action—if a different system for illocutionary action had been in effect than the one that was.

Any system for illocutionary action whose scope consists exclusively of actions of signifying something with something I shall call a *system for signifying*. The *stock* of such a system will consist exclusively of item/usage actions. For one signifies one thing with another by using the latter in a certain manner and circumstance. Specifically, one performs the action of signifying x with I by performing some 2-degree action (usage) on I. Thus a system for signifying is an ordered pair whose first member is a set of item/usage actions, and whose second member is a function which assigns to each of the first some action of signifying something with something, in accordance with this rule: To an action σ is assigned the action of signifying x with I only if an item/usage pair associated with σ has I as member, plus some usage U.

Now consider any system S for signifying. And consider any action σ from the stock of S. σ will be comprised of some usage U and some item I. And the function-member of S will assign to σ some action of signifying something with I. Suppose it assigns to σ the action of signifying E with I. Let us then say that σ *denotes E* in S.[14] (We shall also say that the pair, $\langle I, U \rangle$, *denotes E* in S. The pair, $\langle I, U \rangle$, is of course an item/usage pair associated with σ.)

So suppose that some system S for signifying is in effect. Suppose further that some action σ from the stock of S is comprised of the usage of *uttering* plus the item 'the door'. And suppose that in S, the action of uttering 'the door' denotes my study's door. Then by performing the action of uttering the words 'the door' I generate the action of signifying my study's door with the words 'the door'.

It is important to notice that on this concept it is *actions* which denote—specifically, item/usage actions—not merely items of one sort or another. If systems for signifying were such that, in each system, each member of the stock which shared some item I in its associated item/usage pair denoted the very same thing, this would be an idle point. We could simply speak of what was assigned to each *item* in the system. But most emphatically that is not the case. 'The door' can be used, in English, to signify any

---

[14] Thus for any item/usage system S for signifying, there is a function—call it the denoting function for S—which assigns to each member σ of the stock of S whatever it may be that σ denotes in S. We may, accordingly, form the concept of the denotation system associated with S, where S is any item/usage system for signifying. The denotation system associated with S is an ordered pair whose first member is the set of all those actions which belong to the stock of S, and whose second member is the denoting function for S, assigning to each member σ of the stock of S whatever σ denotes in S.

door whatsoever. Which door it is in fact used to signify on a given occasion depends on manner and circumstance of usage. In English, there is no one thing such that it is what 'the door' is used to signify. Correspondingly, in English there is no one thing denoted by every member of the stock which has the word 'the door' in its associated item/usage pair. What is the case, though, is that in English an uttering in some specific manner and circumstance of 'the door' denotes my study door, and not any other.

Now I shall henceforth speak of someone as *referring* to something only if he not only signifies it but poses something of it (and thereby performs some mood-action). No referring without posing. Accordingly, I must move on to an explanation of the concept of posing.

XII. *Posing*

When a person performs the illocutionary action of asserting something he also, in many cases, performs the illocutionary action of *asserting something about something*. For example, if one asserts that the door will be closed then also one asserts, about the door, that it will be closed.

It is tempting to identify every action of the form *asserting that x is φ* with the corresponding action of the form *asserting of x that it is φ*. But that such pairs of actions are indeed pairs—actions distinct from each other—can be seen in the following way. Consider some specific asserting-that action—say, asserting that Nixon was the first person to resign the United States presidency. Now if someone asserts that Nixon was the first person to resign the United States presidency, then necessarily he also performs the action of asserting *of* Nixon that he was the first person to resign the United States presidency. But the converse is not true. For suppose that I assert that the 37th United States president was the first person to resign the United States presidency. Then again I would have asserted *of* Nixon that he was the first person to resign the United States presidency. For Nixon is identical with the 37th president of the United States. I would in this second case have asserted the same thing of the same person as I did in the first case. But my action of asserting that would not be the same as it was in the

first case. The action of asserting that the 37th president of the
United States was the first person to resign the United States
presidency is not the same action as the action of asserting that
Nixon was the first person to resign the United States presidency, since what I assert in the one case might be true and the
other false—if, for example, Nixon had never been president.
So it is possible to assert *of* Nixon that he was the first person to
resign the United States presidency without asserting *that*
Nixon was the first person to resign the United States presidency. That is enough to show distinctness of actions.

There is nothing peculiar about the example we have used.
So in general it can be said that an action of the form *asserting
that x is* ϕ is not to be identified with the corresponding action of
the form *asserting of x that it is* ϕ, since one can perform the latter
without performing the former. Asserting-that is intensional.
Asserting-of is not.

That which can be asserted is a proposition (state of affairs).
That which can be asserted-of is like a proposition except that it
has in it a hole, an opening, a slot—a phenomenon which has
its linguistic reflection in the fact that the 'it' functions like a
variable, being governed by different antecedents in different
contexts of use. In an earlier day such entities were thought of
as functions, and were specifically called propositional functions by Russell, on the ground that the value of any such
function, for a given argument, is always a proposition. Suppose that we use this phrase 'propositional function' with
ontological neutrality, simply to stand for whatever it is that
can be asserted-about. I am inclined to think that any propositional function *that it is* ϕ, is identical with the corresponding
property of *being* ϕ. If so, propositional functions are just
occurrables of degree 1 or greater.

So to return to our opening point: corresponding to, but
distinct from, the action of asserting that the door is closed is
this action:

(1) asserting, concerning the door, that it will be closed.

But 1-degree actions of asserting-that are not at all peculiar
among mood-actions in having such counterparts. For consider
the following:

(2) commanding, with respect to the door, that it be closed,
(3) expressing the wish, with respect to the door, that it (would) be closed,
(4) asking, with respect to the door, that it be closed, and
(5) promising, with respect to the door, that it (will) be closed.

In all these cases we obviously have a 1-degree action which is the same sort of counterpart to a corresponding 1-degree mood-action as (1) was to the corresponding 1-degree mood-action of asserting that the door will be closed.

So consider the set of 2-degree mood-actions which are incomplete with respect to agent and state of affairs. This will have such members as *asserting that*, *commanding that*, etc. What we have just seen leads to the conclusion that many (if not all) of these will have 3-degree counterparts, thus: the 2-degree mood-action of x *asserting that* p has the 3-degree counterpart of x *asserting of* y *that it is* ϕ; the 2-degree mood-action of x *commanding that* p has the 3-degree counterpart of x *commanding of* y *that it is* ϕ; etc.

Now just as it was convenient to use the word 'introduce' to cover all species of mood-actions, so also it will be convenient to have some word to cover all such mood-action counterparts. Let us use the word 'pose of'. Thus asserting something concerning something is one species of posing something of something; commanding something concerning something is another species of posing something of something; etc. Any species of posing always comes in a certain 'moods', though the concept of *posing-of* is itself mood-neutral, as is the concept of *introducing*.

When I speak of someone posing of x that it is ϕ, many writers would probably speak instead of someone *predicating* of x that it is ϕ. When we are dealing with assertive posing, this is an appropriate word to use. If I assertively pose of the door that it will be closed, then I predicate of the door that it will be closed. But only in the case of asserting-of is it appropriate, in normal English, to speak of predicating. The concept of *predication* has built into it a limitation to actions of asserting-of. If I express the wish, concerning the door, that it would be closed, I do not then predicate of the door that it will be closed. Thus if we were to use the word 'to predicate' for our purposes here we would have to stretch its sense; and always there would be the danger of its being understood in its normal English sense rather than in its stretched sense.

The concept of a system for posing-of is now easily formed. It is a system for illocutionary action whose scope consists entirely of actions of the form 'f-ly posing *being-ϕ* of x'—that is, entirely of 1-degree posing-of actions such as: assertively posing *smiling* of Carter, interrogatively posing *being a skilled general* of Napoleon, imperatively posing *being closed* of my study door, fictively posing *being melancholy* of Bathsheba, etc.

Often posing ϕ of x, and using some sign I to refer to x, go hand in hand. One's referring serves as indicator of what it was that ϕ was posed of. But there seems to be no necessity in this. In principle one could perform some action which counts as fictively posing of Bathsheba that she is melancholy without using some item to refer to (stand for) Bathsheba.

XIII. *Postlude*

The media are many by which world-projection can be accomplished. It does not require, for its performance, that one confine oneself to producing occurrences of those visual/auditory designs which are words in some language or other. True, the examples offered along the way have mainly been verbal examples. But nothing in the formulation and nothing in the theory limits them to words. By doing such things as picturing something, playing a dramatic role, and performing a piece of music, one can also project a world. The crux, of course, is whether by performing such actions one can perform some mood-action. If so, then perforce by the performance of such actions one can project a world.

So as to give my theory some concreteness I shall now turn to showing how the theory applies to two of the non-literary arts. In Part Five I will apply it to role-playing as that occurs in drama, and in Part Six to pictorial representation.

The Medium of Dramatic Performance

A theory of world-projection has now been constructed that is neutral both as to the medium used for the projection and as to the mood-stance taken up toward the world projected. Along the way we have seen how the theory fits diverse mood-stances. What must now be done is to see how it applies to various media. In this Part I shall discuss how it applies to the medium of dramatic performance.

Suppose that an author has composed some dramatic work and that we now want to perform it. What must we do?

Of course it's true that a musical performance can be dramatic. And it's true that a particular execution of the Greek Orthodox liturgy can be dramatic. In saying this, I am refer-ring to the building up and relaxation of tension in the sequence of sounds or liturgical actions.[1] A performance of a dramatic work can also be dramatic in that sense, and apparently Aristo-tle was of the view that all such performances *should be* dramatic in that sense. But when I asked what it is to perform a dramatic work, I was not using the word 'dramatic' in *that* sense. My interest here is not in what constitutes a dramatic performance of a musical work or of the Orthodox liturgy. Rather, a specific instance of my question is this: What is it to perform Arthur Miller's classic dramatic work, *Death of a Salesman*?

I think it best for our purposes here to set off to the side all cases of filmed versions of dramatic works. For these raise quite special problems of their own, due both to the fact that visual representation is involved and to the fact that often such films

---

[1] Some *parts* of the liturgy are perhaps dramatic in the other sense. They may constitute a dramatic representation. And there are some writers on liturgy who hold that the *entire* liturgy should be seen as a highly symbolic or allegorical dramatic representation.

are made, as well as shown, without any performance of the work, in the strict sense of the word 'performance', taking place at all. (Cf. Section IX of Part Two.)

For the performance of dramatic works, even for their correct performance, one does not always needs actors or actresses playing the role of characters. Sometimes puppets will do: sometimes indeed puppets are required. And sometimes mannikins. Our discussion will proceed more smoothly and lucidly, though, if we set the puppets and mannikins off to the side for a while, coming back to them later, and consider those works whose correct performance requires actors or actresses to play the role of characters. *Death of a Salesman* will do nicely as an example, since for a correct performance of this work one needs one actor to play the role of Willie Loman, another to play the role of his son Biff, and so forth.

In saying that one needs someone to play the role of Willie Loman I am, of course, not using the name 'Willie Loman' to refer to some person, claiming that one needs someone to play the role of *that person*. Rather, my claim is that one needs an actor to play the role of the Willie-Loman-in-*Death of a Salesman* character. One needs an actor to play the role of that particular *character* which is a component in the world of *Death of a Salesman* and which has essential within it the property of *being named 'Willie Loman'*. It's true, indeed, that even in works which require actors and actresses for correct performances it will often be the case that there are characters which are components in the world of the work such that the work can be correctly performed without anyone playing those characters. These are characters that never 'appear on stage'. But as we all know, that's not the case for the character Willie Loman. If *Death of a Salesman* is to be performed correctly, someone has to play the role of that character.

So what must an actor do to play the role of a certain character? If we can answer that, we will have got deep into the heart of how dramatic performance works as a medium of world-projection.

The answer for the Willie Loman case can be simply and briefly stated: the actor plays the role of the Willie Loman character by *pretending* to be an *example* of the Willie Loman character. Not, notice, by pretending to *be Willie Loman*. For the name 'Willie Loman' names a character; and only in the very oddest cases would anyone pretend to be a character. Rather, by pretending to be *an example* of the character. Characters, remember, are kinds: entities capable of having examples.

Not quite every case of an actor playing the role of some character is accomplished by the actor pretending to be an example of the character. So we cannot straightforwardly generalize from the Willie Loman case. But far and away most cases are of this sort. Furthermore, a close scrutiny of this sort of case will lead us into the exceptions. So let us try to understand what it is to pretend to be an example of a character.

But first, what about the case in which an actor 'plays a real person', as we say? Isn't that an exception to the rule that the actor plays the role of a character by pretending to be an example of it? Must we *wait* to find exceptions? Aren't they immediately at hand in this phenomenon?

Well, suppose that some dramatic work *W* has a character Henry Kissinger as component—that is, suppose it has among its components a character which has essential within it the property of *being named 'Henry Kissinger'*, plus a great many other properties that our well-known Kissinger has. If this work is to be performed someone has to play the role of Kissinger. But that is really no different in structure from someone playing the role of Willie Loman. For there is, after all, the Kissinger-in-work-*W* character; and it is this that the actor pretends to be an example of. The real Henry Kissinger may in fact be an example of that character, or he may not be. His properties may at no point diverge from those essential within the character, or here and there they may diverge. But that will make no difference to the actor's pretending to be an example of the character, and thus to his playing the role.

But suppose Henry Kissinger *himself* played the role of the Kissinger character. Wouldn't pretence then be left behind? Wouldn't we then have an actor playing a role without *pretending* to be an example of the character, instead, *being* an example? Not necessarily. Unless our play *W* is very unusual, essential within our Kissinger-in-*W* character will be actions of making such-and-such assertions by uttering such-and-such words. But more than likely Kissinger, when playing the part of Kissinger, will not make those assertions. He will only pretend to do so. Uttering those words and thereby making those assertions may even be something that Kissinger actually once did—when addressing, let us say, the North Vietnamese in Paris. But more than likely he would not actually be making those assertations, *now*, *on stage*. He would only pretend to be doing so. In short, playing a real person, even when the real person in question plays the real person, is normally accomplished by the actor's pretending to be an example of the character.

Not only must the actor who plays Willie Loman pretend that he is an example of that character if *Death of a Salesman* is to be correctly performed. He must also pretend that the other actors and actresses are examples of the characters that they are playing, and they must return the favour to him. There must be joint and interacting pretence. And all together the actors and actresses must act as if certain items to be found on and about the stage are examples of some of the non-character kinds which are components in the world of *Death of a Salesman*. We shall have more to say about this last point later, namely, about the role of props in dramatic performances. But first let us scrutinize this action of *pretending* which we have placed near the centre of our theory.

In saying that the actor pretends to be an example of the Willie Loman character, haven't we fallen into the old theory of drama as trickery, as illusion? Aren't we implying that to play the role of Willie Loman is to *fool* people, or at least to *try* to fool people, into believing that one is an example of the Willie Loman character?

Not at all. There are many different things that one can do *by* pretending; and there are many different things that one can *aim* to do *by* pretending. It's true, indeed, that one can pretend to have a toothache for the reason that it is one's aim to fool people into believing that one has a toothache; and *by* thus pretending one can *in fact* thus fool people. But pretending that so-and-so is not always aimed at fooling people into believing that so-and-so, nor does it *in fact* always fool people into believing that so-and-so. (Cf. Part Four, Section VII.) So too for the actor. Though the actor pretends, normally he does not aim to deceive by his pretending, neither does he normally in fact deceive by his pretending. And even when he does, that is irrelevant to how dramatic performance works as a medium of world projection.

But what then is the characteristic aim, and the characteristic outcome, of the actor's pretending? Well, notice in the first place that to pretend is always to pretend *that so-and-so*. We may indeed say it differently. We may speak of someone pretending *to have* a toothache, rather than of his pretending *that he has* a toothache. But the phenomenon remains the same. Pretending always consists of pretending that some proposition is true—that some state of affairs is occurring. The actor pretends *that he is* an example of the character. And to do that is to pretend that the state of affairs of his being an example of the character *is* occurring, *is* true.

Now what the actor characteristically does and aims to do, by pretending that he is an example of the character, is perform the action of taking up a certain mood-stance toward the very same state of affairs that he pretends to be occurring. His aim is to perform the action of taking up a mood-stance toward the state of affairs of his being an example of the Willie Loman character, and his characteristic way of trying to achieve that aim is to perform the other, distinct, action of *pretending* that he is an example of the character. Put it like this: his aim is that his act of pretending that he is an example of the character shall *count as* an act of his taking up a certain mood-stance toward his being an example of the character. The stance in question is the *fictive* stance, that is, the stance of presenting to us a state of affairs for our consideration. The actor's aim, in pretending that he is an example of the Willie Loman character, is that his pretending shall count-generate his taking up a fictive stance toward the state of affairs of his being an example of the character. His aim in pretending is to present to us for our consideration that very same state of affairs that he pretends to be true. He presents that state of affairs to us for our consideration *by* pretending that it is occurring. In other artistic media that very same state of affairs might be presented to us for our consideration; but if so, it would be done in other ways than by thus pretending.

It is of prime importance to notice the following peculiarities in all this. One actor pretends that he is an example of the Willie Loman character, another, that he is an example of the Biff character, and so forth. And by all together doing their pretending, thereby taking up a fictive stance toward their being examples of the characters they are playing, they fictionally project the world of the work (once the function of the props is added in). But though Sidney Lumet, say, pretends that he is an example of the Willie Loman character, and thereby takes up a fictive stance toward his being an example of the Willie Loman character, yet *that* state of affairs is not included in the world of *Death of a Salesman*. The world of *Death of a Salesman* does not include the state of affairs of Sidney Lumet being an example of the Willie Loman character. For it is not necessary, if the work's world is to occur, that Sidney Lumet be an example of the Willie Loman character. Indeed, it's not even necessary that Sidney Lumet exist. The world of the work is not anchored to Sidney Lumet. All that's necessary is that *someone* be an example of the Willie Loman character. So too, when Olivier plays Hamlet he pretends that *he* is an example of the Hamlet character. Thereby he presents for consideration that very same state of affairs that he pretends to be true, namely that of his being an example of the Hamlet character. He takes up a fictive stance toward that. His pretending that he is an example of the Hamlet character *counts as* his taking up a fictive stance toward the state of affairs of his being an example of the Hamlet character. But that state of affairs is not included within the world of the play *Hamlet*; for the world of *Hamlet* could occur without Olivier being an example of the Hamlet character, indeed, without Olivier ever existing. The world of *Hamlet* is not anchored to Olivier. All that is necessary, if the world of *Hamlet* is to occur, is that there be *someone* who is an example of the Hamlet character, *it makes no difference who*.

So this is the situation: When a fully correct performance of a dramatic work takes place, *two distinct* worlds are fictionally projected. One is a world anchored to the actors and the props. That we may call 'the world of the performance'. The other is the world of the work. The theory of dramatic performance that I am proposing is thus a *two-world* theory. In fictionally projecting the world of the performance, the actors and director fictionally project the world of the work.

The logical relation between these two worlds is relatively clear. Part of it consists in there being states of affairs in the performance-world which are *instances*, *instantiations*, of states of affairs in the work's world. In the work's world one finds the state of affairs of *someone* being an example of the Willie Loman character. In the performance-world one finds the state of affairs of *Sidney Lumet* being an example of the Willie Loman character. And the latter is an instance of the former. But that is not the whole of the matter. For almost always there will be many states of affairs that the actor pretends to be true, and by pretending to be true, fictionally projects, which are not instances of states of affairs indicated by the author. That is because the actor fleshes out the character he is playing beyond what the text prescribes. As part of his interpretation of his character he may, let us say, pretend to have a limp, though that is not so much as hinted at in the script. In this way, the world of the performance is more detailed, more rich, than the world of the work. (Incidentally, it is mainly for this reason that the world of the work cannot be inferred from the world of the performance.)

Now in a case of an actor's thus fictionalizing about himself, accomplished by his pretending to be an example of a character, the actor and director do not concern themselves with *all* the attributes essential within the character. There are vastly too many for that. Fortunately, however, there will always be various subsets of that totality of attributes, such that, if someone had all the members of the subset, he would have all the attributes essential within the character. Call such a subset, a *crucial* subset for that character. The actor and director concern themselves with the members of some such crucial subset, realizing full well that the other attributes will take care of themselves.

And what do actor and director characteristically do, with respect to some crucial subset for the character, so as to bring it about that the actor plays the role of a character by pretending to be an example of it? Well, with respect to some of the properties belonging to a crucial subset actor and/or director by intent bring it about that the actor actually *has* those properties. For example, essential within the Willie Loman character is the property of being male. The director sees to it that the actor he chooses actually *has* that property. With respect to others of the properties belonging to a crucial subset actor and/or director by intent bring it about that the actor *has the appearance* of having them if he does not actually have them. For example, if the actor is young, he will be made up so as to have the appearance of being middle-aged, for that is a property essential within the Willie Loman character. Thirdly, with respect to some of the *actions* belonging to a crucial subset, actor and/or director by intent bring it about that the actor actually performs those actions. Actions of uttering certain sentences are good examples. In most cases, actions of uttering certain sentences are essential within the character, and the actor will actually perform those actions. Lastly, with respect to others of the actions belonging to a crucial subset of the character, actor and/or director by intent bring it about that the actor *pretends* to perform those actions. Actions of asserting something are good examples. To be an example of the Willie Loman character one must assert various things. But seldom if ever will an actor in playing the role of Willie Loman actually assert those things. He will, instead, pretend to do so.

In summary, what characteristically happens when an actor plays the role (part) of a certain character by pretending to be an example of the character is that he in conjunction with the director by intent brings it about that some of the properties essential within the character are ones the actor actually has, that others he puts on the appearance of having, that some of the actions essential within the character are ones that he actually performs, and that others are ones that he *pretends* to perform.

Now it is this *last* phenomenon—that, namely, of pretending to perform some action—that is requisite to pretending to be a character. If there is nothing that the actor pretends to do, then he is not pretending to be an example of a character.

Yet even so he may play the role of a character, may he not? We begin finally to catch sight of the exceptions to the rule that the actor plays his character by pretending to be an example thereof.

Suppose that in order to perform a certain drama we need an actor who will sit silently and motionlessly on a sofa throughout the entire performance. Suppose further that the character he plays has essential within it the properties of being male and of being middle-aged, and that the actor who plays the role is in fact male but not middle-aged, being instead young, and is accordingly made up so as to have the appearance of being middle-aged. Though having such-and-such an appearance is still relevant in this case, plus various beings and doings, all pretence has now disappeared. The actor is no longer pretending to be an example of the character he is playing. At most he *puts on the appearance* of being an example of it. Yet he is in fact playing the role of a certain character which is a component in the work's world.

We can go yet farther. Imagine a work of avant-garde drama whose entire dramatic action consists of two actors carrying out onto the stage fifty chairs, carefully arranging them into seven concentric semicircles, then taking them all back. (The work might be called *Semicircles*.) And suppose that the actors are in their own ordinary street clothes and are not in any way made up. In such a case there might well be nothing by way of pretence, and also nothing by way of the actors putting on the appearance of having various properties that they do not in fact have. But still they are playing the role of two characters. By doing what they do they are taking up a fictive stance toward their being examples of the two characters in the work's world. The oddity of the case is that they *are in fact* examples of the characters. It's rather like a novel so realistic that the entire world projected actually occurred, and both author and readers *know* that it did.

While on this topic we ought to take note of yet one other related phenomenon. In my discussion thus far I have focused my attention exclusively on Western drama of the past several centuries. But if one looks further afield into other cultures one frequently finds actors and actresses made up in certain ways but not made up so as to have the appearance of possessing such-and-such properties essential within the character, rather made up so as to have an appearance *conventionally associated* in dramatic performances with those properties. Similarly, one finds actors and actresses who aim neither at performing nor at pretending to perform some action essential within the character, but rather at performing some action *conventionally* connected in dramatic performances with that action.

So what now is left? Have all my theses died the pitiful lingering death of a thousand qualifications? Not at all. What remains is this central point: given that a dramatic work is being correctly performed, for actors and actresses to play the role of characters which are components in the world of the work is for them (along with the director) to adopt the fictive stance toward *their being* examples of those characters—and to do so in what may now be called 'the dramatic way': namely, by having, or being made to appear to have, or being made to have properties conventionally connected in dramatic performances with having, all the *properties* in a crucial subset for the character; and to perform, or pretend to perform, or do what is conventionally connected in dramatic performance with performing, all the *actions* in the same crucial subset for the character. It is for them to take up, in the dramatic way, the fictive stance toward the state of affairs of their being examples of the characters they are playing. *In* so doing (once the function of the props is added in) they fictionally project the world of the performance. And therein, they fictionally project the world of the work.

By us in the modern West, playing the role of a character is characteristically done by way of the actors and actresses pretending to be examples of their characters. We have seen, though, that there are other ways of doing it. But whether it is done by *pretending* to be examples, or by merely *putting on the appearance* of being examples, or by *actually being* examples, or by performing the actions and putting on the appearances *conventionally connected in dramatic performances with* being examples, what remains true is that if an actor is to play the role of a character in a work's world he, in conjunction with whoever else is responsible, must in the dramatic way take up a fictive stance toward his being an example of that character—makes no difference whether in fact he is or isn't.

Of course only *some* of the actor's beings and doings, and only *some* of his appearings and pretendings, *count as* his taking up a fictive stance toward his being and doing so-and-so. And to know what is included within the world of a dramatic performance we must be able to tell whether the actor, by being or doing or appearing to be or pretending to do so-and-so, has or has not taken up a fictive stance toward his being or doing so-and-so. The young actor who plays the part of Willie Loman has the property of *being made up so as to have the appearance of a middle-aged man*. But his having that property does not count as his taking up a fictive stance toward his having it. Further, unless his makeup is applied with extraordinary skill, he also has the property of *appearing to many in the audience to be made up so as to have the appearance of a middle-aged man*. But his having that property also does not count as his taking up a fictive stance toward his having it. It is not included within the world of the performance. A fictive stance is taken up toward Sidney Lumet's being called 'Willie Loman', not toward Sidney Lumet's being called 'Sidney Lumet'; toward Sidney Lumet's being a middle-aged man, not toward Sidney Lumet's being made up to have the appearance of a middle-aged man; toward Sidney Lumet's appearing to be a middle-aged man, not toward Sidney Lumet's appearing to be made up so as to have the appearance of being a middle-aged man. In short, to say it once again, some of what the actor is and does and appears to be and pretends to do counts as his taking up a fictive stance toward his being and doing so-and-so, and some of it does not thus count.

Here I shall not delve into the matter of how we tell one way or the other, beyond remarking that the fact that it is the *fictive* stance that the actors take up toward certain states of affairs, and the fact that they take it up toward the states of affairs that they do, are of course connected with the fact that they are performing the particular drama that they are. The fact that our two imagined actors are performing the imagined avant-garde drama *Semicircles* is an important part of what brings it about that their actions *count as* their taking up a fictive stance toward their being examples of the characters.

Thus far I have limited myself to speaking of those cases in which we need actors and actresses playing the roles of characters if the work is to be performed. Let me now relax this limitation, and pick up the puppets who have been made to sit off on the side long enough by now. Notice first that in dramatic performances the responsibility for projecting the world that is in fact projected is shared among actors, actresses, director, and even, I suppose, assistants. In spite of the centrality of actors and actresses, it does not belong solely to them. Seeing that, we also see how to handle the puppet case. In a puppet performance of a dramatic work no fictive stance is taken up toward some actor's being an example of one of the work's characters; for there are no actors. Instead, a fictive stance is taken up toward some *puppet*'s being an example of one of the characters. And the one who takes up that stance, the one who presents that state of affairs to us for our consideration, is of course the puppeteer. By his moving the puppets as he does, by his uttering the words he does, he presents for our consideration the state of affairs, say, of one of his puppet being an example of the Punch character.[2]

From puppets we are naturally led on to props. When a dramatic work is performed, it is typically not only the case that persons or puppets play the role of characters, but also that objects play the role of various non-person types which are components of the work's world.[3] The structure of such objective role-playing does not differ in essentials from that of actors and puppets playing the role of characters. When an object plays the role of a certain component in the work's world, a fictive stance is taken up in the dramatic way toward the state of affairs of that object's being an example of that component of the work's world. For example, a fictive stance is taken up in the dramatic way toward the state of affairs of some fake plastic trees being examples of the Birnam-Wood-in-*Macbeth* type, toward the state of affairs of some table which was recently made in Zeeland, Michigan, being an example of the banqueting-table-in-*Macbeth* type, and so forth. Furthermore, what characteristically takes place with respect to some at least of the props is that the actors *treat* those objects as examples of components of the work's world, this treating-as sometimes consisting in *pretending that they are* examples. However, such treating-as does not seem necessary for non-personal, objective role-playing. A vase of flowers can play the role of a vase-of-flowers component, even though none of the actors *treats it as* a vase of flowers. It may stand unremarked in the background. And that leads on to the remark that the ultimate avant-garde

[2] A sort of intermediate case between the actor case and the puppet case would occur if some dramatic work were performed by getting small children to engage in rote behaviour. In such a case it might well be that the children were not really pretending, and were not really taking up a fictive stance toward their being examples of the work's world's characters. Rather it would be the producer who would be the responsible agent. The children would hardly be actors. They would be 'puppets', albeit live human ones.

[3] *Persons* can also play the role of non-person-types. They can play the role of animals, even of trees.

dramatic work would be one for whose performance one would need nothing *but* props. The props would be set in place; at the beginning of the work the curtain would be drawn up; it would be lowered at the end of the first act; the props would then be rearranged a bit, the curtain would then be drawn up again to begin the second act, and so forth.[4]

A few pages back I stated what was left at that point by way of solid thesis amidst all the qualifications. It came to this: when a dramatic work is being correctly performed, in order for an actor or actress to play the role of a certain character the fictive stance must be taken up in the dramatic way toward the state of affairs of the actors and actresses themselves being examples of the characters whose roles they are playing. Now we can drop the limitation to actors and actresses: in order for an entity to play the role of a type which is a component in some dramatic work's world, the fictive stance must be taken up in the dramatic way toward *that entity*'s being an example of the type which it is playing the role of. Pretence, appearance, actors, actresses—each falls away as inessential. What is left is that the fictive stance is taken up in the dramatic way toward an entity's being an example of that type whose role it is playing—plus of course our two-worlds theory of dramatic performance. That too is left. Whenever a dramatic work is performed, then two worlds will always be projected at once, connected in the way indicated earlier, with the world of the work being projected in the projection of the world of the performance.

And now we are at a point where I can also put forth this final thesis: for a dramatic work to be performed, role-playing understood as above must take place. The essence of dramatic performance is role-playing.

One large, important, and fascinating question still looms before us. Children often engage in games of pretence—they pretend to do various things that they do not do, they make

---

[4] Objective role-playing shades almost indiscernibly into an object's being merely a feature of the total performance situation and having no role-playing function whatsoever. It may be, for example, that both the world of the work and the world of the performance can occur without there being any vase of flowers; yet a vase of flowers may be standing in the background. Likewise the music that accompanies dramatic performances often plays no representing function whatsoever with respect to either the world of the work or the world of the performance. Its function is rather to be expressive of the same qualities that the work or the performance is expressive of, thus in its inner character to be fitting or congruent to the character of work or performance.

themselves up and dress up so as to put on the appearance of having properties that they do not have, and in general, they pretend to be of a type, a sort, a kind, that they are not at the moment an example of—to be an example of the type: Teacher, when they are not. Furthermore, by their pretending they take up a fictive stance toward their being examples of the types in question. Yet, no work is thereby performed. Why not? What more must be done to perform a work? What makes an array of actions on the stage into a performance of *Death of a Salesman*, rather than just an intensely interesting game of pretence? Why is it that when we engage in the role-playing of ordinary life—psychologists and sociologists tell us that we all do—we are not performing dramatic works? I said that the director and actors by intent aim to bring it about that, with respect to some properties, the actor will have them, with respect to others, that he will appear to have them, with respect to some actions, that he will perform them, with respect to others, that he will pretend to perform them. Couldn't their intentions and accomplishments with respect to those properties and actions be just exactly as they are and yet the work not be performed?

I called that a 'large, important and fascinating question'. But the answer, in all its essentials, is already before us. For in Part Two already we discussed what it is to perform a work of music, there unearthing the difference between performing a piano sonata and just making the sounds of that sonata at the piano. The situation for dramatic performance is not, in its essentials, any different from what it is for musical performance. Accordingly the reader is referred to that earlier discussion, with just this reminder: when we were discussing what it is to perform a musical work, the works we were discussing were not ones by whose performance *worlds* were projected. And so it must be kept in mind that in this crucial respect dramatic works are different. What we said as to the nature of musical performance will have to be *adapted* by the reader.

PART SIX

The Medium of Pictures

I. *Preliminaries*

In this Part I shall analyse in detail the working of pictorial representation as a medium of world projection, thus providing a second illustration of the general theory developed in Parts One–Four. Along the way it will emerge that world projection is not incidental, but *essential*, to pictorial representation. For it is not the case that sometimes one pictures without projecting a world while at other times one pictures and thereby projects a world. Rather, no picturing without projection.

We must remind ourselves of a distinction made in Part One. There I observed that Rembrandt both represented Bathsheba and represented Hendrickje with his painting *Bathsheba*. I also observed in saying this the word 'represent' is being used to express two distinct concepts.

Rembrandt represented Hendrickje in the sense that she was Rembrandt's *model* for his production of the painting. Or to put it in other words, Rembrandt created the painting by producing a *rendering* of Hendrickje. Using something as a model, that is, producing a rendering of something, is a form of guided making. The relation between Rembrandt, Bathsheba, and the painting is different. Bathsheba did not function as a model for Rembrandt in the creation of his painting. Rather, Rembrandt's representing Bathsheba involved his using part of his pictorial design to *stand for* Bathsheba. And the action of using (part of) a pictorial design to stand for something is a count-generated action.

What points up with particular clarity the difference between the relation of Rembrandt, Hendrickje, and the painting, and the relation of Rembrandt, Bathsheba, and the painting, is this: if the world projected by way of the painting is to occur, Bathsheba must exist and must be as the painting shows her to be. But Hendrickje need not exist. The world of the work is anchored to Bathsheba. It is not anchored to Hendrickje.[1]

In what follows I shall not explore representation as rendering. Thus the phenomenon of Rembrandt representing Hendrickje will fall outside my purview. My concern will rather be to account for such phenomena as that of Rembrandt representing Bathsheba. Not everything said in the preceding paragraphs concerning Rembrandt's representing of Bathsheba will hold, *mutatis mutandis*, for all the cases of representation that I will explore. Not always, for example, when a woman is represented will there exist (or have existed) a woman whom part of the design is used to stand for, and not always will there exist (or have existed) a woman to whom the world of the work is anchored. However, the cases of representation that fall within my purview will all be ones that are *count*-generated. Representation *qua* modelling falls outside my purview because it is not a count-generated action.

II. *Goodman's Observations*

In his discussion on representation in *Languages of Art* Nelson Goodman makes several observations that will prove of central importance in our discussion. To gain access to these observations, a few distinctions must first be made.

When I speak of pictorial representation, it is an action of human beings that I have in mind. When Goodman speaks of representation, it is symbols that he has in mind as being what represents. Now in fact there is the phenomenon of a symbol representing something and also the phenomenon of some person performing the action of representing something—both the phenomenon of something being a picture of something and the phenomenon of someone picturing something. In the theory I shall develop, I shall offer an account of both phenomena. But unlike Goodman I shall take as basic the phenomenon of someone performing the count-generated action of representing something.

[1] In Section IV of Part One I took note of the fact that the distinction between rendering and representing applies as much to photographs as to artist-produced pictures. Thus the theory I develop applies and is meant to apply as much to still photographs and moving pictures as to paintings, even though in what follows I shall seldom take explicit note of them.

This difference in strategy reflects the fact that I am approaching the phenomena of pictures and picturing from within the context of an action-generation theory. Goodman, by contrast, approaches it from within the context of a general theory of symbols. He stands in the grand contemporary tradition of semiotic theories of art. A consequence of this difference in approach is that at several points we shall find ourselves in the position of being able to *learn from* Goodman without actually *adopting* what he says.

An initial comment must also be made about the concept of a picture. I shall assume throughout my discussion that accord-¹ ing to the primary concept of a picture, an instance of a certain design is a picture of so-and-so just in case the person who produced or presented it *pictured* so-and-so by so doing. When in the American south-west we come across some incised pattern on a rock and wonder whether or not it is a picture, we are wondering whether someone pictured something by incising this pattern. And when we go on to ask whether it is, say, a picture of a condor or of a horse, the answer to our question is determined by reference to what its maker pictured thereby. We may for years take it to be a picture of a horse. But if someone then presents evidence to show that probably its maker pictured a condor thereby, that establishes that probably it is a picture of a condor and not of a horse. The primary concept of a *picture of X* is thus parasitic on the concept of *someone picturing X*. It's true that we speak of 'seeing pictures' in the clouds—or on damp walls. But in speaking thus we are using a secondary sense of 'picture', according to which one can see a picture of so-and-so in such-and-such without there being a picture that one sees. I shall eventually explain what such *seeing* amounts to.

On Goodman's concept of a picture, it is only *in* a certain system that a symbol is a picture of so-and-so. A symbol that is a picture in one system may be a non-picture in another; and what a symbol pictures in one system may differ from what it pictures in another. More directly relevant, on Goodman's view a symbol is a picture in a certain system whether or not that system is now, or ever, in effect—and whether or not, that system being in effect, that symbol has ever been used to *picture* anything. Here, then, is a significant difference in assumptions between myself and Goodman. For this reason too we shall find ourselves learning from Goodman without actually adopting what he says.

One of the important points which Goodman makes and which any theory of representation must take account of is expressed in Goodman's words as follows:

From the fact that P is a picture of or represents a unicorn we cannot infer that there is something that P is a picture of or represents. Furthermore, a picture of Pickwick is a picture of a man, even though there is no man it represents. Saying that a picture represents a so and so is thus highly ambiguous as between saying what the picture denotes and saying what kind of picture it is. Some confusion can be avoided if in the latter case we speak rather of a 'Pickwick-representing-picture' or, for short, of a 'Pickwick-picture' or 'unicorn-picture' or 'man-picture'. Obviously a picture cannot, barring equivocation, both represent Pickwick and represent nothing. But a picture may be of a certain kind—be a Pickwick-picture or a man-picture—without representing anything.[2]

Let me articulate and adapt Goodman's point. Suppose that someone, looking at Titian's painting *Charles V* (hanging in the Prado), says that Titian has represented a man on a horse. In saying this, he may be claiming that there did or does exist a man and a horse such that Titian represented *that* man and *that* horse, and furthermore, represented that man *as on* that horse. His claim, in short, may be expressible with the following existentially quantified sentence, in which we quantify over things represented:

$(\exists x)$ $(\exists y)$ (x is a man and y is a horse and Titian represented x and represented y and represented x as on y).

But our museum-goer *need* not be making such a claim with those words. For one can just make a picture of a man on a horse without there *existing* any man and any horse which one has pictured. Of course, if our museum-goer happens to notice the title of Titian's painting, he will probably suspect that there actually did exist a man whom Titian represented. (About the horse he may well keep an open mind.) But none the less,

[2] Nelson Goodman, *Languages of Art*, p. 22.

when he says that Titian represented a man on a horse he *need not* be claiming that there existed a man whom Titian represented.

This point is clearer, perhaps, though in essence no different, in the case of representations of things of a sort that don't and never did exist. For example, it is clear that the people who created the Unicorn Tapestry, now hanging in the Cloisters in New York, represented a unicorn thereby. But when I say this, I don't mean to claim that there existed a unicorn which they represented. For I believe that there have never existed any unicorns, and thus, that there have never existed any which have been represented. So if that was what I had been claiming, I would have been speaking falsely. But in fact I am making a true claim when I say that a unicorn was represented by the makers of this tapestry. In saying that a unicorn was represented one can make a true claim even though there never existed any unicorns, and thus, even though there never existed any which were represented. But so too, in saying that a horse was represented I can be making a claim which is true even though there existed no horse such that it was represented. In such a case, of course, the 'failure' does not stem from the fact that there have never existed any horses *to be* represented, but rather from the fact that of the horses that exist, none was in this case represented. One can just make a picture of a horse without there existing any horse which one has represented. But once one sees that one can say truly that someone represented a horse even when there neither did nor does exist a horse which he represented, then one can see that such a non-quantificational claim can be truly made even when, as a matter of fact, one could also claim truly that there existed a horse such that it was represented.

These reflections lead to the conclusion that our word 'represent', when applied to those who picture, expresses two quite different concepts (and, correlatively, that it also expresses two quite different concepts when applied to pictures). When applying the one concept we are making a claim to the effect that some existent entity was represented. When applying the other, we are making no such claim. It will be convenient henceforth to call the former concept—i.e., that concept of representation which allows for quantification in the way indicated—*q-representation*; and to call the other concept, *p-representation*.[3]

Goodman, in the passages quoted, does not only distinguish between p-representation and q-representation. He goes beyond that to offer a theory as to the nature of p-representation. On his view, p-representation of a horse consists in the instantiation of a visual design of a certain sort—one, namely, which we just so happen to call 'a picture of a horse'. It has nothing whatsoever to do, he says, with the look of the picture or the look of the pictured. Or to shift the example: it is Goodman's view that when I say that someone represented a unicorn, meaning thereby that he p-represented it, I am simply making a claim about the *kind* of picture that he produced—specifically, that it is a picture which exhibits a visual design of a certain sort. We English-speaking people just so happen to apply the term 'picture of a unicorn' to pictures that exhibit designs of the sort that this one does. It would be less misleading if we called them 'unicorn-pictures' rather than 'pictures of a unicorn'; for this latter phrase tempts us to search for the unicorns represented when there are none.

We can turn to the history of art for an illustration showing that this will not do. In the early medieval period one finds artists producing pictures which might appropriately be called 'Apollo-pictures'. For these pictures instantiate a very distinct sort of design whose provenance lies in designs of that sort having been regularly used by classical artists to represent Apollo. Now suppose we grant Goodman that to represent Apollo is to engage in p-representation. The medieval artists, though they used the Apollo-design, did not use it as did the classical artists, to p-represent Apollo. They used it to represent Christ. And that at once shows that p-representing Apollo is distinct from producing an Apollo-picture. Goodman's identification of these two phenomena cannot be correct. When we claim that p-representation took place, we are claiming that a design was *used* in a certain way. We are not (simply) making a claim about the kind of design used.

The same point could have been made by reference to ambiguous designs. Many designs are such that they can be

[3] I adapt this terminology from Kendall Walton in his 'Are Representations Symbols?' *The Monist* (April 1974).

used to represent a variety of things. Yet on a given occasion it may be decisively one thing and not another that is represented. One of my children once drew a series of pictures of a family of lions—father, mother, children. He concluded the series with a picture of the hole in which they lived. The design he drew was just a circle—a highly ambiguous design with respect to what it represents. Yet I take it that he did in fact represent the hole in which a family of lions lived. Such p-representation—for that is what it is—cannot be explicated simply by appeal to the kind of design instantiated.[4]

Goodman tacitly affirms—and I think he is right in so doing—that necessarily if one q-represents some entity x, then there are some attributes such that one represents x as *having* those attributes. One cannot q-represent Napoleon without representing him as a man, or as a general, or as obese, or as standing, or whatever. It's true that one may use a sign to represent some entity without representing it *as* anything. One may use a circle to represent Napoleon and not have represented him as anything. But such representation is not picturing; whereas q-representation is of course a mode of picturing. One cannot *picture* some entity (pictorially q-represent it) without representing it *as* having certain attributes. Further, the attributes that one pictures an entity as having will be ones that it either does or does not have at a certain time. In that way,

[4] I have discriminated q-representation from p-representation by noting that if an action satisfies the concept of q-representation, then there *exists* something which has been represented; whereas an action can satisfy the concept of p-representation without there existing anything which has been represented. Recently a theory of representation has been developed by Robert Howell in which it is assumed that whenever representation occurs, there *is* something which is represented—though the entity represented may or may not *exist*. ('The Logical Structure of Pictorial Representation' in *Theoria*, xl (1974), Part 2, pp. 76–109.) If I represent Venus, then there *is* something which I have represented, namely Venus—though indeed Venus has never existed. If I represent a unicorn, then there *is* something which I have represented, namely a certain unicorn—though indeed there has never existed that nor any other unicorn. On this theory, what differentiates q-representation from p-representation is just that in the former case the entity represented exists, in the latter case, the entity represented has being without existence. Throughout my discussion in this essay I am taking for granted that there are no entities which do not exist. Consequently Howell's theory, though developed in a most interesting way, falls outside my purview. Howell's way of answering the question, 'How can we identify the non-existent entities represented in a painting?' is especially ingenious. His solution, though, seems to me to yield the consequence that if the world of a painting is to occur, the painting's picture-plane (its physical surface) must exist. That seems to me definitely false.

representation-as will be either correct or incorrect, for a given time in the career of the represented entity.

Concerning the nature of representation-as, Goodman holds that this phenomenon is related to q-representation and p-representation in the following manner: 'An object *k* is represented as a soandso by a picture *p* if and only if *p* is or contains a picture that as a whole both denotes *k* and is a soandso-picture.'[5] In other words, and without the qualifications: one q-represents *x* as a thing which is-*f* if and only if one q-represents *x* with a picture whereby one p-represents a thing which is-*f*.

Even when this thesis has all the qualifications built into it, it proves untenable for an interesting reason—namely, it ignores metaphorical pictures, ironic pictures, etc. Of course it's true that never does q-representation take place without p-representation taking place. But consider, for example, Jan van Eyck's altarpiece in St Bavo, Ghent. I think it is correct to say that therein, by way of the lamb in the centre of the picture, Christ is represented as a lamb. But he is not represented as having the property of being a lamb. Rather, he is represented as being *metaphorically* a lamb. Yet it is a lamb that is p-represented—literally so. Christ is represented as being metaphorically a lamb with a picture which p-represents what is literally a lamb. Or consider an ironic or sarcastic picture, in which one represents Joe as being excessively fat with a picture which p-represents a skinny person. Here too we have discrepancy between p-representation and representation-as: the person is represented as being fat with a picture which p-represents not a fat but a skinny person. As part of our general theory of representation we shall want to come to some understanding of metaphorical pictures, ironic pictures, etc.

It may be, in the case of our ironic picture, that it is correct both to say that the artist represented Joe as fat and that he represented Joe as skinny. So whenever there is any chance of confusion, let me say that he represented Joe as *being* fat and as *pictorially* skinny. Similarly, when there is any chance of confusion I shall say that van Eyck represented Christ as *being* a

[5] Nelson Goodman, op. cit., pp. 28–9.

lamb, metaphorically speaking, and as *pictorially* a lamb, literally speaking.

III. *The Bennett Theory*

On the topic of pictorial representation, Goodman does more than make certain insightful observations and draw certain important distinctions. He develops a *theory* as to the nature of pictorial representation—both q-representation and p-representation. Already we have glanced at part of his theory of p-representation. However, to consider, at this point, his theory of representation as a whole would seriously disrupt the flow of the argument. Accordingly I shall discuss it in detail in an Appendix to this Part. The same cannot be said concerning a theory as to the nature of pictorial representation which has been proposed by John G. Bennett in his essay 'Depiction and Convention'. A consideration of his theory will naturally flow into the presentation of my own.

At the centre of his discussion Bennett places the observation that pictures when combined with labels can, like sentences, be used to assert something which is either true or false. Goodman observed that one can q-represent something either correctly or incorrectly. Bennett goes beyond that and claims—correctly—that one can use pictures to make assertions. This is what he says:

Consider a picture postcard. It has on one side a picture of a sunny beach with a large modern hotel in the background. On the face of the postcard there is the written phrase, 'Diddle Beach.' I get the impression that Diddle Beach is a sunny place with a fancy modern hotel and a pleasant beach. Later, when I go out of my way to visit it, I find nothing of the sort; Diddle Beach consists entirely of sharp rocks, the largest building within twenty miles is a rundown gas station, and the sun hasn't shown there in the memory of anyone living. I have been misled ...

The picture by itself would not have misled me ... The label, 'Diddle Beach' was necessary. On the other hand, the label without the picture could not have given me the false belief ... It was the combination of the label and the picture which led me to have false beliefs ...

I believe that we have found something which can be true or false; the combination of a picture and a label. Our examples suggest that in these cases the picture is analogous to a *predicate* and the label analogous to a name ... Combining the predicate and the label gives something which can be true or false, like a sentence.[6]

Following out these thoughts, Bennett constructs a formal semantic theory for predicates and for names, and then for combinations thereof. That done, he then goes beyond the semantic theory to propose an analysis of what it is for an abstract language to be used by the members of a population. Bennett thus recognizes the need for something more than a semantic if picturing is to be fully understood.

Bennett's central idea is that a picture is a predicate, and that a predicate is something for which there is, for every possible world, a set of possible objects which is the extension of the predicate for that world. (The set may be empty.) For example, in English the extension of the predicate 'is a man on horseback' for any possible world W is just the set of all those possible objects each of which would be a man on horseback if W obtained. Let us see how Bennett develops this central idea.

We can begin with his definition of 'a language':

A *language* is any ordered pair consisting, first, of a set S of sets of objects, and second, of a function f from S into the set of all sets of possible worlds.

The sets which go to make up the first member of the pair which is a language may be called the *sentences* of the language. For example, in the language which we might call *Written German*, the function-member assigns to the set of objects which constitutes the sentence 'Der Schnee ist weiss' the set of all possible worlds in which snow is white. (Bennett regards this last as identical with the proposition that snow is white.)

In fact, of course, those sets which satisfy Bennett's concept of a *sentence* need be nothing like what we ordinarily call sentences; nor need those sets which satisfy Bennett's concept of a language be anything like what we ordinarily call languages. Accordingly, when I use 'sentence' in Bennett's special sense I shall put it in double quotes; and I shall do the same for 'language' when I use it in Bennett's special sense.

[6] John G. Bennett, 'Depiction and Convention', in *The Monist*, lviii, No. 2 (April 1974), pp. 259–69.

Truth in a "language" can then be explained as follows:

> "Sentence" s is *true in* "language" L, where $L = \langle S, f \rangle$, if and only if the actual world is a member of the set $f(s)$.

This explains what it is for a "sentence" of a "language" to be true in that set which is the "language". It does not explain what it is for a set α of objects to be true for a certain group of people. That has to do with whether or not α belongs to a "language" in use among those people.

> A set of objects α is *true for* a certain group M if and only if the members of M use a "language" L in which α is a true "sentence".

And in turn:

> The members of some group M *use* some "language" L if and only if it is a convention among the members of M for someone to produce a "sentence" of L only if he believes it to be true in L, and for someone to respond to someone's production of a "sentence" of L by coming to believe that it is true in L.

Next we introduce the concept of a *scheme of predication*. Informally this may be explained as consisting of a set of objects along with a function which assigns to each of these objects an "extension" in every possible world. The actual definition goes as follows:

> R is a scheme of predication if and only if R is an ordered pair, $R = \langle P, g \rangle$, such that P is a set of objects and g is a binary function taking as arguments members of P and possible worlds and yielding as values sets of possible objects.

Bennett adds that if R is a scheme of predication and $R = \langle P, g \rangle$, then the members of the set P will be called the *predicates of R*. And if p is a predicate of R and W is a possible world, then g (p, W) will be called *the extension of p at W in R*.

That, then, is the concept of *predicate* that Bennett will use in his claim that pictures are predicates. Something is never a "predicate" *tout court*, but a "predicate" of a certain predication scheme. And to be a "predicate" of a certain predication scheme consists just of being assigned, by the function of that scheme, a set of possible objects for every possible world. The definition of "predicate" makes no use of our ordinary concept of predicating something of something.

Bennett refers, in his definition, to *possible objects*. The informal idea is that, in one scheme for predication, to the words 'is red' are assigned, for some possible world W, the set of whatever entities would be red if W obtained. But it may well be that not all the entities that would be red if W obtained, exist (in the actual world). Thus it is that Bennett speaks of 'possible objects'. Since there are no unicorns, for no world does the set assigned to 'is a unicorn' contain any objects that exist in the actual world. And for the actual world, the set assigned to it is empty. But for various possible worlds, the set assigned to 'is a unicorn' contains various possible unicorns.

We move, next, to the concept of a *labelling scheme*. Informally, this consists of a set of objects together with a function which assigns to each of the objects a "designation" in every possible world. The definition runs as follows:

> D is a labelling scheme if and only if D is an ordered pair, $D = \langle T, h \rangle$, such that T is a set of objects and h is a binary function from members of T and possible worlds to possible objects.

Bennett adds that if $D = \langle T, h \rangle$ is a labelling scheme, then the members of T will be called the *labels of D*; and if l is a label of D and W is a possible world, then h (l, W) will be called *the object designated by l at W in D*. It must be emphasized that Bennett's concept of *designation* has nothing to do with our ordinary concept of designating one thing with another. It is a concept merely of an entity occupying a position of a certain sort in a set of a certain sort.

The next steps are to show how a "language" can be constructed from a scheme of predication and a labelling scheme, and to explain what it is for a scheme of predication R *to be used* in a certain population M. Nothing essential for our purposes will be missed if we do not follow Bennett into these explanations, but observe, merely, that on his analysis a scheme of predication is used in a population only if a language made from it is used in that population.

Bennett's main thesis then is this: *pictures are predicates in schemes of predication which are actually used.* That is to say, pictures are combined with labels to make up the "sentences" of "languages" such that, in some population, it is a convention for someone to produce a "sentence" of the "language" only if he thinks the "sentence" is true in that "language", and to respond to someone's production of a "sentence" of that "language" by coming to believe that that "sentence" is true in the "language". Let me quote Bennett for an illustrative example:

Consider a picture of Napoleon, such as might appear in a book of history. The picture shows Napoleon on a horse and has a caption consisting of the words 'Napoleon Bonaparte'. On the theory presented above we can say various things about this picture. First, the combination of the picture and the label makes something which is true or false ... The caption is the label, the picture the predicate. It is the predicate whose extension in any possible world is just the set of all men who are riding horses and who look exactly as the picture pictures Napoleon as looking ... The label in this example is the phrase 'Napoleon Bonaparte'. It designates Napoleon Bonaparte in every possible world in which he exists ... In this case the combination is true if and only if the actual historical person, Napoleon Bonaparte, looked the way the picture pictures him ... The combination of picture and caption is part of a larger scheme concerning which there are conventions of truthfulness and trust.[7]

Bennett does not develop an account of the difference between those predicates which are pictures and those which are not. On this matter he follows Goodman and holds that a "predicate" is a picture if and only if it belongs to a dense and relatively replete scheme of predication. (See the Appendix to this Part.) Thus on his theory, for a picture to p-represent a unicorn for us is for that picture to be a predicate in a dense and relatively replete scheme of predication which is used among us and which is such that everything in the picture's extension for any possible world W is a unicorn at W. For the actual world, that extension would be empty, since in our world there exist no unicorns. But for any possible world such that if it obtained unicorns would exist, the extension of the predicate for that world is the set of those possible non-actual objects which

[7] John G. Bennett, op. cit., p. 263.

would be the unicorns that would exist if that world obtained. And in general, 'a picture is a soandso picture if and only if anything in the extension of the picture at a possible world is a soandso at that world' (Bennett, p. 265). 'Many pictures which are soandso pictures will have empty extensions in the actual world. They are soandso pictures because everything in their extensions at any possible world is a soandso, even though there are soandsos in these extensions only in nonactual worlds' (p. 266).

This theory of what it is to be a picture is both imaginative and elegant. Unfortunately, it does not prove satisfactory. It will be instructive to see why not. In the first place, the theory exacts an exceedingly heavy payment in ontological commitment. It requires us to acknowledge that there are possible but non-existent objects. Given the deep difficulties in such a view (cf. Chaps. 7 and 8 in Alvin Plantinga's *The Nature of Necessity*) that seems too high a price to pay for a theory of representation.

Yet even this price is not high enough; for the theory runs aground with those pictures which p-represent impossible things. Various prints of M. C. Escher, for example, p-represent a variety of impossible buildings. So consider two such prints representing distinct impossible buildings. On Bennett's line of thought, those pictures are to be thought of as predicates; and accordingly, we are to regard each as assigned, for each possible world W, a set (possibly empty) of possible objects such that, if W occurred, those objects would exist and the picture would apply to them. But since our two prints p-represent impossible buildings, the extension of each at all possible worlds will be empty. Thus these two prints will be undifferentiated as to what they p-represent. And that difficulty is an exact counterpart of Goodman's original problem: 'how to distinguish between a picture of a unicorn and a picture of a hippogryph when there is nothing which either represents.

The thought which comes naturally to mind is that *impossible* objects should be added to the ontology, to accompany the possible non-actual objects which we already have. But if acknowledging the being of non-actual possible objects is a heavy price to pay for a theory of representation, then acknowledging the being of *impossible* objects is a vastly heavier price. In addition, if impossible objects are to be made available for functioning in the semantics, then that semantics will require a great deal of revision. Bennett assumes that for each possible world there is a *domain*, that domain consisting of the set of all and only those objects that would exist if that world occurred. And then he introduces the notion of a predicate's extension at any possible world, explaining that the extension of a predicate at a possible world is either empty or has as members a selection from that world's domain. Obviously this way of thinking will require sizeable revision if impossible objects are introduced and allowed to occur in the extensions of predicates.

Thirdly, we must take note of the curious fact that q-representation virtually disappears from view in Bennett's theory. Consider once more Rembrandt's *Bathsheba*. Bennett rightly asks us to take note of the fact that the caption 'Bathsheba' stands for, or denotes, Bathsheba. Likewise he rightly asks us to take note of the fact that the picture p-represents a woman sitting on a couch bathing. And he constructs a theory which he intends to yield an account of both these facts. What is also true, though, is that *the figure of the woman* in the picture q-represents Bathsheba. That is to say: not only does the caption denote Bathsheba. The *picture* represents Bathsheba. Of this fact, however, Bennett gives us no account. He does suggest in one place that a given picture may be both a predicate and a label. But he does not develop the suggestion. There is, in Bennett, no theoretical account of q-representation.

Fourth, Bennett's account of a language scheme, coupled with his account of what it is for a language scheme to be in use, yields the consequence that probably no sentences of English are "sentences" of any "language" in use among, say, midwestern Americans. This is ironic, since Bennett's basic strategy was to develop a theory such that both the English sentence 'Diddle Beach is a sunny sandy beach,' and a picture p-representing a sunny sandy beach and bearing the caption 'Diddle Beach', would be "sentences" of a "language" in use. Let us see how this consequence ensues.

On Bennett's theory, if a sentence of English is to be in use among mid-western Americans it must be a convention among them for someone to produce an occurrence of such a sentence only if he believes that the proposition associated with it in English is true.[8] So consider the English sentence 'Diddle Beach is a sunny sandy beach'. The first thing to note is that there may well be no one proposition associated with this sentence in English. For it may well be the case that many things are named 'Diddle Beach'. Secondly, one may produce an occurrence of this sentence—as I did just above—without conventions of truthfulness and trust even being relevant. One may produce an example merely to illustrate a point. For this pair of reasons, then, it is false that there is some proposition p such that it is a convention among mid-western Americans for someone to produce an occurrence of the sentence 'Diddle Beach is a sunny sandy beach' only if he believes that p is associated with that sentence in English and believes that p is true. Though there are some sentences to which the first of these reasons does not pertain—e.g., 'snow is white'—there is none to which the second does not pertain. The sentences of English do not qualify as the "sentences" of a Bennett "language" in use among mid-western Americans.

No doubt Bennett believes that producing a sentence for which his specified conventions of truthfulness and trust hold is what it is to make an *assertion* by producing an occurrence of the sentence. The two points made above can then be put somewhat more lucidly thus: using English, we can assert many different propositions by producing an occurrence of 'Diddle Beach is a sunny sandy beach'. But also, we may assert nothing at all thereby, nor perform any other mood-action.

A dialect of English at a certain moment in its history can indeed be conceived as an ordered pair, consisting first of a certain set of entities and second of a certain function. But the set of entities is a set of *sentence-usages*, not of sentences. And the function assigns to each such sentence-usage not a certain proposition but a certain *speech-action*. It is such a system which is in effect among mid-western Americans. Further, it is used by

[8] Incidentally, Bennett gives no explanation of 'produce' as used in this formula. For ordinary sentences it is easy to see what he has in mind: To produce a sentence is to produce an occurrence of it. But what 'produce' can mean in general, for all the things that can be "sentences" in Bennett "languages", I do not know. The moral I draw is that an adequate theory will have to speak of diverse *usages*, not merely of *symbols*.

them. That is, they instantiate elements of the stock of the system; and an act of someone's doing so counts as an act of his performing whatever speech action is assigned by the language's function to that member of its stock.

Though English sentences do not qualify as the "sentences" of a "language" in use among us, thus at once breaking down Bennett's supposed analogy, may it none the less be the case that *pictures combined with captions* constitute "sentences" of "languages" in use among us? Take, for example, our now familiar Rembrandt painting showing a woman sitting on a couch and bearing the caption 'Bathsheba'. Is it a convention among us not to produce such a painting-cum-caption unless we believe that Bathsheba sat on a couch? Certainly not. Pictures when coupled with captions can indeed be used to make assertions; Bennett is quite right to take note of this. But they can be used to perform other mood-actions as well. And my guess is that Rembrandt, by producing and labelling his painting, was taking up a *fictive* rather than an assertive stance toward Bathsheba's sitting on a couch. He may or may not actually have believed this state of affairs to have occurred. But even if he did not, none the less in producing his captioned painting he would not have violated any conventions of truthfulness and trust. Pictures-cum-captions are not "sentences" of "languages" in use, for basically the same reason that English sentences are not.

Bennett does not actually say what he takes representation-as to be. But it is easy to see what his theory would lead him to say; namely, that one represents *x* as being so-and-so just in case one actually produces a picture-cum-caption such that it is a convention in one's group not to do so unless one believes that *x* is so-and-so. It is easy to see, though, given the foregoing, that this will not do. Rembrandt represented Bathsheba as sitting on a couch. But the supposed convention does not exist.

Lastly, there is one important respect in which pictures differ decisively from the predicates of sentences. The predicate 'is a hat worn by a man on a horse' is true only of hats. The predicate 'is a man on a horse wearing a hat' is true only of men. And the predicate 'is a horse being ridden by a man wearing a hat' is true only of horses. But a *picture* of a man on a horse wearing a hat is *also* a picture of a hat being worn by a man on a horse, and is also a picture of a horse being ridden by a man wearing a hat. So what then is to be counted as constituting the extension of this picture for our actual world? The set of all hat-wearing horse-riding men, or the set of all man-on-a-horse-worn hats, or the set of all man-wearing-a-hat-ridden horses?

One suggestion which comes to mind is that the extension of this picture for our actual world is to be taken as the *union* of the set of all hat-wearing horse-riding men, plus the set of all man-on-a-horse-worn hats, plus the set of all man-wearing-a-hat-ridden horses. But then one of the advantages which Bennett claims for his theory is lost. For suppose that the picture is labelled 'Napoleon'. Bennett wants to say that this picture-cum-label asserts that Napoleon is (was) a man wearing a hat and riding a horse, by virtue of the label standing for something that belongs to the extension of the picture. But on the proposed revision, the extension of the picture includes not just men but also horses and hats; consequently attaching the label gives us at best the assertion that Napoleon was a man of a certain sort or a horse of a certain sort or a hat of a certain sort.

Now the state of affairs of a man wearing a hat riding a horse, is also the state of affairs of a hat being worn by a man riding a horse, and is also the state of affairs of a horse being ridden by a man wearing a hat. The thought is irresistible: the fundamental role of pictures is to pick out states of affairs, not properties or extensions. In their fundamental role they are to be compared to sentences, not to predicates. That is the clue I shall follow in developing my theory. In doing so, I shall want to keep in mind that pictures are not only used to make assertions—the point Bennett emphasizes—but also to issue commands, to ask questions, to make promises, to give instructions, etc. I shall develop a theory as to the role of pictures in mood-actions generally.

IV. *P-Representation*

Let me begin the exposition of my theory of pictorial represen-tation with an analysis of p-representation. For this is basic. Never does representation occur without p-representation occurring.

What, then, is the nature of p-representation? Well, suppose

I wish to assert that the door to my study is closed. In the appropriate circumstances I might do so by drawing a picture of a closed door. The act of my drawing the picture in that particular manner and circumstance would *count as* an act of my asserting that my study door is closed. If I perform the action while believing that my study door is not closed, I will have lied. One can commit perjury by drawing a picture.

We in our culture are surrounded by examples of assertions being made by producing occurrences of pictorial designs. Consult any guide for the field identification of flora or fauna. Characteristically for each species the guide will contain both a paragraph describing properly formed members of the species, and a design picturing a properly formed member of the species. The design functions exactly like the paragraph. By producing it, or arranging to have it produced, the author asserts, say, that the common loon looks thus-and-so. Accordingly he can make a mistake with his pictorial design as well as with his paragraph. Again, in a handbook on grafting the author may wish to explain what the *veneer crown graft* (Tittel's graft) is like. He may do so either with a pictorial design or with a paragraph, or with both.

What I have said about asserting something by producing a picture applies, *mutatis mutandis*, to issuing commands, to asking questions, to making promises. By producing a picture of a closed door I can command that my study door be closed, or ask whether it is closed, or promise that it will be closed. Likewise by producing a picture of a closed door I can invite others to take up a fictive stance toward the state of affairs of my study door's being closed. Is this not how the illustrations accompanying some work of novelistic fiction are to be taken? The illustrator is not asserting, commanding, asking, or promising. He is inviting us to take up a fictional attitude toward certain states of affairs. He is doing so by producing a picture rather than a sentence. And to a considerable extent the states of affairs that he presents for our consideration are the very same as those that the novelist presents. The point is too obvious to labour: by producing a picture one can perform a mood-action.

This same point is made by Ernst Gombrich in an interesting passage in his *Art and Illusion*. The point is made, however, in a slightly askew fashion; and it will help to get matters straight before us to consider what he says. In discussing *The Lacka-wanna Valley* by the nineteenth-century American painter George Inness, Gombrich says about the painting that it

was commissioned in 1855 as an advertisement for a railroad. At the time there was only one track running into the roundhouse, 'but the president insisted on having four or five painted in, easing his consci-ence by explaining that the road would eventually have them'. Inness protested, and we can see that when he finally gave in for the sake of his family, he shamefacedly hid the patch with the non-existent tracks behind puffs of smoke. To him this patch was a lie ...

But, strictly speaking, the lie was not in the painting. It was in the advertisement, if it claimed by caption or implication that the paint-ing gave accurate information about the facilities of the railway's roundhouses ...

... the terms 'true' and 'false' can only be applied to statements, propositions. And whatever may be the usage of critical parlance, a picture is never a statement in that sense of the term. It can no more be true or false than a statement can be blue or green. Much confusion has been caused in aesthetics by disregarding this simple fact. It is an understandable confusion because in our culture pictures are usually labelled, and labels, or captions, can be understood as abbreviated statements.[9]

When Gombrich says that 'the lie was not in the painting' he surely speaks truth. A painting tells no lies. For it tells nothing at all. But rather than saying that the lying is done by someone making and presenting that painting in a certain manner and circumstance, Gombrich seems to locate the lie in the accom-panying words. That is because he assumes that in this respect sentences are different from pictures—that sentences can tell lies. In fact, that visual design which is the sentence 'The door is closed' no more states anything than does a picture of a closed door. It is we who use it to assert true things—and false things. Of course, one might wish to say that a sentence is *true on some occasion* just in case by the uttering of it on that occasion one would assert something true. But then the same can be said for the picture.

There is also the suggestion behind Gombrich's words that it is *only* when words are added, or introduced, that pictures are

<hr />

[9] Ernst Gombrich, *Art and Illusion* (Princeton Univ. Press: Princeton, 1969), pp. 67–8.

used to assert. That likewise seems false. Certainly it is true that when by producing a picture of something one asserts something, the particular manner and circumstance in which it is produced often incorporates the use of words. But that seems not at all essential. Further, in all such cases one might cast the situation in the opposite light: It is by incorporating some picture into the manner and circumstance in which we use certain words that we assert something. Lastly, it is regularly the case that when we assert something by uttering some sentence in a certain manner and circumstance, that circumstance incorporates the use of other, explanatory words. Individual isolated sentences are scarcely more satisfactory for the performance of mood-actions than are individual isolated pictures.

And now I can present my thesis as to the fundamental nature of p-representation. Always when someone pictures (p-represents) something, he performs a mood-action on certain states of affairs. (We may say, as before, that he *introduces* those states of affairs.) The way I presented the examples above may have encouraged the conclusion that the introduction of some state of affairs is incidental to picturing. In fact it is essential. If we assume, as I do, that states of affairs and propositions are identical, we can say that p-representation is always *de dicto*. And since a world is projected whenever states of affairs are introduced, what we can also say is that there is no p-representation without world-projection. Always when p-representation takes place, a world is projected.

Specifically, in picturing a man on a horse one introduces the state of affairs of *there being a man on a horse*. And likewise, in picturing a unicorn one introduces the state of affairs of *there being a unicorn*.[10] Unicorns have never existed. None the less

---

[10] The principle espoused above is that one p-represents a *k* only if one takes up a mood-stance toward the state of affairs of *there being a k*. This principle needs a slight qualification. I assume that if one p-represents a man wearing a hat riding a horse, then also one p-represents a hat. Now suppose that the mood-stance one takes up in this case of representation is that of asserting. The picturer asserts that there is a man wearing a hat riding a horse. It's not so clear, though, that he has *also* asserted that there is a hat—even though what he has asserted entails this. Nor is it clear that he has performed any other mood-action on that state of affairs. Accordingly the above should read as follows: one p-represents a *k* only if one takes up a mood-stance toward the state of affairs of *there being a k* or to something entailing *there being a k*. In the text subsequently I shall not introduce this qualification, since I think it would never do anything more than complicate the discussion.

there is the state of affairs, or proposition, that there is a unicorn—this proposition being false. And so at once we see how a *de dicto* theory of p-representation can handle, with ease, those special cases of 'representation of what never existed' in which the 'thing represented' is impossible of existing. Though there cannot be such buildings as Escher represents, none the less there is the proposition that there is a building of such-and-such an impossible sort. It just happens to be a necessarily false proposition.

A *de dicto* theory of p-representation also handles with ease the objection lodged against Bennett's theory. In p-representing a woman sitting on a couch, Rembrandt also represented a couch being sat on by a woman. And so his picture both p-represented a woman sitting on a couch and a couch being sat on by a woman. Pictures are multi-directional. In this fundamental fact lay the downfall of Bennett's predicate-theory of p-representation. The predicate 'is a woman sitting on a couch' is distinct in extension from the predicate 'is a couch being sat on by a woman'. What the one can be truly predicated of, the other cannot be. No counterpart distinction is available for pictures. Pictures lack extensions. By contrast, a *de dicto* theory of p-representation has no difficulty whatsoever with the multi-directionality of pictures. For the state of affairs of *a woman sitting on a couch* is the very same state of affairs as that of *a couch being sat on by a woman*.[11]

States of affairs, I have said, are on my view identical with propositions. And a normal way of specifying a proposition is with a 'that'-clause. Accordingly in what follows I shall often make explicit my understanding of p-representation by speaking not of p-representing *a k* but rather of *representing that there is a k*. Also, it will sometimes be convenient to call p-representation, *picturing*.

But why hold that one cannot p-represent something without taking up a mood-stance toward some state of affairs? Consider once again the *Bathsheba* painting; and suppose that Rembrandt in making it had not q-represented Bathsheba nor anything

---

[11] In giving states of affairs a central role in my theory of representation, I am agreeing with Kendall Walton and Robert Howell. See Walton, 'Pictures and Make-Believe' in *Philosophical Review* (July 1973); and Howell, 'The Logical structure of Pictorial Representation' in *Theoria*, xl (1974), Part 2. Walton's theory I shall discuss in more detail later.

else. Suppose that he had just p-represented a woman sitting on a couch bathing. Why not regard what he has thereby done as produce an occurrence of a visual design which *could* be used to q-represent something as a woman sitting on a couch bathing, which *could* be used to q-represent something as a couch being sat on by a woman bathing, etc.? Why not regard what Rembrandt would have done, if he had used his painting only for p-representation, as like inscribing the sentence 'This is a woman sitting on a couch bathing' without performing any illocutionary action thereby? This sentence *could be* used to perform some illocutionary action. But one can also *just* inscribe it. Isn't p-representation like that?

Before I answer this query, notice first that we *do* regularly produce, without q-representing anything, occurrences of visual designs which could also be used to p-represent something. Indeed, we probably produce few visual designs which are not of this sort—which are not, as we may call them, *pictorial* designs. A circle may be drawn and thereby an egg p-represented as seen from end on, or the hole in which a family of gophers live, or a doorknob. So a circle is a pictorial design. But a circle may also be drawn without p-representing anything whatsoever thereby. My contention is not that one cannot produce an occurrence of a pictorial design without thereby taking up a stance toward some state of affairs. Certainly one can. My contention is that one cannot *p-represent* something without taking up a stance toward some state of affairs.

With that clarification in mind, suppose that I now draw a circular shape and thereby p-represent something—specifically, a hole in which a family of gophers live. This is to do more than draw a circular shape. It is to p-represent one specific state of affairs, when a host of others, or none at all, might have been pictured with the very same design. The instance of the design is in this case *functioning* in picturing. So it is not like merely inscribing the visual design 'This is a woman sitting on a couch bathing.' Even when used as a sentence of English this sentence can function to assert an immense variety of states of affairs. Merely inscribing it resolves none of that diversity of potential. For to merely inscribe it is not to *use* it to assert anything. But in p-representing a gopher hole by inscribing a circular design, I do resolve the diversity of potential of this circular design. I represent that there is a gopher hole when I might have represented other things by producing this design, or nothing at all. And by doing this I, say, *assert* that there is a gopher hole (perhaps in the neighbouring field), when instead I might have taken up some other mood-stance. It is this 're-solution of diverse potential' which makes it clear that p-representation consists of more than producing an occur-rence of a design which *could* be used to q-represent some entity as being so-and-so.

V. *Seeing As*

If pictures and words alike can be used to assert that there is a horse, and to invite one's audience to take up a fictional attitude toward there being a horse, etc., then wherein lies the difference between using a picture to assert that there is a horse and using words to do so? For that there is a difference is obvious. Or, to use another example, wherein lies the difference between the pictures and the paragraphs in a field identification guide for birds, if both are used to assert propositions?

Suppose that someone has performed some action which *counts as* his performance of some mood-action on some prop-osition (state of affairs). Specifically, suppose it counts as his introduction of the proposition *that there is a unicorn.* What is necessary for his act of so doing to be a case of *picturing*?

Obviously one thing necessary is that his generating act consist in the *instantiation* of some *visual design* in a certain context. Picturing does not occur apart from performing a certain type of action on a visual design—namely, an action of *instantiating* a design in a certain context.[12] But more is necess-ary than this. What is also necessary, I suggest, is that the design in question *look like* a unicorn—that it *be capable of being seen as* a unicorn. Only with a visual design that can be seen as a unicorn can one p-represent a unicorn. If the instantiated design cannot be seen as a unicorn, then one has not pictured a unicorn by instantiating that design.

But what is it to *see* a design *as* a unicorn? To answer that

[12] Or alernatively, displaying an already instantiated design.

question we shall have to dip into a corner of the psychology of perception. Consider the following array of curved lines:

A fundamental fact about us human beings, explored especially by the Gestalt psychologists of perception, is that we tend to see this not as an array of independent lines but rather as an instance of a certain pattern. Specifically, we tend to see it *as a circle*. In fact, the sheet of paper being seen by the reader does not exhibit a circle; nor, more importantly, does it look as if it does. Clearly it exhibits only an array of definitely distinct curved lines. In spite of that, we see the array as a circle—or at least, there seems no better way of describing our experience. Seeing-as of this sort consists of two-dimensional pattern completion.

A different situation is presented to us by the following design:

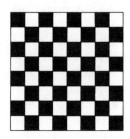

We can see this either as an array of crosses having black arms and white centres or as an array of crosses having white arms and black centres. To see it in the former way is definitely to see it differently from seeing it in the latter way. One has a peculiar sense of 'switching' when one changes the way in which one sees it—partly due to the fact that one's visual focus moves from one set of points in the design to another. The design itself is ambiguous; it can be seen either way.

This second case of seeing-as consists then of two-dimensional pattern *resolution* rather than of two-dimensional pattern *completion*. What makes the resolution case different from the completion case is that what we see really does have the look of cross-shaped designs with black arms and white centres, or cross-shaped designs with white arms and black centres; whereas, by contrast, what we see does not really have the look of a circle.

But now consider this array of lines:

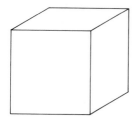

We are all capable of seeing this as a cube—that is, as an object of cube shape. Indeed, most of us find it difficult to look at this and *not* see it as a cube. And if we do not see it as a cube, we probably see it as an empty box with three of its sides missing, seen from below left and looking into the box.

Now there is probably no strong experiential sense of a difference between seeing this array of lines as a cube and seeing that array above as a circle. But there is in fact a striking difference between the two cases which shows up on analysis. I can actually see a circle (i.e., circular design) on a sheet of paper—or at least something which so far as I can see is a circle. For a circle is a two-dimensional shape which can be instantiated or exhibited on a plane surface. Accordingly when a piece of paper contains a design which is not actually a circle, and when I then see the design as a circle, I see it as something that a piece of paper *could* exhibit or instantiate. But a cube—a three-dimensional object of cube-shape—is obviously something that that design on paper cannot be. So when I see the design as a cube, I am seeing it as an object of a sort that an inscription of a design on a plane surface cannot be identical with. Let us call this latter sort of seeing-as, *two-dimensional representational seeing*. Two-dimensional representational seeing consists of seeing a design on plane surface as a three-dimensional object or spatially related array of three-dimensional objects; or alternatively, it consists of seeing a design on plane surface as a number of plane surfaces related recessively, or as a plane surface part of which is nearer the viewer than another part. One of the goals of certain twentieth-century painters—a goal which has proved surprisingly difficult to achieve—has been to produce canvases which not only do not invite, but are not even susceptible of, two-dimensional representational seeing. (It should be noted that seeing-as, in the sense of pattern resolution, is also relevant within the context of representational seeing. Our cube design can be seen either as a cube or as an incomplete box.)

Perhaps an example of planar recession would be helpful. Consider this design:

This can be seen just as a triangle. But also it can be seen as a figure on a ground—as a triangular shaped plane surface in front of a white background. And yet another way of seeing it is just the reverse: one can see it as a triangular hole in the plane of the paper, through which we see another plane behind it. Of course one does not need nicely outlined shapes in order to see what occurs on a flat surface as a figure on a ground. One could just have amorphous patches of colour—a black surface, say, with an amorphous blob of red in the centre. In such a case it takes little effort to see the red as in front of the black. Incidentally, it's also possible to see our triangular design not as an example of planar recession but as a three-dimensional object: one can see it as a road receding into space.

An even more interesting example of planar recession is this:

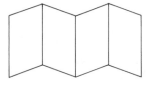

It is almost impossible not to see this as a corrugated surface alternately advancing from and receding toward the ground of the paper's plane (or, as alternately receding from and advancing toward the viewer, and 'standing on' the ground of the paper's plane so that the vertical lines are at right angles to this plane). In this case, however, what we see as plane surfaces are seen as lying at something other than a right angle with respect to the plane of the paper's surface. There are, indeed, two ways of seeing it thus. One can either see it as the parallelogram on the left having its right edge ahead of its left, the one to the right of it as having its left edge ahead of its right, etc. Or one can see it in just the reverse fashion—as the parallelogram on the left having its left edge ahead of its right, etc.

The phenomenon of seeing a design as a three-dimensional object or array of three-dimensional objects, and that of seeing a design as planes receding in space, can be combined. Our cubic design can be seen as a cube in front of the plane surface of the paper. Central in the artistic endeavours of the Western Renaissance 'perspectivists' was their attempt to bring these two phenomena together. It was consistently their goal, however, so to construct their paintings that we would see the objects as *behind* the plane of the painting's surface rather than in front of it. The picture was to be seen as a window onto the reality beyond. In that way they differed from the Byzantine artists, who wished their designs to be seen as objects in front of the plane of the surface.

Go back now to our cube design. It is extremely difficult not to see this representationally. And if one sees it representationally, it is most readily seen as a cube. But now suppose that we wish to describe more closely that particular representational seeing of it. What we can say is that we see it as a cube viewed from slightly above and to the right, with the plane of two of its façades parallel to the plane of the paper. In short, we see it as something *viewed from a certain angle*. When, in a case of representational seeing, we see the design in question as a k *viewed from such-and-such an angle*, let us say that that case of representational seeing has an *implied visual angle*. In particular, the implied visual angle of our representational seeing of that design as a cube is from slightly above and from slightly to the right and with the plane of two of its façades parallel to the plane of the paper.

For most cases of representational seeing there is an implied visual angle. But there are exceptions. If, in a particular case of representational seeing, I see a design as a uniformly coloured sphere—nothing more—then though I see it as a sphere I do not see it as a sphere *viewed from some particular angle*. The reason of course is that a uniformly coloured sphere provides us with no way whatsoever of specifying angles of vision. (If the sphere is shaded, I may see it as viewed from some angle with respect to the line of the light falling upon it.)

It may be noted, while we are on the matter, that in that form of seeing-as which is pure two-dimensional pattern completion, there is never an implied visual angle. I see the array as a circle, say. But I do not see it as a circle *viewed from such-and-such an angle*. Of course I do actually view the design on paper from a particular angle. So *the actual visual angle* from which a design on plane surface is seen on a given occasion must be sharply distinguished from *the implied visual angle* of a given case of representational seeing of that design. I may see the paper with the cube design on it from head-on, so that the line from midway between my eyes to the centre of the design is at right angles to the plane of the paper. None the less I see the design as a cube *viewed from above and to the right*.

What must be added at once is that the actual visual angle at which I see the design on paper has an impact on my representational seeing of the design. If the angle is acute enough I may be able still to see the design but not to see it representationally. And conversely, in the case of certain anamorphic designs, I can see them representationally only if I view them at very acute angles.[13] Further, some designs on paper are such that if I view them with the paper at one angle I representationally see one thing, and if at another angle, I representationally see something different. There is a charming anecdote from the history of art which nicely illustrates this point—though it happens to be concerned with sculpture rather than with two-dimensional designs:

The Athenians intending to consecrate an excellent image of Minerva upon a high pillar, set Phidias and Alcamenes to work, meaning to chuse the better of the two. Alcamenes being nothing at all skilled in

---

[13] Cf. *Hidden Images*, text by Fred Leeman; concept, production, and photographs by Joost Elffers and Mike Schuyt (Harry Abrams: New York, 1976).

Geometry and in the Optickes made the goddesse wonderfull faire to the eye of them that saw her hard by. Phidias on the contrary ... did consider that the whole shape of his image should change according to the height of the appointed place, and therefore made her lips wide open, her nose somewhat out of order, and all the rest accordingly ... When these two images were afterwards brought to light and compared, Phidias was in great danger to have been stoned by the whole multitude, untill the statues were at length set on high. For Alcamenes his sweet and diligent strokes beeing drowned, and Phidias his disfigured and distorted hardnesse being vanished by the height of the place, made Alcamenes to be laughed at, and Phidias to bee much more esteemed.[14]

To give a detailed description of what we see a design as, when seeing it representationally, we must often, of course, adopt strategies beyond that of specifying the implied visual angle. Let us see how such descriptions might go, observing first that any such description can always be fitted into this general structure: I see this design as a k which is ϕ viewed by a person of sort P under conditions of sort C. (Implied visual angle fits under the conditions.)

Sometimes we can increase the specificity of our description by attaching (additional) modifiers to the common noun for which 'a k' stands. There's not much of this sort that we can do in describing more closely what we see our cube-design as. But if one representationally sees a design as a man, it may be that one sees it not *just* as a man but as a man who is standing, with one arm raised above his head, etc. Secondly, we can sometimes specify, or describe with greater specificity, the sort of person. It may be that one sees the design not just as a k but as a k viewed by a person with astigmatic vision, or by a person intensely interested in the textures and the lighting of things. Thirdly, we can sometimes specify, or describe with greater specificity, the sort of conditions. One may see the design not just as a k but as a k viewed in a fog, or viewed from a considerable distance. Parts of Turner's paintings can be seen as ships viewed in a fog; and often parts of Brueghel's paintings can be seen as people viewed from a great distance. In this last case, we might say that for the representational seeing in question there is an *implied visual distance*; and we might put implied visual angle and

[14] Ernst Gombrich, op. cit., pp. 191–2.

implied visual distance together and call it *implied visual vantage point*.

Suppose that we see a given visual design as not just one object but as an *array* of objects, and that for our representational seeing of each of these there is an implied visual angle and distance. It may be that these implied visual vantage points all converge, so that there is just one, convergent, implied visual vantage point for the entire design. With their experiments in vanishing perspective the Western Renaissance painters attempted to construct their canvases in such a way as to force us, the viewers, to see their designs as an array of objects viewed from one, single, convergent, implied visual vantage point, and as receding from the plane of the picture's surface. Thereby, of course, they at once gave a powerful unity to their productions. But we must never so fall under their spell as to think that a condition for aesthetic excellence in representational painting is that there be a single implied visual vantage point. In Hugo van der Goes's masterpiece in the Uffizi, *The Adoration of the Shepherds*, the implied visual vantage point floats around in a most marvellous way.

Obviously what some design is representationally seen as will often depend a great deal on surrounding designs. The very design which in one context we see as a man viewed from a considerable distance may, if put into a different context, be seen as a man viewed from relatively close up.[15]

In our attempt to give a close description of what a given design is representationally seen as we can often choose from a variety of combinations as among the phrases replacing 'a k which is ϕ' in our formula, the phrases specifying the sort of person, and the phrases specifying the sort of conditions. When I see a certain design as a cube-shaped object, I may, to describe the matter more closely, say either that I see it as a serrated-edge cube viewed by a person of normal vision, or as a smooth-edged cube viewed by a person of astigmatic vision. These may be two equally correct descriptions of the very same case of representational seeing. They need not be descriptions of two different cases of representational seeing. I do not think it will ever happen, though, that a case of seeing our design as a cube-shaped object will also be a case of seeing our design as a

---

[15] Cf. Ernst Gombrich, op. cit., p. 232.

three-sided box. 'I see it as a cube' and 'I see it as a three-sided box' will never both be correct descriptions of one case of representational seeing of our design. For one can only engage in seeing it as a cube and seeing it as a three-sided box in succession, not simultaneously. That is enough to show their distinctness.

Instead of saying that I see some two-dimensional visual design as a horse, I might say that it *looks (to me) like a horse*. How is such a claim to be understood? Well, it too, I think, should be understood as a description of how I see the design in a given case of representational seeing. For I am not saying that that design, or that design on that paper, looks as a horse would look. On some occasion, staring off into the distance while out in the country, I may see some objects and say, 'They look to me like horses.' What I would mean is that they look to me as horses would look under these circumstances. (I might, in addition, be *suggesting* that they *are* horses.) But that is not what I would mean in the case before us. For only under the most extraordinary circumstances would a sheet of white paper with some pencil marks on it look as a horse would look under these circumstances. Neither am I saying that I apprehend some (relatively close) similarity in the design before me and a design characteristically instantiated by horses. For I might in fact apprehend that there is some such similarity, yet the design not look to me like a horse. It is rather that upon seeing the design representationally—as an object—I describe more closely what I see it as by saying that it 'looks like a horse'. And that is to say nothing different from saying that I see it as a horse.

It might be thought that a mark of a significant difference is the fact that when using the 'looks like' locution we can speak of degrees: 'It looks quite a bit like a horse.' 'It looks very much like a horse.' One cannot more or less see a design as a horse, nor can one see a design as more or less of a horse. One can, though, see it as something quite a bit like a horse. And that is no different from its looking quite a bit like a horse. So both 'something quite a bit like a horse' and 'something which looks like a horse' can replace the 'a *k*' in our formula. And, when thus replacing it, they would mean the same thing.

No doubt people differ in their tendencies to representational seeing. A design that one person tends readily to see as so-and-so, another person may not tend to see representationally at all, or may tend to see representationally as something else, or may see as so-and-so only with difficulty. No doubt it is also true that what one person can representationally see as so-and-so, another person cannot see that way at all. Probably there are differences from culture to culture on these matters as well. For it's worth noting that representational seeing is in part a matter of training and of psychological set. Probably some readers never saw our cube-design as a three-sided box until we pointed out that it could be seen that way. Perhaps our remark prodded some of those who had never seen it thus, to do so. Though doing so, they may have done so only with difficulty. But then one can practise seeing it thus; and gradually one will become more and more adept at doing so.

I have concentrated my attention on visual designs on plane surfaces and on the correlate of these, two-dimensional representational seeing. But one can also see a block of wood as a horse. In the relevant sense of 'look like', it can look like a horse. So from all the cases of *seeing-as*, we can pick out, as cases of *three*-dimensional representational seeing, those in which we see some three-dimensional object as a so-and-so, when it neither is that nor looks to us as if it is. With the obvious modifications, most of what I have said about two-dimensional representational seeing applies also to three-dimensional representational seeing. There are some interesting differences, though, the principal one being that implied visual vantage point disappears in full-bodied sculpture. Though I see the block of wood as a horse, I do not see it as a horse viewed from some angle or other, or from some distance or other. I do of course actually see the lump of wood from some angle and distance; and perhaps some angle and some distance are aesthetically preferable. But though my seeing of the lump of wood will always have an *actual* visual vantage point, my representational seeing of it will never have any implied visual vantage point. I am inclined, indeed, to think that implied perceptual conditions in general—not just implied visual vantage point—become irrelevant when we deal with sculpture. However, conditions concerning the nature of the implied perceiver remain relevant. We can see the block of wood as a horse viewed by someone totally uninterested in texture.

For each of us, then, there is a stock of visual designs which we *tend* to see representationally, whether ambiguously or not; and an even greater stock which we are *able* to see representationally, given the right assistance and training and effort. Though one person's stock, with respect both to ability and tendency, differs from another person's stock, there is also, within a given society, a massive overlap in both respects. And surely there is also a large overlap between the members of almost any pair of societies that one could pick.

It is from the stock of designs that can be seen representationally by human beings that the artist who pictures must choose his designs—on pain of not picturing. It's true that a given artist's range of options is narrower than this. He must choose from a subset thereof; and we shall see what that subset is, for a given artist. But those are the outer limits. Because of this intimate relation between picturing and representational seeing, Leonardo da Vinci was giving good advice to the fledgeling artist when he advised him, in a famous passage, to practise seeing things wherever he happened to be:

You should look at certain walls stained with damp, or at stones of uneven colour. If you have to invent some backgrounds you will be able to see in these the likeness of divine landscapes, adorned with mountains, ruins, rocks, woods, great plains, hills and valleys in great variety; and then again you will see there battles and strange figures in violent action, expressions of faces and clothes and an infinity of things which you will be able to reduce to their complete and proper forms. In such walls the same thing happens as in the sound of bells, in whose stroke you may find every named word which you can imagine.[16]

VI. *Representational Seeing and Picturing*

Having explained what it is for a design to *look like* a unicorn, or in other words, to be capable of being seen as a unicorn, I can now return to the thesis I put forth as to the connection between pictures and what is pictured. It was this: only with a visual design that can be seen as a unicorn can one p-represent a unicorn. If the instantiated design cannot be seen as a unicorn, then one has not pictured that there is a unicorn by instantiating that design.

[16] Quoted in Gombrich, op. cit., p. 188.

But *who* must be capable of seeing that design as a unicorn? For as we saw earlier, what one person is capable of seeing as a so-and-so, another may not be capable of so seeing. So whose ability for representational seeing is relevant to the determination as to whether picturing has occurred?

'The artist's,' one is initially inclined to say. 'The artist's abilities for representational seeing are the relevant ones.' Suppose, though, that an artist *does* have the ability to see some design as a unicorn but that he has never, in fact, seen it thus, and doesn't *know* that he is capable of seeing it thus. Suppose that he doesn't know that *anyone* is capable of seeing it thus. The potential of the design for being thus seen is simply unknown to him. I think the proper conclusion is that that design can then not be used by him to picture a unicorn.

Are we, perhaps, to demand that the artist *actually have seen* the design as a unicorn? No, that will also not do. Suppose, for example, that an artist produces a large-scale design which he knows can be seen as a unicorn, by himself and others, but which he has never in fact seen thus, never having stood far enough back to get the necessary perspective. Surely he might none the less have pictured a unicorn.

Closer to the truth, I think, is this: if an artist is to picture a unicorn, he must instantiate a design which he *knows* can be seen by him as a unicorn. But even this seems too constrictive. For might an artist not picture a unicorn by instantiating a design which he knows can be seen by many in his society as a unicorn but which he is incapable of seeing thus? Perhaps his vision is no longer keen enough, or perhaps he suffers from the quirk of just not being able to see this particular design as a unicorn. It would seem that none the less he can use this design to picture a unicorn. Accordingly, I suggest that if an artist is to p-represent a unicorn, he must instantiate a visual design which he knows that he or others in his society can see as a unicorn.

In the light of these conclusions let me introduce the concept of a *pictorial arrangement* (an arrangement for p-representation). Given that certain visual designs which can be seen by one person as a so-and-so cannot be thus seen by another, the concept will have to be relative to a person at a time. Suppose, then, that some action, ψ-ing, can be generated by the performance of some action ϕ-ing, so that $\langle\phi$-ing, ψ-ing$\rangle$, is an arrangement for ψ-ing. Suppose, further, that the generating action, ϕ-ing, consists of instantiating (in a certain sort of context) a visual design D. And suppose that to perform the generated action, ψ-ing, is to perform some illocutionary action on the proposition *that there is a k*. Then the arrangement, $A = \langle\phi$-ing, ψ-ing$\rangle$, is a pictorial arrangement, relative to person P at time t, if and only if P at t knows that he or others in his society can see D as a k. And we may say that a system for mood-action is a *pictorial system*, relative to person P at time t, if and only if its function-member is such that all the pairs of which it is comprised are pictorial arrangements, relative to P at t.

From our preceding discussion it follows that P at t pictures a k only if P at t uses an arrangement for the performance of some illocutionary action on *there being a k* which, relative to him at that time, is a pictorial arrangement. It would be pleasant if this were a sufficient as well as a necessary condition for picturing. Unfortunately, it is not. For suppose that P is using a language some of whose sentences are pictorial designs—designs which can be seen by P and/or members of his society as three-dimensional objects. Specifically, suppose that in this language the sentence normally used to assert that there is a unicorn looks like a unicorn. Suppose, further, that P knows it can be seen thus. Now suppose that in the course of using this language P asserts, in the fashion normal for that language, that there is a unicorn. His inscribing of that unicorn-like design counts as his asserting that. He has then made use of an arrangement for indicating that there is a unicorn which is, for him at that time, a pictorial arrangement. Yet I take it that he has not pictured a unicorn. It is sheer coincidence that in this language the sentence to use for asserting that there is a unicorn looks like a unicorn. One cannot in this fashion, coincidentally, picture a unicorn.

Why not? What is missing? What is missing, I suggest, is a certain intention. For picturing to take place, the agent must *intend* that his indication of the state of affairs of *there being a unicorn* shall be performed by the instantiation of a design that looks like a unicorn. It is this *intention* that is missing in our case of the man who coincidentally uses a design that looks like a unicorn. He may well have intended to indicate the proposition that there is a unicorn. And he may well have intended to inscribe the visual design that he did. What is missing is the intention that his indication of that state of affairs shall be performed by the inscription of a design that looks like a unicorn. And if, on the contrary, this intention is present, then he has pictured a unicorn.

A point made persuasively by Ernst Gombrich, in *Art and Illusion*, is that, as a matter of psychological fact, an artist never has available to him, for the purpose of constructing his pictures, the whole stock of visual designs which can be used to picture. On the contrary, even the most facile of artists works with a surprisingly limited subset of these. The members of the particular subset that an artist works with are called, by Gombrich, his artistic *schemata*. The repertoire of schemata that an artist works with is in part the result of his being influenced by the particular artistic tradition in which he stands; but in part it is also the result of his own idiosyncrasies. Sometimes artists are selfconsciously aware of these schemata. Their awareness will come out in rules for drawing that they offer to fledgeling artists, in canons of proportion that they formulate, etc. For example, some at least of the Byzantine icon painters were aware of the fact that they were working with a canon of proportion according to which the distance from hair-line to crown of head always constituted about a third of the face in their paintings. Other times, artists have been totally unaware of their particular schemata.

Gombrich theorizes that an artist's repertoire of schemata influences what he tries to picture and how he pictures it. Actually Gombrich has two somewhat different things in mind when he says this, for by an artist's 'schemata' he means two rather different things. Sometimes his point is that the artist's rendering and picturing is influenced by what one might call *pictorial motifs* which are acquired from here and there in the history of art and which retain considerable invariance across their occurrence in different styles. After giving some examples of this tendency he says that

These examples demonstrate, in somewhat grotesque magnification, a tendency which the student of art has learned to reckon with. The familiar will always remain the likely starting point for the rendering of the unfamiliar; an existing representation will always exert its spell over the artist even while he strives to record the truth. Thus it was remarked by ancient critics that several famous artists of antiquity had made a strange mistake in the portrayal of horses; they had represented them with eyelashes on the lower lid, a feature which belongs to the human eye but not to that of the horse.[17]

On other occasions when speaking of schemata for picturing, what Gombrich calls a 'schema' is not a stylistically invariant pictorial motif but rather the style of an artist. His point then is that an artist's style influences what he tries to picture and how he pictures it. In considering a painting by the Chinese artist Chiang Yee of a scene in Derwentwater we find Gombrich saying this:

We see how the relatively rigid vocabulary of the Chinese tradition acts as a selective screen which admits only the features for which schemata exist. The artist will be attracted by motifs which can be rendered in his idiom. As he scans the landscape, the sights which can be matched successfully with the schemata he has learned to handle will leap forward as centers of attention. The style, like the medium, creates a mental set which makes the artist look for certain aspects in the scene around him that he can render. Painting is an activity; and the artist will therefore tend to see what he paints rather than to paint what he sees.[18]

What we find clearly stated in this quotation, and hinted at in the preceding one, is Gombrich's additional theory that artistic motifs and styles function as *visual stereotypes*. Motifs and styles influence how that which is seen is pictured. But also they influence how that which is pictured is seen. Indeed, they influence our seeing, whether or not we try to picture. They influence the visual perception of beholders as well as that of artists. Having looked at Piranesi, we find that London has acquired here and there a Piranesian look. Having looked at the Dutch landscape paintings, we find that the sky of western Michigan on occasion has the look of the sky in a Dutch landscape. Neither the artist nor anyone else approaches visual reality with naked eye. And part of what influences how we all—artists and spectators alike—see the reality around us is the motifs and styles in the pictures we have seen.

Thus Gombrich theorizes that the artist, head and eye filled

[17] Gombrich, op. cit., p. 82.
[18] Ibid., pp. 85–6.

with artistic schemata, allows these to function both as visual and as pictorial stereotypes, only now and then noticing, and recording, the discrepancy between stereotype and reality. Speaking about 'the procedure of any artist who wants to make a truthful record of an individual form', Gombrich says this:

He begins not with his visual impression but with his idea or concept: The German artist with his concept of a castle that he applies as well as he can to that individual castle, Merian with his idea of a church, and the lithographer with his stereotype of a cathedral. The individual visual information, those distinctive features I have mentioned, are entered, as it were, upon a pre-existing blank or formulary.[19]

VII. *How to Tell What's Pictured*

In the preceding sections I have considered matters from the side of the artist, asking what conditions must be satisfied if he is to picture. Let me now shift perspective and consider matters from the side of the spectator. What are some of the characteristic problems which arise when we, the spectators, try to tell what has been pictured—that is, what the artist is to be counted as having indicated pictorially? In other words, what are some of the characteristic problems that arise when we try to decide which pictorial arrangement was used in a given case? Of course this is to presuppose that it has in fact been determined, in a given situation, that picturing was taking place. And often *that* determination is itself a difficult, problematic matter.

(1) For one thing, it is often unclear which visual design is functioning as a sign. A picture—a concrete physical object—instantiates many designs. And though sometimes it will be clear which is the functioning design, other times it will not be. Two roots of such obscurity are worth singling out for attention.

A picture will not display the functioning sign to all observers under all conditions. It will display it only if someone of a rather definite sort looks at it under conditions of a rather definite sort. What goes into being a person of the requisite sort is having the requisite perceptual apparatus, but also having the appropriate

[19] Ibid., p. 73. Cf. p. 88.

visual training so that one knows what to focus on. And what belong to the requisite conditions are such matters as being seen in the proper light, being seen from the proper angle and distance, etc. We might say that for each case of picturing there is a *canonical mode of apprehension*—the way the picture must be seen if the functioning design is to be apprehended.

This point—that for cases of picturing there are canonical modes of apprehension—is especially evident from that little anecdote about Phidias and Alcamenes which we cited a few sections back. Looking at Phidias' statue from ground level did not fall within its canonical mode of apprehension. If it had, Phidias would justly have been accused of representing a woman with lips wide open. But in fact he is not to be accused of that. The canonical mode of apprehension for his statue includes seeing it from well below. Only then can one apprehend the functioning design. Other examples of picturing which make it clear that cases of picturing have canonical modes of apprehension are the already mentioned anamorphic pictures. To view them so as to apprehend the functioning design one must see them at extremely acute angles, or in curved mirrors, and so forth.

How do we determine the canonical mode of apprehension for a given case of picturing? How do we know that looking at an etching from fifty feet off is outside the canonical mode of apprehension? How do we know that looking at a painting by late Titian from close up with a magnifying glass is outside the canonical mode of apprehension? How did the Athenians know that the canonical mode of apprehension for Phidias' statue was from well below? The clues are of many different sorts. But often what is involved is the existence of certain conventions for looking at art of different styles—that is, the existence of certain co-ordinations of action as between the picturer and his public. Such conventions, where they exist, constitute part of the context within which the picturer works. Of course a given artist may choose to depart from all the extant conventions by painting in a radically new style for which there are no such conventions. He may then either inform people of the canonical mode of apprehension for his pictures; or he may leave them to find out for themselves. And if the latter, the public may be perplexed until finally they arrive at a way of apprehending the

paintings which makes good sense of them. Either way, characteristically the artist's new style will induce the birth of new
conventions for looking at paintings in this fresh style. A great
deal of what goes into learning to appreciate representational
art, contemporary as well as traditional, is learning and practising the canonical modes of apprehension for different styles of
painting.

But then secondly, even when the picture in a given case of
picturing is being viewed within its canonical mode of
apprehension, we may still not know, fully, what is the functioning design. For we may not know which features of the object
and of how we see it are functioning representationally and
which are there for other reasons—perhaps to make the painting's surface aesthetically worthwhile, or perhaps because they
are unavoidable features of the medium used. Those wide black
bands surrounding the figures in Rouault's paintings are not
functioning representationally; they are not part of the picturing design. And that swirling, jabbing, highly three-
dimensional texture of the paint in Van Gogh's late paintings
was—usually at least—also not functioning representationally. It was not part of the picturing design. Its function was to
give to the surface of the painting an intensely expressive,
highly textured quality so as thereby to make that surface
aesthetically important in its own right.

(2) Sometimes we do not know what is the artist's repertoire
of pictorial designs—that is, which of all the designs which *can*
be used to picture are available to him within his schemata.
We do not know which designs belong within his representational style, and we do not know his skill in using his style. This
too can lead to uncertainty as to what the picturer is to be
counted as having pictured. Suppose that we come across some
petroglyphs in the south-western United States, left by some
primitive Indian tribe. We may have concluded that what is
here pictured is a condor with wings outspread. But the picture
is in the 'stick' style. So that leaves us with the question of
whether it is the *skeleton* of a condor that is pictured or a
full-fleshed condor. If we know that the picturer was not limited
in his repertoire to such stick designs, then we would probably
conclude one thing. If we know that he was limited to that, then
we would conclude a different thing. So too, if we know that the

repertoire of the late Byzantine icon painters was limited to designs in which the distance from hair-line to crown was one third of the entire face, we will not count them as picturing a narrow range of rather strange looking human faces. And if we know that in Duccio's repertoire there were no devices for showing shadows, we will not count him as always showing the Madonna in a blaze of absolutely uniform illumination. Rembrandt's repertoire—both in terms of designs available to him within his style and in terms of his skill in putting down those designs—was immense. And so the very same design produced by his hand and by the hand of a primitive Indian would rightly lead to different conclusions.

(3) What may be called the *pictorial situation* of the picturer differs from artist to artist; and our knowledge of that situation also enters into our judgement as to what to count the artist as having pictured. If we do not know the relevant part of his pictorial situation, we are often left with uncertainty.

Given the facts about our human make-up, there are for every artist, at a given time, many pictureable states of affairs which he himself cannot picture at that time, even if he had the total repertoire of visual designs at his command; for he is not aware of them. And within the set of ones that he can picture at a given time, there are ones that he would be very unlikely to have pictured at that time. By the *pictorial situation* of a given artist at a given time I mean, then, the states of affairs which at that time he could have pictured and which he would not have been unlikely to have tried to picture.

There being unicorns did not belong to the pictorial situation of the south-western Indians; but *there being condors* did. *There being such a god as Olmec* did not belong to the pictorial situation of the European medieval painters; but *there being unicorns* did. And in the pictorial situation of the Aztecs there were gods of the sort described in their myths. Knowing the pictorial situation of a picturer often helps us to know what he is to be counted as having pictured. And conversely, if we do not know what the pictorial situation of an artist was like in relevant respects, we will often be at a loss to tell what he pictured.

One last comment should be made concerning the viewer's attempt to figure out what the artist has pictured. The public of the artist will have a tendency to representationally see his designs in certain ways even though it is possible to see them in various other ways as well. Often the artist will know about these tendencies. If the artist then produces a design which can be seen by his audience as a three-sided empty box but which they will tend to see as a cube, and if the artist knows about this tendency on their part and does nothing to try to counteract it, then what he does is to be counted as picturing a cube. The reason for this lies in that obligation to act in trust which lies at the root of all count-generation. Essentially the same thing holds for language. Suppose that I utter a certain sentence and that everybody in my audience strongly tends to think that I am using it in sense S, and so asserting P. Suppose, though, that it has another sense S', such that if I had used it in that sense I would have asserted P'. Suppose, further, that this is an exotic sense. No one, in the context, would tend to think I was using it in sense S'. And suppose that I knew this, and did nothing to counteract the tendency of my public to think that I was using it in sense S. Then what I did would *count as* my asserting P. And my plea that this sentence has another sense, and that I should be taken as having asserted P', is of no avail. In a court of law one cannot get out of a perjury charge by arguing that one of the words one used has a sense, albeit a minor and unusual one, such that in that sense one told the truth.

Often, of course, what serves to clarify and resolve what is pictured is accompanying words, or other features of the context. But sometimes it remains incurably ambiguous and unclear what was pictured. No investigations along any of the above lines, nor any other lines, help at all. And sometimes—as in the case of picture puzzles—such ambiguity is deliberate. But we should not exaggerate the unclarity and ambiguity. It is perfectly clear that Rembrandt has pictured a woman bathing. So clear is this that if seventeenth-century Amsterdam had had a law again picturing women bathing, Rembrandt would indisputably have violated it. He could no more have got out of the charge by claiming that he was merely making a design, or picturing something else than a woman bathing, than someone can get out of a perjury charge by claiming that he just happened to be rolling certain English sentences over his tongue, or just happened to be using the sounds of English to assert something quite different from what his accusers suppose. So too, it was often perfectly clear in ancient Byzantium that the iconoclast laws had been violated; and often it was perfectly clear in Jewish communities that their laws against the making of images had been broken.

VIII. *What's to be Found in the World of the Picture*

Consider some two-dimensional design which, when seen representationally, tends to be seen as a serrated-edged cube viewed by someone with normal vision from slightly above and to the right—alternatively described, as a straight-edged cube viewed by someone with astigmatic vision from slightly above and to the right. Such a design can be used to picture that there is a cube. So suppose we did use it thus. Would we then picture that there is a straight-edged cube, or would we picture that there is a serrated-edged cube? If the state of affairs pictorially introduced were to occur, would there have to be a cube with straight edges, or would there have to be a cube with serrated edges?

Well, sometimes the one and sometimes the other. Given that the look of the design can be described with equal correctness in either of the two suggested ways, one can use it to picture that there is a serrated-edged cube and one can use it to picture that there is a straight-edged cube. And sometimes it will decisively be *one* of these actions that one has performed, at other times, the other.

Though it's clear that the design can be used to picture that there is a serrated-edged cube, perhaps it's not so clear that it can be used to picture that there is a straight-edged cube. So let us reflect for a moment on what is to be said in favour of the claim that it can be so used. One can picture a straight-edged cube as it would appear to a person of normal vision viewing it through clear air from above right. Equally, one can picture a straight-edged cube as it would appear to a person of normal vision viewing it through clear air from below left. In short, one can picture a straight-edged cube as it would appear when viewed from various distinct angles of vision. But if the 'how' of picturing straight-edged cubes can tolerate variation in angles of vision, then it seems reasonable to allow that it can also tolerate other sorts of variations in conditions of viewing. It would seem, for example, that one can picture a straight-edged cube as it would appear to a person of normal vision viewing it from above right *through a fog*, or *through a piece of distorting glass*. In turn, if the 'how' of picturing straight-edged cubes can tolerate variations in the conditions of viewing, then it seems reasonable to allow that it can also tolerate variations in the perceptual state of the perceiver. One can picture a straight-edged cube as it would appear to a person of normal vision; why not also, as it would appear to a person of *astigmatic* vision? If we should find some artist producing an occurrence of our serrated-edged cube design and labelling it: 'Straight-edged cube—as seen by an astigmatic,' it seems reasonable to conclude that he has pictured that there is a straight-edged cube.

There is, admittedly, another way of construing the situation in which an artist inscribes our serrated-edged cube design and labels it 'Straight-edged cube—as seen by an astigmatic.' Perhaps he has not pictured *that there is a cube* but rather, *that this is how a cube would appear to an astigmatic*. At the end of this section I shall consider the tenability of this alternative construal.

It's worth noting explicitly that since the very same design can be used either to picture there being a straight-edged cube or there being a serrated-edged cube, what accounts for its being the one rather than the other that has been pictured is not the fact that this particular design has been used to do the picturing. That this particular design was instantiated does not, *by itself*, constitute the statal indicator of the particular arrangement for picturing which was used. Some other feature of the generating act is involved as well. And so it always is, at least for arrangements for picturing which are at all like our normal ones. *Merely* from the design used one cannot read off what is represented.

Now look back once again at the claim that the artist has pictured a straight-edged cube as it would appear to someone viewing it who is an astigmatic. For the world of the picture to occur there must be a straight-edged cube. But must there also be a person with astigmatic vision who is viewing a straight-edged cube and to whom the cube appears as the design looks? Surely not. The occurrence of the world of the work is compatible with there being no astigmatic person viewing a cube. Indeed, it is compatible with there being no astigmatic person at all.

But granted that there need be no astigmatic person, let alone an astigmatic person actually viewing a straight-edged cube; must there none the less be *someone* viewing a straight-edged cube, and must it appear to him as the picture looks? Does the world of a picture always include an implicit viewer? No, not that either. There needn't even be someone to whom a straight-edged cube *would* appear, under *some conditions or other*, as the design looks. The world of a picture can include *there being a cube* without including *there being a perceiver*. What *is* the case, however, is that if the world of a picture includes there being a straight-edged cube, then it will also include a number of counterfactuals of the following sort, pertaining to the 'look' of the cube: if someone with the visual capacities of normal persons in the actual world would look at the cube under such-and-such conditions, it would appear so-and-so; if someone with the visual capacities of astigmatic persons in the actual world would look at the cube under such-and-such conditions, it would appear thus-and-thus; etc.

In his well-known essay, 'Style and Medium in the Motion Picture',[20] Erwin Panofsky remarks that a distinguishing feature of motion pictures is what he calls 'dynamization of space'. He explains this by saying that in movies, the visual vantage point moves around. Of course he does not mean that we, the viewers, change our vantage point. Neither, I think, does he mean that if the world of the film were to occur there would have to be, for each frame, someone to whom things appear as the picture looks; and that this person, or these persons, characteristically move around in the world projected. That may be true for the entirety of a few films. And it is true of passages in many films; they present things as they appear to one of the characters in the film. But this is not in general true. Consider, for example, those many scenes in Kubrick's *Barry Lyndon* in which the camera begins by shooting an actor from very close up and then, keeping him in focus, moving backward. (That, at least, would be one way of getting the result.) One frame pictures a person as he would appear to someone seeing him

[20] In *Critique*, i, No. 3 (1947).

from close up, a later frame pictures that same person as he would appear to someone seeing him from slightly less close up, etc, In that way, space is dynamized. But it is not dynamized in the sense that for the world of *Barry Lyndon* to occur, there must repeatedly occur the phenomenon of someone looking at someone else from close up, and then, with gaze fixed firmly upon him, moving backward into the distance. In *Barry Lyndon* we are repeatedly confronted with a peculiarity in the manner of the picturing rather than with a peculiarity in the content of the pictured.[21] The dynamization of space in movies pertains to the 'how' of the picturing, not to the 'what' of the pictured.

We have seen that an artist may represent a straight-edged cube as it would appear to an astigmatic viewer while yet the world of his work does not include there being a person, and thus does not include there being a person of astigmatic vision. All that is necessary is that there be a straight-edged cube. But what then is the force of adding 'as it would appear to an astigmatic viewer'? For surely it may in fact sometimes be correct to say that an artist has represented a straight-edged cube *as it would appear to an astigmatic viewer*, or a tree *as it would appear through a piece of distorting glass*, or a liver cell *as it would appear through a 60 power microscope*. Indeed, we can always, in principle, fill out our description of a case of picturing along such lines. That is to say, if someone has pictured an object, then always some proposition of the following form will be true: He has pictured a *k* (which is ϕ) *as it would appear to a person of sort P viewing it under conditions of sort C*.

I suggest that to claim that someone has pictured a cube which has straight edges as it would appear to an astigmatic is to claim:

(i) that he has pictured that there is a cube which has straight edges, and

(ii) that the design he has used is such that (in the actual world) if an astigmatic looked at a cube which has straight edges, it would appear as this design looks.[22]

---

[21] In some recent essays of his Kendall Walton has taken the opposite position from that which I am here espousing. He has held that the world of a picture does, in a certain way, always involve an observer. In Section X I propose to consider this matter in more detail in the context of scrutinizing Walton's theory of representation.

[22] Perhaps sometimes it is to claim, thirdly, that the artist *by intent* used a design having this property.

Accordingly, it pertains to the *content* of one's picturing that one has pictured a straight-edged cube, whereas it pertains to the *manner* of one's picturing that one has pictured it as it would appear to a person of astigmatic vision viewing it through clear air from above and to the right.

In the light of this conclusion, a small refinement can now be introduced into one of my conclusions in the preceding sections. There I contended that to picture a cube which has straight edges one must use a design which one knows can be seen by oneself or others as a cube with straight edges. We can now add this: one must use a design which one knows can be seen by oneself or others as how a cube which has straight edges would appear (in the actual world) to some sort of percipient viewing it under some sort of conditions.

Most of the time when a so-and-so is p-represented, it is represented as it would appear to a person of normal vision under fairly ordinary conditions. There are, of course, exceptions. In his 'The Dead Christ', Mantegna pictured a corpse as seen from its feet looking toward its head, and from just slightly above the feet, so that the picture is an example of extreme foreshortening. Turner was fond of representing things as seen in fog (perhaps not a non-ordinary condition, in his locale!). And scientific texts are filled with pictures of things as viewed through microscopes and telescopes. Still, most of the time when someone pictures that there is a k which is ϕ, the design used is one which can be seen as how a k which is ϕ would appear (in the actual world) to normal observers under rather ordinary conditions.

Not only is this how things are *usually* done. I think that there is a convention in force among us, roughly to the following effect:[23] if an artist wishes to picture a k, and if he wishes to use a design which does not have the look of how a k appears (in the actual world) to normal observers under ordinary conditions, and if he knows that it has the look instead of how something else, a k^*, appears to normal observers under ordinary conditions, then he will in some way give us a clue that he is not using the design to picture a k^*. Mantegna need not give us a clue that he is picturing a human corpse, since, odd as the

[23] This is really a specific version of the point made at the end of the preceding section.

perspective is, what else would anyone see this design as? But if our tendency had been, say, to see it as a pelican as viewed by a normal observer under ordinary conditions, and if he knew that, then he would have violated a convention in effect among us if he had not given us a clue that he did not mean to be picturing a pelican. Perhaps even—in spite of whatever protestations he might mount—what he would have done would have counted as representing a pelican and not as representing a corpse. Perhaps, in short, a certain arrangement for picturing would have been in effect for him by virtue of convention regardless of his own private intentions.

The fact that the convention indicated is often in effect for us is of fundamental importance when we try to figure out just what it is that the artist has represented. We know, let us say, that the artist has p-represented *something*. But *what*? What sort of object must there be if the world of the picture is to occur? Very often we make our inferences on the assumption that the convention cited has been respected. We know that if something would appear (in the actual world) to someone of normal vision under ordinary conditions as this design looks, then it would be, say, a brown horse standing upright. And so we flesh out the world by invoking that counterfactual. Similarly, if we are told that the artist has pictured a liver cell as seen through a 60 power microscope, then we flesh out the world by invoking such a counterfactual as this: if a liver cell appeared to a person of normal vision through a 60 power microscope as this design looks, then that cell would have properties F, G, H, etc.[24]

---

[24] When in Part Three I explored the idea of the world of a work, I took literature as my prime example, and distinguished between interpretation and extrapolation. Interpretation consists of finding out what states of affairs the author indicated (mentioned or suggested). Extrapolation consists of figuring out what else the world contains. It proceeds by asking: what else would occur if the states of affairs indicated were to occur? Thus extrapolation essentially involves an appeal to counterfactuals. A counterpart distinction applies to picturing. But I think that it presents us with many more borderline examples, perhaps so many as to make it a distinction not worth using. Confronted with Titian's painting *Charles V*, the conclusion that the world of the work includes *there being a horse* is arrived at by something very like interpretation, whereas the conclusion that it includes *there being a horse which was born at some time* is arrived at by supplementing interpretation with something very much like extrapolation. But what about the conclusion that it includes *there being a horse which has a heart*? Is this also interpretation supplemented with something like extrapolation, or is it just interpretation? We have seen above that in our attempt to figure out what the world of a picture includes we appeal to counterfactuals from the very beginning, counterfactuals which

And now, in conclusion, we must return to an issue raised early in this section but then set to the side for the time being. Suppose that an artist instantiates a serrated-edged cube design and labels his picture: 'A straight-edged cube—as it would appear to an astigmatic.' I argued that it seems reasonable to conclude that in such a case the artist has pictured *that there is a cube which has straight edges*. And an implication of what I later contended is that by thus labelling it, he is claiming that the design used has the property of looking as does a straight-edged cube (in the actual world) to an astigmatic viewer. But I added that another way of construing the situation is that the artist has pictured this last-mentioned proposition, namely *that this is how a straight-edged cube would appear to an astigmatic viewer*. And this interpretation seems quite compelling when we notice that the artist might well have labelled his picture: 'How a straight-edged cube would appear to an astigmatic viewer' (instead of: 'A straight-edged cube—as it would appear to an astigmatic viewer').

To make sure that we have the issue clearly before us, let me construct an additional example. Suppose that in some scientific text we find a picture with this caption: 'Liver cell ($\times 60$).' One interpretation of this situation would be that what is here pictured is that there is a liver cell, so that the world of the picture includes that state of affairs; and that, in addition, it is being claimed that the design is such that it looks as a liver cell would appear (to a normal observer) when magnified 60 times. But another interpretation is that what is here pictured is itself this last proposition, namely that this design looks as a liver cell would appear to a normal observer when magnified 60 times. Or to state it a bit more amply: That this design has the property of having a look which is like that which, in the actual world, a liver cell would present to a person of normal vision viewing it under a 60 power microscope. On this alternative

---

refer to the properties of the look of the design in our actual world. Now we could distinguish such counterfactuals from those which do not refer to such properties. And perhaps we get to the conclusion that the world of the work includes there being a horse by appealing to counterfactuals which make such reference, while, given that inclusion, we get to the further conclusion that the world contains an object which was born at some time, by appealing to counterfactuals which do not make such reference. But it looks to me as if the distinction leaves many ambiguous cases. And it does not seem to me especially interesting to try to refine it so as to make it yield fewer such.

interpretation, if that which is pictured is to occur, there must be this design and it must have this property. But there need not be a liver cell.

So our questions are these: is it a liver cell which is pictured, or how a liver cell would appear when magnified 60 times? Is it a straight-edged cube which is pictured, or how a straight-edged cube would appear to an astigmatic viewer?

Well, suppose that in some newly designed typeface, the O has an egg shape. That is, suppose that the O has a look which is like that which (in the actual world) an egg presents to a person of normal vision who views it from the side through clear air. I can then, pointing to one of those O's on a page, say truly, 'This is how an egg looks.' But I would not then be claiming that the typesetter has pictured how an egg looks. For surely the typesetter has not *pictured* anything at all with that O. Would I not simply be remarking that that design has the property of looking a certain way in the actual world? So too, then, if someone draws a certain design and *himself says* that it is how a liver cell looks when magnified 60 times, should we not avoid concluding that he has pictured that this is how a liver cell looks when magnified 60 times, should we not conclude rather that he has simply instantiated a certain design and coupled that action with the claim that this design has the property of looking a certain way in the actual world?

A reply to these seemingly rhetorical questions is possible, however. Notice, in the first place, that to use a design to picture something, one need not oneself produce an occurrence of that design. Under certain circumstances one can do so with an occurrence of the design that someone else has produced. Keeping that in mind, the following view seems coherent: the typesetter by producing occurrences of that egg-shaped O has indeed not pictured that that is how an egg looks, even though it's true that that *is* how an egg looks. But if I now point to one of those O's and say, 'This is how an egg looks,' perhaps that is sufficient to bring it about that *I* have used the design to picture something. And if so, is there really anything against the suggestion that what I have pictured is that this is how an egg looks?

This does indeed seem to me to be a coherent answer. And I judge that we are now at a stalemate. Sometimes one uses an

egg-shaped design to picture that there is an egg. But sometimes, perhaps, one uses it simply to picture that this (design) is
how an egg looks. If so, then often, no doubt, it will not be clear
which of the two has been done.[25]

IX. *Pictorial Perspective*

The matters discussed in the last several sections have a particularly interesting application in the case of pictorial perspective. The Quattrocento painters and their successors in the
West became intensely interested in capturing the spatial
recession of objects. They wanted to picture there being an
array of objects receding in space. For this they needed *designs*
which can be seen representationally as an array of objects
receding into space. Now in fact a fairly large number of quite
different sorts of designs will fill the bill. The genius of the
Renaissance painters was that they hit on a very extraordinary
set of rules for constructing the requisite designs. It would be a
mistake to think that their attempt to capture spatial recession
depended entirely on their use of these rules; it depended also
on their capturing of texture, of light, etc. But certainly these
rules and the attempt to follow them drew the focus of their
attention. The rules I have in mind are of course the now-
traditional rules of perspective, these being a set of rules of
projection from objects to representing images.

The Renaissance painters justified their particular rules of
projection—the now-traditional rules of perspective—as
follows. Take an array of objects, and place images representing those objects on a surface according to the rules. Then look
at the picture under certain conditions, and the array of objects
under rather similar conditions; and the picture will look just
like the array of objects with respect to the sight-lines of the
spatially receding objects. It will look just like it in the sense

[25] If the world of the work includes
    (i) there being an egg,
then I think it will also include
    (ii) this design's being how an egg looks when seen from the side by a normal
         observer.
For if it includes (i), then surely by extrapolation it will also include the counterfactual,
    (iii) that if someone with normal vision would look at the egg from the side it would
          appear as this design looks.
And (iii) directly entails (ii).

that one cannot tell any difference. The two sets of conditions in question are stated succinctly by Goodman:

The picture must be viewed through a peephole, face on, from a certain distance, with one eye closed and the other motionless. The object also must be observed through a peephole, from a given (but not usually the same) angle and distance, and with a single unmoving eye.[26]

It should be noted how absolutely extraordinary this all is. The rules of perspective are justified by claiming that they give us a look alike, with respect to the lines of sight, between the peephole appearance of the painting and the peephole appearance of the array of objects. But rarely do we look at objects through peepholes. And rarely do we look at pictures through peepholes. Nor did the Renaissance painters regard peephole appearances of their paintings as defining the limits of the *canonical range of appearances* of their paintings. Yet they were right. A design so constructed *can* be seen, even when viewed under circumstances canonical for the picture, as an array of objects receding into space. Indeed, *so* right were they that even when viewing a design so constructed under normal, 'canonical', circumstances, it is very difficult *not* to see it as an array of objects receding into space. Such a design is thus a very fit candidate indeed for picturing there being an array of objects receding into space.

Many writers have pointed out that the justification offered for the traditional rules of pictorial perspective does not in fact justify those rules in all respects. When the traditional rules are faithfully followed, they yield, at certain junctures, pictures which are not peephole look-alikes of their peephole representata. This is most clearly seen by considering the traditional rules for drawing the façades of buildings. It is a law of optical geometry that as parallel lines recede from the point of vision, they appear to converge. Thus the vertical lines in a building's façade appear to converge as they recede upward from the viewer, and the horizontal lines appear to converge to the left and to the right of the viewer. This, incidentally, is also how a camera will record the situation. The traditional rules of perspective for the drawing of façades are quite different, how-

---

[26] Nelson Goodman, op. cit., p. 12.

ever. They stipulate that if a head on view of a façade is being rendered or represented, the vertical and horizontal lines in the façade should both be represented with parallel lines in the picturing design.

Now one response to this situation is that, *mirabile dictu*, the traditional rules are just wrong. And indeed, assessed by reference to the justification offered, they are wrong. By reference to the justification offered, the 'correct' rules would be those which follow the laws of optics—parallel lines receding should be represented or rendered with converging lines. Any hesitation on this point is due, as Goodman points out, to confusions over the conditions of observation. Yet most observers in our western tradition would agree that if we use those 'correct' rules in the drawing of façades, we end up with something which 'looks wrong'. So much is this true that cameras designed for architectural photography use 'corrective' devices. But how are we to understand this claim, that if we use the 'correct' rules—correct by reference to the justification offered—rather than the traditional rules, we wind up with something which looks wrong? For in the peephole appearance of the picture we would not wind up with something which looks wrong. On the contrary, it would look just like the peephole appearance of the objects. Well, what is meant, surely, is that under *canonical* appearances of the painting, it is hard to see a design with lines converging above and to the sides *as* a rectangular façade. And that, of course, is why the traditional rules diverge at this point from the 'correct' rules.

Seeing the matter in this way enables us to adjudicate the dispute as to whether the rules of pictorial perspective are merely conventions or whether they offer a natural way of transcribing the appearance of objects. Gibson, for example, says '. . . it does not seem reasonable to assert that the use of perspective in paintings is merely a convention, to be used or discarded by the painter as he chooses . . . When the artist transcribes what he sees upon a two-dimensional surface, he uses perspective geometry, of necessity.'[27] And likewise Gombrich, holding that 'the theory of perspective is in fact perfectly valid,' hotly disputes the idea 'that perspective is

[27] James J. Gibson, 'Pictures, Perspective, and Perception', in *Daedalus* (Winter 1960), p. 227. Quoted by Goodman in op. cit., p. 11.

merely a convention and does not represent the world as it looks.'[28]

Whether these remarks are true or not depends on what is being claimed. If the claim is that the traditional rules of perspective give a way of producing a picture which, when observed under peephole conditions, will be a look-alike match to an array of objects observed under peephole conditions, then the claim is nearly, but not quite, true. It would be fully true for the traditional rules *corrected* in the respects discussed. By following the *corrected* traditional rules it is in fact theoretically possible to produce a design which will be a look-alike under the conditions specified. And that this is possible is a straightforward consequence of the laws of geometrical optics. In this sense the corrected traditional rules are natural rules.

But if one does not take the canonical range of appearance of one's painting to be the peephole range of appearances; and if one's concern is not to picture an array of objects receding into space as this would appear to a normal perceiver under peephole conditions but to a normal observer under ordinary conditions; then it is hard to see wherein lies the inherent preferability or 'naturalness' of perspective designs. The person who argues for the naturalness of perspective designs by reference to the laws of optical geometry will have to acknowledge the fact that in the drawing of façades the traditional rules depart from the correct rules, and that if they did not, the designs produced would look wrong when viewed under canonical conditions. But more generally, the fact that we in the West under canonical conditions so easily see perspective designs as objects receding into space, and less readily see the tiered designs of the Chinese as objects receding into space, is probably only a matter of habituation on our part. From the Renaissance up to the twentieth century, the systems for picturing spatial recession which have been in effect for us in the West have almost invariably been ones which used perspective designs; and mainly these systems have been in effect for us by virtue of convention. As a consequence, our eyes have become habituated. But the eyes of the Chinese have been habituated along different lines.

So who is right on this issue of the status of the rules of

[28] Ernst Gombrich, op. cit., p. 248 and 254.

perspective, the conventionalists or the anti-conventionalists? The issue is to be resolved by locating the precise point at which convention, and habituation, enter.

X. *The Walton Theory*

In a series of recent articles Kendall Walton has developed an interesting theory of picturing which, while it has some basic affinities with mine, is yet very different. We both place states of affairs (propositions) at the centre of our theories. But from this common centre we travel in different directions. Walton's theory grounds picturing in what *beholders* do. Mine grounds picturing in what *artists* do.

Before I begin the exposition of Walton's theory I think it may be helpful to indicate its general drift. Imagine a performance of a play in which the background scenery includes a window framing a painted landscape. In the course of the play one of the actors may look in the direction of the painted scene and pretend to be seeing trees, cows, and so forth, off in the distance. Now in effect Walton says: why not think of all representational paintings as functioning in fundamentally the same way as that painted background in that play? Why not regard what it is for a design to be a picture as involving, in a certain way, the potential for persons looking at it and, in so doing, pretending to see real objects? If this guiding idea is kept firmly in mind, the reader will find the elements of Walton's theory falling quite readily into place.

Fundamental in Walton's discussion is the concept of a proposition's being *fictionally true*. From all he says it is clear that fictional truth is not some special kind of truth. The clue to what he means lies in the fact that, on occasion, he speaks of a proposition as being true in the world of some work of fiction in place of speaking of it as being fictionally true. That makes it clear that his concept of *fictionally true* is really an amalgam of two distinct concepts that I have been using all along: the concept of *a proposition's being included in the world* associated with some artefact or activity, and the concept of *a world's being fictionally projected* by some activity. I think clarity will be gained, in stating Walton's theory, if we unravel his concept of *fictionally true* into these two constituent concepts. I should add that Walton, like almost all theorists of representation, speaks not of human beings as using designs to represent things, but rather of *designs* themselves as representing things. In stating his theory, I shall follow him in that. (Actually, he usually speaks of *pictures*—occurrences of pictorial designs—as representing things.)

Novels and pictures are alike in fictionally projecting worlds. But wherein lies their essential difference? That is one of the principal questions Walton poses. The beginning of his answer is this: when someone is viewing a *picture* of a man, his performance of visual actions such as looking at the picture *generates* its being fictionally true that he is seeing a man; whereas when someone is viewing a novel about a man, that is not so. In other words, what is peculiar to a picture of a man, as distinguished from a novel about a man, is that someone's performance of visual actions such as looking at the picture *count-generates* his fictionally projecting that he is seeing a man.[29]

But why does this particular form of count-generation take place? Why is it that by looking at a certain sort of design one takes up a fictive stance toward one's seeing a man? Because, says Walton, there is a certain 'game' which our society plays, defined by certain rules, pictures being 'props' in this 'game'. What this suggestion amounts to, I think, is that the count-generation in question occurs because there is a certain action-generation system in effect in our society, that it is in effect by virtue of convention; and that, specifically, it is an item/usage system in which pictures are the items. There is an action-generation system, in effect in our society by virtue of convention, such that our looking (under appropriate conditions) at those objects which we call pictures *counts as* our fictionally

[29] Walton does not articulate a theory of count-generation, nor does he articulate a theory of action-generation in general. However, by placing his theory explicitly in the context of my theory of count-generation I think I am being faithful to his intent, though indeed giving it considerably more articulation than he himself does. It is interesting to note that he himself uses both the word 'generates' and the word 'counts as' in this connection. He says, for example, that 'a viewer's action of perceiving a man-painting (in the normal way) generates the fictional truth that he perceives a man.' (Kendall Walton, 'Points of View in Narrative and Depictive Representation', *Nous*, x, No. 1, March 1976, p. 60.) For examples of the use of 'counts as' see his 'Pictures and Make-Believe' (in *Philosophical Review*, lxxxii, No. 3, July 1973) throughout, but especially pp. 304, 312, 313.

projecting that we are seeing what those pictures p-represent. Pictures, as Walton puts it, are props in games of make-believe.

I suggest that representational pictures are distinguished from novels mainly by their role in a game of make-believe of a certain kind—a game which allows for our performing various make-believe visual actions . . . There is no non-arbitrary way to specify precisely which and how many make-believe visual actions must be provided for . . . What novel characters lack, if they do not happen to be pictured in illustrations, is the possibility of being objects of make-believe *visual* actions.[30]

So given that a certain convention is in effect, by looking at a picture (in appropriate ways) one count-generates the action of fictionally projecting various propositions. But which sort of propositions? Some clues as to what Walton would say in answer to that question can be culled from what I have already quoted and reported him as saying. But let us look more carefully at what he says.

On Walton's view, a picture always presents *a look of things*. It presents *that there are things which look a certain way*. If the world of a picture is to occur, there must be things which look a certain way; and that there are things which look that way is what the picture presents. Furthermore, what is *directly* presented by a picture if *only* a look of things. From a picture's presenting that things *look* thus-and-so we can usually extrapolate, says Walton, to how things *actually are* in the world projected by the picture. For often it will be true that if things *look* a certain way, then they *are* thus-and-so. But all inference to how things *are* in the projected world begin from the picture's direct presentation of how things look in that world.

The only primary fictional truths generated by a depiction are that things *look* a certain way; whatever is fictionally true about how things are is implied by fictional truths about how they look.[31]

Now 'how things look', says Walton, 'depends on the person and his circumstances. The primary fictional truths which a depiction generates are merely that things appear certain ways

---

[30] 'Pictures and Make-Believe', op. cit., p. 303. In stating Walton's theory in terms of an action-generation system being in effect by virtue of *convention*, I am again going beyond what Walton explicitly says. But again, I think that placing it in this context is faithful to his intent, merely giving his intent more articulation than he himself gives it.

[31] 'Points of View . . .', op. cit., p. 58.

to *some* sort of person under *some* conditions or other.'[32] From just these words it is not clear how Walton intends this sentence to be quantified. Does he mean that if what is directly presented is to occur, there must *be* an object, there must *be* a person, and there must *be* conditions of viewing, such that that person *does in fact view* that object under those conditions and the object looks as the picture presents things as looking? Or, more weakly, does he mean that there must *be* an object and there must *be* a person and there must *be* conditions of viewing such that the object *would* look as the picture presents things as looking *if* that person would look at that object under those conditions? Or, more weakly yet, does he mean that there must *be* an object such that it is *possible* that there be a person and conditions for viewing such that if the person viewed the object under those conditions it would appear as the picture presents things?

It is clear from the rest of what he says that Walton holds the first of these three possibilities. Indeed, he holds something even stronger than the first. He does not merely hold that if the world of the picture is to occur there must be an object, a person, and conditions of viewing such that that person views that object under those conditions. He holds that *there actually exists* a person such that if the world of the work is to occur, there must be an object and conditions of viewing such that this existent person views that object under those conditions and . . .

We want to see who, on Walton's view that person might be, for a given picture. But before doing so, I wish to cast some doubt on one of the claims which, a few paragraphs above, I reported Walton as making. What a picture directly presents, says Walton, is just that there is some person and some object and some conditions for viewing such that that person views that object under those conditions and the object looks as the picture presents things as looking. From this directly presented proposition, says Walton, we then extrapolate to what an object must actually be like for the world of the work to occur. Surely, however, the truth is that only rarely can we make any such inference from such thin information. For an object which is in fact so-and-so can look almost any way you please to *some* sort of perceiver under *some* sort of conditions. Accordingly, if Wal-

[32] Ibid., p. 59.

ton's theory were correct, it would rarely be the case that objects were represented as actually being so-and-so.

But let us return to the point which momentarily we left. In the course of his discussion as to the sorts of propositions directly presented by pictures, Walton says this:

As in the real world, one can infer from the way things appear, what sort of person things appear that way to, and in what circumstances they do, as well as what the things are like. Brueghel's *The Death of Icarus* generates fictional truths about how things look to a person with normal vision seeing them from above in full daylight, as well as the fictional truth that what appears so is a man floundering in the bay. A depiction's perspective on the fictional world is a matter of what the relevant sort of person and circumstances are: Brueghel's painting portrays Icarus from the perspective of a person with normal vision, looking from above, etc.[33]

After saying this, Walton then goes on to ask, 'But *who* is it to whom things fictionally appear in a certain way? Who fictionally sees Icarus from above in broad daylight?'[34] His answer is: The actual person who is looking at the depiction. If I am looking at *Death of Icarus*, then things must look *to me* as the picture presents things as looking, if what is made fictionally true by my looking is actually to occur. 'I would say that it is fictionally true', says Walton, 'of a person viewing Brueghel's painting, that he sees Icarus from above, etc., and that Icarus appears a certain way to him.'[35]

Why does Walton give this answer? Why does he assume that when I look at *Death of Icarus*, it becomes fictionally true of me that I see a certain sort of object under certain sorts of conditions and that it looks to me as that picture presents things as looking? Why not make the weaker assumption that there must be *someone* who views . . .? The answer lies way back in Walton's guiding idea: something's being a picture of a man consists in the fact that there is a convention in effect such that if *I* view the picture in an appropriate way, then thereby I am pretending that *I* am seeing a man. (Pretending is of course, for Walton, one way of making a proposition fictionally true.)

---

[33] Ibid., p. 59.
[34] Ibid.
[35] Ibid., p. 60.

We can now put all the pieces together. Suppose that D is a picture, for a society S, of a man as viewed by a person of sort P under conditions of sort C. Walton's view, as I understand it, is that that consists in D's being an object such that in society S there is an action-generation system in effect by virtue of convention such that if someone looks at D in a way specified by the convention, his doing so count-generates the action of his taking up a fictive stance toward the proposition that he himself is of sort P and is seeing a man under circumstances of sort C.[36]

Though Walton does on several occasions speak of the world of a work, it should be noted that we cannot immediately get from the above way of thinking of how pictures work to a concept of the world of a picture. For suppose that I am looking at *Death of Icarus*. If the body of fictional truths which Walton sees as then involved is to occur, *I* would have to see an example of the Icarus character floundering in a bay, and *I* would have to see it from a great distance and from far up above the bay. But surely we do not want to say that the world of the work is anchored to *me*. Or, if we do say that it is anchored to me, we would have to say, for similar reasons, that it is likewise anchored to every other viewer (either to everyone who has ever viewed it, or to everyone who is now viewing it, depending on how one chooses to develop the theory). And that seems absurd. So what directly emerges from Walton's way of thinking of how pictures work is not the concept of the world of a work W as such, but the concept of the world of W *with respect to viewer* V. However, the concept of the world of W as such can probably be derived from the concept of the world of W with respect to V. I shall not attempt actually to construct the derivation. But whereas the world of *'Death of Icarus' with respect to me* would require, for its occurrence, that things appear to *me* as the picture presents things as looking, the world W as such would perhaps require just that things appear to someone or other in that way. Accordingly, though the world of *'Death of Icarus' with respect to me as viewer* requires that I, looking on from a considerable distance way up above, see an example of the Icarus character floundering in a bay, it will not be the case that

---

[36] For a fully accurate statement of Walton's thought, certain qualifications not relevant to our purposes here would have to be added.

the world of the work itself is anchored to me. Nor will it be the case that it is anchored to any other actual viewer.

Certainly this is an imaginative theory of what it is for something to be a picture. I do not think that it is an acceptable theory, however. Let us see why.

As I indicated at the beginning of this discussion of Walton's theory, I think it sometimes happens that a person, upon looking at a p-representation of a k, *pretends* that he is seeing a k. But though this sometimes happens, I doubt that it very regularly happens. Rather more often it happens, so it seems to me, that upon looking at a p-representation of a k we *imagine* that we are seeing a k. But even this, I judge, by no means always happens—perhaps not even usually. Sometimes upon looking at a picture of a mountain I imagine that I am seeing a mountain, but certainly not always. Now it should be noticed, however, that Walton's theory does not depend on either or both of these always happening. He claims that what does invariably and necessarily happen when I view, in the conventionally prescribed way, a p-representation of a k, is that I *fictionally project* that I am seeing a k. And though he would agree that pretending that I am seeing a k is one mode of fictionally projecting a k, there are others as well.[37]

But what reason is there to suppose that by looking in the standard way at a p-representation of a k, we *do* fictionally project that we are seeing a k? And what reason is there to suppose that there *is* any such convention in effect as Walton claims, bringing it about that such count-generation takes place? The supposition that there is such a convention in effect seems not to explain anything. And conversely, all the phenomena of picturing can be explained without supposing that there is any such convention in effect among us, or in any other society.

The truth of these two points can be seen as follows. Whenever a certain action-generation system is in effect for a person by virtue of convention, it is always possible for that person to put (or have put) that system out of effect for himself on a given occasion—for example, by announcing his

---

[37] In fact I do not think that either pretending that one is seeing a k or imagining that one is seeing a k is an action which can be count-generated. But even if true, this is not a decisive objection to Walton's theory as a whole.

repudiation of it on that occasion. So let us go along with Walton and suppose that in our society there is a certain system in effect for us by virtue of convention such that, by looking at Rembrandt's *St Paul* in the requisite manner, we take up a fictive stance toward our seeing a man. Suppose that on a certain occasion I then announce that no such convention will be in effect for me, and then proceed to look at the painting. What now has changed? Might I not still see the design as a man? Might Rembrandt not still have p-represented a man with it? Might I not *know* that he did? In short, nothing is different. Or to put it the other way round: nothing is explained by supposing that my looking at a picture generates my taking up a certain fictive stance. And conversely, everything about representation can be explained without supposing that (normally) one takes up a fictive stance toward one's seeing a man by looking at a picture which p-represents a man. Even the fact that we often *say* that we see a man when we look at such a picture can be explained. We are not then asserting that we are taking up a fictive stance toward our seeing a man. We are asserting that we are seeing a certain visual design *as* a man.

Though I see no reason for supposing that I am taking up a fictive stance toward my seeing a man when I look in appropriate ways at the *St Paul*, I do not doubt that my looking at something *could* count as my performing some action, and it could do so by virtue of convention. In particular, my looking at something could count as my performance of some mood-action, and yet more particularly, it could count as my taking up a fictive stance toward my seeing a man. My looking at a p-representation of a man could count as my taking up a fictive stance toward my seeing a man. But the truth is that, for any object whatsoever at which I can look, there could be a system in effect for me (by virtue of convention) such that my looking at that object count-generates the act of my taking up a fictive stance toward my seeing a man. The object need not have any particular look. And it is interesting that Walton himself attaches no conditions to what an object must look like to be a picture of a man. On his view, an object is a picture of a man for a certain society just in case there is a system in effect for that society such that if someone looks at it, his doing so counts as his taking up a fictive stance toward his seeing a man. A novel could satisfy this condition as well as a picture. But here we are on the track of a second objection to Walton's theory. Suppose that in a particular society it is not designs like our pictures that are used as items (props) in the relevant game of make-believe, but rather designs like our words. As we have seen, there is nothing impossible in this—and it is not prevented by any of the qualifications that Walton attaches.[38] I submit that in spite of there being such a system in effect in that society, these would not be pictures in that society. And the reason for their not being pictures is that they don't have the right look. The word 'man' cannot be seen as a man. That is why it cannot be a picture of a man, even though looking at it could be made to count as taking up a fictive stance toward one's seeing a man. Walton has not succeeded in differentiating words from pictures.

Thirdly, as I argued in Section VIII, many pictures are such that for the world of the picture to occur there need not be any perceiver at all, let alone any perceiver to whom some thing appears as the picture looks. For the world of *Death of Icarus* to occur it is sufficient that an example of the Icarus character fall into a bay surrounded by high cliffs. It is not necessary that there be someone high up to whom things appear as the picture looks. A picture does not present a look of things in the sense that something must actually look that way to someone if the world of the work is to occur.

This is particularly evident for films. Is it at all plausible to hold that if the world projected in the beginning sequence of *Straw Dogs* is to occur, there must be someone who looks at an English village out of focus from high up and then gradually descends? Or in a film-sequence presenting an intimate love scene, is it plausible to think that if the world thereby projected is to occur there must be a third person very close by to whom things appear as the picture presents things as looking? If so, how is it that the two lovers take no notice of this blatant intruder?

[38] The relevant qualification to consider is the qualification to the effect that the rules must be 'internalized' enough so that people do not have to explicitly infer that their looking counts as, say, taking up a fictive stance toward their seeing a lion rather than toward their seeing a horse. I do not see that this qualification comes anywhere near forestalling the objection. It is obvious that the rules for our handling of word-designs can be deeply internalized.

XI. *Q-Representation*

It is time to turn our attention to q-representation. Consider once again Rembrandt's painting *Bathsheba*. By producing the painting, Rembrandt q-represented Bathsheba. But not only did Rembrandt q-represent Bathsheba. He q-represented Bathsheba *as being* (among other things) a woman sitting on a couch bathing. How are such phenomena of q-representation, and of q-representation-as, to be analysed?

Let us begin by reviewing some of the key facts which a theory of q-representation must organize.

(1) One cannot q-represent Bathsheba without q-representing her *as* being or doing something or other—without q-representing her as having certain properties or engaging in certain actions. There is no q-representation without representation-as.[39]

(2) In q-representing Bathsheba as a woman sitting on a couch bathing, Rembrandt may have asserted of Bathsheba that she was a woman sitting on a couch bathing. But he need not have done so. He may have taken up some other mood-stance instead—say, the fictive stance.

(3) Rembrandt's painting is as much a picture of a couch with a woman sitting on it bathing, as it is of a woman sitting on a couch bathing. Pictures are, in this multi-directionality of theirs, significantly different from predicates. The predicate 'is

---

[39] Perhaps it is worth repeating here a point made earlier. There is a sense of the word 'represent' such that, in that sense, if I claim that *P* represents *x*, the proposition asserted entails that *x* exists, while yet it is true that there is nothing which I represent *x* as being. 'Represent', in this sense, means the same as 'denote'. Anything can be used to denote anything. And in particular, a pictorial design, as well as a concrete picture, can be used to denote anything whatsoever. I can use Rembrandt's *Bathsheba* painting to denote the North Pole, if I wish. One wants to say that then no pictorial design that the painting instantiates is *functioning* pictorially. Indeed. And the clue is that the North Pole is not being represented as anything.

I think that pictorial designs are more often used to represent in this sense of *merely denoting* than one might expect. When the medievals drew a picture of a man holding a key, they were usually representing St Peter thereby. But probably sometimes there was nothing at all that they were representing him *as*. Probably sometimes a picture of a key alone would have done as well. Pictorial *symbols* are pictorial designs used to represent something without representing it *as* anything. The man-holding-a-key design was probably sometimes used merely as a pictorial symbol for St Peter. Of course, for *P* to be a symbol for *x*, there must be some appropriateness, some fittingness, between *P* and *x*.

a woman sitting on a couch bathing' expresses the property of being a woman sitting on a couch bathing, and has only women in its extension. By contrast, the predicate 'is a couch with a woman sitting on it bathing' expresses the property of being a couch with a woman sitting on it bathing, and has only couches in its extension.

(4) Even when Rembrandt used his painting to q-represent Bathsheba as a woman sitting on a couch bathing, he did not cease to use it to p-represent there being a woman sitting on a couch bathing. And indeed, only if he used it to p-represent there being a woman sitting on a couch bathing, could he use it to q-represent Bathsheba as a woman sitting on a couch bathing.

(5) With the very same pictorial design Rembrandt might have p-represented there being a woman sitting on a couch bathing and not have q-represented Bathsheba, or anything else, as a woman sitting on a couch bathing. To q-represent Bathsheba as a woman sitting on a couch bathing he must do something *more* than p-represent there being a woman sitting on a couch bathing. In Rembrandt's case, that something more was achieved by affixing the name 'Bathsheba' to the painting.

(6) Rembrandt used part of the total design on his painting to q-represent Bathsheba. And indeed, only if he did so could he have q-represented Bathsheba as a woman sitting on a couch bathing.

(7) Rembrandt can q-represent Bathsheba as a woman sitting on a couch bathing even if Bathsheba never did sit on a couch bathing—even if Bathsheba had not been a woman.

Our challenge now is to fit all these facts together into a coherent general theory of q-representation.

Suppose Rembrandt had p-represented that there is a woman sitting on a couch bathing. What he has then represented is a proposition, a state of affairs, which can be expressed with the following quantificational sentence:

(A) $(\exists x)$ (x is a woman and x is sitting on a couch bathing).

Now consider the sentence:

(B) Bathsheba is a woman and Bathsheba is sitting on a couch bathing.

The proposition expressed by (B) is, of course, a singular instance of the general proposition expressed by (A). Noticing this, the thought comes to mind: could it be that q-representing Bathsheba as a woman sitting on a couch bathing consists of introducing by pictorial means *that Bathsheba is a woman sitting on a couch bathing?* And is the situation just that p-representation consists of introducing by pictorial means a general state of affairs, whereas q-representation-as consists of introducing by pictorial means some singular state of affairs which is an instance of a p-represented state of affairs?

There is an attractive elegance in this idea. But I do not think that as a general theory of q-representation-as it will work, for the following reason. It is a fact that

(i) Rembrandt has q-represented Bathsheba as a woman sitting on a couch bathing.

It is also a fact that

(ii) Bathsheba was identical with the wife of Uriah.

I take it as following from these two facts that

(iii) Rembrandt has q-represented the wife of Uriah as sitting on a couch bathing.

Now suppose that to q-represent A as a k which is ϕ were to introduce (by pictorial means) the proposition that A is a k which is ϕ. Then (i) could be expressed thus:

(iv) Rembrandt has represented (pictorially introduced) that Bathsheba is a woman and is sitting on a couch bathing.

And then (iii) could be expressed thus:

(v) Rembrandt has represented (pictorially introduced) that the wife of Uriah is a woman and is sitting on a couch bathing.

But even though (ii) is true, none the less the proposition

(vi) that Bathsheba is a woman sitting on a couch bathing

is distinct from the proposition

(vii) that the wife of Uriah is a woman sitting on a couch bathing.

For Bathsheba might not have been the wife of Uriah. If so, then (vi) might have been true and (vii) not, as well as (vii) true and (vi) not. And that is enough to show distinctness of propositions. But if (vi) and (vii) are distinct propositions, there is no reason to suppose that (iv) plus (ii) entails (v). In general, if p and q are distinct propositions, then one of them can have the property of being introduced by so-and-so and the other lack that property. Yet (i) plus (ii) *does in fact* entail (iii). So I conclude that (i) is not to be identified with (iv), nor (iii) with (v). We need a theory of q-representation which will account for the fact that (i) plus (ii) entails (iii). Compare the situation here to a closely related one. Suppose I have asserted proposition (vi). From that fact, plus (ii), it does *not* follow that I have asserted proposition (vii).

But now a distinction is in order. The concept of *assertion* which I used in the last two sentences of the preceding paragraph is such that, on this concept, it is *propositions* which are the entities asserted. But there is another concept of assertion. Suppose that I utter, 'Bathsheba is a woman and is sitting on a couch bathing.' In doing so I may have asserted, *of* Bathsheba, *that she is a woman sitting on a couch bathing.* But Bathsheba is identical with the wife of Uriah. And so it follows that I will have asserted, of the wife of Uriah, that she is a woman sitting on a couch bathing. If I, Bathsheba, and the 'propositional function', *that x is a woman sitting on a couch bathing*, stand in the relation of the first of these asserting the third of these of the second, then of course the second of these, Bathsheba, has the property of having that 'propositional function' asserted of her by me. And if Bathsheba has that property, then by Leibniz's Law, anything identical with her has that property. So Uriah's wife has it. Uriah's wife will have the property of having me assert of her *that she is a woman and is sitting on a couch bathing.*

Put it like this: *asserting that p*, is assertion *de dicto*. *Asserting of x that it is* ϕ, is assertion *de re*.

The similarity between these facts concerning asserting-of, and the fact that (iii) follows from (i) plus (ii), is striking. So here we have the clue to be followed out in our analysis.

Q-representing Bathsheba as a woman sitting on a couch bathing is not like asserting (the proposition) that Bathsheba is a
woman sitting on a couch bathing. Rather, it is like asserting *of*
Bathsheba that she is a woman sitting on a couch bathing.
Q-representation is representation *de re*, in distinction from
p-representation which is representation *de dicto*. Sometimes, to
make this structure of q-representation explicit, I shall speak of
q-representing of A that it is a k which is ϕ, rather than speaking
of q-representing A as a k which is ϕ.

We saw above that if q-representation were *de dicto*, there
would be no reason whatsoever to suppose that (iv) follows
from (i) plus (ii). The reason it does in fact follow lies in the *de re*
character of q-representation. If Rembrandt has represented of
Bathsheba that she is a woman sitting on a couch bathing, then
Bathsheba has the property of Rembrandt having represented
of her that she is a woman sitting on a couch bathing. And since
Uriah's wife is identical with Bathsheba, Uriah's wife will also
have that property, by Leibniz's Law. And if Uriah's wife has
the property of Rembrandt having represented of her that she is
a woman sitting on a couch bathing, then Rembrandt has the
property of representing of Uriah's wife that she is a woman
sitting on a couch bathing. And that conclusion is just proposition (iii). The argument is of course general in its import.
Any co-designative term can be substituted, *salve veritate*, for
'Bathsheba' in (i). And so it is in general for terms occupying
the y-position in sentences of the form 'x q-represented y as
being ϕ.'

Now asserting of A that it is a k which is ϕ, is a species of what
earlier I called posing of A that it is a k which is ϕ. (See Part
Four, Section XII.) And posing, remember, is stance-neutral in
the way that introducing is, whereas asserting-of (predicating-
of) is stance-specific in the way that asserting-that is stance-
specific. Now *q-representing-of* must likewise be understood as
stance-neutral. For though one can use a pictorial design to
assert of Bathsheba that she is sitting on a couch bathing, one
can also use a pictorial design, even the very same pictorial
design, to inquire concerning Bathsheba whether she is a
woman and is sitting on a couch bathing; etc. Thus
q-representing of something that it is a k which is ϕ is a species
of *posing of* something that it is a k which is ϕ—specifically, that

species which occurs when the medium is pictorial. Q-representation-of is neutral as to mood-stance but committed as to medium. Let me add here that I shall assume that to pose of A that it is a k which is ϕ, is the same as to pose of A the property of being K which is ϕ.

Now as we have seen, whenever q-representation takes place, then p-representation also takes place. And the p-representation which takes place will always be such that there is some proposition of existentially quantified form which has been pictured (pictorially introduced). Actually there will always be *many* which have been pictured, of the form $(\exists x)$ (x is a k which is ϕ). So consider some such pictured proposition of that form. Call it α. And then consider the corresponding property β of the form:

being a k which is ϕ,

Call β, a property-associate of α. There may, of course, be many property-associates of α. For suppose α is: $(\exists x)$ (x is a woman and x is sitting on a couch bathing). A property-associate of this is: *being a woman who is sitting on a couch bathing.* Now this particular proposition is identical with the proposition $(\exists x)$ (x is a couch and x is being sat on by a woman bathing). And a property-associate of this is: *being a couch sat on by a woman bathing.* But this property is distinct from that of being a woman sitting on a couch bathing.

And now I can explain what it is to q-represent of A the property of being a k which is ϕ (i.e., to q-represent A as a k which is ϕ). It is to count-generate the action of posing of A that it has the property of being a k which is ϕ. And it is to do so (i), by using some design D to p-represent that there is a k which is ϕ, and (ii), by denoting A with design D or some part thereof—the denoting design being such that it can be seen (in the context of the whole design) as a k which is ϕ. The property which one will have q-represented of A will be a property-associate of one of the propositions that one will have p-represented.

A few explanatory comments should be made about this analysis. In the first place, an essential part of the analysis is that initial proviso to the effect that he has *posed* of A that it has the property of being a k which is ϕ. It is *not* my contention that the second proviso by itself is sufficient to ensure q-representation. In general, it is not the case that *if* one uses a design D to p-represent that there is a k which is ϕ, and *if* a part of D which can be seen in context as a k which is ϕ is used to denote A, *then* A has been q-represented as a k which is ϕ. For imagine a design used to p-represent a fully clothed person—clothed in monk's habit, let us say. I can see a part of the design as a person who is fully clothed in monk's habit. But alas I can see that very same part as a monk's habit worn by a person. (These would be alternative descriptions of the same act of representational seeing.) Now suppose that that design is used to denote St Francis. Obviously I have not—normally anyway—q-represented of St Francis that he is a monk's habit worn by a person.[40]

Secondly, the reason for speaking always of how *a part of* the design is seen *in context* is this: if one takes *just* that part of the image which denotes Bathsheba, and so excludes that part which is seen as a couch, one does not see that part as a woman sitting on a couch. But obviously that part in context is seen as a woman sitting on a couch. That leads into this additional explanatory comment. Suppose that with a given picture, two women are p-represented, the one being a woman sitting on a couch bathing, the other not. Then I would have p-represented that there is a woman sitting on a couch bathing. Now suppose that the image of the woman *not* sitting on a couch bathing is used to denote Bathsheba. In such a case I would not, of course, have q-represented of Bathsheba that she is a woman sitting on a couch bathing. For me to q-represent of Bathsheba that she is a woman sitting on a couch bathing, I must p-represent that there is a woman sitting on a couch bathing; and that part of the design used to denote Bathsheba must be a part which I not only see in context as a woman, but which I see in context as a woman sitting on a couch bathing.

I have offered an account of what it is to q-represent x as so-and-so. What remains is to say what it is to q-represent x. Not, that is to say, what it is to q-represent Bathsheba as sitting on a couch bathing; but just what it is to q-represent Bath-

---

[40] Thus we avoid the first of the objections which Howell lodges against Goodman's theory of representation in footnote 3 of his article, 'The Logical Structure of Pictorial Representation', op. cit.

sheba. But that is now easy. Q-representing an entity x never takes place outside the context of q-representing something of x. And to q-represent x is to denote x in the context of q-representing something of x.

What are some of the ways in which it is brought about, when one has p-represented something, that one has also used some part of the picturing design to q-represent some entity?

Well, sometimes nothing is needed beyond a certain picturing arrangement's being in effect and being used, in a particular circumstance. The picturer's doing what he has done in that circumstance counts as his having q-represented something. Suppose, for example, that some political cartoonist in the last days of the Nixon administration had pictured a swarthy, jowly cheeked, bulbous nosed, person rushing frantically from closed door to closed door in a room. And suppose that there were no accompanying words whatsoever. I think it clear that his act of so doing in that circumstance would count as his q-representing of Nixon that he is rushing about from door to door. And no doubt that is because his pictorial situation is severely limited—namely, to widely-known political events and figures.

Rembrandt's q-representation of Bathsheba is an example of a different sort. Clearly Rembrandt used part of his picturing design to denote Bathsheba. And the decisive thing he did was affix the title *Bathsheba* to the painting. Of course, it is by virtue of various features of his entire circumstance that his producing an occurrence of 'Bathsheba' counts as his naming the Old Testament personage Bathsheba. And naturally we have to surmise that it is 'the woman in the picture' and not, say, 'the couch in the picture' which denotes Bathsheba. But this then is one standard strategy: affixing titles. And more generally, it may be by virtue of what the picturer says with words about his design that what he has done counts as q-representing so-and-so.

Yet another strategy, common among medieval artists but now fallen into disuse, is that of having pictorial emblems or symbols for certain very commonly represented persons. The emblem for St John, for example, was that of a picture of a person holding a lamb. And if, in certain circumstances, an instance of a picturing design included a picture of a man holding a lamb, one knew that that part of the design was being used to denote St John.[41]

One final point must be made about q-representation. Botticelli, with his *Birth of Venus*, represented Venus as having long flowing tresses, as standing on a giant sea-shell floating on the sea, etc. How are we to understand this? And in general, how are we to understand the representation of fictitious entities?

Well, my theory of characters (Part Three) suggests immediately that what is going on in this case is that Botticelli is q-representing, of Venus, that she has long flowing tresses. For there is in fact such a fictional (mythological) entity as Venus, this being a certain person-type. Venus is available as an object for q-representation. However, to q-represent of Venus that she has long flowing tresses is not to pose of that type that it *has* the property of having long flowing tresses. Rather, it is to pose of that type that the property of having long flowing tresses is *essential within* it. So given my theory of characters, my theory of q-representation handles, with suitable minor adjustments, the q-representation of fictional 'persons' as well as it does that of actual persons.

XII. De Dicto *Representation*

I must now correct an impression which, for pedagogical reasons, I have allowed my discussion to leave in the reader. Beginning with Section IV of this Part, I inquired into the nature of p-representation. My fundamental suggestion was that to p-represent a *k* is to introduce, pictorially, the proposition *that there is a k*. Thus my suggestion was that p-representation is always *de dicto*. In the course of the discussion we also saw, however, that sometimes what is represented is perhaps not a proposition of the form *that there is a k* but rather a proposition of the form, *that this is how a k would look to such-and-such an observer under such-and-such conditions*. After having scrutinized p-representation at some length, I then turned my

---

[41] Howell, op. cit., holds that if I am to depict something of *b*, *b* must figure causally in the production of the picture. He does not explain *just how* it must figure causally. But I suspect that what leads him to believe that there is *some sort* of causal connection is a confusion between representation as depiction and representation as *rendering*.

attention, in Section XI, to q-representation, arguing that such representation is always *de re*.

But once we see clearly that some representation is *de dicto*, some *de re*, then the question comes to mind: how is p-representation to be conceived? Is p-representation just representation *de dicto*? If so, then we have already seen that propositions of two fundamentally different forms can be p-represented. Alternatively, is p-representation to be conceived as *de dicto* representation in which the form of the proposition represented is *that there is a k*? If so, then what are we to do with representation *de dicto* in which the proposition represented is of that other form which I noted?

Of course, nothing of theory depends on how we sort out our terminology here. It will be simplest, though, if we just take p-representation to be representation *de dicto*. And whatever impression I may have given, that in fact is how I have been conceiving it. That form of representation *de dicto* in which the proposition represented is of the existentially quantified form, *that there is a k (which is φ)*, may then be called *the standard form* of p-representation. We have already seen that some p-representation is not of the standard form.

But there are non-standard forms of p-representation in addition to that one which I have already noted. Let us then look at one or two of these others. Characteristic of them is that they never occur except in the context of p-representation of the standard form.

In the preceding section I argued that q-representing Bathsheba as a woman sitting on a couch bathing is not to be construed as pictorially introducing the singular proposition *that Bathsheba is a woman sitting on a couch bathing*. None the less, it would seem that one *can* pictorially introduce that singular proposition. Certainly it would be odd if one could not. Of course, if one can, then surely it will often not be clear which of these two the artist has done, whether he has pictorially introduced that proposition, or whether he has pictorially posed, of Bathsheba, that she is a woman sitting on a couch bathing. If he has done the latter, then *also* he has posed of the wife of Uriah that she is a woman sitting on a couch bathing; whereas if he has done the former, he will not also have introduced the proposition that the wife of Uriah is sitting on a couch bathing.

But this difference is subtle. Often we won't be able to tell decisively which of these has gone on, or whether both have. And sometimes our inability to tell decisively one way or the other will be rooted in the fact that it's not decisively true that the one has gone on, nor decisively true that the other has. It may be noted that exactly the same sort of haziness turns up in our attempt to apply the distinction between asserting a proposition of the form *that A is* ϕ, and asserting of *A* that it is ϕ.

The workings of this particular non-standard form of p-representation can be readily explained by reference to the workings of the standard form, plus reference to the workings of q-representation. For this particular non-standard form will never occur outside the context of those two. It will always consist of the introduction of a singular proposition by way of an interconnected exercise of p-representation of the standard form, plus q-representation. I shall not bore the reader with the details of the analysis.

What about universally quantified propositions, of the form *that all k's are* ϕ? Can such propositions also be p-represented? Can one p-represent that all pine siskins have brownish stripes on their breasts? Well, perhaps we are stretching ordinary usage here. I can picture a pine siskin, without there being any pine siskin of which I have drawn a picture. So also I can picture how a pine siskin looks. And I can picture that particular pine siskin on my bird-feeder. But can I picture all pine siskins as having brownish stripes on their breasts? Perhaps ordinary usage does not allow us to say that I can. But certainly I can use a picture to introduce that proposition—to assert it, to ask whether it is true, etc. And it is more important to see how that works than to uncover the refinements of ordinary usage.

By the use of a picture with which I p-represent a bird with brownish stripes on its breast, I can claim that all (well-formed) pine siskins have brownish stripes on their breasts. How can such a situation best be analysed? Consider some occasion on which I p-represent with some visual design *D* the state of affairs of there being a *k* which is ϕ. Now suppose there exists the event of *A*'s being a *k* which is ϕ. That event will be what I called an *occurrence* of the state of affairs. (See Part Three.) Let me now introduce one more bit of terminology. Let us say, when there is that event, that *A matches* the state of affairs.[42]

The application of these distinctions and this terminology to the situation at hand then goes as follows. Suppose that in a case of standard form p-representation I have introduced the state of affairs of there being a bird with brownish stripes on its breast. To use that picture of a bird to claim that all (well-formed) pine siskins have brownish stripes on their breasts consists then in using that picture to claim that all (well-formed) pine siskins *match* that pictorially introduced state of affairs. That is what is going on when we use a visual design to claim that *all* so-and-so's are such-and-such. We are claiming that all so-and-so's match one (or more) of the p-represented states of affairs. Obviously a directly analogous analysis is to be given of our use of pictures to say that *some* so-and-sos are such-and-such, and that *no* so-and-sos are such-and-such.

XIII. *Non-Literal Representation*

In developing my theory of representation, I have focused exclusively on literal representation. It is time now, as I bring our discussion to its conclusion, to say a few words about the workings of metaphorical representation, ironic representation, and so forth.

It was common practice among radical anti-establishment groups in the United States in the late 1960s to speak of policemen as *pigs*. Of course, the people who spoke thus were not claiming that policemen were literally pigs. They were using 'pig' metaphorically. They were indicating certain states of affairs toward which they were taking up an assertive stance; and their method of doing so involved using 'pig' metaphorically.

Now suppose that some such person wished to q-represent some policeman as metaphorically a pig.[43] Suppose, that is, that he wished to q-represent of some policemen that he is metaphorically a pig. What he might very well do is produce a design which we all tend to see as a pig, and he might produce it

---

[42] The use of the word 'match' in this sort of context I take over from Walton, though the concept I attach to it is rather different from his. See K. Walton, 'Are Representations Symbols?' in *The Monist* (April 1974), pp. 238–9.

[43] By the locution 'is metaphorically a pig' I mean, has that property which is expressed by the predicate 'is a pig' when those words are used metaphorically.

in such a way that his doing so counts as his introducing that there is something which is metaphorically a pig. (Perhaps also it might count as his introducing the *singular* proposition that person *P* is metaphorically a pig.) Such a case of introducing some state of affairs by using a pictorial design may be called a case of *metaphorical p-representation*. And in general, metaphorical p-representation occurs when someone produces a design which we all tend to see as a *k*, and thereby introduces the proposition that there is something which is metaphorically a *k* (along perhaps, with some singular proposition of the form that *x* is metaphorically a *k*).

Having introduced, with a design which we all tend to see as a *k*, there being something which is metaphorically a *k*, one may then in the usual fashion allow part of the design which we see as literally a *k* to denote something. By thus introducing and denoting, one may pose of some policeman the property of being metaphorically a *k*. Such posing-of, we may call *metaphorical q-representation*.

Ironic p- and q-representation fit into the structure I have developed in a manner wholly parallel to the way in which metaphorical representation fits in. There is no point in elaborating further. The reader will be able, given the hints offered, to work out for himself the details of how these and all other modes of non-literal p- and q-representation work.

The examples cited above of non-literal representation—that of metaphorically p-representing that there is something which is metaphorically a pig, and that of metaphorically q-representing of some policeman that he is metaphorically a pig—are not only bizarre but insulting. But we should not let this obscure from us the fact that metaphorical p- and q-representation are common phenomena in the visual arts. As observed earlier, in his great altarpiece in St Bavo, Ghent, Jan van Eyck metaphorically q-represented Christ as a lamb. The design which denotes Christ in the painting tends to be seen by all of us as a lamb. But obviously van Eyck is not p-representing that there is something that is literally a lamb, nor that Christ is literally a lamb, but rather that there is something which is metaphorically a lamb. (Perhaps also that *Christ* is metaphorically a lamb.) Thus he q-represents of Christ that he is a lamb—but *metaphorically* a lamb, not *literally*.

It should not go unnoticed that by virtue of metaphorical representation one can represent that which cannot be perceived—that which has no appearances. Time can be metaphorically q-represented as (metaphorically) a skeleton with a scythe in hand. God can be metaphorically q-represented as (metaphorically) a stern father. Thus at a stroke the non-visual is made available for visual representation.

XIV. Appendix on Goodman's Theory

Here in this Appendix to my discussion on representation I wish to scrutinize the theory which Goodman constructs to account for the various phenomena of picturing. Perhaps it should be said in advance that though Goodman does indeed set his analysis of representation within the context of a general theory of symbols, he nowhere gives a full systematic and sequential presentation of that embracing semiotic theory. One has to piece it together from remarks scattered throughout the text. On several crucial points the theory is present more by allusion than by exposition. Further, these remarks are often as obscure in their meaning as they are arresting in their rhetoric. Thus what follows is as much a construal as a report of what Goodman says.

Goodman's basic idea concerning representation is that a picture is a character in a representational symbol system. So begin with the idea of a symbol system. 'A symbol system', says Goodman, 'consists of a symbol scheme correlated with a field of reference.'[44] But what, then, is a *symbol scheme*? This: 'Any symbol scheme consists of characters, usually with modes of combining them to form others. Characters are certain classes of utterances or inscriptions or marks.'[45]

Having said this, Goodman adds in the footnote on page 131 that he 'prefers' to 'dismiss' characters altogether—by which he presumably means that in his theory he prefers not to commit himself to the existence of characters but only to the existence of utterances, inscriptions, and marks. This statement is one of many manifestations of the nominalist impulse

---

[44] *Languages of Art*, p. 143.
[45] Or, as he makes clear on p. 139, of 'time-slices' of such. Ibid., p. 131.

which pervades Goodman's book. But in spite of his nominalist longings, Goodman does not provide us with an articulate theory which avoids commitment to characters and of which his 'characters language' can be viewed as a loose though convenient expression. On the basis of what he says we have no reason for supposing that he is thinking with the learned while speaking with the vulgar—let alone any evidence for what those learned thoughts might be. We have no choice but to regard him as reluctantly forsaking his nominalism and committing himself to the view that there are characters and that symbol schemes consist of characters.[46]

Goodman does not explain what he means by saying that a symbol scheme 'consists' of characters. The most natural interpretation, though, is that he means to say that characters are *members of* symbol schemes, and that, correspondingly, symbol schemes are *sets* of characters. If so, then, given his view as to the nature of characters, symbol schemes are sets of sets.

Return, now, to our opening quotation: 'A symbol system consists of a symbol scheme correlated with a field of reference.' Hearing these words of Goodman, and a good many others, one naturally wonders whether a symbol *system* should be thought of along lines made familiar by logicians in their offering of semantic interpretations of elementary languages: a symbol system is an ordered pair whose first member is a set of characters (i.e., a symbol scheme) and whose second member is a function which assigns sets to at least some of the characters.

Before we conclude that this eminently natural interpretation of Goodman's words is in fact the correct interpretation, however, we should consider the following passage (in which 'compliant' is used as a synonym of 'denotatum'): 'Inscriptions

---

[46] Surely, though, characters are not classes. Whatever inscriptions a character has, it has contingently. Whatever members a class has, it has necessarily. Characters are *kinds* rather than classes. (I do not suppose that Goodman would agree with these points.)

One might also question the assumption that symbols are always characters. Why must this be? Goodman himself offers the example of a briefing officer using the paintings in a captured museum to indicate enemy positions, (p. 41). Presumably in the system then being used, the paintings refer to enemy positions. And is it not those very paintings—those particular concrete objects—that thus refer? One could save the theory by insisting that in this case it is the unit sets of the paintings which refer. But Goodman himself says on p. 5 that 'almost anything may stand for almost anything else'. This would scarcely be true if the only things that can refer are characters.

without compliants may be called *vacant*. Vacancy may arise either from a character having been assigned no compliant, or from there being no such compliants as are called for, or from explicit stipulation that the character have no compliant.'[47] If a Goodman symbol system is just an ordered pair, whose first member is a set of characters and whose second member is a function on that set, then how are we to distinguish the three cases which Goodman notes? A function either assigns some entity to some character or it does not. How then can Goodman's three types of vacancy be distinguished?

Well, a function may be only partially defined on a certain set of characters, and may on that account make no assignments whatever to a certain character. That is one case. Secondly, the function can assign the null set to some character. That gives us a second case. Thirdly, once a primary function has assigned entities to characters, then a secondary function may, on the basis of the primary function, make assignments of combinations of those characters; and some of these secondary assignments may be to the null set. For example, once a primary function has assigned to 'snake' the set of all snakes, and to 'hairy' the set of all hairy things, there may then be a secondary function which assigns to 'hairy snake' the intersection of those two sets. And that, as it so happens, is the null set, since there are no hairy snakes. This third situation (provided the primary assignments are to something other than the null set) gives us a distinct third case.

Can we then identify the first of these cases with the first of the situations that Goodman had in mind, the second with the third, and the third with the second? Well, the first two of these suggestions seem plausible. But what about the third? The description Goodman *gave* of the third case he had in mind was that in this case there is an 'explicit stipulation that the character have no compliant'. And the proposal we are considering is that this case be identified with the situation in which a function assigns the null set to a character. Are these not incompatible,

---

[47] Op. cit., p. 145. Compare this passage: 'Having an established null denotation is quite a different matter from not having any established denotation.' (n. 26, p. 75.) And this: 'The rule for correlating symbols with denotata may result in no assignment of any actual denotata to any symbol, so that the field of reference is null; but elements become representations only in conjunction with some such correlation actual or in principle.' (p. 228.)

having no compliant and *being assigned the null set?* Not at all. Denotation, as Goodman thinks of it, is a species of reference. And if the function in a certain system assigns to 'horse' the set of all horses, Goodman would not say that 'horse' refers to that set but rather that it refers to the horses. The horses are the denotata, the compliants, the referents, of 'horse'. So too, if in a certain system the function assigns the null set to 'unicorn', Goodman would not say that 'unicorn' then refers to (has as compliant, as denotatum) the null set but rather that it does not refer to anything. When a character is assigned the null set, it does not denote that set but rather does not denote anything.

So I think we *can* regard Goodman symbol systems as ordered pairs of the sort indicated. (At least, the simplest ones will be of that sort. There may well be some of greater internal complexity.) Goodman's words quite naturally suggest this interpretation. And I know of no passage which decisively contradicts it. And in fact, Goodman follows the customary practice of calling the set of all things assigned to a symbol σ in a system *GS* the *extension* of σ in *GS*. (Or in case the mode of reference is denotation, the extension is also called the compliance-class of σ in *GS*. If the extension of σ in *GS* has no members and the mode of reference is denotation, Goodman says that σ has null-denotation in *GS*.)

But more must be said if we are to understand what Goodman has in mind by a symbol system. For I doubt that Goodman would regard every ordered pair of the sort we have been considering, a symbol system. The crux is that he seems to have more in mind by 'reference' than just the relation that a term has to the members of its extension in such a set. Reference, as he seems to understand it, is something effected by what we human beings do. *We* bring it about that certain characters refer to certain things. And I think that Goodman requires that an ordered pair of the sort indicated somehow involve reference if it is to be a symbol system.

In what way must it involve reference? Well, if an ordered pair of the sort indicated is such that all the characters which are assigned an extension in that set also *refer to* the members of the extension, then it will of course be a symbol system. But there will be more symbol systems than these. For we have seen that some of those ordered pairs in which some (or all) of the characters do not in fact refer to anything would also be regarded by Goodman as symbol systems. Still, for those it will be the case that someone will have done to some of those characters the sort of thing which, if the world were appropriately different, would have resulted in those characters referring to something. If the world had been appropriately different, 'unicorn' would have referred to something. In fact it doesn't. But we human beings have done to it what would be sufficient to make it refer to unicorns if there were any. So perhaps we can say this: if an ordered pair, whose first member is a symbol scheme and whose second member is a function which assigns sets to some at least of the characters, is to be a *symbol system*, the characters to which the function assigns sets must be such that either they do refer to the members of the sets assigned to them or, in case the set assigned is empty, they enter into human practice in such a way that they *would* refer to something if the world were appropriately different.

But what then does Goodman take reference to be? And what brings it about, on his view that characters refer to things, and that some of those that don't refer *would* do so if the world were appropriately different?

To the second question Goodman's answer is clearly that a character σ refers to something on account of the emergence of certain *habits* (*practices*, he also sometimes calls them) with respect to σ, or alternatively on account of persons assenting to certain *stipulations* with respect to σ. He says, for example, '. . . there are countless alternative systems of representation and description. Such systems are the products of stipulation and habituation in varying proportion.'[48] He speaks of 'a term with an extension established by habit'.[49] And speaks of alphabetical notation as correlated with sound-events 'according to the usual practice of pronunciation' and as correlated with objects 'according to the usual practice of application'.[50] So on Goodman's view, σ refers to x only if either persons have a habit of doing some thing with respect to σ, or persons assent to the stipulation *to do* something with respect to σ.

[48] Ibid., p. 40.   [49] Ibid., p. 71.

[50] Ibid., p. 144. Compare this: '. . . what counts is not whether anyone calls the picture sad but whether the picture is sad, whether the label "sad" does in fact apply. "Sad" may apply to a picture even though no one ever happens to use the term in describing the picture; and calling a picture sad by no means makes it so. This is not to

But a habit of doing *what* with σ? And a stipulation for doing *what* with σ? Goodman never says. Possibly he means: a habit of *using σ to refer*, and a stipulation to *use σ to refer*. If so, then here at ground-point there is an appeal to the *count-generated action of someone using something to refer to something*. But before we thus interpret Goodman let us drop this matter for the moment and take up the other question posed, namely, what concept of *reference* is Goodman using? Since Goodman never says, the evidence for the answer to this question will have to lie almost exclusively in the examples of reference that he offers.

Goodman distinguishes between reference and what he calls denotation, denotation being a species of reference. He explains his usage in this passage: '... "denotation" must be taken somewhat more broadly than is usual, to cover a system where scores are correlated with performances complying with them, or words with their pronunciations, as well as a system where words are correlated with what they apply to or name. Partly as a way of keeping this in mind, I shall use "complies with" as interchangeable with "extension". Compliance requires no special conformity; whatever is denoted by a symbol complies with it.'[51]

Apart from some cautionary comments, what we are offered in this passage is examples of denotation. Goodman cites the phenomena of a musical performance complying with a score, of an utterance being a pronunciation of a word, and of an entity being such that a word applies to it or names it. Another example, not mentioned in this passage but fundamental to Goodman's entire essay, is the phenomenon of a picture representing something. And in the following passage one is offered an assortment of yet other examples: 'A gesture, too, may denote ... Nods of agreement or dissent, bows, pointings, serve as labels ... An orchestra conductor's gestures denote sounds to be produced but are not themselves sounds ... The same is true of such activities in response to music as foot- and

[51] Ibid., pp. 143–4. Cf. p. 200: 'Offhand, indeed, the relation between a term and what it denotes appears quite different from that between a score and its performances or between a letter and its utterances; but no very clear principle seems to underlie this distinction.'

say that whether a picture is sad is independent of the use of "sad" but that given, by practice or precept, the use of "sad," applicability to the picture is not arbitrary.' (p. 88.)

finger-tappings, head-bobbings, and various other minor motions. That these are called forth by the music, while the conductor's gestures call it forth, does not affect their status as labels ...'[52]

Keeping these examples of denotation in mind, let us turn, secondly, to a species of reference that Goodman calls exemplification, distinct from denotation though in his view dependent upon it. What is exemplified is always a property. And he says that an entity *exemplifies* a certain property just in case it possesses that property and also refers to it. Mere possession is not enough, nor is mere reference enough. What is required is possession plus reference. 'To have without symbolizing is merely to possess, while to symbolize without having is to refer in some other way than by exemplifying.'[53] An example of exemplification which Goodman himself offers is that of a tailor's sample exemplifying various properties of the cloth from which it is cut.

Saying only this does not explain how on Goodman's view exemplification is connected with denotation. Goodman's conception of the connection presupposes his nominalism. He regards 'possesses redness' as synonymous with 'is denoted by some label coextensive with "red".' And in general, he regards a locution of the form 'possesses f-ness' as synonymous with 'is denoted by some label coextensive with "is-f".' Thus for a tailor's sample to exemplify redness is for the sample to be denoted by some label coextensive with 'red' and to refer to some such label.[54]

And now we can look at some of the examples Goodman offers of exemplification. He says that 'an Albers painting may pretty clearly *exemplify* certain shapes and colors and interrelationships between them, while it merely possesses the property of being exactly 24½ inches high ...';[55] that Bach's *Goldberg Variations* and Jackson Pollock's paintings exemplify various formal relationships;[56] that the word 'ping' exemplifies being quick, light, and sharp and the word 'pong', being slow, heavy, and dull;[57] that 'a glue factory ... exemplifies being a glue

---

[52] Ibid., pp. 61–2.   [53] Ibid., p. 53.

[54] Relevant to the attempt to comprehend Goodman's concept of denotation is a passage in which he says that sometimes the distinction between denotation and exemplification becomes arbitrary. See pp. 58–9.

factory';[58] and that 'fictive description and fictive representation reduce to exemplification of a special kind. "Centaur" or a picture of a centaur exemplifies being a centaur-description or a centaur-picture ...'[59]

Our question was this: what is the concept of reference that Goodman is using? Since Goodman does not define 'reference', we decided to look at the examples he offers, to see if we could surmise what concept he is using. I think, however, that the net effect of this canvas of examples is that our question remains unanswered. What does Goodman mean by 'reference' when, for example, he claims that a glue factory refers to the property of being a glue factory? An Albers painting may of course be used to *perform the action* of referring to one of the shapes which it exhibits. But so too it may be used to perform the action of referring to its size. However, Goodman in the passage quoted neither affirms the former of these points nor denies the latter. For when he speaks of reference he is speaking not of an action of persons but of a relation between a symbol and what it is a symbol of. And it is his view that Albers paintings refer to the shapes that they exhibit though not to their sizes. But then what relation, of an Albers painting to its exhibited shapes, might it be that Goodman has in mind?

One suggestion comes to mind. Possibly a symbol's referring to so-and-so consists, for Goodman, in its capacity for suggesting so-and-so, in its disposition to bring so-and-so to mind. Possibly it is the capacity of an Albers painting for *suggesting* certain of its exhibited shapes, acquired on Goodman's view by habit (practice) or by assenting to stipulation, that constitutes what Goodman means when he speaks of the painting as referring to those shapes. Some slight evidence in favour of this interpretation is the following passage—slight since there is no other passage like it: 'Among the countless properties, most of them usually ignored, that a picture possesses, it expresses

[55] Ibid., p. 90.   [56] Ibid., p. 93.   [57] Ibid., p. 75.   [58] Ibid., p. 91.

[59] Ibid., p. 66. There is also this mystifying passage: 'Some elements of the dance are primarily denotative ... But other movements, especially in the modern dance, primarily exemplify rather than denote. What they exemplify, however, are not standard or familiar activities, but rather rhythms and dynamic shapes ... To regard these movements as illustrating verbal descriptions would of course be absurd; seldom can the just wording be found. Rather, the label a movement exemplifies may be itself ...' (pp. 64–5). Why is it that Goodman thinks movements of modern dance typically refer to anything at all, let alone to themselves?

only those metaphorical properties it refers to. Establishment of the referential relationship is a matter of singling out certain properties for attention, of selecting associations with certain other objects. Verbal discourse is not least among the many factors that aid in founding and nurturing such associations.'[60]

Just possibly then Goodman's view on reference is that a character σ refers to so-and-sos just in case σ has acquired the capacity to suggest so-and-sos. And σ acquires such capacity by virtue of a habit being built up or a stipulation being assented to. If this is indeed Goodman's view, then much could be said in critique of it. But since there is only the thinnest of evidence that it is his view, what is more relevant is just the observation that Goodman's concept of reference remains deeply obscure.

With this discussion behind us of what Goodman has in mind by a *symbol system*, let us now proceed to ask what he has in mind by a *representational* symbol system. For his concept of such a system enters crucially into his theory of representation.

In the first place, 'A system is representational only insofar as it is dense. . . .'[61] But what is it for a system to be *dense*? A dense system will be, for one thing, *syntactically* dense. It will have a dense scheme of characters. And 'A scheme is syntactically dense if it provides for infinitely many characters so ordered that between each two there is a third.'[62] For example, our scheme of whole numerals, on the usual ordering, is not syntactically dense; '2' and '3' are both characters in the scheme, but between them there is nothing else which is a character. On the other hand, our scheme of arabic fractions, on the usual ordering, *is* syntactically dense. (Goodman does not say whether the syntactic density requirement on representational systems is satisfied simply by there being *some ordering or other* on which the scheme is dense. However, he probably has in mind normal, ordinary, orderings.) Goodman makes it clear that on his concept of syntactic density, a scheme may be dense even though it does not contain an infinite number of characters. What is crucial is that it *provide* for infinitely many characters ordered in the requisite way. He remarks that 'So long as the scheme

[60] Ibid., p. 88.   [61] Ibid., p. 226.
[62] Ibid., p. 136.

provides for a dense set of characters, we need not actually have any pictures or images that are difficult to discriminate in height. All that is required here of a representational scheme is that it prescribe a dense ordering for characters—that its character specifications be dense-ordering.'[63] And then he remarks in a footnote that 'a dense-ordering specification does not imply that there are such characters as are specified.'[64]

Secondly, a system, to be dense, must be *semantically* dense. That is, the system must provide for a set of compliance-classes so ordered that between each two there is a third. Here too it must be remarked that what is necessary is only that the system *provide for* such a set, not that there *be* such a set. 'The semantic requirement for a representational system no more calls for an actually dense set of compliance classes than the syntactic requirement calls for a dense set of characters, but again calls only for a dense-ordering specification.'[65]

On Goodman's view, more is required of a system, if it is to be representational, than that it be dense. Density is only a necessary condition. What must be added is that if a system is to be representational it must have a scheme which is *relatively replete*:

The difference between representations and diagrams is syntactic: The constitutive aspects of the diagrammatic as compared with the pictorial character are expressly and narrowly restricted. The only relevant features of the diagram are the ordinate and abscissa of each of the points the center of the line passes through. The thickness of the line, its color, and intensity, the absolute size of the diagram, etc., do not matter; whether a purported duplicate of the symbol belongs to the same character of the diagrammatic scheme depends not at all upon such features. For the sketch this is not true. Any thickening or thinning of the line, its color, its contrast with the background, its size, even the qualities of the paper—none of these is ruled out, none can be ignored ... While there is an at least theoretically sharp line between dense and articulate schemes, among dense schemes the difference between the representational and the diagrammatic is a matter of degree.[66]

Thus for a scheme to be relatively replete, there must be a relatively large number of property categories, such that if two

[63] Ibid., p. 227.
[65] Ibid., p. 226.
[64] Ibid., p. 227 n.
[66] Ibid., pp. 229–30.

inscriptions differ with respect to any properties in any of these property categories, they will be inscriptions of two different characters in the scheme.

It should be emphasized that 'although representation thus depends upon a relationship among symbols rather than upon their relationship to denotata, it nevertheless depends upon their use as denotative symbols. A dense set of elements does not constitute a representational scheme unless at least ostensibly provided with denotata. The rule for correlating symbols with denotata may result in no assignment of any actual denotata to any symbol, so that the field of reference is null; but elements become representations only in conjunction with some such correlation actual or in principle.'[67]

In summary, then, a symbol system is *representational* just in case it is syntactically and semantically dense, and has a relatively replete symbol scheme.

Having in mind Goodman's concept of a representational system puts us in a position where two of his fundamental theses concerning pictures can be enunciated. One is this: a character of a system is a representation (picture) in that system if and only if the system as a whole, or that part of the system to which the character belongs, is representational. And the second is: no character is a representation (picture) as such; characters are representations (pictures) only relative to particular systems.

Obviously this view of what it is to be a picture is a view of considerable originality, particularly in its abolition of any appeal to what a character *looks like*. Goodman himself describes it, with evident relish, as 'open heresy'. And concluding a summary of views he has rejected he says: 'Nothing [in my theory] depends upon the internal structure of a symbol; for what describes in some systems may depict in others. Resemblance disappears as a criterion of representation, and structural similarity as a requirement upon notational or any other languages. The often stressed distinction between iconic and other signs become transient and trivial; thus does heresy breed iconoclasm.'[68]

We have seen the theoretical answer that Goodman gives to

---

[67] Ibid., pp. 227–8.
[68] Ibid., pp. 230–1.

the question: 'What is a picture?' We must now see how he tries to fit the phenomena of q-representation and of p-representation into his theoretical structure.

'The plain fact,' says Goodman, 'is that a picture, to represent an object, must be a symbol for it, stand for it, refer to it ... A picture that represents—like a passage that describes —an object refers to and, more particularly, *denotes* it. Denotation is the core of representation...'[69]

And what, then, is p-representation? The view which comes first to mind is that a character σ which is a picture in the scheme of system S p-represents ks in S if and only if σ refers to ks in S. But on this view, there would be no difference between a p-representation of a unicorn and a p-representation of a hippogryph, since neither refers to anything. In fact Goodman makes it clear that p-representation has nothing at all to do with the semantic function of a character. It has nothing to do with what may be assigned to it in some symbol system. As we saw in Section II of this Part, it has to do only with the *kind* of visual design that the picture is an example of:

Since there is no Pickwick and no unicorn, what a picture of Pickwick and a picture of a unicorn represent is the same. Yet surely to be a picture of Pickwick and to be a picture of a unicorn are not at all the same.

The simple fact is that much as most pieces of furniture are readily sorted out as desks, chairs, tables, etc., so most pictures are readily sorted out as pictures of Pickwick, of Pegasus, of a unicorn, etc., without reference to anything represented ... A picture may be of a certain kind—be a Pickwick-picture or a man-picture without representing anything.[70]

Just as objects are classified by means of, or under, various verbal labels, so also are objects classified by or under various pictorial labels. And the labels themselves, verbal or pictorial, are in turn classified under labels, verbal or nonverbal ... The labeling of labels does not depend upon what they are labels for. Some, like 'unicorn,' apply to nothing; and as we have noted, not all pictures of soldiers are soldier-pictures. Thus with a picture as with any other label, there are always two questions: what it represents (or describes) and the sort of representation (or description) it is. The first question asks what objects, if any, it applies to as a label; and the second asks about which among certain labels apply to it.[71]

[69] Ibid., p. 5.   [70] Ibid., p. 21–2.   [71] Ibid., pp. 30–1.

In short, for a character to p-represent something or other it must be a representation, a picture; and it will be a picture if and only if it is a character in a representational system. For the character, then, to p-represent specifically a unicorn instead of a hippogryph—that has nothing whatsoever to do with its role in any scheme or system. That consists just in its being a design of a certain kind—a design of a kind which we happen to describe with the words 'picture of a unicorn'. And Goodman resists saying that its being thus described has something to do with how it looks, or with the properties that something would have·to have to be a unicorn. 'The way pictures and descriptions are thus classified into kinds, like most habitual ways of classifying, ... resists codification ... [T]he canons of the classification are less clear than the practice.'[72]

There we have the essentials of Goodman's theory of representation. What, by way of response, is to be said concerning its acceptability?

In the first place, Goodman's theory of p-representation is definitely unsatisfactory. Goodman holds that our description of certain pictures as p-representations of a man has nothing at all to do with what the pictures look like and also nothing at all to do with what men are like. I, on the contrary, have argued that the look of a picture and the properties of the pictured have a great deal to do with each other. Given the nature and appearance of horses and of roosters, we could not just as well call p-representations of horses, pictures of roosters; and vice versa.[73]

Secondly, p-representation is clearly not simply a matter of the kind of design that a picture is an instance of, for the reason

---

[72] Ibid., p. 23.

[73] In this connection I find the following passage totally baffling: 'The difference between a man-picture and a picture of a man has a close parallel in the difference between a man-description (or man-term) and a description of (or term for) a man. "Pickwick", "the Duke of Wellington", "the man who conquered Napoleon", "a man", "a fat man", "the man with three heads", are all man-descriptions, but not all describe a man.' (p. 23.) Can it really be the case that those six expressions are all classed as man-descriptions just because they are characters of a certain kind? Is it not obvious that they are so classed because of the *semantic* fact about each, that if it applied to anything, it would apply to a man? And why does Goodman say, on the following page, that 'in English, "a man" is a man-description'? English, after all, is a *semantic* *system*. What he should say, given his theory, is that 'a man' is described, in English, as a man-description.

already offered in Section II of this Part. We can pick out the Apollo-designs in early medieval art. They constitute, in a quite straightforward sense, a *kind* of design. Yet the medieval artists were most emphatically not p-representing Apollo, as can be seen by contrasting the use of that very same design by the Greek artists to represent Apollo. By the medievals this design was used to q-represent Christ. The same point can be made by reference to ambiguous designs. A single 'kind' of design can be *used* to p-represent a variety of different things. P-representation cannot be explicated simply by appeal to the kind of character used.

Thirdly, Goodman's account of what it is to be a picture is unsatisfactory. Consider a denotative system of the following sort. The material with which one works is two foot by three foot grids, each having units of $\frac{1}{8}$ inch square. The rule is that to produce a symbol one must completely fill every square in the grid, either with black or with white. The simplest way of analysing this scheme into its characters is to regard each different way of completing the grid as a distinct character. If we are uncertain as to whether a certain unit in what purports to be an inscription is filled or not, or if we are uncertain as to whether a certain unit is filled with black or white, then we are uncertain as to whether we do or do not have an inscription of a character from the system.

This is beyond doubt both a non-dense scheme and one relatively unreplete. So the question is whether any of the character-inscriptions could be used to picture something, and so whether any could be pictures. It seems to me obvious that they could. The effect would be rather like that of tapestries and of samplers—and on a large scale, of newspaper pictures. Thus it is possible for characters of syntactically non-dense and relatively unreplete schemes to be representations.

Next, I do not think that Goodman's theory gives a satisfactory account of q-representation. It is Goodman's claim that if a symbol belonging to the scheme of a representational system *denotes* something in some system, then in that system it q-represents that thing. But consider some representational system which contains an eagle-picture—a design which would be classed by all of us as an eagle-picture. And suppose that in that system the design denotes, say, some naked-nosed wombat. Does it follow that the design q-represents that wombat? Certainly not. It may merely denote it, merely stand for it. For it may not represent that wombat *as* anything whatsoever; and accordingly, may not pictorially represent it. Thus Goodman's account of q-representation does not discriminate between the case in which a symbol in a representational system q-represents something, and the case in which it merely denotes something without pictorially representing it. It does not discriminate between pictures merely *standing for* something and pictures pictorially representing something.[74]

It follows straightforwardly that Goodman's theory does not discriminate between the case in which a symbol in a representational system merely denotes something, and the case in which that very same symbol represents something *either correctly or incorrectly*. At one point Goodman says, 'The two pictures just described are equally correct, equally faithful to what they represent, provide the same and hence equally correct information ... For a picture to be faithful is simply for the object represented to have the properties that the picture in effect ascribes to it.'[75] It is abundantly clear, then, that the

[74] Even though Goodman's theory cannot account for the difference between using a picture merely to denote something and using it to represent something as having certain properties, he himself recognizes the difference and the need to account for it. He says that 'denotation by a picture does not always constitute depiction; for example, if pictures in a commandeered museum are used by a briefing officer to stand for enemy emplacements, the pictures do not thereby represent these emplacements. To represent, a picture must function as a pictorial symbol; that is, function in a system such that what is denoted depends solely upon the pictorial properties of the symbol.' (p. 42.) And again, 'pictures when taken as mere markers in a tactical briefing or used as symbols in some other articulate scheme do not function as representations.' (p. 231.) But there is nothing in Goodman's *theory* to achieve the differentiation which he himself sees as necessary.

[75] Ibid., p. 36. Compare: 'Almost any picture may represent almost anything; that is, given picture and object there is usually a system of representation, a plan of correlation, under which the picture represents the object. How correct the picture is under that system depends upon how accurate is the information about the object that is obtained by reading the picture according to that system.' (p. 38.) This passage raises another difficulty: Goodman seems to say here that for a given eagle-picture there could be a plan of correlation such that it represents a certain wombat wholly correctly. Yet on his theory of representation-as, it would be representing that wombat as being an eagle. How can both of these claims be true? Correctness of representation, says Goodman here, is relative to a system. Yet representation-as is explicated by reference to p-representation; and p-representation has nothing to do with the semantic function of a symbol whatsoever. So all we have, on Goodman's theory, is that a certain design denotes a certain thing in a certain system. There simply is no room for the distinction

phenomenon of a picture representing something either correctly or incorrectly has not escaped Goodman's attention. Yet
his theory does not discriminate between the case in which a
picture merely denotes something, and the case in which, representing something *as* so-and-so, it represents it either correctly or incorrectly.

Lastly, we might ask whether Goodman's theory can give a
theoretical articulation of the fact that I can p-represent a lion
without q-representing anything whatsoever, including lions
—that in spite of the fact that there are lions. I think the answer
is 'Yes'—Goodman could say that in such a case I am using a
system in which my character is a picture, that it is in fact the
lion-picture kind of design, and that in the system used, the
character does not refer to anything. But though this answer is
available to Goodman, offering it as answer points up a fundamental defect in his theory: Goodman gives us no account
whatsoever of what it is for a system to be in effect, and what it is
for a system actually to be used. How do I tell what system I am
using on a given occasion? When I p-represent a lion without
q-representing anything, *just what* system am I using, and *what*
in the system is assigned to the character I use? To these basic
queries Goodman offers no answer whatsoever.

The conclusion must be that at crucial points the Goodman
theory of representation is unsatisfactory. And if we now look
back to survey the deficiencies, we will see that at several points
the root of the difficulty lies in the fact that Goodman's theory,

---

between merely denoting it, on the one hand, and on the other hand, representing it
correctly or incorrectly.

Compare also this passage: 'A picture that under one (unfamiliar) system is a correct
but highly realistic representation of an object may under another (the standard)
system be a realistic but very incorrect representation of the same object. Only if
accurate information is yielded under the standard system will the picture represent the
object both correctly and literally.' (n. 30, p. 38.)

When Goodman says on p. 70 that 'falsity depends upon misassignment of a label',
he clearly slips into an alternative and better account of correctness and incorrectness.
The idea here is that falsity depends upon ascribing a predicate to something it does not
denote. Thus falsehood is seen as inhering in ascribing to a non-k, a predicate which
denotes ks, rather than as inhering in a k-predicate denoting a non-k. This will not do as
a general account of falsehood. But it is an improvement in so far as it makes reference
to the action of ascribing, and does not try to explain falsehood purely in terms of
predicates. The same understanding of falsehood is alluded to on p. 79.

being a purely semantic theory, is unable to cope with the many different ways in which pictures *are used*. Our scrutiny of Goodman's theory confirms us in the conviction that we must go beyond semantics into pragmatics if we wish to have anything near a satisfactory theory of picturing.

PART SEVEN

Projected and Actual

I have abstracted the action of world-projection from the totality of human action and developed a theory concerning its
nature. Let me now in conclusion make clear, by considering
some of the ways in which world-projection is related to human
life as a whole, that it is indeed an abstraction I have performed.
I have also distinguished between, on the one hand, the projected worlds of works of art and, on the other, the actual world;
and I have looked intensely at the former. Let me now in
conclusion take note of some of the principal ways in which the
worlds of works of art, as I have conceived them, are related to
the actual world.

Projected worlds, in the first place, exist—that is, they
actually exist. There are those states of affairs that constitute
these worlds. And likewise there are those kinds of persons,
those person-kinds, with which characters are to be identified.
The artist, in his projection of worlds and his delineation of
characters, is dealing with what does actually exist. And the
claims that you and I make as to the states of affairs included in
some projected world, along with the claims that we make as to
the properties belonging to some character, are either true or
false—that is, true or false in the actual world.

Further, projected worlds are always *anchored to* entities existing in the actual world. They are anchored to such necessarily
existing entities as states of affairs and kinds. But characteristically they are also anchored to such contingently existing
entities as cities, countries, events, and persons. The world of
David Copperfield could not occur without London existing—*actually* existing. Likewise the *laws* that hold in projected
worlds, the laws on the basis of which we do our extrapolating,
are, in what we called α-worlds, laws that hold in the actual
world. In many of the worlds other than α-worlds they are,
though not that, still laws that one or another person or group of

persons *believes* to hold in the actual world. In all these ways, projected worlds are tied with adamantine chains to the actual world.

There is yet another relationship to which it is worth calling attention. Characteristically the world of a work of art does not, *as a whole*, occur; and in some cases it *could not* as a whole occur. It exists, indeed. But it does not actually occur. Invariably, though, *some* of the states of affairs *included within* the work's world do actually occur. And this, I suggest, is how we should construe the claim, so frequently made by critics, that worlds of works of art are *true to* reality in various respects. Our theory yields a straightforward construal of such claims. The 'respects' in question are states of affairs included within the world of the work. And for the world of a work to be *true to* reality (actuality), with respect to some state of affairs included within it, is for that state of affairs actually to occur—that is, to occur in the actual world. Of course, even when a projected world is not true to actuality in a certain respect, it may yet be true in that respect to some person's *view* concerning actuality—which is just to say that that person believes that that state of affairs does actually occur. In the fact that invariably the world of a work of art is true to reality in an indefinitely large number of respects lies the potential of works of art for illuminating us, and for confirming us in the knowledge we already have.

Just as the world of a work is true to actuality in various respects, so in a similar way characters are, in various respects, *accurate portrayals* of actual persons. Normally a character will not as a whole be exemplified; sometimes in fact it *could not* be. Usually, though, there will be less determinate person-kinds within which a work's characters are included; and many of these will be such that some person actually exemplifies them. In that way characters are, in various respects, accurate portrayals of those persons.

That speaks of the relation of projected worlds to the actual world. What, next, can be said in summary fashion about the relation of the *action* of world-projection to life as a whole?

One thing to be mentioned here is a reminder of what we have already seen: the artist, by projecting a world, may assert something, may issue a condemnation, may express a wish, and in general, may count-generate some action or other.

He may, in the strictest sense, *say* something. But since this point has already been discussed (Part Three, Section I; Part Four, Section X), let me here pass it by without further comment.

Over and over when surveying the world's representational art we are confronted with the obvious fact that the artist is not merely projecting a world which has caught his private fancy, but a world true in significant respects to what his community believes to be real and important. Since in most communities it is the religion of the people which above all is important in their lives, this implies that much of the world's representational art is explicitly *religious* art. To understand the art of ancient and medieval South and Central America, the art of India, the art of medieval Europe, one must set off to the side our contemporary image of the alienated artist who has a prophetic insight to deliver or a stinging condemnation to issue to his fellow human beings, and one must instead see the artist as one who is allied in fundamental conviction with his community. The stories, the dramas, the paintings, the sculptures, serve more as an expression of the convictions of the artist's community, and to confirm that community *in* those convictions, than to lead it into new ones. What Geerhardus vander Leeuw says concerning what he calls the 'sacer ludus' in his *Sacred and Profane Beauty* is illustrative:

The dramatic scheme which follows is found in numberless instances among cultured peoples, and still has power today among the primitives and in folk customs. From the group of young people, either girls alone or together with young men, a single individual, the dance leader, separates himself, gradually assuming more and more the role which actually is appropriate to the entire youth of the village or tribe, that of the bearer of life, the bringer of new life, the savior. He or she is led about in triumph, but comes to an unhappy, a mock end, banished, drowned, or burned. That is new life which ages and dies. Just as frequently, however, the concern is with old life that dies but rises again. The bearer of life is dressed as an old man or an old woman, is ridiculed or maltreated, is finally killed, but rises again after a short while. This is naturally only a schema. In reality, the *sacer ludus* occurs in innumerable variations. Often there are two actors, the one representing life, the other death; or better, the one the life which dies, the other the life which awakens. Then the theme of resurrection is dropped, and the drama takes on the form of a battle, a battle between two gods, summer and winter, death and life. The climax of the drama still remains invariably the same, the transition from death to life, and vice versa. That is also the significance of the stereotyped ending of many Greek tragedies, that drama which developed from a dance with animal masks to the highest of arts, but which always finally returns to a unity from the multiplicity and confusion of human affairs. This unity is brought about by a *deus ex machina*, or remains limited to a formula:

> A manifold form has the will of the gods,
> Their counsel is done without man's expectation,
> And what you imagined comes never to pass.
> The impossible yields its path to a god.
> Thus this event has its finish.

The protagonist was originally a god or a daemon whose suffering and death represented the tragic element, and whose resurrection represented the joyous element. Greek tragedy is rooted in the sacral representation of the sufferings of Dionysus. The comedy is the other, the bright side.[1]

What is important in the life of a community, in addition to its religion, is its image of itself, including especially its remembered history, with its great figures, its decisive events, its crucial artefacts. Indeed, usually a community's remembered history, and certainly its self-image, is inextricably interwoven with its religion. Thus much of the world's art is national art, art which celebrates the nation, art which invokes the people's remembered (or fabled) history. The artist, counting himself a member of his people, serves its cause by projecting worlds true in significant respects to the people's image of itself, serving in that way, too, more to confirm than to illuminate.

But even religious and national art do not, by any means, exhaust the examples of projected worlds which are true in significant respects to what the artist's community takes to be real and important. The wall paintings of Thera and Herakleion are evidence of the importance assigned to upper-class social life by those for whom these ancient artists were working. The Greek sculptures are evidence of the importance assigned by the Greeks generally to the human body. And the landscape painting of the West, from the late Renaissance on into the early

---

[1] G. vander Leeuw, *Sacred and Profane Beauty* (Holt, Rinehart & Winston: New York, 1963), p. 80.

twentieth century, reflects the fact that Western man for some four centuries now has been passionately interested in nature—*physical* nature. Indeed, for many Westerners nature has been a matter of far more passionate interest than the Christian religion, or the history of their own people. And this interest has been served by our artists. From Giorgione to Cézanne our painters have tried to capture the physical world surrounding us, to make their works true to Mont St-Victoire, to a lily pond in France, to the Dutch or English landscape.

But why? Why this persistent impulse of the artist to project worlds true in significant respects to what his community finds real and important? Obviously because his community finds it desirable and beneficial to have such works. But that just moves the question over one step. Why does the community find it desirable and beneficial? Why was medieval European man not content with Bible and sermon and devotional book? Why all those dramas? Why all those paintings? Why all those sculptures?

For one thing, one cannot escape the impression that there is in man a deep desire for *concreteness*, that there is in man a deep dissatisfaction with merely holding *in mind* his religion, the history of his people, his convictions as to what is important, and a passionate wish instead to make all this concrete, in story and play, song and dance, painting and sculpture. Aristotle sets us on the wrong track with his suggestion that the principal benefit of dramatic tragedy lies in the emotional purging we undergo by virtue of the fear and pity induced in us by the drama. Surely what above all gripped the Greeks in watching the tragedies of their dramatists was that there, before their eyes, were being unfolded the stories and histories so important to them as a people.

No doubt there are other reasons as well why societies have prized the availability of works of art whose worlds are true in significant respects to what the people regarded as real and important. One that we are inclined to overlook, because it no longer plays any role whatsoever in our thinking, is the conviction of people in earlier cultures that in *representing* something one somehow *realizes* it. A public drama was thought of not merely as a representation of certain sacred events but as a *re-enactment* of those events. And sacred visual representations were regarded as invocations of the presence of the represented being. The ancestor was 'present' in the mask, the god in the idol, the saint in the icon.

One cannot help noticing, though, that even when the artist put himself at the service of his community, projecting worlds true in significant respects to what his community regarded as real and important, at the same time aesthetic and artistic concerns shaped the world he projected and his manner of projecting it. We need not doubt that Mantegna was producing genuinely religious art in his *The Dead Christ*—that is to say, we need not doubt that he aimed to create a painting true in important respects to the religion of his people. Yet what strikes any viewer is the extraordinary foreshortening in his drawing of the dead Christ. Surely this reflects an *artistic* concern on the part of Mantegna, a concern shared, no doubt, by the members of the art community in which he was a participant. This same tendency to allow the content and manner of world-projection to be shaped by artistic and aesthetic concerns is carried farther by later artists, until in the twentieth century we are repeatedly confronted by artists to whom the subject-matter itself means little, artists for whom the subject-matter is a mere prop on which to hang the artistic and aesthetic concerns of themselves and their art community. And just as the subject-matter becomes a mere prop for our artists, so too the subject-matter of prior art in good measure loses its interest for us the viewers. André Malraux, in the famous opening of the *Voices of Silence*, states the point well:

A Romanesque crucifix was not regarded by its contemporaries as a work of sculpture; nor Cimabue's *Madonna* as a picture. Even Pheidias' *Pallas Athene* was not, primarily, a statue. So vital is the part played by the art museum in our approach to works of art today that we find it difficult to realize that no museums exist, none has ever existed, in lands where the civilization of modern Europe is, or was, unknown; and that, even amongst us, they have existed for barely two hundred years. They bulked so large in the nineteenth century and are so much part of our lives today that we forget they have imposed on the spectator a wholly new attitude towards the work of art. For they have tended to estrange the works they bring together from their original functions and to transform even portraits into 'pictures'.... Until the nineteenth century a work of art was essentially a representation of something real or imaginary, which conditioned its existence *qua* work of art. Only in the artist's eyes was painting specifically painting, and often, even for him, it also meant a 'poetic' rendering of his subject.[2]

But there is another and more fundamental way in which the artist of our century differs from his traditional predecessors. Whereas the traditional artist aimed to produce a work true in significant respects to what his community found real and important, our high-art artist in the modern contemporary West characteristically sets himself *over against* his society, or at least against large segments of it. He aims not to *confirm* them in their convictions but to *alter* their convictions, by *showing* them how things are, so as thereby to awaken them from their somnolence or release them from their self-indulgent ideology, to illuminate them, or energize them into action, or console them. Or perhaps even it is no concern of the artist to alter the convictions of his compatriots. Perhaps his goal is simply to *express* his own vision—to give it concrete embodiment by composing a world true in significant respects to that vision. In any case, instead of seeking to produce works true in significant respects to what his society finds real and important, our contemporary high-art artist aims to produce works true in significant respects to what *he himself in distinction from his society* finds real and important.

To describe the difference between the traditional artist and the contemporary high-art artist thus, however, is actually to paint the difference in starker tones than is justified. What is true of our advanced contemporary societies is that they are all—to a greater or lesser degree—pluralistic. In each there coexist a number of distinct and competing fundamental visions of life. It is true that an outside observer, noticing that these competing visions often have long traditions behind them, will observe that when these traditions are thrown together into one society they tend to adapt to each other and to look more and more alike. Still, the pluralism of our societies is as evident as the move toward accommodation. What is characteristic of our modern high-art artists, then, is not that they with their private visions stand in agonized prophetic

---

[2] André Malraux, *The Voices of Silence*, transl. by Stuart Gilbert (Paladin: St Albans, 1974).

opposition to their society as a whole. What is rather the case is that they give expression to the vision of a certain *sub-community*. And characteristically they have given expression to the vision of the cultural élite, in opposition to that of the bourgeoisie. They have produced art which is true in significant ways to what the cultural élite regards as real and important. One result is that ours has become more and more a *secularized* art, while at the same time our veneration for art has acquired religious overtones. Again Malraux is worth quoting:

The gestures we make when holding pictures we admire (not only masterpieces) are those befitting precious objects: but also, let us not forget, objects claiming veneration. Once a mere collection, the art museum is by way of becoming a sort of shrine, the only one of the modern age; the man who looks at an *Annunciation* in the National Gallery of Washington is moved by it no less profoundly than the man who sees it in an Italian church. True, a Braque still life is not a sacred object; nevertheless, though not a Byzantine miniature, it, too belongs to another world and it is hallowed by its association with a vague deity known as Art, as the miniature was hallowed by its association with Christ Pantocrator ... From the Romantic period onward art became more and more the object of a cult.[3]

The world of a work of art can be true, I have said, in various respects to actuality; likewise it can be true to what one and another person *takes* actuality to be. In these facts lies the potential of art for altering our convictions and for confirming us in the ones we already have. Over and over this potential is in fact, and by intent, realized by our artists. But the worlds of works of art can also be *false* to actuality in various respects, and false in various respects to one and another person's settled convictions about reality. And sometimes we prize the world of a work of art for its *falsehood* in various respects to what we believe actuality to be like. We want for a while to burrow into a world significantly different from our actual world. We want for a while to escape the drudgery and pain, the boredom, perplexity, and disorder of real life. There is that about our actual world which distresses us. And the artist presents us with a world which we judge to be, in one way or another, better. We wish things actually were like that. J. R. R. Tolkien speaks vividly on the matter in his essay 'On Fairy-Stories':

[3] Op. cit., pp. 600–1.

I have claimed that Escape is one of the main functions of fairy-stories, and since I do not disapprove of them, it is plain that I do not accept the tone of scorn or pity with which 'Escape' is now so often used ... Why should a man be scorned, if, finding himself in prison, he tries to get out and go home? Or if, when he cannot do so, he thinks and talks about other topics than jailers and prison-walls?

For a trifling instance: not to mention (indeed not to parade) electric street-lamps of mass-produced pattern in your talk is Escape (in that sense). But it may, almost certainly does, proceed from a considered disgust for so typical a product of the Robot Age, that combines elaboration and ingenuity of means with ugliness, and (often) with inferiority of result. These lamps may be excluded from the tale simply because they are bad lamps; and it is possible that one of the lessons to be learnt from the story is the realization of this fact ...

And if we leave aside for a moment 'fantasy', I do not think that the reader or the maker of fairy-stories need even be ashamed of the 'escape' of archaism: of preferring not dragons but horses, castles, sailing-ships, bows and arrows; not only elves, but knights and kings and priests ...

But there are also other and more profound 'escapisms' that have always appeared in fairy-tale and legend. There are other things more grim and terrible to fly from than the noise, stench, ruthlessness, and aimlessness of the internal-combustion engine. There are hunger, thirst, poverty, pain, sorrow, injustice, death. And even when men are not facing hard things such as these, there are ancient limitations from which fairy-stories offer a sort of escape, and old ambitions and desires (touching the very roots of fantasy) to which they offer a kind of satisfaction and consolation. Some are pardonable weaknesses or curiosities: such as the desire to visit, free as a fish, the deep sea; or the longing for the noiseless, gracious, economical flight of a bird, that longing which the aeroplane cheats, except in rare moments seen high and by wind and distance noiseless, turning in the sun: that is, precisely when imagined and not used. There are profounder wishes: such as the desire to converse with other living things. On this desire, as ancient as the Fall, is largely founded the talking of beasts and creatures in fairy-tales, and especially the magical understanding of their proper speech. This is the root, and not the 'confusion' attributed to the minds of men of the unrecorded past, an alleged 'absence of the sense of separation of ourselves from beasts.' A vivid sense of that separation is very ancient: but also a sense that it was a severance: a strange fate and a guilt lies on us. Other creatures are like other realms with which Man has broken off relations, and sees now only from the outside at a distance, being at war with them, or on the terms of an uneasy armistice ...

And lastly there is the oldest and deepest desire, the Great Escape: The Escape from Death. Fairy-stories provide many examples and modes of this—which might be called the genuine *escapist*, or (I would say) *fugitive* spirit.[4]

Sometimes our prizing of the world of a work of art is grounded in the fact that we are persuaded, or become persuaded, that in significant respects the world of the work is true to actuality. Sometimes it is grounded in the fact that we are persuaded, or become persuaded, that in significant respects it is *false* to actuality. But sometimes it is grounded in the fact that we don't know one way or the other. We desperately *hope* that the work shows how actuality is. Or we *fear* that it does; and, strangely, the evocation of this fear is what grips us in the work.

Some of the consequences flowing from world-projection, and some of the purposes underlying it, presuppose that worlds of works of art are true and false in various respects to actuality and to what we take actuality to be. I have been calling attention to some of these. Likewise I have suggested, though without developing the point, that projected worlds may satisfy our aesthetic interests, and that from the artist's side they also often mark the attempt to conquer certain artistic challenges and problems that the artist has set for himself: to render the glow of a setting sun in paint, as Claude Lorraine attempted in so many of his paintings, to give novelistic expression to one's way of seeing life, etc. I have set off to the side Aristotle's assignment of central position to the emotions evoked by the projected worlds of dramatic tragedy.

But of course it's true that our apprehension of projected worlds does, over and over, evoke emotions in us; and that often this contributes to what we find gripping and compelling about them. The artist, by his projection of worlds, alters and confirms us in our beliefs, such confirmation and alteration in turn altering our attitudes, our commitments, our actions. But also the artist, by his projection of worlds, affects our emotional life.

[4] In Essays Presented to Charles Williams, ed. by C. S. Lewis (Eerdmans Publ. Co.: Grand Rapids, 1956), pp. 75–81.

Almost everything about this phenomenon remains mysterious. Plato already insisted that representational art has some special impact on our emotions. This insistence remained a persistent, though sub-dominant, theme in Western culture until, since the turn of our century, it has risen in influence to become a standard dogma concerning the arts. But in spite of the long tradition and the massive popularity of this conviction, virtually no theoretical illumination has been shed on the linkage between art and the emotions. How does one explain the fact that the world of a painting, of a film, of a novel, of a play, moves one profoundly, inducing fear, grief, exhilaration, etc., all the while never stirring one from the conviction that what is represented never happened, and certainly is not happening now. Why do children weep over the fate of Pinocchio? Why do adults feel terror in the face of the blackbirds in Hitchcock's *The Birds*? To these questions we have, I say, no good answers —and remarkably little attempt even to find answers. A good beginning has recently been made, however, by Kendall Walton in his 'Fearing Fictions'.[5] And one must hope that this large untracked terrain will shortly be explored in depth by serious aestheticians.

One more connection between world-projection and life should be noted. Psychologists by now have accumulated a great deal of experimental and field-study evidence concerning what is called *modelling*. Repeatedly it has been shown that (under certain conditions) when a person A observes a person B performing some action, that serves to develop in A the *ability* to perform that same action, if he did not already have it, and in many cases it serves also to produce in A the *tendency* to perform that action in the relevant circumstances. Further, it has been shown that it matters very little whether the model is presented live or represented. In general, pictorially or dramatically represented models seem more effective than purely literary ones; but these latter are by no means without their effect. To be a bit more specific, it has been shown that cinematically-represented incidents of violence tend to increase incidents of violence among certain sorts of viewers, and that dramatically-represented discrepancy between preaching and practice on some moral issue tends to increase the incidence among viewers

[5] In *Journal of Philosophy*, lxxv, No. 1 (January 1978), pp. 5–25.

of someone preaching this way while acting that way. Plato already warned against the effects of those works of art in which evil actions are represented. He was convinced that such works have a tendency to produce in viewers an inclination to act similarly. Contemporary psychology tells us that Plato's fears have a sound basis in fact.

I have been pointing out some of the ways in which the action of world-projection is involved in the lives of us human beings, both artists and beholders. The artist, by virtue of projecting a world, alters or confirms us in our beliefs, this in turn having a ripple-effect throughout our lives. He alters or confirms us in our abilities and tendencies. He evokes emotions in us. He gives to us aesthetic satisfaction, and delight in observing how well he has met the demands and resolved the problems of his craft. He gives expression to his own self.

Or, to look at it all with the structure in mind that I outlined in our opening Part: the artist by his projection of worlds count-generates such actions as asserting and warning. Likewise he *causally*-generates, both intentionally and non-intentionally, both knowingly and non-knowingly, such actions as evoking emotions and altering our tendencies to action. In turn, his projection of a world is itself generated by such actions as rendering or 'capturing' one and another facet of the world around him. And through it all he reveals and expresses himself—his emotions, his beliefs, his commitments.

Always it is the temptation of writers on the arts to reduce the richness and diversity of ways in which world-projection enters our lives—to say that the 'real' benefit of art lies in *this* one thing, that the 'real' purpose of art lies in *that* one thing. I have indicated a wide variety of ways in which world-projection enters our lives. But this is still only a selection. And even where I have selected, my selection has been highly general and schematic. The purposes, the benefits, the consequences of world-projection in one of the arts are not the same as those in another of the arts. Neither are they the same in one age and culture as they are in another. But even in one art, in one age, in one culture, the projection of worlds enters in countless significant ways into the fabric of our human existence.

Subject Index

Index of Artists Cited

Index of Theorists Cited